KETO DIET

COOKBOOK

~ 600+ ~

Quick, Easy and Healthy Keto Diet Recipes for Beginners: Healthy and Fast Meals with 30 Day Recipe Meal Plan For Whole Family

By

RILEY SANDERS

TABLE OF CONTENTS

DESCRIPTION

So, you've decided and you're ready to begin a Ketogenic alimentary program. What do you need to do? Above all, you need to eat the right foods and the correct amount of those foods. You also will need to be aware that you may experience symptoms as you reduce the amount of your carbohydrate intake. Initially you may experience maybe a little fatigue or even haziness, but that's just your body adjusting to your new dietary program. Drink more water, increase your fat intake and increase your sodium, potassium and magnesium to help your body adapt to its new alimentary regime.

This book has that 600+ keto diet recipes and a 30-day meal plan. You can comfortably prepare all recipes at home with so much ease. They include the following meals:

- Breakfast
- Main dishes
- Side dishes
- Seafood
- Poultry
- Vegetables
- Eggs and diary
- Soups and stews
- Fat bombs
- Keto favorites
- Snacks and
- Desserts

I hope you are set to begin a new lifestyle by embracing keto diet and making this guide your all time cooking companion. Happy cooking!!!!

INTRODUCTION

Strict diets are often met with criticism, and the keto diet is not immune to controversy. In particular, some have raised concerns about the high fat intake that keto requires, as fatty foods are known to raise cholesterol and cause heart disease. However, studies have shown that when carefully planned and adhered to, low-carb regimens win out against all others. They are not only advantageous to those trying to lose weight but come with a whole host of extra health benefits that will improve your overall well-being. In some cases, the keto diet can even reduce your cholesterol levels. Let's delve deeper into the various perks of the keto diet.

The main process at play with the ketogenic diet is ketosis. Entering this metabolic state has been shown to positively impact the body in a number of ways, even if you are only on the diet for a brief period of time. Ketosis itself has a number of benefits. It has been shown to:

- Improves the body's ability to draw on fats as an energy source.
- Spare your proteins, as your body starts to use ketones as fuel instead.
- Lower insulin levels in the body, which influences the secretion of growth hormones.

BREAKFAST

01. Anaheim pepper Gruyere Waffles

Preparation Time: 16 MIN
Serve: 2

Ingredients:

- 1 small Anaheim pepper
- 3 eggs
- 1/4 cup cream cheese
- 1/4 cup Gruyere cheese
- 1 tbsp coconut flour
- 1 tsp Metamucil powder
- 1 tsp baking powder
- Salt and pepper to taste

Directions:

1. In a blender, mix together all ingredients except for the cheese and Anaheim pepper. Once the ingredients are mixed well, add cheese and pepper. Blend well until all ingredients are mix well.
2. Heat your waffle iron; pour on the waffle mix and cook 5-6 minutes. Serve hot.

Nutritional Value:

Calories 223.55
Total Fats 17g
Net Carbs: 5.50g
Protein 11g

02. Nutty Cocoa Cereal

Preparation Time: 12 MIN
Serve: 2

Ingredients:

- 3 tsp organic butter
- ¾ cup toasted walnuts, roughly chopped
- ¾ cup toasted macadamia nuts, roughly chopped
- ½ cup coconut shreds, unsweetened
- ½ tbsp stevia (optional
- 2 cups almond milk
- 1/8 tsp salt

Directions:

1. Melt the butter in a pot over the medium heat. Add the toasted nuts to the pot and stir for 2 minutes.
2. Add the shredded coconut into the pot and continue stirring to make sure to not burn the ingredients.
3. Drizzle with stevia (if using and then pour the milk into the pot. Add salt. Stir again and turn the heat off.
4. Allow resting for 10 minutes to allow the ingredients to soak in the milk before serving.

Nutritional Value:

Calories 515
Total Fats 50.3g
Net Carbs: 14.4g
Protein 6.5g | Fiber: 7.3g

03. Breakfast Tacos

Preparation Time: 25 MIN
Serve: 3

Ingredients:

- 3 strips bacon
- 1 cup mozzarella cheese, shredded
- 2 tbsp butter
- 6 eggs
- Salt and pepper
- ½ avocado, cubed
- 1 oz cheddar cheese, shredded

Directions:

1. Cook bacon until crisp, put aside until needed.
2. Heat a non-stick pan and place 1/3 cup mozzarella into the pan and cook for 3 minutes until browned around the edges. Place a wooden spoon in a bowl or pot and use tongs to lift cheese 'taco from the pot. Repeat with leftover cheese.
3. Melt butter in a skillet and scramble eggs; use pepper and salt to season.
4. Spoon eggs into hardened shells and top

with avocado and bacon.

5. Top with cheddar and serve.

Nutritional Value:

Calories 443
Total Fats 36.2g
Net Carbs: 3g
Protein 25.7g | Fiber: 1.7g

04. Cheesy Bacon and Chive Omelet

Preparation Time: 30 MIN
Serve: 1

- **Ingredients:**
- 2 eggs, large
- Salt and pepper
- 1 tsp bacon fat
- 1 oz cheddar cheese
- 2 slices bacon, cooked
- 2 stalks chives

Directions:

1. Beat eggs together and add pepper and salt to taste. Chop chives and shred cheese.
2. Heat skillet and cook bacon fat until hot.
3. Add eggs to pot and top with chives. Cook until edges start to set then add bacon and cook for 30-60 seconds.
4. Add cheese and a few additional chives. Use a spatula to fold in half. Press to seal and flip over.
5. Serve immediately.

Nutritional Value:

Calories 463
Total Fats 39g
Net Carbs: 1g
Protein 24g
Fiber 0g

05. Pizza Waffles

Preparation Time: 30 MIN
Serve: 2

Ingredients:

- 1 tbsp psyllium husk
- 1 tsp baking powder
- Salt
- 3 oz cheddar cheese
- 4 eggs, large
- 3 tbsp almond flour
- 1 tbsp butter, organic
- 1 tsp Italian seasoning
- 4 tbsp parmesan cheese
- ½ cup tomato sauce

Directions:

1. Add all ingredients to a bowl except cheese and tomato sauce. Use mixer or immersion blender to combine until mixture is thick.
2. Heat waffle iron and use mixture to make two waffles.
3. Place waffles onto a lined baking sheet and top with tomato sauce and cheese (divide evenly. Broil for 3 minutes or until cheese melted.
4. Serve.

Nutritional Value:

Calories 525.5
Total Fats 41.5g
Net Carbs: 5g
Protein 29g
Fiber 5.5g

06. Anchovy, Spinach and Asparagus Omelet

Preparation Time: 23 MIN
Serve: 2

Ingredients:

- 2 oz anchovy in olive oil
- 2 organic eggs
- 3/4 cup of spinach
- 4 marinated asparagus
- Celtic Sea salt
- Freshly ground black pepper

Directions:

1. Preheat the oven to 375 F.
2. In the bottom of the baking pan place the anchovy.

3. In a bowl, beat the eggs and pour on top of the fish. Add the spinach and the chopped asparagus on top.
4. Season with salt and pepper to taste.
5. Bake in preheated oven for about 10 minutes.
6. Serve hot.

Nutritional Value:

Calories 83
Total Fats 4.91g
Net Carbs: 2.28g
Protein 7.5g

07. Autumn Keto Pumpkin Bread

Preparation Time: 1 HR 30 MIN
Serve: 2

Ingredients:

- 3 egg whites
- 1/2 cup coconut milk
- 1 1/2 cup almond flour
- 1/2 cup pumpkin puree
- 2 tsp baking powder
- 1 1/2 tsp Pumpkin pie spice
- 1/2 tsp Kosher Salt
- Coconut oil for greasing

Directions:

1. Preheat your oven to 350F. Grease a standard bread loaf pan with melted coconut oil.
2. Sift all dry ingredients into a large bowl.
3. In another bowl, add pumpkin puree and coconut milk and mix well. In a separate bowl, beat the egg whites. Fold in egg whites and gently fold into the dough.
4. Spread the dough into the prepared bread pan.
5. Bake the bread for 75 minutes. Once ready, remove bread from the oven and let cool.
6. Slice and serve.

Nutritional Value:

Calories 197
Total Fats 16g
Net Carbs: 8.18g
Protein 7.2g

08. Frozen Ketoccino

Preparation Time: 10 MIN
Serve: 1

Ingredients:

- 1 cup cold coffee
- 1/3 cup heavy cream
- 1/4 tsp xanthan gum
- 1 tsp pure vanilla extract
- 1 tbsp xylitol
- 6 ice cubes

Directions:

1. Place all of the ingredients in your blender.
2. Blend until all ingredients are well combined and become smooth.
3. Serve and enjoy.

Nutritional Value:

Calories 287
Total Fats 29g
Net Carbs: 2.76g
Protein 1.91g

09. Sweet & Creamy Eggs

Preparation Time: 17 MIN
Serve: 1

Ingredients:

- 2 organic eggs
- 1/3 cup heavy cream, preferably organic
- ½ tbsp stevia
- 2 tbsp organic butter
- 1/8 tsp cinnamon, ground

Directions:

1. In a small bowl, whisk the eggs, whipping cream, and sweetener.
2. Melt the organic butter in a pan over medium heat and then pour in the egg mixture.
3. Stir and cook until the eggs start to thicken and then transfer into a bowl.
4. Sprinkle with cinnamon on top before serving.

Nutritional Value:

Calories 561
Total Fats 53.6g
Net Carbs: 6.4g
Protein 15g

10. Breakfast Protein Bread

Preparation Time: 50 MIN
Serve: 9

Ingredients:

- 12 egg whites, organic
- 1 cup whey protein
- 4 oz softened cream cheese

Directions:

1. Set the oven at 325 F.
2. Pour the egg white and whey protein into a bowl and whisk using a hand mixer until the whites are stiff.
3. Gently fold in the cream cheese into the mixture and pour over 2 greased bread pans.
4. Place in the oven to cook for 40 minutes or until the bread is golden brown.
5. Allow the bread to cool before cutting into slices. Serve or store the bread in the freezer.

Nutritional Value:

Calories 144
Total Fats 11.5g
Net Carbs: 0.9g
Protein 9.4g

11. Keto Oatmeal

Preparation Time: 20 MIN
Serve: 5

Ingredients:

- 1/3 cup almonds, flaked
- 1/3 cup unsweetened coconut flakes
- ¼ cup chia seeds
- 2 tbsp erythritol
- ¼ cup coconut, shredded, unsweetened
- 1 cup almond milk
- 1 tsp vanilla, sugar-free
- 10 drops stevia extract
- ½ cup heavy whipping cream, whipped

Directions:

1. Place almonds and coconut flakes in a pot and toast for 3 minutes until fragrant.
2. Place toasted ingredients into a bowl along with chia seeds, erythritol, and shredded coconut; mix together to combine.
3. Top with milk and stir. You can use hot or cold milk based on your preference.
4. Add vanilla and stevia, stir and set aside for 5-10 minutes.
5. Serve topped with whipped cream.

Nutritional Value:

Calories 277
Total Fats 25.6g
Net Carbs: 16.4g
Protein 5.5g | Fiber: 7.5g

12. Batter Coated Cheddar Cheese

Preparation Time: 23 MIN
Serve: 1

Ingredients:

- 1 large egg
- 2 slices Cheddar cheese
- 1 tsp ground walnuts
- 1 tsp ground flaxseed
- 2 tsp almond flour
- 1 tsp hemp seeds
- 1 tbsp olive oil
- Salt and pepper to taste

Directions:

1. In a small bowl, whisk an egg together with the salt and pepper.
2. Heat a tbsp of olive oil in a frying pan, on medium heat.
3. In a separate bowl, mix the ground flaxseed with the ground walnuts, hemp seeds, and the almond flour.
4. Coat the cheddar slices with the egg mix, then roll in the dry mix and fry cheese for about 3 minutes on each side. Serve hot.

Nutritional Value:

Calories 509
Total Fats 16g
Net Carbs: 2g
Protein 21g

13. Cheesy Boiled Eggs

Preparation Time: 27 MIN
Serve: 2

Ingredients:

- 3 eggs
- 2 tbsp almond butter, no-stir
- 2 tbsp cream cheese, softened
- 1 tsp whipping cream
- Salt and pepper to taste

Directions:

1. In a small saucepan hard boil the eggs.
2. When ready, wash the eggs with cold water, peel and chop them. Place eggs in a bowl; add in the butter, cream cheese and whipping cream.
3. Mix well and add salt and pepper to taste. Serve.

Nutritional Value:

Calories 212
Total Fats 19g
Net Carbs: 0.75g
Protein 7g

14. Mahón Kale Sausage Omelet Pie

Preparation Time: 40 MIN
Serve: 8

Ingredients:

- 3 chicken sausages
- 2 1/2 cups mushrooms, chopped
- 3 cups fresh spinach
- 10 eggs
- 1/2 tsp black pepper and celery seed
- 2 tsp hot sauce
- 1 tbsp garlic powder
- Salt and pepper to taste
- 1 1/2 cups Mahón cheese (or Cheddar

Directions:

1. Preheat oven to 400 F.
2. Chop up the mushroom and chicken sausage thin and place them in a cast iron skillet. Cook on a medium-high heat for 2-3 minutes.
3. While the sausages are cooking, chopped spinach, then add spinach and mushrooms to the skillet.
4. In a meanwhile, in a bowl mix eggs with black pepper and celery seed, spices, and hot sauce. Scramble all mixture well.
5. Mix your spinach, mushrooms, and sausages so that the spinach can wilt completely. Season with salt and pepper to taste.
6. Finally, add the cheese to the top.
7. Pour eggs over the mixture and combine well.
8. Stir the mixture for a few seconds, and then place your skillet in the oven. Bake for 10-12 minutes, and then broil the top for 4 minutes.
9. Let cool for a while, cut into 8 slices and serve hot.

Nutritional Value:

Calories 266
Total Fats 17g
Net Carbs: 7g
Protein 19g

15. Monterey Bacon-Scallions Omelet

Preparation Time: 30 MIN
Serve: 2

Ingredients:

- 2 eggs
- 2 slices cooked bacon
- 1/4 cup scallions, chopped
- 1/4 cup Monterey Jack cheese
- Salt and pepper to taste
- 1 tsp lard

Directions:

1. In a frying pan heat lard in on medium-low heat. Add the eggs, scallions and salt and pepper to taste.

2. Cook for 1-2 minutes; add the bacon and sauté 30 - 45 seconds longer. Turn the heat off on the stove.
3. On top of the bacon place a cheese. Then, take two edges of the omelet and fold them onto the cheese. Hold the edges there for a moment as the cheese has to partially melt. Make the same with the other egg and let cook in a warm pan for a while.
4. Serve hot.

Nutritional Value:

Calories 321
Total Fats 28g
Net Carbs: 1.62g
Protein 14g

16. Smoked Turkey Bacon and Avocado Muffins

Preparation Time: 45 MIN
Serve: 16

Ingredients:

- 6 slices smoked turkey bacon
- 2 tbsp butter
- 3 spring onions
- 1/2 cup cheddar cheese
- 1 tsp baking powder
- 1 1/2 cups coconut milk
- 5 eggs
- 1 1/2 tbsp Metamucil powder
- 1/2 cup almond flour
- 1/4 cup flaxseed
- 1 tsp minced garlic
- 2 tsp dried parsley
- 1/4 tsp red chili powder
- 1 1/2 tbsp lemon juice
- Salt and pepper to taste
- 2 medium avocados

Directions:

1. Preheat oven to 350 F.
2. In a frying pan over medium-low heat, cook the bacon with the butter until crisp. Add the spring onions, cheese, and baking powder.
3. In a bowl, mix together coconut milk, eggs, Metamucil powder, almond flour, flax, spices and lemon juice. Switch off the heat and let cool. Then, crumble the bacon and add all of the fat to the egg mixture.
4. Clean and chop avocado and fold into the mixture.
5. Measure out batter into a cupcake tray that's been sprayed or greased with nonstick spray and bake for 25-26 minutes.
6. Once ready, let cool and serve hot or cold.

Nutritional Value:

Calories 184
Total Fats 16g
Net Carbs: 5.51g
Protein 5.89g

17. Hot n' Spicy Scramble

Preparation Time: 25 MIN
Serve: 4

Ingredients:

- 1 green bell pepper, chopped
- 1 onion, chopped
- 1 cup cooked ham, diced
- 1 cup pepper jack cheese, shredded
- 8 organic eggs
- ½ tsp chili powder
- 1 tsp Sriracha sauce
- ¼ cup coconut milk
- Salt and pepper to taste
- 2 tbsp ghee

Directions:

1. Heat the ghee in a non-stick pan over medium fire.
2. Add the onions and bell pepper to the pan and sauté for 5 minutes.
3. Season with salt and pepper and add the diced ham into the pan.
4. Meanwhile, in a large bowl, whisk together the eggs, chili powder, Sriracha sauce, and coconut milk.
5. Gradually add the shredded cheese into

the bowl with eggs. Set aside.

6. Reduce the heat to low and then pour the egg mixture into the pan with the bell peppers and cook for 2 minutes.
7. Flip and then cook again until the eggs are done.
8. Serve.

Nutritional Value:

Calories 545
Total Fats 53.6g
Net Carbs: 10g
Protein 35g

18. Chorizo Breakfast Peppers

Preparation Time: 25 MIN
Serve: 2

Ingredients:

- ½ tbsp ghee
- 1 onion, chopped
- 2 cloves of garlic
- 6 organic eggs
- ¼ cup almond milk, unsweetened
- 1 cup cheddar cheese, shredded
- Salt and pepper to taste
- 3 large bell peppers, cut in half, core and seeds removed
- ½ lb. spicy chorizo sausage, crumbled

Directions:

1. Set oven to 350 F.
2. Heat the ghee in a non-stick pan over medium heat and cook the chorizo crumbles. Set aside
3. Using the same pan, add the onions and garlic and sauté for a few minutes. Turn off the heat and set aside.
4. In a bowl, stir together the eggs, milk, cheddar, and season with salt and pepper.
5. Add the chorizo into the bowl with the eggs and stir well.
6. Place the bell pepper halves in an oven-safe dish filled with a ¼ inch of water.
7. Scoop the chorizo and egg mixture into the bell peppers and place the dish into the oven to bake for 35 minutes.
8. Serve warm.

Nutritional Value:

Calories 631
Total Fats 46g
Net Carbs: 13g
Protein 44g
Fiber: 3.5 g

19. Breakfast Bread Pudding

Preparation Time: 30 MIN
Serve: 2

Ingredients:

- 4 slices of the Protein Loaded bread, chopped into small bites
- 2 organic eggs
- 2 tbsp heavy cream
- 2 tbsp stevia
- 1 tsp cinnamon, ground
- 1 tbsp organic butter

Directions:

1. Set oven to 350 F.
2. In a bowl whisk the eggs with heavy cream and stevia.
3. Place the chopped bread into an oven-safe dish and pour over the egg mixture. Sprinkle with cinnamon.
4. Bake in the oven for 15 minutes or until the pudding has set.
5. Allow to cool before serving warm.

Nutritional Value:

Calories 278
Total Fats 19.5g
Net Carbs: 4.1g
Protein 22.4g
Fiber: 5.4 g

20. Creamy Chocó & Avocado Mousse

Preparation Time: 50 MIN
Serve: 2

Ingredients:

- 2 ripe avocados
- 1/3 cup cocoa powder
- ½ tsp chia seeds
- 1 tsp vanilla extract

- 10 drops Stevie
- 3 tbsp coconut oil

Directions:

1. Place all the ingredients in a blender and blend until smooth.
2. Pour the mixture into a bowl and place in the fridge to chill for 40 minutes or more.
3. Serve chilled.

Nutritional Value:

Calories 462
Total Fats 46g
Net Carbs: 15g
Protein 6g
Fiber 1.2 g

21. Sour Cream Cheese Pancakes

Preparation Time: 30 MIN
Serve: 2

Ingredients:

- 2 eggs
- 1/4 cup cream cheese
- 1 tbsp coconut flour
- 1 tsp ground ginger
- 1/2 cup liquid Stevie
- Coconut oil
- Sugar-free maple syrup

Directions:

1. In a deep bowl, beat together all of the ingredients until smooth.
2. Heat up a frying skillet with oil on medium-high. Ladle the batter and pour in hot oil.
3. Cook on one side and then flip. Top with a sugar-free maple syrup and serve.

Nutritional Value:

Calories 170
Total Fats 13g
Net Carbs: 4g
Protein 6.90g

22. Vesuvius Scrambled Eggs with Provolone

Preparation Time: 15 MIN
Serve: 2

Ingredients:

- 2 large eggs
- 3/4 cup Provolone cheese
- 1.76 oz. air-dried salami
- 1 tsp fresh rosemary (chopped
- 1 tbsp olive oil
- Salt and pepper to taste

Directions:

1. In a small pan with olive oil fry the chopped salami.
2. In the meantime, in a small bowl whisk the eggs, then add the salt, pepper and fresh rosemary.
3. Add in the provolone cheese and mix well with a fork.
4. Pour the egg mixture into the pan with salami and cook for about 5 minutes. Serve hot.

Nutritional Value:

Calories 396
Total Fats 32.4g
Net Carbs: 2.8g
Protein 26.1g
Fiber: 0.3 g

23. Adorable Pumpkin Flaxseed Muffins

Preparation Time: 25 MIN
Serve: 2

Ingredients:

- 1 egg
- 1 1/4 cups flax seeds (ground
- 1 cup pumpkin puree
- 1 tbsp pumpkin pie spice
- 2 tbsp coconut oil
- 1/2 cup sweetener of your choice
- 1 tsp baking powder
- 2 tsp cinnamon
- 1/2 tsp apple cider vinegar
- 1/2 tsp vanilla extract
- Salt to taste

Directions:

1. Preheat your oven to 360 F.
2. First, grind the flaxseeds for several seconds.
3. Put together all the dry ingredients and stir.
4. Then, add your pumpkin puree and mix to combine.
5. Add the vanilla extract and the pumpkin spice.
6. Add in coconut oil, egg and apple vinegar. Add sweetener of your choice and stir again.
7. Add a heaping tbsp of batter to each lined muffin or cupcake and top with some pumpkin seeds.
8. Bake for about 18 - 20 minutes. Serve hot.

Nutritional Value:

Calories 43
Total Fats 5.34g
Net Carbs: 3g
Protein 1g
Fiber: 1 g

24. Baked Ham and Kale Scrambled Eggs

Preparation Time: 40 MIN
Serve: 2

Ingredients:

- 5 ounces ham diced
- 2 medium eggs
- 1 green onion, finely chopped
- 1/2 cups kale leaves, chopped
- 1 garlic clove, crushed
- 1 green chili, finely chopped
- 4 ready-roasted peppers
- Pinch cayenne pepper
- 1 tbsp olive oil
- 1/2 can water

Directions:

1. Heat oven to 360 F.
2. Heat the oil in a small ovenproof frying pan. Add green onion and cook for 4-5 minutes until softened.
3. Stir in the garlic and chili, and cook for a couple minutes more.
4. Add the 1/2 cup water. Season well and stir in the ready-roasted peppers and ham. Bring to a simmer and cook for 10 minutes.
5. Add the kale, stirring through to wilt.
6. In a small bowl, beat the eggs with a pinch of cayenne and pour in frying pan together with other ingredients.
7. Transfer the frying pan to the oven and bake for 10 minutes.
8. Serve hot.

Nutritional Value:

Calories 251
Total Fats 15.74g
Net Carbs: 3.8g
Protein 22g
Fiber: 0.8g

25. Bell Pepper and Ham Omelet

Preparation Time: 30 MIN
Serve: 2

Ingredients:

- 4 large eggs
- 1 cup green pepper, chopped
- 1/4 lb ham, cooked and diced
- 1 green onion, diced
- 1 tsp coconut oil
- Salt and freshly ground pepper to taste

Directions:

1. Wash and chop vegetables. Set aside.
2. Into a small bowl beat the eggs. Set aside.
3. Heat a non-stick skillet over medium heat and add coconut oil. Pour half of the beaten eggs into the skillet.
4. When the egg has partially set, add half of the vegetables and ham to one-half of the omelet and continue to cook until the egg is almost fully set.
5. Fold the empty half over top of the ham and veggies using a spatula.
6. Cook for 2 minutes more and then serve.
7. Serve hot.

Nutritional Value:

Calories 225.76
Total Fats 12g
Net Carbs: 6.8g
Protein 21.88g
Fiber: 1.4g

26. Sausage Casserole

Preparation time: 10 minutes
Cooking time: 30 minutes
Servings: 4

Ingredients:

- 6 sausages, sliced
- 3 carrots, chopped
- 4 eggs, whisked
- 2 tablespoons tomato sauce
- 1 teaspoon sweet paprika
- 10 ounces canned tomatoes, chopped
- A pinch of salt and black pepper

Directions:

1. In a pan, combine the sausages with the carrots, tomato sauce, paprika, tomatoes, salt and pepper and stir.
2. Add the eggs, whisk everything, introduce in the oven and cook at 370 degrees F for 30 minutes.
3. Slice, divide between plates and serve.
4. Enjoy!

Nutritional Value:calories 287, fat 6, fiber 5, carbs 16, protein 11

27. Green Onions Omelet

Preparation time: 10 minutes
Cooking time: 10 minutes
Servings: 4

Ingredients:

- 4 eggs, whisked
- ½ teaspoon olive oil
- A pinch of salt and black pepper
- 6 green onions, chopped
- 1 cup almond milk

Directions:

1. Heat up a pan with the oil over medium-high heat, add eggs, salt, pepper, onions and almond milk, whisk a bit, spread into the pan, cook for 10 minutes, divide between plates and serve for breakfast.
2. Enjoy!

Nutritional Value:calories 270, fat 10, fiber 6, carbs 9, protein 15

28. Bok Choy and Eggs Mix

Preparation time: 10 minutes
Cooking time: 20 minutes
Servings: 4

Ingredients:

- 1 teaspoon red chili flakes
- 2 red bell peppers, chopped
- ½ teaspoon chili powder
- 1 tablespoon olive oil
- A pinch of salt and black pepper
- 3 bunches bok choy, trimmed and chopped
- 1 teaspoon ginger, grated
- 4 eggs, whisked

Directions:

1. Heat up a pan with the oil over medium-high heat, add bell peppers, stir and cook for 2-3 minutes.
2. Add chili flakes, chili powder, salt, pepper, bok choy and ginger, stir and cook for 5 minutes more.
3. Add the eggs, toss, cook for 7 minutes, divide between plates and serve.
4. Enjoy!

Nutritional Value:calories 208, fat 14, fiber 5, carbs 11, protein 14

29. Breakfast Chia Pudding

Preparation time: 10 minutes
Cooking time: 15 minutes
Servings: 3

Ingredients:

- 2 tablespoons coffee
- 2 cups water
- 1/3 cup chia seeds
- ¼ cup coconut cream

- 1 tablespoon stevia
- 1 tablespoon vanilla extract
- 2 tablespoons chocolate chips
- ¼ cup coconut cream

Directions:

1. Heat up a small pot with the water over medium heat, bring to a boil, add coffee, simmer for 15 minutes, take off heat and strain into a bowl,
2. Add vanilla extract, coconut cream, stevia, chocolate chips and chia seeds, stir well, cover, leave aside for 10 minutes, divide into bowls and serve cold for breakfast.
3. Enjoy!

Nutritional Value:calories 200, fat 4, fiber 4, carbs 9, protein 5

30. Apple Bowls

Preparation time: 10 minutes
Cooking time: 15 minutes
Servings: 3

Ingredients:

- 2 apples, cored and chopped
- 2 cups coconut milk
- ½ cup flax meal
- ½ teaspoon vanilla extract
- 1 tablespoon stevia
- ¼ cup walnuts, chopped

Directions:

1. Heat up a small pot with the milk over medium heat, add apples, flax meal, vanilla, stevia and walnuts, stir, cook for 15 minutes, divide into bowls and serve for breakfast.
2. Enjoy!

Nutritional Value:calories 200, fat 4, fiber 6, carbs 12, protein 6

31. Mexican Bowls

Preparation time: 10 minutes
Cooking time: 20 minutes
Servings: 6

Ingredients:

- 4 ounces canned green chilies, chopped
- 3 tomatoes, chopped
- 1 green bell pepper, chopped
- 1 yellow onion, chopped
- 1 red bell pepper, chopped
- ½ teaspoon oregano, dried
- 2 teaspoons chili powder
- A pinch of salt and black pepper
- 1 tablespoon olive oil

Directions:

1. Heat up a pan with the oil over medium heat, add the onion, bell peppers, tomatoes, oregano, salt, pepper and chili powder, stir and cook for 10 minutes.
2. Add chilies, stir, cook for 10 minutes, divide into bowls and serve.
3. Enjoy!

Nutritional Value:calories 200, fat 7, fiber 2, carbs 11, protein 11

32. Almond Squash Bowls

Preparation time: 10 minutes
Cooking time: 15 minutes
Servings: 4

Ingredients:

- ½ cup walnuts, soaked for 12 hours and drained
- ½ cup almonds
- 1 butternut squash, peeled and cubed
- 1 teaspoon cinnamon powder
- 1 tablespoon stevia
- 1 cup almond milk

Directions:

1. In a pot, combine the walnuts with almonds, squash, cinnamon, stevia and milk, stir, bring to a simmer, cook for 15 minutes, divide into bowls and serve.
2. Enjoy!

Nutritional Value:calories 202, fat 3, fiber 7, carbs 14, protein 6

33. Quick Cauliflower Mix

Preparation time: 10 minutes

Cooking time: 15 minutes
Servings: 2

Ingredients:

- 1 egg, whisked
- A pinch of salt and black pepper
- 2 cups cauliflower florets
- 1 red bell pepper, chopped
- 1 tablespoon onion, chopped
- ½ tablespoon olive oil
- 1 tablespoon goat cheese, crumbled

Directions:

1. Heat up a pan with the oil over medium heat, add the onion, stir and cook for 1-2 minutes.
2. Add cauliflower, bell pepper, salt and pepper, stir and cook for 7 minutes.
3. Add the egg and the cheese, toss, cook for 2 minutes more, divide between plates and serve for breakfast.
4. Enjoy!

Nutritional Value:calories 200, fat 4, fiber 7, carbs 11, protein 9

34. Taco Bowls

Preparation time: 10 minutes
Cooking time: 20 minutes
Servings: 6

Ingredients:

- 1 cup celery, peeled and cubed
- 4 eggs
- ¼ cup yellow onion, chopped
- 1 jalapeno, chopped
- 6 ounces ham, chopped
- A pinch of salt and black pepper
- ¼ teaspoon chili powder
- ¾ teaspoon taco seasoning

Directions:

1. In a bowl, mix eggs with onion, jalapeno, celery, ham, salt, pepper, chili powder and taco seasoning, stir and pour into a casserole.
2. Introduce in the oven and cook at 380 degrees F for 20 minutes.
3. Slice, divide between plates and serve for breakfast.
4. Enjoy!

Nutritional Value:calories 233, fat 4, fiber 6, carbs 10, protein 7

35. Bacon, Sausage and Ham Casserole

Preparation time: 10 minutes
Cooking time: 35 minutes
Servings: 4

Ingredients:

- ½ cup coconut milk
- A pinch of salt and black pepper
- 6 eggs, whisked
- 4 bacon slices, chopped
- 1 cup sausage, chopped
- ½ cup ham, chopped
- 2 green onions, chopped
- 1 cup cheddar cheese, shredded
- Cooking spray

Directions:

1. In a bowl, mix eggs with salt, pepper, milk, sausage, bacon, ham, green onions and cheese, stir well and pour into a casserole greased with cooking spray.
2. Introduce in the oven and cook at 350 degrees F for 35 minutes.
3. Enjoy!

Nutritional Value:calories 271, fat 3, fiber 3, carbs 15, protein 6

36. Almond Waffles

Preparation time: 10 minutes
Cooking time: 10 minutes
Servings: 4

Ingredients:

- 5 eggs, yolks and whites separated
- 3 tablespoons almond milk
- 1 teaspoon baking powder
- 3 tablespoons stevia
- 4 tablespoons coconut flour
- 2 teaspoon vanilla extract

- 4 ounces ghee, melted

Directions:

1. In a bowl, whisk egg whites with your mix
2. In another bowl mix flour with stevia, baking powder, egg yolks, vanilla, ghee, milk and egg whites and stir gently everything.
3. Divide the mix into your waffle iron and cook until the waffles are done.
4. Divide between plates and serve for breakfast.
5. Enjoy!

Nutritional Value:calories 200, fat 13, fiber 2, carbs 15, protein 7

37. Kale Bowls

Preparation time: 5 minutes
Cooking time: 0 minutes
Servings: 2

Ingredients:

- 2 cups coconut milk
- 1 cup kale, torn
- ¼ cup cocoa nibs
- 1 cup cherries, pitted and chopped
- ¼ cup cocoa powder
- 1 small avocado, pitted and peeled

Directions:

1. In a bowl, combine the coconut milk with avocado, cocoa powder, cherries, kale and cocoa nibs, stir, divide into smaller bowls and serve for breakfast.
2. Enjoy!

Nutritional Value:calories 190, fat 3, fiber 2, carbs 12, protein 8

38. Beef Patties

Preparation time: 10 minutes
Cooking time: 25 minutes
Servings: 6

Ingredients:

- 1 pound beef meat, ground
- A pinch of salt and black pepper
- 1 tablespoon garlic, minced
- 1 tablespoon Italian seasoning
- 2 tablespoons homemade mayonnaise
- 2 tablespoons olive oil
- 1 yellow onion, chopped

Directions:

1. In a bowl, combine the beef with salt, pepper, onion, Italian seasoning, garlic and mayo, stir and shape 6 patties
2. Heat up a pan with the olive oil over medium-high heat, add the beef patties, cook them for 5 minutes on each side, divide between plates and serve for breakfast.
3. Enjoy!

Nutritional Value:calories 180, fat 8, fiber 1, carbs 4, protein 20

39. Breakfast Salad

Preparation time: 10 minutes
Cooking time: 25 minutes
Servings: 4

Ingredients:

- 1 and ½ pound beef steak, thinly sliced
- 3 tablespoons olive oil
- A pinch of salt and black pepper
- ¼ cup balsamic vinegar
- 6 ounces sweet onion, chopped
- 1 lettuce head, chopped
- 2 garlic cloves, minced
- 4 ounces mushrooms, sliced
- 1 yellow bell pepper, sliced
- 1 orange bell pepper, sliced
- 1 teaspoon Italian seasoning
- 1 teaspoon red pepper flakes

Directions:

1. In a bowl, mix steaks with salt, pepper and vinegar and toss to coat.
2. Heat up a pan with the oil over medium heat, add mushrooms, garlic and onion, stir, cook for 20 minutes and take off heat.
3. Season steak slices with pepper flakes and

Italian seasoning, place them in a broiling pan, introduce in preheated broiler and cook for 5 minutes.

4. In a salad bowl, combine the lettuce with bell peppers and mushroom mix.
5. Add steaks, toss, divide between plates and serve for breakfast.
6. Enjoy!

Nutritional Value:calories 235, fat 23, fiber 7, carbs 10, protein 15

40. Chicken, Walnuts and Fennel Salad

Preparation time: 10 minutes
Cooking time: 0 minutes
Servings: 4

Ingredients:

- 3 chicken breasts, boneless, skinless, cooked and chopped
- 2 tablespoons olive oil
- ¼ cup walnuts, toasted and chopped
- 1 and ½ cup fennel, chopped
- 2 tablespoons lemon juice
- ¼ cup homemade mayonnaise
- Salt and black pepper to the taste

Directions:

1. In another bowl, mix mayo with salt, pepper, oil, lemon juice and whisk.
2. In a salad bowl, combine the chicken with fennel and walnuts, add the mayo dressing, toss, divide between plates and serve for breakfast.
3. Enjoy!

Nutritional Value:calories 270, fat 10, fiber 6, carbs 14, protein 5

41. Chicken Pate

Preparation time: 10 minutes
Cooking time: 0 minutes
Servings: 2

Ingredients:

- 4 ounces chicken livers, cooked
- ½ tablespoon thyme, chopped
- ½ tablespoon oregano, chopped
- Salt and black pepper to the taste
- 3 tablespoons ghee, melted

Directions:

1. In your food processor, mix chicken livers with thyme, oregano, ghee, salt and pepper, blend well for a few minutes, divide into small cups and serve for breakfast.
2. Enjoy!

Nutritional Value:calories 380, fat 10, fiber 5, carbs 15, protein 11

42. Mini Egg Muffins

Preparation Time: 40 minutes
Serves: 5

Ingredients

- 1 tbsp olive oil
- 1 onion, chopped
- 1 bell pepper, chopped
- 6 slices bacon, chopped
- 8 eggs, whisked
- 1 cup gruyere cheese, shredded
- Salt and black pepper, to taste
- ¼ tsp rosemary
- 1 tbsp fresh parsley, chopped

Directions

1. Set oven to 390°F. Place cupcake liners to your muffin pan. In a skillet over medium heat, warm the oil and sauté the onions and bell pepper for 4-5 minutes, as you stir constantly until tender.
2. Stir in bacon and cook for 3 more minutes. Add in the rest of the ingredients and mix well. Set the mixture to the lined muffin pan and bake for 23 minutes; let muffins cool, before serving.

Nutritional Value: Calories 261; Fat: 16g, Net Carbs: 7.6g, Protein: 21.1g

43. Cheesy Bites with Turnip Chips

Preparation Time: 25 minutes
Serves: 8

Ingredients

- 1 cup Monterey Jack cheese, shredded
- ½ cup natural yogurt
- 1 cup pecorino cheese, grated
- 2 tbsp tomato puree
- ½ tsp dried rosemary leaves, crushed
- 1 tsp dried thyme leaves, crushed
- Salt and black pepper, to taste
- 1 pound turnips, sliced
- 2 tbsp olive oil
- Salt and black pepper, to taste

Directions

1. In a mixing bowl, mix cheese, tomato puree, black pepper, salt, rosemary, yogurt, and thyme. Place in foil liners-candy cups and refrigerate until ready to serve.
2. Set oven to 430°F. Coat turnips with salt, pepper and oil. Arrange in a single layer on a cookie sheet. Bake for 20 minutes, shaking once or twice. Dip turnip chips in cheese cups.

Nutritional Value: Calories 177; Fat: 12.9g, Net Carbs: 6.8g, Protein: 8.8g,

44. Baked Chicken Legs with Cheesy Spread

Preparation Time: 45 minutes
Serves: 4

Ingredients

- 4 chicken legs
- ¼ cup goat cheese
- 2 tbsp sour cream
- 1 tbsp butter, softened
- 1 onion, chopped
- Sea salt and black pepper, to taste

Directions

1. Set oven to 360°F. Bake legs for 25-30 minutes until crispy and browned. In a mixing bowl, mix the rest of the ingredients to form the spread. Serve alongside the prepared chicken legs.
2. Nutritional Value: Calories 119; Fat: 10.5g, Net Carbs: 1.1g, Protein: 5.1g

45. Juicy Beef Cheeseburgers

Preparation Time: 20 minutes
Serves: 6

Ingredients

- 1 pound ground beef
- ½ cup green onions, chopped
- 2 garlic cloves, finely chopped
- ¼ tsp black pepper
- Sea salt and cayenne pepper, to taste
- 2 oz mascarpone cheese
- 3 oz pecorino romano cheese, grated
- 2 tbsp olive oil

Directions

1. Using a mixing bowl, mix ground meat, garlic, cayenne pepper, black pepper, green onions, and salt. Shape into 6 balls; then flatten to make burgers.
2. In a separate bowl, mix mascarpone with grated pecorino romano cheese. Split the cheese mixture among prepared patties. Wrap the meat mixture around the cheese to ensure that the filling is sealed inside. Warm oil in a skillet over medium heat. Cook the burgers for 5 minutes each side.

Nutritional Value: Calories 252; Fat: 15.5g, Net Carbs: 1.2g, Protein: 26g

46. Cilantro & Chili Omelet

Preparation Time: 15 minutes
Serves: 2

Ingredients

- 2 tsp butter
- 2 spring onions, chopped
- 2 spring garlic, chopped
- 4 eggs, beaten
- 1 cup sour cream, divided
- 2 tomatoes, sliced
- 1 green chili pepper, minced
- 2 tbsp fresh cilantro, chopped
- Salt and black pepper, to taste

Directions

1. Set a pan over high heat and warm the butter. Sauté garlic and onions until tender and translucent.
2. Whisk the eggs with sour cream. Pour into the pan and use a spatula to smooth the surface; cook until eggs become puffy and brown to bottom. Add cilantro, chili pepper and tomatoes to one side of the omelet. Add in pepper and salt. Fold the omelet in half and slice into wedges.

Nutritional Value: Calories 319; Fat: 25g, Net Carbs: 10g, Protein: 14.9g

47. Bacon Balls with Brie Cheese

Preparation Time: 15 minutes
Serves: 5

Ingredients

- 3 ounces bacon
- 6 ounces goat's cheese
- 1 chili pepper, seeded and chopped
- ¼ tsp parsley flakes
- ½ tsp paprika

Directions

1. Set a frying pan over medium heat and fry the bacon until crispy; then chop it into small pieces. Place the other ingredients in a bowl and mix to combine well. Refrigerate the mixture. Create balls from the mixture. Set the crushed bacon in a plate. Roll the balls around to coat all sides.

Nutritional Value: Calories 206; Fat: 16.5g, Net Carbs: 0.6g, Protein: 13.4g

48. Jamon & Queso Balls

Preparation Time: 15 minutes
Serves: 8

Ingredients

- 1 egg
- 6 slices jamon serrano, chopped
- 6 ounces cotija cheese
- 6 ounces Manchego cheese
- Salt and black pepper, to taste
- ¼ cup almond flour
- 1 tsp baking powder
- 1 tsp garlic powder

Directions

2. Set oven to 420 °F.
3. Whisk the eggs; place in the remaining

ingredients and mix well. Split the mixture into 16 balls; set the balls on a baking sheet lined with parchment paper. Bake for 13 minutes or until they turn golden brown and become crispy.

Nutritional Value: Calories: 168; Fat 13g, Net Carbs 2.5g, Protein 10.3g

49. Cajun Crabmeat Frittata

Preparation Time: 25 minutes
Serves: 3

Ingredients

- 1 tbsp olive oil
- 1 onion, chopped
- 4 ounces crabmeat, chopped
- 1 tsp cajun seasoning
- 6 large eggs, slightly beaten
- ½ cup Greek yogurt

Directions

1. Set oven to 350°F and set a large skillet over medium heat and warm the oil. Add in onion and sauté until soft; place in crabmeat and cook for 2 more minutes. Season with Cajun seasoning. Evenly distribute the ingredients at the bottom of the skillet.
2. Whisk the eggs with yogurt. Transfer to the skillet. Set the skillet in the oven and bake for about 18 minutes or until eggs are cooked through. Slice into wedges and serve warm.

Nutritional Value: Calories 265; Fat: 15.8g, Net Carbs: 7.1g, Protein: 22.9g

50. Garlick & Cheese Turkey Slices

Preparation Time: 20 minutes
Serves: 4

Ingredients

- 1 tbsp olive oil
- 1 pound turkey breasts, sliced
- 2 garlic cloves, minced
- ½ cup heavy cream
- ⅓ cup chicken broth
- 2 tbsp tomato paste
- 1 cup cheddar cheese, shredded

Directions

1. Set a pan over medium heat and warm the oil; add in garlic and turkey and fry for 4 minutes; set aside. Stir in the broth, tomato paste, and heavy cream; cook until thickened.
2. Return the turkey to the pan; spread shredded cheese over. Let sit for 5 minutes while covered or until the cheese melts. Place in the refrigerator for a maximum of 3 days or serve instantly.

Nutritional Value: Calories 416; Fat: 26g, Net Carbs: 3.2g, Protein: 40.7g

51. Prosciutto & Cheese Egg Cups

Preparation Time: 30 minutes
Serves: 9

Ingredients

- 9 slices prosciutto
- 9 eggs
- 4 green onions, chopped
- ½ cup cheddar cheese, shredded
- ¼ tsp garlic powder
- ½ tsp dried dill weed
- Sea salt and black pepper, to taste

Directions

1. Set oven to 390°F and grease a 9-cup muffin pan with oil. Line one slice of prosciutto on each cup. In a mixing bowl, combine the remaining ingredients. Split the egg mixture among muffin cups. Bake for 20 minutes. Leave to cool before serving.

Nutritional Value: Calories 294, Fat: 21.4g, Net Carbs: 3.5g, Protein: 21g

52. Zucchini with Blue Cheese and Walnuts

Preparation Time: 15 minutes + chilling time
Serves: 6

Ingredients

- 1 tbsp butter

- 6 zucchinis, chopped
- 2 tsp powdered unflavored gelatin
- 1 ⅓ cups heavy cream
- 1 cup sour cream
- 8 ounces blue cheese
- 1 tsp Italian seasoning
- ¼ cup walnut halves

Directions

1. Set a pan over medium heat and warm butter; add in zucchini and sauté for 4 minutes as you stir. Place in heavy cream and gelatin and cook to boil.
2. Transfer from heat; add the Italian seasoning, cheese and sour cream. Evenly layer the mixture in 6 glasses. Place in the refrigerator for at least 5 hours. Serve decorated with walnut halves.

Nutritional Value: Calories 489; Fat: 47.4g, Net Carbs: 6.9g, Protein: 12.7g

53. Carrot & Cheese Mousse

Preparation Time: 15 minutes + cooling time
Serves: 6

Ingredients

- 1 ½ cups half & half
- ½ cup cream cheese
- ½ cup erythritol
- 3 eggs
- 1 ¼ cups canned carrots
- ½ tsp ground cloves
- ½ tsp ground cinnamon
- ¼ tsp grated nutmeg
- A pinch of salt

Directions

1. Using a pan, mix erythritol, cream cheese, and half & half, and boil. Beat the eggs; slowly place in ½ of the hot cream mixture to the beaten eggs. Pour the mixture back to the pan. Cook for 2 to 4 minutes, until thick. Kill the heat; add in carrots, cinnamon, salt, nutmeg, and cloves. Blend with a blender and split the mixture among serving plates and refrigerate.

Nutritional Value: Calories 368, Fat: 33.7g, Net Carbs: 5.6g, Protein: 13.8g

54. Vanilla-Coconut Cream Tart

Preparation Time: 30 minutes
Serves: 6

Ingredients

- ½ cup butter
- ⅓ cup xylitol
- ¾ cup coconut flour
- ⅓ cup coconut shreds, unsweetened
- 1 ¼ cups double cream
- 3 egg yolks
- ⅓ cup coconut flour
- ¾ cup water
- ½ tsp ground cinnamon
- ½ tsp star anise, ground
- ½ tsp vanilla extract
- 1 cup double cream
- 2 tbsp coconut flakes

Directions

1. Set a pan over medium heat and warm butter. Stir in xylitol and cook until fully dissolved.
2. Add in coconut shreds and coconut flour and cook for 2 more minutes. Scrape the crust mixture into the bottom of a baking dish. Refrigerate the mixture.
3. Preheat the pan over medium-low heat; place in 1 ¼ cups of double cream and cook. Fold in egg yolks and mix thoroughly. Mix in water and coconut flour until thick. Place in cinnamon, vanilla extract, and anise star. Cook until thick. Let cool for 10 minutes; sprinkle over the crust. Place in the refrigerator for some hours.
4. Beat 1 cup of the cream until stiff peaks start to form. Apply a cream topping to the cake. Spread coconut flakes on top and serve when chilled well.

Nutritional Value: Calories 305, Fat: 30.6g, Net Carbs: 9.7g, Protein: 4.6g

55. Berry Pancakes with Coconut

Topping

Preparation Time: 20 minutes
Serves: 4

Ingredients For the Batter:

- 5 eggs
- 6 ounces cream cheese, room temperature
- 1 tsp baking powder
- 3 tbsp coconut oil
- A pinch of salt
- For the Topping:
- 1 cup fresh mixed berries
- ¼ tsp freshly grated nutmeg
- 2 tbsp swerve
- ½ cup natural coconut yogurt

Directions

1. Use an electric mixer to beat the eggs, cream cheese, baking powder, and salt. Set a frying pan over medium heat and brush lightly with oil. Ladle a small amount of the batter into the pan and cook for 3 minutes for each side until golden; remove to a plate. Repeat for the remaining pancakes.
2. Serve the pancakes in plates and scatter over fresh berries. Sprinkle with swerve and ground nutmeg, and finish with a dollop of coconut yogurt.

Nutritional Value: Calories 237, Fat: 16.3g, Net Carbs: 8.5g, Protein: 14.5g

56. Goat Cheese Muffins with Ajillo Mushrooms

Preparation Time: 45 minutes
Serves: 6

Ingredients

- 1 ½ cups double cream
- 5 ounces goat cheese, crumbled
- 3 eggs, beaten
- Salt and black pepper, to taste
- 1 tbsp butter, softened
- 2 cups mushrooms, chopped
- 2 garlic cloves, minced

Directions

1. Preheat the oven to 320°F. Insert 6 ramekins into a large pan. Add in boiling water up to 1-inch depth.In a pan, over medium heat, warm double cream. Set heat to a simmer; stir in goat cheese and cook until melted.
2. Set the beaten eggs in a bowl and place in 3 tablespoons of the hot cream mixture; combine well. Place the mixture back to the pan with hot cream/cheese mixture.
3. Sprinkle with pepper and salt. Ladle the mixture into ramekins. Bake for 40 minutes.
4. Melt butter in a pan over medium heat. Add garlic and mushrooms, season with salt and pepper and sauté for 5-6 minutes until tender and translucent.
5. Spread the ajillo mushrooms on top of each cooled muffin to serve.

Nutritional Value: Calories 263, Fat: 22.4g, Net Carbs: 6.1g, Protein: 10g

57. Chili Chicken Breasts Wrapped in Bacon

Preparation Time: 35 minutes
Serves: 6

Ingredients

- 6 chicken breasts, flatten
- 1 tbsp olive oil
- 2 tbsp fresh parsley, chopped
- 3 garlic cloves, chopped
- 1 chili pepper, chopped
- 1 tsp tarragon
- Salt and black pepper, to taste
- 1 tsp hot paprika
- 6 slices bacon

Directions

1. Set oven to 390°F and season with fresh parsley each fillet. Mix chopped garlic, tarragon, hot paprika, salt, chili pepper, and black pepper; rub onto chicken and roll fillets in the bacon slices.
2. Arrange on a greased with the olive oil baking dish and bake for 30 minutes.

Plate the chicken and serve sprinkled with fresh parsley.

Nutritional Value: Calories 275, Fat: 9.5g, Net Carbs: 1.3g, Protein: 44.5g

58. Spanish Salsa Aioli

Preparation Time: 10 minutes
Serves: 8

Ingredients

- 1 tbsp lemon juice
- 1 egg yolk, at room temperature
- 1 clove garlic, crushed
- ½ tsp salt
- ½ cup olive oil
- ¼ tsp black pepper
- ¼ cup fresh parsley, chopped

Directions

1. Using a blender, place in salt, vinegar, garlic, and egg yolk; pulse well to get a smooth and creamy mixture. Set blender to slow speed.
2. Slowly sprinkle in olive oil and combine to ensure the oil incorporates well.
3. Stir in parsley and black pepper. Refrigerate the mixture until ready.

Nutritional Value: Calories 116; Fat: 13.2g, Net Carbs: 0.2g, Protein: 0.4g

59. Herbed Keto Bread

Preparation Time: 40 minutes
Serves: 6

Ingredients

- 5 eggs, separated
- ½ tsp cream of tartar
- 2 cups almond flour
- 3 tablespoons butter, melted
- 3 tsp baking powder
- 1 tsp salt
- 1 tsp dried rosemary
- ½ tsp dried oregano
- 1 tbsp sunflower seeds
- 2 tbsp sesame seeds

Directions

1. Set oven to 360ºF. Use a cooking spray to grease a loaf pan.
2. Combine the eggs with cream of tartar until the formation of stiff peaks happens. In a food processor, place in the baking powder, flour, salt, and butter and blitz to incorporate fully. Add in the egg white mixture while stirring. Ladle the batter into the prepared loaf pan.
3. Spread the loaf with sesame seeds, dried rosemary, sunflower seeds, and oregano and bake for 35 minutes. Serve alongside butter!

Nutritional Value: Calories 109, Fat: 10.2g, Net Carbs: 1g, Protein: 3.9g

60. Cheese Ciabatta with Pepperoni

Preparation Time: 30 minutes
Serves: 6

Ingredients

- 10 ounces cream cheese, melted
- 2 ½ cups mozzarella cheese, shredded
- 4 large eggs, beaten
- 3 tbsp Romano cheese, grated
- ½ cup pork rinds, crushed
- 2 ½ tsp baking powder
- A pinch of salt
- ½ cup tomato puree
- 12 large slices pepperoni

Directions

1. Combine eggs, mozzarella cheese and cream cheese. Place in baking powder, pork rinds, and grated Romano cheese. Season with salt.
2. Set a nonstick pan over medium heat. Cook each ciabatta for 2 minutes per side. Sprinkle tomato puree over each one; apply a topping of 2 slices of pepperoni and serve while warm.

Nutritional Value: Calories 464, Fat: 33.6g, Net Carbs: 9.1g, Protein: 31.1g

61. Italian Cakes with Gorgonzola

and Salami

Preparation Time: 25 minutes
Serves: 5

Ingredients

- 3 slices salami
- 4 eggs, beaten
- ½ cup coconut flour
- 1 tsp baking powder
- 1 cup gorgonzola cheese, diced
- A pinch of salt
- A pinch of grated nutmeg

Directions

1. Set a frying pan over medium heat. Add in salami and cook as you turn with tongs until browned; use paper towels to drain the salami. Chop the salami and stir with the other ingredients to mix.
2. Grease cake molds. Fill them with batter (¾ full). Set oven to 390°F and bake for 15 minutes.

Nutritional Value: Calories 240, Fat: 15.3g, Net Carbs: 10g, Protein: 16.1g

62. One-Pot Cheesy Cauliflower & Bacon

Preparation Time: 15 minutes
Serves: 4

Ingredients

- 1 tbsp butter
- ½ pound bacon, cut into strips
- 1 head cauliflower, broken into florets
- ¼ cup sour cream
- ¾ cup heavy whipping cream
- 1 tsp smashed garlic
- 2 tbsp apple cider vinegar
- ½ cup queso fresco, crumbled

Directions

1. Set a frying pan over medium heat and melt the butter; brown the bacon for 3 minutes. Set aside. Cook cauliflower in pan drippings until tender.
2. Add in the whipping and sour creams, then the vinegar and garlic; cook until warmed fully. Take the reserved bacon back to the pan. Fold in queso fresco and cook for 2 minutes, or until cheese melts.

Nutritional Value: Calories 323, Fat: 24g, Net Carbs: 7.4g, Protein: 18.8g

63. Chorizo Egg Balls

Preparation Time: 35 minutes
Serves: 6

Ingredients

- 2 eggs
- ½ cup butter, softened
- 8 black olives, pitted and chopped
- 3 tbsp mayonnaise
- Salt and crushed red pepper flakes, to taste
- 3 slices cooked chorizo, chopped
- 2 tbsp chia seeds

Directions

1. In a food processor, place eggs, olives, pepper, mayonnaise, butter, and salt and blitz until everything is incorporated. Stir in the chopped chorizo. Refrigerate for 30 minutes. Form balls from the mixture.
2. Set the chia seeds on a serving bowl; roll the balls through to coat. Place in an airtight container and place in the refrigerator for 4 days.

Nutritional Value: Calories 174, Fat: 15.2g, Net Carbs: 4.3g, Protein: 5.9g

64. Ginger & Walnut Porridge

Preparation Time: 25 minutes
Serves: 2

Ingredients

- 3 eggs
- 4 tbsp swerve
- ½ cup double cream
- 1 ½ tbsp coconut oil
- ½ tsp ginger paste
- ¼ tsp turmeric powder
- ¼ cup walnuts, chopped

Directions

1. In a mixing bowl, mix swerve, eggs and double cream.
2. Set a pot over medium heat and warm coconut oil; add in egg/cream mixture and cook until cooked through. Kill the heat and place in turmeric and ginger.
3. Split the porridge into individual bowls, spread the top with chopped walnuts and serve.

Nutritional Value: Calories 430, Fat: 41.1g, Net Carbs: 9.8g, Protein: 11.4g

65 Crabmeat & Cheese Stuffed Avocado

Preparation Time: 25 minutes
Serves: 4

Ingredients

- 1 tsp olive oil
- 1 cup crabmeat
- 2 avocados, halved and pitted
- 3 ounces cream cheese
- ¼ cup almonds, chopped
- 1 tsp smoked paprika

Directions

1. Set oven to 425°F. Grease oil on a baking pan.
2. In a bowl, mix crabmeat with cream cheese. To the avocado halves, place in almonds and crabmeat/cheese mixture and bake for 18 minutes. Decorate with smoked paprika and serve.

Nutritional Value: Calories 264, Fat: 24.4g, Net Carbs: 11g, Protein: 3.7g

66. Pureed Broccoli with Roquefort Cheese

Preparation Time: 15 minutes
Serves: 4

Ingredients

- 1 ½ pounds broccoli, broken into florets
- 2 tbsp olive oil, divided
- 1 tsp crushed garlic
- 1 rosemary sprig, chopped
- 1 thyme sprig, chopped
- 2 cups roquefort cheese, crumbled
- Black pepper to taste

Directions

1. Place salted water in a deep pan and set over medium heat. Add in broccoli and boil for 8 minutes. Remove the cooked florets to a casserole dish.
2. In a food processor, pulse ½ of the broccoli. Place in 1 tablespoon of oil and 1 cup of the cooking liquid. Do the same with the remaining water, broccoli, and 1 tablespoon of olive oil. Stir in the remaining ingredients and serve.

Nutritional Value: Calories 230, Fat: 17.7g, Net Carbs: 7.2g, Protein: 11.9g

67. Cauliflower Gouda Casserole

Preparation Time: 21 minutes
Serves: 4

Ingredients

- 2 heads cauliflower, cut into florets
- ⅓ cup butter, cubed
- 2 tbsp melted butter
- 1 white onion, chopped
- Pink salt and black pepper to taste
- ¼ almond milk
- ½ cup almond flour
- 1 ½ cup grated gouda cheese
- Water for sprinkling

Directions

1. Preheat oven to 350°F and put the cauli florets in a large microwave-safe bowl. Sprinkle with water, and steam in the microwave for 4 to 5 minutes.
2. Melt the ⅓ cup of butter in a saucepan over medium heat and sauté the onions for 3 minutes. Add the cauliflower, season with salt and black pepper and mix in almond milk. Simmer for 3 minutes.
3. Mix the remaining melted butter with almond flour. Stir into the cauliflower as well as half of the cheese. Sprinkle the top with the remaining cheese and bake for 10 minutes until the cheese has

melted and golden brown on the top. Plate the bake and serve with arugula salad.

Nutritional Value: Calories 215, Fat 15g, Net Carbs 4g, Protein 12g

68. Zucchini Lasagna with Ricotta and Spinach

Preparation Time: 50 minutes
Serves: 4

Ingredients

- Cooking spray
- 2 zucchinis, sliced
- Salt and black pepper to taste
- 2 cups ricotta cheese
- 2 cups shredded mozzarella cheese
- 3 cups tomato sauce
- 1 cup packed baby spinach

Directions

1. Preheat oven to 370°F and grease a baking dish with cooking spray.
2. Put the zucchini slices in a colander and sprinkle with salt. Let sit and drain liquid for 5 minutes and pat dry with paper towels. Mix the ricotta, mozzarella, salt, and pepper to evenly combine and spread ¼ cup of the mixture in the bottom of the baking dish.
3. Layer ⅓ of the zucchini slices on top spread 1 cup of tomato sauce over, and scatter a ⅓ cup of spinach on top. Repeat the layering process two more times to exhaust the ingredients while making sure to layer with the last ¼ cup of cheese mixture finally.
4. Grease one end of foil with cooking spray and cover the baking dish with the foil. Bake for 35 minutes, remove foil, and bake further for 5 to 10 minutes or until the cheese has a nice golden brown color. Remove the dish, sit for 5 minutes, make slices of the lasagna, and serve warm.

Nutritional Value: Calories 390, Fat 39g, Net Carbs 2g, Protein 7g

69. Vegetable Greek Mousaka

Preparation Time: 50 minutes
Serves: 6

Ingredients

- 2 large eggplants, cut into strips
- 1 cup diced celery
- 1 cup diced carrots
- 1 small white onion, chopped
- 2 eggs
- 1 tsp olive oil
- 3 cups grated Parmesan, divided into 2
- 1 cup ricotta cheese
- 3 cloves garlic, minced
- 2 tsp Italian seasoning blend
- Salt to taste
- Sauce:
- 1 ½ cups heavy cream
- ¼ cup butter, melted
- 1 cup grated mozzarella cheese
- 2 tsp Italian seasoning
- ¾ cup almond flour

Directions

1. Preheat the oven to 350°F. Lay the eggplant strips on a paper towel, sprinkle with salt and let sit there to exude liquid. Heat olive oil in a skillet over medium heat and sauté the onion, celery, and carrots for 5 minutes. Stir in the garlic and cook further for 30 seconds; set aside to cool.
2. Mix the eggs, 1 cup of parmesan cheese, ricotta cheese, parsley, and salt in a bowl; set aside. Pour the heavy cream in a pot and bring to heat over a medium fire while continually stirring. Stir in the remaining parmesan cheese, and 1 teaspoon of Italian seasoning. Turn the heat off and set aside.
3. To lay the mousaka, spread a small amount of the sauce at the bottom of the baking dish. Pat dry the eggplant strips and make a single layer on the sauce. Spread a layer of ricotta cheese on the eggplants, sprinkle some veggies on it, and repeat the layering process from the

sauce until all the ingredients are exhausted.

4. In a small bowl, evenly mix the melted butter, almond flour, and 1 teaspoon of Italian seasoning. Spread the top of the lasagna layers with it and sprinkle the top with mozzarella cheese. Cover the dish with foil and place it in the oven to bake for 25 minutes. Remove the foil and bake for 5 minutes until the cheese is slightly burned. Slice the mousaka and serve warm.

Nutritional Value: Calories 476, Fat 35g, Net Carbs 9.6g, Protein 33g

70. Creamy Vegetable Stew

Preparation Time: 32 minutes
Serves: 4

Ingredients

- 2 tbsp ghee
- 1 tbsp onion garlic puree
- 4 medium carrots, peeled and chopped
- 1 large head cauliflower, cut into florets
- 2 cups green beans, halved
- Salt and black pepper to taste
- 1 cup water
- 1 ½ cups heavy cream

Directions

1. Melt ghee in a saucepan over medium heat and sauté onion-garlic puree to be fragrant, 2 minutes.
2. Stir in carrots, cauliflower, and green beans, salt, and pepper, add the water, stir again, and cook the vegetables on low heat for 25 minutes to soften. Mix in the heavy cream to be incorporated, turn the heat off, and adjust the taste with salt and pepper. Serve the stew with almond flour bread.

Nutritional Value: Calories 310, Fat 26.4g, Net Carbs 6g, Protein 8g

Tofu Sandwich with Cabbage Slaw
Preparation Time: 4 hours 10 minutes
Serves: 4

Ingredients

- ½ lb Firm tofu, sliced
- 4 low carb buns
- 1 tbsp olive oil
- Marinade
- Salt and black pepper to taste
- 2 tsp allspice
- 1 tbsp erythritol
- 2 tsp chopped thyme
- 1 Habanero, seeded and minced
- 3 green onions, thinly sliced
- 2 cloves garlic
- ¼ cup olive oil
- Slaw
- ½ small cabbage, shredded
- 1 carrot, grated
- ½ red onion, grated
- 2 tsp swerve
- 2 tbsp white vinegar
- 1 pinch Italian seasoning
- ¼ cup olive oil
- 1 tsp Dijon mustard
- Salt and black pepper to taste

Directions

1. In a food processor, make the marinade by blending the allspice, salt, black pepper, erythritol, thyme, habanero, green onions, garlic, and olive oil, for a minute. Pour the mixture in a bowl and put the tofu in it, coating it to be covered with marinade. Place in the fridge to marinate for 4 hours.
2. Make the slaw next: In a large bowl, evenly combine the white vinegar, swerve, olive oil, Dijon mustard, Italian seasoning, salt, and pepper. Stir in the cabbage, carrots, and onion, and place it in the refrigerator to chill while the tofu marinates.
3. Frying the tofu: heat 1 teaspoon of oil in a skillet over medium heat, remove the tofu from the marinade, and cook it in the oil to brown on both sides for 6 minutes in total. Remove onto a plate after and toast the buns in the skillet. In the buns, add the tofu and top with the

slaw. Close the bread and serve with a sweet chili sauce.

Nutritional Value: Calories 386, Fat 33g, Net Carbs 7.8g, Protein 14g

71. reamy Cucumber Avocado Soup

Preparation Time: 15 minutes
Serves: 4

Ingredients

- 4 large cucumbers, seeded, chopped
- 1 large avocado, peeled and pitted
- Salt and black pepper to taste
- 2 cups water
- 1 tbsp cilantro, chopped
- 3 tbsp olive oil
- 2 limes, juiced
- 2 tsp minced garlic
- 2 tomatoes, evenly chopped
- 1 chopped avocado for garnish

Directions

1. Pour the cucumbers, avocado halves, salt, pepper, olive oil, lime juice, cilantro, water, and garlic in the food processor. Puree the ingredients for 2 minutes or until smooth.
2. Pour the mixture in a bowl and top with avocado and tomatoes. Serve chilled with zero-carb bread.

Nutritional Value: Calories 170, Fat 7.4g, Net Carbs 4.1g, Protein 3.7g

72. Asparagus and Tarragon Flan

Preparation Time: 65 minutes
Serves: 4

Ingredients

- 16 asparagus, stems trimmed
- 1 cup water
- ½ cup whipping cream
- 1 cup almond milk
- 2 eggs + 2 egg yolks, beaten in a bowl
- 2 tbsp chopped tarragon, fresh
- Salt and black pepper to taste
- A small pinch of nutmeg
- 2 tbsp grated Parmesan cheese
- 3 cups water
- 2 tbsp butter, melted
- 1 tbsp butter, softened

Directions

1. Pour the water and some salt in a pot, add the asparagus, and bring them to boil over medium heat on a stovetop for 6 minutes. Drain the asparagus; cut their tips and reserve for garnishing. Chop the remaining asparagus into small pieces.
2. In a blender, add the chopped asparagus, whipping cream, almond milk, tarragon, ½ teaspoon of salt, nutmeg, pepper, and parmesan cheese. Process the ingredients on high speed until smooth. Pour the mixture through a sieve into a bowl and whisk the eggs into it.
3. Preheat the oven to 350°F. Grease the ramekins with softened butter and share the asparagus mixture among the ramekins. Pour the melted butter over each mixture and top with 2-3 asparagus tips. Pour the remaining water into a baking dish, place in the ramekins, and insert in the oven.
4. Bake for 45 minutes until their middle parts are no longer watery. Remove the ramekins and let cool. Garnish the flan with the asparagus tips and serve with chilled white wine.

Nutritional Value: Calories 264, Fat 11.6g, Net Carbs 2.5g, Protein 12.5g

73. Vegetable Tempeh Kabobs

Preparation Time: 2 hours 26 minutes
Serves: 4

Ingredients

- 10 oz tempeh, cut into chunks
- 1 ½ cups water
- 1 red onion, cut into chunks
- 1 red bell pepper, cut chunks
- 1 yellow bell pepper, cut into chunks
- 2 tbsp olive oil

- 1 cup sugar-free barbecue sauce

Directions

1. Bring the water to boil in a pot over medium heat and once it has boiled, turn the heat off, and add the tempeh. Cover the pot and let the tempeh steam for 5 minutes to remove its bitterness.
2. Drain the tempeh after. Pour the barbecue sauce in a bowl, add the tempeh to it, and coat with the sauce. Cover the bowl and marinate in the fridge for 2 hours.
3. Preheat a grill to 350°F, and thread the tempeh, yellow bell pepper, red bell pepper, and onion.
4. Brush the grate of the grill with olive oil, place the skewers on it, and brush with barbecue sauce. Cook the kabobs for 3 minutes on each side while rotating and brushing with more barbecue sauce.
5. Once ready, transfer the kabobs to a plate and serve with lemon cauli couscous and a tomato sauce.

Nutritional Value: Calories 228, Fat 15g, Net Carbs 3.6g, Protein 13.2g

74.. Lemon Cauliflower "Couscous" with Halloumi

Preparation Time: 5 minutes
Serves: 4

Ingredients

- 4 oz halloumi, sliced
- Cooking spray
- 1 cauliflower head, cut into small florets
- ¼ cup chopped cilantro
- ¼ cup chopped parsley
- ¼ chopped mint
- ½ lemon juiced
- Salt and black pepper to taste
- Sliced avocado to garnish

Directions

1. Place a non-stick skillet over medium heat and lightly grease it with cooking spray.
2. Add the halloumi and fry for 2 minutes on each side to be golden brown, set aside. Turn the heat off.
3. Next, pour the cauli florets in a bowl and steam in the microwave for 2 minutes. They should be slightly cooked but crunchy. Remove the bowl from the microwave and let the cauli cool. Stir in the cilantro, parsley, mint, lemon juice, salt, and pepper.
4. Garnish the couscous with avocado slices and serve with grilled halloumi and vegetable sauce.

Nutritional Value: Calories 185, Fat 15.6g, Net Carbs 2.1g, Protein 12g

75. Parmesan Roasted Cabbage

Preparation Time: 25 minutes
Serves: 4

Ingredients

- Cooking spray
- 1 large head green cabbage
- 4 tbsp melted butter
- 1 tsp garlic powder
- Salt and black pepper to taste
- 1 cup grated Parmesan cheese
- Grated Parmesan cheese for topping
- 1 tbsp chopped parsley to garnish

Directions

1. Preheat oven to 400°F, line a baking sheet with foil, and grease with cooking spray.
2. Stand the cabbage and run a knife from the top to bottom to cut the cabbage into wedges. Remove stems and wilted leaves. Mix the butter, garlic, salt, and black pepper until evenly combined.
3. Brush the mixture on all sides of the cabbage wedges and sprinkle with parmesan cheese.
4. Place on the baking sheet, and bake for 20 minutes to soften the cabbage and melt the cheese. Remove the cabbages when golden brown, plate and sprinkle with extra cheese and parsley. Serve warm with pan-glazed tofu.

Nutritional Value: Calories 268, Fat 19.3g, Net Carbs 4g, Protein 17.5g

76. Avocado and Tomato Burritos

Preparation Time: 5 minutes
Serves: 4

Ingredients

- 2 cups cauli rice
- Water for sprinkling
- 6 zero carb flatbread
- 2 cups sour cream sauce
- 1 ½ cups tomato herb salsa
- 2 avocados, peeled, pitted, sliced

Directions

1. Pour the cauli rice in a bowl, sprinkle with water, and soften in the microwave for 2 minutes.
2. On flatbread, spread the sour cream all over and distribute the salsa on top. Top with cauli rice and scatter the avocado evenly on top. Fold and tuck the burritos and cut into two.

Nutritional Value: Calories 303, Fat 25g, Net Carbs 6g, Protein 8g

77. Briam with Tomato Sauce

Preparation Time: 70 minutes
Serves: 4

Ingredients

- 3 tbsp olive oil
- 1 large eggplant, halved and sliced
- 1 large onion, thinly sliced
- 3 cloves garlic, sliced
- 5 tomatoes, diced
- 3 rutabagas, peeled and diced
- 1 cup sugar-free tomato sauce
- 4 zucchinis, sliced
- ¼ cup water
- Salt and black pepper to taste
- 1 tbsp dried oregano
- 2 tbsp chopped parsley

Directions

1. Preheat the oven to 400°F. Heat the olive oil in a skillet over medium heat and cook the eggplants in it for 6 minutes to brown on the edges. After, remove to a medium bowl.
2. Sauté the onion and garlic in the oil for 3 minutes and add them to the eggplants. Turn the heat off.
3. In the eggplants bowl, mix in the tomatoes, rutabagas, tomato sauce, and zucchinis. Add the water and stir in the salt, pepper, oregano, and parsley. Pour the mixture in the casserole dish. Place the dish in the oven and bake for 45 to 60 minutes. Serve the briam warm on a bed of cauli rice.

Nutritional Value: Calories 365, Fat 12g, Net Carbs 12.5g, Protein 11.3g

78. Spicy Cauliflower Steaks with Steamed Green Beans

Preparation Time: 20 minutes
Serves: 4

Ingredients

- 2 heads cauliflower, sliced lengthwise into 'steaks'
- ¼ cup olive oil
- ¼ cup chili sauce
- 2 tsp erythritol
- Salt and black pepper to taste
- 2 shallots, diced
- 1 bunch green beans, trimmed
- 2 tbsp fresh lemon juice
- 1 cup water
- Dried parsley to garnish

Directions

1. In a bowl, mix the olive oil, chili sauce, and erythritol. Brush the cauliflower with the mixture. Place them on the grill, close the lid, and grill for 6 minutes. Flip the cauliflower, cook further for 6 minutes.
2. Bring the water to boil over high heat, place the green beans in a sieve and set over the steam from the boiling water. Cover with a clean napkin to keep the steam trapped in the sieve. Cook for 6 minutes. After, remove to a bowl and

toss with lemon juice.

3. Remove the grilled caulis to a plate; sprinkle with salt, pepper, shallots, and parsley. Serve with the steamed green beans.

Nutritional Value: Calories 118, Fat 9g, Net Carbs 4g, Protein 2g

79. Tofu Sesame Skewers with Warm Kale Salad

Preparation Time: 2 hours 40 minutes
Serves: 4
Ingredients

- 14 oz Firm tofu
- 4 tsp sesame oil
- 1 lemon, juiced
- 5 tbsp sugar-free soy sauce
- 3 tsp garlic powder
- 4 tbsp coconut flour
- ½ cup sesame seeds
- Warm Kale Salad:
- 4 cups chopped kale
- 2 tsp + 2 tsp olive oil
- 1 white onion, thinly sliced
- 3 cloves garlic, minced
- 1 cup sliced white mushrooms
- 1 tsp chopped rosemary
- Salt and black pepper to season
- 1 tbsp balsamic vinegar

Directions

1. In a bowl, mix sesame oil, lemon juice, soy sauce, garlic powder, and coconut flour. Wrap the tofu in a paper towel, squeeze out as much liquid from it, and cut it into strips. Stick on the skewers, height wise. Place onto a plate, pour the soy sauce mixture over, and turn in the sauce to be adequately coated. Cover the dish with cling film and marinate in the fridge for 2 hours.
2. Heat the griddle pan over high heat. Pour the sesame seeds in a plate and roll the tofu skewers in the seeds for a generous coat. Grill the tofu in the griddle pan to be golden brown on both sides, about 12 minutes in total.
3. Heat 2 tablespoons of olive oil in a skillet over medium heat and sauté onion to begin browning for 10 minutes with continuous stirring. Add the remaining olive oil and mushrooms. Continue cooking for 10 minutes. Add garlic, rosemary, salt, pepper, and balsamic vinegar. Cook for 1 minute.
4. Put the kale in a salad bowl; when the onion mixture is ready, pour it on the kale and toss well. Serve the tofu skewers with the warm kale salad and a peanut butter dipping sauce.

Nutritional Value: Calories 263, Fat 12.9g, Net Carbs 6.1g, Protein 5.6g

80. Cheesy Cauliflower Falafel

Preparation Time: 15 minutes
Serves: 4

Ingredients

1 head cauliflower, cut into florets
⅓ cup silvered ground almonds
½ tsp mixed spice
Salt and chili pepper to taste
3 tbsp coconut flour
3 fresh eggs
4 tbsp ghee

Directions

1. Blend the cauli florets in a food processor until a grain meal consistency is formed. Pour the puree in a bowl, add the ground almonds, mixed spice, salt, chili pepper, and coconut flour, and mix until evenly combined.
2. Beat the eggs in a bowl until creamy in color and mix with the cauli mixture. Shape ¼ cup each into patties and set aside.
3. Melt ghee in a frying pan over medium heat and fry the patties for 5 minutes on each side to be firm and browned. Remove onto a wire rack to cool, share into serving plates, and top with tahini sauce.

Nutritional Value: Calories 315, Fat 26g, Net Carbs 2g, Protein 8g

81. Portobello Mushroom Burgers

Preparation Time: 15 minutes
Serves: 4

Ingredients

- 4 low carb buns
- 4 portobello mushroom caps
- 1 clove garlic, minced
- ½ tsp salt
- 2 tbsp olive oil
- ½ cup sliced roasted red peppers
- 2 medium tomatoes, chopped
- ¼ cup crumbled feta cheese
- 1 tbsp red wine vinegar
- 2 tbsp pitted kalamata olives, chopped
- ½ tsp dried oregano
- 2 cups baby salad greens

Directions

1. Heat the grill pan over medium-high heat and while it heats, crush the garlic with salt in a bowl using the back of a spoon. Stir in 1 tablespoon of oil and brush the mushrooms and each inner side of the buns with the mixture.
2. Place the mushrooms in the heated pan and grill them on both sides for 8 minutes until tender.
3. Also, toast the buns in the pan until they are crisp, about 2 minutes. Set aside.
4. In a bowl, mix the red peppers, tomatoes, olives, feta cheese, vinegar, oregano, baby salad greens, and remaining oil; toss them. Assemble the burger: in a slice of bun, add a mushroom cap, a scoop of vegetables, and another slice of bread. Serve with cheese dip.

Nutritional Value: Calories 190, Fat 8g, Net Carbs 3g, Protein 16g

82. Zesty Frittata with Roasted Chilies

Preparation Time: 17 minutes
Serves: 4

Ingredients

- 2 large green bell peppers, seeded, chopped
- 4 red and yellow chilies, roasted
- 2 tbsp red wine vinegar
- 1 knob butter, melted
- 8 sprigs parsley, chopped
- 8 eggs, cracked into a bowl
- 4 tbsp olive oil
- ½ cup grated Parmesan
- ¼ cup crumbled goat cheese
- 4 cloves garlic, minced
- 1 cup loosely filled salad leaves

Directions

1. Preheat the oven to 400°F. With a knife, seed the chilies, cut into long strips, and pour into a bowl.
2. Mix in the vinegar, butter, half of the parsley, half of the olive oil, and garlic; set aside. In another bowl, whisk the eggs with salt, pepper, bell peppers, parmesan, and the remaining parsley.
3. Now, heat the remaining oil in the cast iron over medium heat and pour the egg mixture along with half of the goat cheese. Let cook for 3 minutes and when it is near done, sprinkle the remaining goat cheese on it, and transfer the cast iron to the oven.
4. Bake the frittata for 4 more minutes, remove and drizzle with the chili oil. Garnish the frittata with salad greens and serve for lunch.

Nutritional Value: Calories 153, Fat 10.3g, Net Carbs 2.3g, Protein 6.4g

83. Vegan Mushroom Pizza

Preparation Time: 35 minutes
Serves: 4

Ingredients

- 2 tsp ghee
- 1 cup chopped button mushrooms
- ½ cup sliced mixed colored bell peppers
- Pink salt and black pepper to taste
- 1 almond flour pizza bread
- 1 cup tomato sauce

- 1 tsp vegan Parmesan cheese
- Vegan Parmesan cheese for garnish

Directions

1. Melt ghee in a skillet over medium heat, sauté the mushrooms and bell peppers for 10 minutes to soften. Season with salt and black pepper. Turn the heat off.
2. Put the pizza bread on a pizza pan, spread the tomato sauce all over the top and scatter vegetables evenly on top. Season with a little more salt and sprinkle with parmesan cheese.
3. Bake for 20 minutes until the vegetables are soft and the cheese has melted and is bubbly. Garnish with extra parmesan cheese. Slice pizza and serve with chilled berry juice.

Nutritional Value: Calories 295, Fat 20g, Net Carbs 8g, Protein 15g

84. Sausage and Shrimp Stew

Preparation time: 10 minutes
Cooking time: 1 hour
Servings: 6

Ingredients:

- 1 pounds spicy sausage, sliced
- 1 yellow onion, roughly chopped
- 2 celery stalks, chopped
- 2 garlic cloves, minced
- 1 pound shrimp, peeled and deveined
- 1 green bell pepper, chopped
- 28 ounces canned tomatoes, chopped
- A pinch of salt and black pepper

Directions:

1. Heat up a pot over medium-high heat, add sausage, stir and brown for 10 minutes.
2. Add onion, celery, garlic, bell pepper, tomatoes, salt and pepper, bring to a simmer, reduce heat to medium and cook for 45 minutes.
3. Add the shrimp, cover the pot, cook for 5-6 minutes more, divide into bowls and serve for lunch.
4. Enjoy!

Nutritional Value:calories 301, fat 4, fiber 7, carbs 12, protein 8

85. Cauliflower Cream

Preparation time: 10 minutes
Cooking time: 33 minutes
Servings: 4

Ingredients:

- 2 tablespoons olive oil
- 1 small yellow onion, chopped
- 1 cauliflower head, florets separated and chopped
- 3 cups veggie stock
- 1 teaspoon garlic, minced
- A pinch of salt and black pepper
- 1 cup cheddar cheese, shredded
- ½ cup coconut milk

Directions:

1. Heat up a pot with the oil over medium-high heat, add the onion, stir and cook for 2-3 minutes.
2. Add garlic, cauliflower, stock, salt and pepper, stir, bring to a simmer and cook for 30 minutes.
3. Add the milk and the cheese blend the soup using an immersion blender, divide into bowls and serve.
4. Enjoy!

Nutritional Value:calories 271, fat 4, fiber 4, carbs 11, protein 7

86. Indian Chicken Dish

Preparation time: 1 hour
Cooking time: 30 minutes
Servings: 4

Ingredients:

- 2 chicken breasts, skinless, boneless and chopped
- 1 tablespoon lemon juice
- 1 tablespoon garam masala
- ¼ teaspoon ginger, grated
- A pinch of salt and black pepper
- For the sauce:
- 4 teaspoons garam masala

- 4 garlic cloves, minced
- 15 ounces canned tomato sauce
- ½ teaspoon sweet paprika
- ½ teaspoon turmeric powder

Directions:

1. In a bowl, mix chicken with lemon juice, 1-tablespoon garam masala, ginger, salt and pepper, toss well and leave aside in the fridge for 1 hour.
2. Heat up a pot over medium-high heat, add the chicken, stir and cook for 10 minutes.
3. Add 4 teaspoons garam masala, garlic, tomato sauce, paprika and turmeric, stir, cover the pot and cook for 20 minutes.
4. Divide into bowls and serve for lunch
5. Enjoy!

Nutritional Value:calories 252, fat 4, fiber 7, carbs 9, protein 11

87. Creamy Lunch Pork Chops

Preparation time: 10 minutes
Cooking time: 30 minutes
Servings: 4

Ingredients:

- 3 bacon slices, chopped
- 3 garlic cloves, minced
- 1 tablespoon olive oil
- 1 small yellow onion, chopped
- 8 ounces mushrooms, sliced
- 4 pork chops, bone in
- 1 cup veggie stock
- 1 thyme spring, chopped
- 10 ounces coconut cream
- 1 tablespoon parsley, chopped

Directions:

1. Heat up a pot with the oil over medium-high heat, add the bacon, stir and cook for 2 minutes.
2. Add garlic, onion and mushrooms, stir and cook for 3 minutes more.
3. Add pork chops, garlic powder, stock and thyme, stir, bring to a simmer and cook for 30 minutes
4. Add the cream and the parsley, stir, simmer the stew for 10 minutes more, divide into bowls and serve for lunch.
5. Enjoy!

Nutritional Value:calories 270, fat 8, fiber 7, carbs 12, protein 11

88. Tomatillo and Pork Mix

Preparation time: 10 minutes
Cooking time: 45 minutes
Servings: 4

Ingredients:

- 2 pounds pork sirloin roast, cubed
- A pinch of salt and black pepper
- 2 teaspoons garlic powder
- 1 tablespoon olive oil
- 16 ounces green chili tomatillo salsa

Directions:

1. In a bowl, mix pork with cumin, salt, pepper and garlic powder and rub well.
2. Heat up a pan with the oil over medium-high heat, add the pork and brown for 5 minutes on each side.
3. Add the tomatillo mix, stir, bring to a simmer and cook for 35 minutes more.
4. Divide into bowls and serve for lunch.
5. Enjoy!

Nutritional Value:calories 321, fat 7, fiber 6, carbs 10, protein 17

89. Cheesy Meatloaf

Preparation time: 10 minutes
Cooking time: 55 minutes
Servings: 4

Ingredients:

- 2 pounds beef, ground
- ¼ cup parmesan, grated
- 2 yellow onions, chopped
- 1 egg, whisked
- A pinch of salt and black pepper
- 1 tablespoon garlic, minced
- ½ teaspoon thyme, dried
- 1 tablespoon olive oil

- 1 cup tomato paste
- ½ cup beef stock

Directions:

1. In a bowl, mix beef with cheese, 1 onion, egg, thyme, garlic, salt and pepper and stir really well.
2. Shape a meatloaf out of this mix and put it in a baking dish.
3. Heat up a pan with the oil over medium-high heat; add the other onion, stir and sauté for 4-5 minutes.
4. Add stock and tomato paste, stir, simmer for 1-2 minutes more, pour over the meatloaf, cover the dish with tin foil, introduce in the oven and cook at 390 degrees F for 45 minutes.
5. Slice the meatloaf, divide it between plates, drizzle the sauce all over and serve for lunch.
6. Enjoy!

Nutritional Value:calories 383, fat 6, fiber 3, carbs 12, protein 11

90. Shrimp Skillet

Preparation time: 10 minutes
Cooking time: 15 minutes
Servings: 4

Ingredients:

- 8 ounces mushrooms, chopped
- 1 pound shrimp, peeled and deveined
- 1 yellow onion, chopped
- Salt and black pepper to the taste
- 1 butternut squash, peeled and cubed
- 2 tablespoons olive oil
- 2 teaspoons Italian seasoning
- 1 teaspoon red pepper flakes, crushed
- ¼ cup ghee
- 1 cup parmesan, grated
- 2 garlic cloves, minced
- 1 cup coconut cream

Directions:

1. Heat up a pan with oil and ghee over medium-high heat, add mushrooms and onion, stir and cook for 5 minutes.
2. Add pepper flakes, Italian seasoning, salt, pepper and squash, stir and cook for 5-6 minutes more.
3. Add coconut cream, parmesan, garlic and shrimp, stir, cook for 5 minutes, divide between plates and serve for lunch.
4. Enjoy!

Nutritional Value:calories 251, fat 6, fiber 2, carbs 9, protein 10

91. Mexican Chicken Soup

Preparation time: 10 minutes
Cooking time: 30 minutes
Servings: 6

Ingredients:

- 1 and ½ pounds chicken tights, skinless, boneless and cubed
- 15 ounces chicken stock
- 15 ounces chunky salsa
- 8 ounces Monterey jack cheese, shredded

Directions:

1. Put the chicken and the stock in a pot, bring to a simmer over medium heat, add salsa, stir, cover the pot and cook for 30 minutes.
2. Add the cheese, stir, ladle the soup into bowls and serve for lunch.
3. Enjoy!

Nutritional Value:calories 300, fat 6, fiber 3, carbs 9, protein 18

92. Chicken and Tomato Soup

Preparation time: 10 minutes
Cooking time: 30 minutes
Servings: 4

Ingredients:

- 2 chicken breasts, boneless and skinless and cubed
- 3 cups chicken stock
- 16 ounces canned tomatoes, chopped
- 4 ounces canned green chilies, chopped
- Salt and black pepper to the taste
- 2 garlic cloves, minced
- 1 cup white onion, chopped

- 1 teaspoon oregano, dried
- 1 tablespoon cilantro, chopped

Directions:

1. Put the stock in a pot and bring to a simmer over medium heat.
2. Add the chicken, tomatoes, chilies, salt, pepper, garlic, onion and oregano, stir, cover the pot and simmer the soup for 30 minutes.
3. Add the cilantro, stir, ladle the soup into bowls and serve for lunch.
4. Enjoy!

Nutritional Value:calories 261, fat 7, fiber 7, carbs 13, protein 13

93. Meatballs Stew

Preparation time: 10 minutes
Cooking time: 30 minutes
Servings: 6

Ingredients:

- 1 and ½ pounds pork meat, ground
- 1 egg
- 2 tablespoons parsley, chopped
- 4 tablespoons coconut flour
- 2 garlic cloves, minced
- Salt and black pepper to the taste
- ¾ cup veggie stock
- 1 cup tomato sauce
- ½ teaspoon nutmeg, ground
- ½ teaspoon sweet paprika
- 2 tablespoons olive oil
- 2 carrots, chopped

Directions:

1. In a bowl, combine the meat with egg, salt, pepper, parsley, paprika, garlic and nutmeg, stir, shape medium meatballs out of this mix and dust them with the flour.
2. Heat up a pot with the oil over medium-high heat, add the meatballs and brown them for 3-4 minutes on each side.
3. Add carrots, tomato sauce and stock, stir, bring to a simmer, cover the pot and cook the stew for 20 minutes.
4. Divide everything into bowls and serve for lunch.
5. Enjoy!

Nutritional Value:calories 281, fat 8, fiber 6, carbs 10, protein 15

94. Chicken Cream Soup

Preparation time: 10 minutes
Cooking time: 25 minutes
Servings: 6

Ingredients:

- 1 and ½ pounds butternut squash, peeled and cubed
- 1 cup chicken meat, cooked and shredded
- ½ cup green onions, chopped
- 3 tablespoons ghee, melted
- 30 ounces chicken stock
- ½ cup carrots, chopped
- ½ cup celery, chopped
- 1 garlic clove, minced
- ½ teaspoon Italian seasoning
- 15 ounces canned tomatoes, chopped
- Salt and black pepper to the taste
- A pinch of red pepper flakes, dried
- 1 and ½ cup coconut cream

Directions:

1. Heat up a pot with the ghee over medium-high heat, add celery, carrots and onions, stir and cook for 5 minutes.
2. Add garlic, squash, chicken, tomatoes, stock, Italian seasoning, salt, pepper, pepper flakes and nutmeg, stir, bring to a simmer and cook for 15 minutes.
3. Blend soup using an immersion blender, add coconut cream, stir, cook for 5 minutes more, ladle into bowls and serve.
4. Enjoy!

Nutritional Value:calories 282, fat 9, fiber 7, carbs 10, protein 7

95. Asparagus Soup

Preparation time: 10 minutes
Cooking time: 20 minutes
Servings: 5

Ingredients:

- 2 pounds green asparagus, chopped
- 2 tablespoons olive oil
- 5 cups chicken stock
- 1 yellow onion, chopped
- A pinch of salt and black pepper
- ¼ teaspoon lemon juice
- 1 cup coconut cream

Directions:

1. Heat up a pot with the oil over medium-high heat, add the asparagus, onion, salt and pepper, stir and cook for 5 minutes.
2. Add stock, cover the pot, bring to a boil, cook for 15 minutes, transfer everything to your blender, pulse well, add coconut cream and lemon juice, stir, ladle into bowls and serve.
3. Enjoy!

Nutritional Value:calories 250, fat 5, fiber 9, carbs 8, protein 7

96. Fennel Soup

Preparation time: 10 minutes
Cooking time: 25 minutes
Servings: 3

Ingredients:

- 3 fennel bulbs, chopped
- 2 cups veggie stock
- 1 tablespoon olive oil
- Salt and black pepper to the taste
- 2 teaspoons parmesan cheese, grated

Directions:

1. Heat up a pot with the oil over medium-high heat, add the fennel, stir and sauté it for 5 minutes.
2. Add the stock, salt and pepper, stir, bring to a simmer and cook for 20 minutes.
3. Add cheese, stir, ladle into bowls and serve.
4. Enjoy!

Nutritional Value:calories 206, fat 3, fiber 7, carbs 12, protein 5

97. Lunch Chicken and Tomatoes Stew

Preparation time: 10 minutes
Cooking time: 40 minutes
Servings: 6

Ingredients:

- 6 chicken thighs
- 1 teaspoon olive oil
- ¼ pound baby carrots
- Salt and black pepper to the taste
- 1 yellow onion, chopped
- 1 celery stalk, chopped
- 1 tablespoon parsley, chopped
- 2 and ½ cups chicken stock
- 15 ounces canned tomatoes, chopped

Directions:

1. Heat up a pot with the oil over medium-high heat, add the chicken, salt and pepper and brown for 4 minutes on each side.
2. Add celery, onion and carrots, stir and sauté them for 4 minutes.
3. Add stock and tomatoes, stir, bring to a simmer and cook for 25 minutes.
4. Transfer chicken pieces to a cutting board, leave aside to cool down for a few minutes, discard bones, shred meat, return it to the stew, also add the parsley, toss, divide into bowls and serve for lunch.
5. Enjoy!

Nutritional Value:calories 272, fat 4, fiber 4, carbs 7, protein 14

98. Fresh Eggplant Mix

Preparation time: 10 minutes
Cooking time: 10 minutes
Servings: 4

Ingredients:

- 1 eggplant, sliced
- 1 red onion, sliced
- 2 teaspoons olive oil
- 1 avocado, pitted and chopped
- 1 teaspoon mustard

- 1 tablespoon balsamic vinegar
- Zest of 1 lemon, grated
- A pinch of salt and black pepper
- 1 tablespoon fresh oregano, chopped

Directions:

1. Brush the onion slices and eggplant with half of the oil, put them on heated kitchen grill over medium-high heat, cook for 5 minutes on each side, transfer them to a cutting board, roughly chop them, put them in a bowl, add the avocado and toss a bit.
2. In a bowl, mix vinegar with mustard, oregano, lemon zest, the rest of the oil, salt and pepper, whisk well, pour over the eggplant mix, toss, divide into bowls and serve for lunch,
3. Enjoy!

Nutritional Value:calories 250, fat 3, fiber 2, carbs 14, protein 8

99. Fish Soup

Preparation time: 10 minutes
Cooking time: 36 minutes
Servings: 4

Ingredients:

- 1 yellow onion, chopped
- 1 pound white fish, skinless, boneless and roughly cubed
- 10 cups veggie stock
- 1 pound carrots, sliced
- 1 tablespoon olive oil
- Salt and black pepper to the taste
- 2 tablespoons ginger, grated

Directions:

1. Heat up a pot with the oil over medium heat, add onion, stir and sauté for 6 minutes.
2. Add ginger, carrots, salt, pepper, water and stock, stir bring to a simmer and cook for 20 minutes.
3. Add the fish, simmer the soup for 10 minutes more, ladle it into bowls and serve for lunch.
4. Enjoy!

Nutritional Value:calories 200, fat 6, fiber 6, carbs 9, protein 11

100. Bacon Kebabs

Preparation time: 10 minutes
Cooking time: 20 minutes
Servings: 6

Ingredients:

- 1 pound mushroom caps
- 6 bacon strips
- 1 tablespoon olive oil
- Salt and black pepper to the taste
- ½ teaspoon sweet paprika

Directions:

1. Season mushroom caps with salt, pepper and paprika.
2. Spear a bacon strip on a skewer's ends, continue with a mushroom cap and fold over bacon and repeat until you obtain a braid.
3. Repeat with the rest of the mushrooms and bacon strip, brush the kebabs with the oil, place them on preheated kitchen grill over medium heat, cook for 10 minutes on each side, divide them between plates and serve for lunch with a side salad.
4. Enjoy!

Nutritional Value:calories 200, fat 7, fiber 4, carbs 12, protein 10

101. Creamy Pumpkin Soup

Preparation time: 10 minutes
Cooking time: 20 minutes
Servings: 6

Ingredients:

- ½ cup yellow onion, chopped
- 2 tablespoons olive oil
- 1 garlic clove, minced
- 1 teaspoon cumin, ground
- 1 teaspoon coriander, ground
- 2 cups pumpkin puree
- Salt and black pepper to the taste
- 32 ounces chicken stock

- ½ cup coconut cream

Directions:

1. Heat up a pot with the oil over medium heat, add onions and garlic, stir and cook for 4 minutes.
2. Add cumin and coriander, stir and cook for 1 minute more.
3. Add stock and pumpkin puree, stir and cook for 5 minutes.
4. Add salt and pepper and cream, blend soup well using an immersion blender, cook for 10 minutes more and divide into bowls and serve for lunch.
5. Enjoy!

Nutritional Value:calories 270, fat 12, fiber 6, carbs 14, protein 5

102. Pork Pie

Preparation time: 10 minutes
Cooking time: 50 minutes
Servings: 6

Ingredients:

- For the crust:
- 2 cups cracklings
- ¼ cup flax meal
- 1 cup almond flour
- 2 eggs
- For the filling:
- 1 cup cheddar cheese, grated
- 4 eggs
- 12 ounces pork loin, chopped
- ½ cup coconut cream
- 1 red onion, chopped
- ¼ cup chives, chopped
- 2 garlic cloves, minced
- Salt and black pepper to the taste
- 2 tablespoons ghee, melted

Directions:

1. In your food processor, combine the crackings with the flour, flax meal and 2 eggs, blend until you obtain a dough, transfer to a pie pan, press well on the bottom, introduce in the oven at 350 degrees F and bake for 15 minutes.
2. Heat up a pan with the ghee over medium-high heat, add garlic and onion, stir and cook for 5 minutes.
3. Add bacon and pork loin, brown for 5-6 minutes and take off heat.
4. In a bowl, combine 4 eggs with salt, pepper, cheese, chives and cream and blend well.
5. Spread pork into pie pan, add eggs mix, introduce in the oven at 350 degrees F, bake for 25 minutes, slice and serve for lunch.
6. Enjoy!

Nutritional Value:calories 405, fat 14, fiber 3, carbs 13, protein 33

103. Chicken and Mint Sauce

Preparation time: 20 minutes
Cooking time: 25 minutes
Servings: 6

Ingredients:

- 18 chicken wings
- 1 tablespoon turmeric powder
- 1 tablespoon ginger, grated
- 1 tablespoon coriander, ground
- 1 tablespoon sweet paprika
- Salt and black pepper to the taste
- 2 tablespoons olive oil
- For the sauce:
- Juice of ½ lime
- 1 cup mint leaves
- 1-inch ginger, grated
- ¾ cup cilantro
- 1 tablespoon olive oil
- 1 tablespoon water
- Salt and black pepper to the taste

Directions:

1. In a bowl, combine 1 tablespoon ginger with coriander, paprika, turmeric, salt, pepper and 2 tablespoons oil, stir well, add the chicken wings, toss and keep in the fridge for 20 minutes.
2. Heat up your grill over high heat, add the wings, cook for 25 minutes, turning them

from time to time and divide them between plates,

3. In a blender, combine the mint with cilantro, 1-inch ginger, lime juice, 1 tablespoon oil, salt, pepper and water, blend well, spread over the chicken wings and serve for lunch.
4. Enjoy!

Nutritional Value:calories 260, fat 5, fiber 7, carbs 15, protein 11

104. One Pan Chicken Thighs

Preparation time: 10 minutes
Cooking time: 30 minutes
Servings: 4

Ingredients:

- 4 chicken thighs
- 2 cups mushrooms, sliced
- ¼ cup ghee
- Salt and black pepper to the taste
- ½ teaspoon onion powder
- ½ teaspoon garlic powder
- ½ cup water
- 1 teaspoon mustard
- 1 tablespoon parsley, chopped

Directions:

1. Heat up a pan with half of the ghee over medium-high heat, add chicken thighs, salt, pepper, garlic and onion powder, cook for 3 minutes on each side and transfer to a bowl.
2. Heat up the same pan with the rest of the ghee over medium-high heat, add mushrooms, mustard and water, stir and cook for 5 minutes.
3. Return chicken to the pan, stir, cover, cook for 15 minutes, add parsley, toss, divide between plates and serve for lunch.
4. Enjoy!

Nutritional Value:calories 273, fat 32, fiber 6, carbs 12, protein 26

105. Roasted Cauliflower with Serrano Ham & Pine Nuts

Preparation Time: 30 minutes
Serves: 6

Ingredients

- 2 heads cauliflower, cut into 1-inch slices
- 2 tbsp olive oil
- Salt and chili pepper to taste
- 1 tsp garlic powder
- 10 slices Serrano ham, chopped
- ¼ cup pine nuts, chopped
- 1 tsp capers

Directions

1. Preheat oven to 450°F and line a baking sheet with foil.
2. Brush the cauli steaks with olive oil and season with chili pepper, garlic, and salt.
3. Spread the cauli florets on the baking sheet. Roast in the oven for 10 minutes until tender and lightly browned. Remove the sheet and sprinkle the ham and pine nuts all over the cauli. Bake for another 10 minutes until the ham is crispy and a nutty aroma is perceived.
4. Take out, sprinkle with capers and parsley. Serve with ground beef stew and braised asparagus.

Nutritional Value: Calories 141, Fat 10g, Net Carbs 2.5g, Protein 10g

106. Mascarpone Snapped Amaretti Biscuits

Preparation Time: 25 minutes
Serves: 6

Ingredients

- 6 egg whites
- 1 egg yolk, beaten
- 1 tsp vanilla bean paste
- 8 oz swerve confectioner's sugar
- A pinch of salt
- ¼ cup ground fragrant almonds
- 1 lemon juice
- 7 tbsp sugar-free amaretto liquor
- ¼ cup mascarpone cheese
- ¼ cup butter, room temperature
- ¾ cup swerve confectioner's sugar, for topping

Directions

1. Preheat an oven to 300°F and line a baking sheet with parchment paper. Set aside.
2. In a bowl, beat eggs whites, salt, and vanilla paste with the hand mixer while you gradually spoon in 8 oz of swerve confectioner's sugar until a stiff mixture. Add ground almonds and fold in the egg yolk, lemon juice, and amaretto liquor. Spoon the mixture into the piping bag and press out 40 to 50 mounds on the baking sheet.
3. Bake the biscuits for 15 minutes by which time they should be golden brown. Whisk the mascarpone cheese, butter, and swerve confectioner's sugar with the cleaned electric mixer; set aside.
4. When the biscuits are ready, transfer them into a serving bowl and let cool. Spread a scoop of mascarpone cream onto one biscuit and snap with another biscuit. Sift some swerve confectioner's sugar on top of them and serve.

Nutritional Value: Calories 165, Fat 13g, Net Carbs 3g, Protein 9g

107. Cheesy Chicken Fritters with Dill Dip

Preparation Time: 32 minutes + cooling time
Serves: 4

Ingredients

- 1 lb chicken breasts, thinly sliced
- 1 ¼ cup mayonnaise
- ¼ cup coconut flour

- 2 eggs
- Salt and black pepper to taste
- 1 cup grated mozzarella cheese
- 4 tbsp chopped dill
- 3 tbsp olive oil
- 1 cup sour cream
- 1 tsp garlic powder
- 1 tbsp chopped parsley
- 2 tbsp finely chopped onion

Directions

1. In a bowl, mix 1 cup of the mayonnaise, 3 tbsp of dill, sour cream, garlic powder, onion, and salt. Cover the bowl with plastic wrap and refrigerate for 30 minutes.
2. Mix the chicken, remaining mayonnaise, coconut flour, eggs, salt, pepper, mozzarella, and remaining dill, in a bowl. Cover the bowl with plastic wrap and refrigerate it for 2 hours. After the marinating time is over, remove from the fridge.
3. Place a skillet over medium fire and heat the olive oil. Fetch 2 tablespoons of chicken mixture into the skillet, use the back of a spatula to flatten the top. Cook for 4 minutes, flip, and fry for 4 more.
4. Remove onto a wire rack and repeat the cooking process until the batter is finished, adding more oil as needed. Garnish the fritters with parsley and serve with dill dip.

Nutritional Value: Calories 151, Fat 7g, Net Carbs 0.8g, Protein 12g

108. Spinach Turnip Salad with Bacon

Preparation Time: 48 minutes
Serves: 4

Ingredients

- 6 turnips, cut into wedges
- 1 tsp olive oil
- 1 cup baby spinach chopped
- 3 radishes, sliced
- 3 bacon slices, sliced
- 4 tbsp sour cream
- 2 tsp mustard seeds
- 1 tsp Dijon mustard
- 1 tbsp red wine vinegar
- Salt and black pepper to taste
- 1 tbsp chopped chives

Directions

1. Preheat the oven to 400°F. Line a baking sheet with parchment paper, toss the turnips with pepper, drizzle with the olive oil, and bake for 25 minutes, turning halfway. Let cool.
2. Spread the baby spinach in the bottom of a salad bowl and top with the radishes. Remove the turnips to the salad bowl. Fry the bacon in a skillet over medium heat until crispy, about 5 minutes.
3. Mix the sour cream, mustard seeds, Dijon mustard, vinegar, and salt with the bacon. Add a little water to deglaze the bottom of the skillet and turn off the heat.
4. Pour the bacon mixture over the vegetables, scatter the chives over it, and season with black pepper.Serve the salad with grilled pork chops.

Nutritional Value: Calories 193, Fat 18.3g, Net Carbs 3.1g, Protein 9.5g

109. Zucchini Gratin with Feta Cheese

Preparation Time: 65 minutes
Serves: 6

Ingredients

- Cooking spray
- 2 lb zucchinis, sliced
- 2 red bell peppers, seeded and sliced
- Salt and black pepper to taste
- 1 ½ cups crumbled feta cheese
- ⅓ cup crumbled feta cheese for topping
- 2 tbsp butter
- ¼ tsp xanthan gum
- ½ cup heavy whipping cream

Directions

1. Preheat oven to 370°F. Place the sliced

zucchini in a colander over the sink, sprinkle with salt and let sit for 20 minutes. Transfer to paper towels to drain the excess liquid.
2. Grease a baking dish with cooking spray and make a layer of zucchini and bell peppers in the dish overlapping one on another. Season with black pepper, and sprinkle with some feta cheese. Repeat the layering process a second time.
3. Combine the butter, xanthan gum, and whipping cream in a microwave dish for 2 minutes, stir to mix completely, and pour over the vegetables. Top with remaining feta cheese.
4. Bake the gratin for 45 minutes to be golden brown on top. Cut out slices and serve with kale salad.

Nutritional Value: Calories 264, Fat 21g, Net Carbs 4g, Protein 14g

110. Cheesy Cauliflower Bake with Mayo Sauce

Preparation Time: 27 minutes
Serves: 6

Ingredients

- Cooking spray
- 2 heads cauliflower, cut into florets
- ¼ cup melted butter
- Salt and black pepper to taste
- 1 pinch red pepper flakes
- ½ cup mayonnaise
- ¼ tsp Dijon mustard
- 3 tbsp grated pecorino cheese

Directions

1. Preheat oven to 400°F and grease a baking dish with cooking spray.
2. Combine the cauli florets, butter, salt, black pepper, and red pepper flakes in a bowl until well mixed. Mix the mayonnaise and Dijon mustard in a bowl, and set aside until ready to serve. Arrange cauliflower florets on the prepared baking dish.
3. Sprinkle with grated pecorino cheese and bake for 25 minutes until the cheese has melted and golden brown on the top. Remove, let sit for 3 minutes to cool, and serve with the mayo sauce.

Nutritional Value: Calories 363, Fat 35g, Net Carbs 2g, Protein 6g

111. Parmesan Crackers with Guacamole

Preparation Time: 10 minutes
Serves: 4

Ingredients

- 1 cup finely grated Parmesan cheese
- ¼ tsp sweet paprika
- ¼ tsp garlic powder
- 2 soft avocados, pitted and scooped
- 1 tomato, chopped
- Salt to taste

Directions

1. To make the chips, preheat oven to 350°F and line a baking sheet with parchment paper.
2. Mix parmesan cheese, paprika, and garlic powder evenly. Spoon 6 to 8 teaspoons on the baking sheet creating spaces between each mound. Flatten mounds with your hands. Bake for 5 minutes, cool, and remove with a spatula onto a plate.
3. To make the guacamole, mash avocado, with a fork in a bowl, add in tomato and continue to mash until mostly smooth. Season with salt. Serve crackers with guacamole.

Nutritional Value: Calories 229, Fat 20g, Net Carbs 2g, Protein 10g

112. Crunchy Pork Rind and Zucchini Sticks

Preparation Time: 20 minutes
Serves: 4

Ingredients

- Cooking spray
- ¼ cup pork rind crumbs
- 1 tsp sweet paprika

- ¼ cup shredded Parmesan cheese
- Salt and chili pepper to taste
- 3 fresh eggs
- 2 zucchinis, cut into strips

Directions

1. Preheat oven to 425°F and line a baking sheet with foil. Grease with cooking spray and set aside. Mix the pork rinds, paprika, parmesan cheese, salt, and chili pepper in a bowl. Beat the eggs in another bowl. Coat zucchini strips in egg, then in parmesan mixture, and arrange on the baking sheet. Grease lightly with cooking spray and bake for 15 minutes to be crispy.
2. To make the aioli, combine in a bowl mayonnaise, lemon juice, and garlic, and gently stir until everything is well incorporated. Add the lemon zest, adjust the seasoning and stir again. Cover and place in the refrigerator until ready to serve. Arrange the zucchini strips on a serving plate and serve with garlic aioli for dipping.

Nutritional Value: Calories 180, Fat 14g, Net Carbs 2g, Protein 6g

113. Cheesy Green Bean Crisps

Preparation Time: 30 minutes
Serves: 6

Ingredients

- Cooking spray
- ¼ cup shredded pecorino romano cheese
- ¼ cup pork rind crumbs
- 1 tsp garlic powder
- Salt and black pepper to taste
- 2 eggs
- 1 lb green beans, thread removed

Directions

1. Preheat oven to 425°F and line two baking sheets with foil. Grease with cooking spray and set aside.
2. Mix the pecorino, pork rinds, garlic powder, salt, and black pepper in a bowl. Beat the eggs in another bowl. Coat green beans in eggs, then cheese mixture and arrange evenly on the baking sheets.
3. Grease lightly with cooking spray and bake for 15 minutes to be crispy. Transfer to a wire rack to cool before serving. Serve with sugar-free tomato dip.

Nutritional Value: Calories 210, Fat 19g, Net Carbs 3g, Protein 5g

114. Bacon Mashed Cauliflower

Preparation Time: 40 minutes
Serves: 6

Ingredients

- 6 slices bacon
- 3 heads cauliflower, leaves removed
- 2 cups water
- 2 tbsp melted butter
- ½ cup buttermilk
- Salt and black pepper to taste
- ¼ cup grated yellow cheddar cheese
- 2 tbsp chopped chives

Directions

1. Preheat oven to 350°F. Fry bacon in a heated skillet over medium heat for 5 minutes until crispy. Remove to a paper towel-lined plate, allow to cool, and crumble. Set aside and keep bacon fat.
2. Boil cauli heads in water in a pot over high heat for 7 minutes, until tender. Drain and put in a bowl.
3. Include butter, buttermilk, salt, black pepper, and puree using a hand blender until smooth and creamy. Lightly grease a casserole dish with the bacon fat and spread the mash in it.
4. Sprinkle with cheddar cheese and place under the broiler for 4 minutes on high until the cheese melts. Remove and top with bacon and chopped chives. Serve with pan-seared scallops.

Nutritional Value: Calories 312, Fat 25g, Net Carbs 6g, Protein 14g

115. Devilled Eggs with Sriracha Mayo

Preparation Time: 15 minutes
Serves: 4

Ingredients

- 8 large eggs
- 3 cups water
- Ice water bath
- 3 tbsp sriracha sauce
- 4 tbsp mayonnaise
- Salt to taste
- ¼ tsp smoked paprika

Directions

1. Bring eggs to boil in salted water in a pot over high heat, and then reduce the heat to simmer for 10 minutes. Transfer eggs to an ice water bath, let cool completely and peel the shells.
2. Slice the eggs in half height wise and empty the yolks into a bowl. Smash with a fork and mix in sriracha sauce, mayonnaise, and half of the paprika until smooth.
3. Spoon filling into a piping bag with a round nozzle and fill the egg whites to be slightly above the brim. Garnish with remaining paprika and serve immediately.

Nutritional Value: Calories 195, Fat 19g, Net Carbs 1g, Protein 4g

116. Mixed Roast Vegetables

Preparation Time: 40 minutes
Serves: 4

Ingredients

- 1 large butternut squash, cut into chunks
- ¼ lb shallots, peeled
- 4 rutabagas, cut into chunks
- ¼ lb Brussels sprouts
- 1 sprig rosemary, chopped
- 1 sprig thyme, chopped
- 4 cloves garlic, peeled only
- 3 tbsp olive oil
- Salt and black pepper to taste

Directions

1. Preheat the oven to 450°F.
2. Pour the butternut squash, shallots, rutabagas, garlic cloves, and brussels sprouts in a bowl. Season with salt, pepper, olive oil, and toss them. Pour the mixture on a baking sheet and sprinkle with the chopped thyme and rosemary. Roast the vegetables for 15–20 minutes.
3. Once ready, remove and spoon into a serving bowl. Serve with oven roasted chicken thighs.

Nutritional Value: Calories 65, Fat 3g, Net Carbs 8g, Protein 3g

117. Duo-Cheese Chicken Bake

Preparation Time: 30 minutes
Serves: 6

Ingredients

- 2 tbsp olive oil
- 8 oz cream cheese
- 1 lb ground chicken
- 1 cup buffalo sauce
- 1 cup ranch dressing
- 3 cups grated yellow cheddar cheese

Directions

1. Preheat oven to 350°F. Lightly grease a baking sheet with a cooking spray. Warm the oil in a skillet over medium heat and brown the chicken for a couple of minutes, take off the heat, and set aside.
2. Spread cream cheese at the bottom of the baking sheet, top with chicken, pour buffalo sauce over, add ranch dressing, and sprinkle with cheddar cheese. Bake for 23 minutes until cheese has melted and golden brown on top. Remove and serve with veggie sticks or low carb crackers.

Nutritional Value: Calories 216, Fat 16g, Net Carbs 3g, Protein 14g

118. Coconut Ginger Macaroons

Preparation Time: 20 minutes
Serves: 6

Ingredients

- 2 fingers ginger root, peeled and pureed

- 6 egg whites
- 1 cup finely shredded coconut
- ¼ cup swerve
- A pinch of chili powder
- 1 cup water
- Angel hair chili to garnish

Directions

1. Preheat the oven to 350°F and line a baking sheet with parchment paper. Set aside.
2. Then, in a heatproof bowl, whisk the ginger, egg whites, shredded coconut, swerve, and chili powder.
3. Bring the water to boil in a pot over medium heat and place the heatproof bowl on the pot. Then, continue whisking the mixture until it is glossy, about 4 minutes. Do not let the bowl touch the water or be too hot so that the eggs don't cook.
4. Spoon the mixture into the piping bag after and pipe out 40 to 50 little mounds on the lined baking sheet. Bake the macaroons in the middle part of the oven for 15 minutes.
5. Once they are ready, transfer them to a wire rack, garnish them with the angel hair chili, and serve.

Nutritional Value: Calories 97, Fat 3.5g, Net Carbs 0.3g, Protein 6.8g

119. Balsamic Brussels Sprouts with Prosciutto

Preparation Time: 45 minutes
Serves: 4

Ingredients

- 3 tbsp balsamic vinegar
- 1 tbsp erythritol
- ½ tbsp olive oil
- Salt and black pepper to taste
- 1 lb Brussels sprouts, halved
- 5 slices prosciutto, chopped

Directions

1. Preheat oven to 400°F and line a baking sheet with parchment paper. Mix balsamic vinegar, erythritol, olive oil, salt, and black pepper and combine with the brussels sprouts in a bowl.
2. Spread the mixture on the baking sheet and roast for 30 minutes until tender on the inside and crispy on the outside. Toss with prosciutto, share among 4 plates, and serve with chicken breasts.

Nutritional Value: Calories 166, Fat 14g, Net Carbs 0g, Protein 8g

120. Buttery Herb Roasted Radishes

Preparation Time: 25 minutes
Serves: 6

Ingredients

- 2 lb small radishes, greens removed
- 3 tbsp olive oil
- Salt and black pepper to season
- 3 tbsp unsalted butter
- 1 tbsp chopped parsley
- 1 tbsp chopped tarragon

Directions

1. Preheat oven to 400°F and line a baking sheet with parchment paper. Toss radishes with oil, salt, and black pepper. Spread on baking sheet and roast for 20 minutes until browned.
2. Heat butter in a large skillet over medium heat to brown and attain a nutty aroma, 2 to 3 minutes.
3. Take out the parsnips from the oven and transfer to a serving plate. Pour over the browned butter atop and sprinkle with parsley and tarragon. Serve with roasted rosemary chicken.

Nutritional Value: Calories 160, Fat 14g, Net Carbs 2g, Protein 5g

121. Bacon-Wrapped Jalapeño Peppers

Preparation Time: 30 minutes
Serves: 6

Ingredients

- 12 jalapeños
- ¼ cup shredded colby cheese
- 6 oz cream cheese, softened
- 6 slices bacon, halved

Directions

- Cut the jalapeno peppers in half, and then remove the membrane and seeds. Combine cheeses and stuff into the pepper halves. Wrap each pepper with a bacon strip and secure with toothpicks.
- Place the filled peppers on a baking sheet lined with a piece of foil. Bake at 350°F for 25 minutes until bacon has browned, and crispy and cheese is golden brown on the top. Remove to a paper towel lined plate to absorb grease, arrange on a serving plate, and serve warm.

Nutritional Value: Calories 206, Fat 17g, Net Carbs 0g, Protein 14g

122. Herbed Brussels Sprouts Salad

Serves: 6
Preparation: 10 minutes
Cooking: 3 minutes

Ingredients

- 2 lbs Brussels sprouts
- 1 Tbsp fresh parsley finely chopped
- 1 tsp of fresh dill finely chopped
- 1 tsp fresh chives chopped
- Salt and pepper to taste
- 1 cup water
- Salt and ground black pepper to taste
- 2 Tbsp of olive oil for serving
- Lemon juice for serving (freshly squeezed)

Directions:

1. Place Brussels sprouts into your Instant Pot.
2. Add fresh herbs, salt and pepper to taste and pour water.
3. Lock lid into place and set on the MANUAL setting for 3 minutes.
4. When the timer beeps, press "Cancel" and carefully flip the Quick Release valve to let the pressure out.
5. Open the lid and transfer Brussels sprouts in a salad bowl.
6. Drizzle with olive oil and lemon juice, and serve.

Nutritional Value:

Calories: 107 Carbohydrates: 9g Proteins: 5g Fat: 7g Fiber: 6g

123. Warm Bok Choi Salad with Mustard Dressing

Serves: 6
Preparation: 5 minutes
Cooking: 15 minutes

Ingredients

- 1 1/2 lbs of Bok choy, trimmed
- 1 cup or more water
- Seasoned salt to taste
- 1 cup olive oil
- 1 1/2 Tbsp of lime juice
- 2 Tbsp yellow mustard

Directions:

1. Rinse and clean Bok Choy from any dirt.
2. Pour Bok Choy in your Instant Pot, sprinkle with a pinch of seasoned salt and pour water.
3. Lock lid into place and set on the MANUAL setting for 15 minutes.
4. Use Quick Release - turn the valve from sealing to venting to release the pressure.
5. Open lid, and with tongue transfer Bok Choy in a large salad bowl.
6. In a bowl, whisk olive oil, mustard, seasoned salt and lime juice.
7. Pour dressing over Bok choy salad, toss and serve.

Nutritional Value:

Calories: 327 Carbohydrates: 1.5g Proteins: 1g Fat: 37g Fiber: 0.6g

124. Broccoli Salad with Melted Cheese

Serves: 4
Preparation: 15 minutes

Cooking: 3 hours

Ingredients

- 1 1/2 lbs. broccoli florets cut into small pieces
- 1 cup of water
- 1/4 cup olive oil
- 1/2 lemon zest
- 1 1/2 tsp lemon juice, freshly squeezed
- Salt and pepper to taste
- 1 can ground parmesan Cheese

Directions:

1. Wash the broccoli thoroughly and clean from any dirt.
2. Cut the broccoli in florets, and then cut them in small pieces
3. Place broccoli in your oiled Crock Pot.
4. Pour water, oil, lemon zest and lemon juice into Crock Pot.
5. Season salt and black pepper, stir and cover.
6. Cook on LOW for 2-3 hours.
7. Open lid, and sprinkle grated parmesan cheese in your Crock Pot.
8. Cover again, and cook on HIGH for 15 minutes. Serve hot.

Nutritional Value:

Calories: 280 Carbohydrates: 7g Proteins: 15g Fat: 33g Fiber: 0.1g

125. Warm Spinach - Basil and Parmesan Salad

Serves: 6
Preparation: 10 minutes
Cooking: 6 hours

Ingredients

- 2 Tbsp olive oil
- 1 1/2 lbs. spinach chopped
- 1 green onion, diced
- 2 cloves garlic, sliced
- 1/2 cup basil, fresh
- Pinch of ground nutmeg
- 1/4 cup water
- Salt and pepper to taste
- 3/4 cup Parmesan cheese - grated
- 1 lemon wedges for serving

Directions:

1. Grease the bottom and sides of Crock Pot with olive oil.
2. Add all ingredients in Crock Pot and give a good stir.
3. Cover and cook on LOW for 4 - 6 hours.
4. Transfer creamy vegetables on a serving plate.
5. Serve hot with lemon wedges.

Nutritional Value:

Calories: 125 Carbohydrates: 4g Proteins: 9g Fat: 10g Fiber: 3g

126. Bitter Turnip Greens and Almond Salad

Serves: 4
Preparation: 10 minutes
Cooking: 30 minutes

Ingredients

- 1 Tbsp tallow
- 3 cups turnip greens
- 1/2 cup slivered almonds, lightly toasted
- 1/4 tsp of salt and black pepper freshly ground
- 1 Tbsp apple vinegar (optional)

Directions:

1. Rinse and clean the turnip greens from any dirt.
2. Heat tallow in a skillet over medium heat.
3. Add turnip greens; season with the pinch of the salt and pepper and sauté for 20 minutes.
4. Add finely chopped almonds, stir and cook for further 10 minutes; stir.
5. Stir in apple cider vinegar.
6. Taste and adjust salt and pepper.
7. Transfer to the salad bowl, and allow it to cool before serving.

Nutritional Value:

Calories: 113 Carbohydrates: 7.4g Proteins: 6.7g Fat: 9.4g Fiber: 5g

127. Hearty Artichokes, Green Beans and Eggs Salad

Serves: 6
Preparation: 15 minutes
Cooking: 35 minutes

Ingredients

- 4 artichokes (cooked)
- 2 cups green beans (cooked)
- 4 boiled eggs (hard)
- 2 scallions finely chopped
- 2 Tbsp of fresh mint finely chopped
- 2 Tbsp of fresh dill finely chopped
- 3 Tbsp of capers
- 10 olives, pitted, finely chopped (optional)
- Dressing
- 1/2 cup olive oil
- 2 Tbsp of lemon juice
- Sea salt and freshly ground black pepper

Directions:

1. Bring to boil pot with the salted water.
2. Add artichokes and boil for 2 - 3 minutes.
3. Reduce heat; simmer, covered, for about 20 to 30 minutes.
4. Cut artichokes in quarters and place in a salad bowl.
5. Add green beans, eggs quartered, spring onions, dill, mint, caper and olives.
6. For the dressing:
7. In a bowl, combine olive oil, salt, pepper, lemon juice and stir well.
8. Pour dressing over the artichokes salad and toss to combine well.
9. Serve immediately.

Nutritional Value:

Calories: 493 Carbohydrates: 12g Proteins: 21g
Fat: 24g Fiber: 2.4g

128. Lobster, Eggs and Mayonnaise Salad

Serves:
Preparation: 10 minutes

Ingredients

- 2 can (11 oz) lobster meat
- 1 cup mayonnaise
- 2 boiled eggs, finely chopped
- 3 Tbsp scallions, green parts only, chopped
- 1 Tbsp mustard (Dijon, English, or whole grain)
- Salt and ground pepper
- 1 Tbsp capers
- 1 lettuce heart

Directions:

1. Place the lobster meat, mayonnaise, eggs, green onions, mustard in a salad bowl.
2. Stir to combine well.
3. Season the salt and pepper to taste.
4. Sprinkle with a capers and garnish with lettuce hearts.
5. Serve and enjoy!

Nutritional Value:

Calories: 374 Carbohydrates: 9g Proteins: 21g
Fat: 25.5g Fiber: 1
3g

129. Tuna - Avocado Salad with Mayo-Mustard Dressing

Serves: 4
Preparation: 15 minutes

Ingredients

- 1 avocado, sliced
- 6 oz of tuna fish in water
- 1 tomato, coarsely chopped
- 3 Tbs fresh basil, finely chopped
- 1 tsp chives, chopped, for garnish
- For the sauce
- 1 Tbsp stone-ground mustard
- 2 Tbs mayonnaise
- 1 tsp apple cider vinegar
- Sea salt and ground black pepper ti taste

Directions:

1. Place the tuna fish, tomato, onion, avocado, basil in a shallow ball and stir well.

2. For the sauce:
3. In a small bowl stir the mayonnaise, mustard and apple cider vinegar and salt and pepper.
4. Pour the sauce over the salad.
5. Taste and adjust salt and pepper to taste.
6. Sprinkle with chopped chives and serve.

Nutritional Value:

Calories: 292 Carbohydrates: 9g Proteins: 33g Fat: 14g Fiber: 5.4g

130. Chicken Salad with Dandelion Greens & Chicory

Serves: 6

Preparation: 10 minutes

Ingredients

- 10 oz dandelion greens, trimmed and thinly sliced
- 10 oz chicory greens
- 1 chicken breast, cooked and sliced
- 1/4 cup extra-virgin olive oil
- 3 Tbsp of fresh lemon juice (about 2 lemons)
- Sea salt and freshly ground black pepper, to taste

Directions:

1. Clean and rinse from any dirt dandelion greens and chicory, and add in a large salad bowl.
2. Add sliced chicken breast in a salad bowl; toss. Season the chicken with the salt.
3. Whisk the olive oil and lemon juice and pour over the salad; toss to combine well.
4. Serve immediately.

Nutritional Value:

Calories: 182 Carbohydrates: 5.6g Proteins: 18g Fat: 10g Fiber: 3g

131. Delicious Avocado Puree

Serves: 8

Preparation: 15 minutes

Ingredients

- 4 ripe avocados
- Juice of 1 lemon
- 1 onion finely chopped
- 1 ripe tomato finely chopped
- Salt to taste
- 1 cup of fresh parsley finely chopped

Directions:

1. Peel and cut avocado in the middle.
2. Remove the pit with a teaspoon, remove the flesh and place into a bowl.
3. Add the onion and tomato and drizzle with lemon juice.
4. Place the mixture in a blender and blend until softened.
5. Season with the salt and blend for 20 further seconds.
6. Transfer the avocado pour into glass bowl and sprinkle with chopped parsley.
7. Refrigerate until serving.

Nutritional Value:

Calories: 159 Carbohydrates: 8.8g Proteins: 2.4g Fat: 14g Fiber: 7g

132. Festive Red Cabbage Salad

Serves: 6

Preparation: 15 minutes

Ingredients

- 1 lb red cabbage, finely chopped or shredded
- 2 garlic cloves, finely sliced
- 4 slices crispy bacon, crumbled
- 1/2 cup olive oil
- 2 Tbsp of fresh lemon juice
- 1/2 tsp of mustard seeds
- 1/2 tsp of tarragon

Directions:

1. Rinse cabbage and clean from any dirt or yellow outer leaves.
2. Place the cabbage in a food processor and finely chopped or shred.
3. Place shredded cabbage in a large salad bowl.
4. Sprinkle with the salt and pepper; add crumbled bacon and sliced garlic. Toss to combine well.
5. In a small bowl, whisk the olive oil,

lemon juice, mustard seeds and tarragon.

6. Pour dressing over cabbage salad, and toss to combine well.
7. Serve.

Nutritional Value:

Calories: 200 Carbohydrates: 8.5g Proteins: 6.3g Fat: 15.5g Fiber: 4.3g

133. Garlic Sauce for Poultry

Serves: 6

Preparation: 5 minutes

Ingredients

- 1 cup olive oil
- 1/2 cup fresh lemon juice
- 6 large garlic cloves, finely chopped
- Salt and freshly ground black pepper to taste
- 1 peel from one lemon
- 1/4 tsp dried sage
- 1/4 tsp dried marjoram
- 1/4 tsp of nutmeg

Directions:

1. Add all ingredients in a high-speed blender; blend for 15 - 20 seconds or until all ingredients combined well.
2. Pour in a glass container, cover and refrigerate before serving.
3. Serve with any kind of poultry.

Nutritional Value:

Calories: 328 Carbohydrates: Proteins: 2.6g Fat: 36g Fiber: 0.3g

134. Green Salad a la Italian

Serves: 8

Preparation: 10 minutes

Ingredients

- 10 oz green salads such as lettuce, cos, romain
- 1 can (11 oz) artichoke hearts, drained and quartered
- 1 can (11 oz) tuna in water or oil, drained, flaked
- 1/2 lb green beans, cooked, drained
- 1 pinch salt to taste
- 1 cup Italian dressing

Directions:

1. Place all ingredients from the list above in a large salad bowls.
2. Pour Italian dressing, and gently stir to combine evenly.
3. Taste and adjust salt if needed.
4. Serve immediately.

Nutritional Value:

Calories: 167 Carbohydrates: 7.6g Proteins: 12 g Fat: 9.8g Fiber: 2.8g

135. Hearty Autumn Salad

Serves: 4

Preparation: 10 minutes

Ingredients

- For the salad:
- 3/4 lb of lettuce salad
- 1 avocado
- 1 carrot
- 1/2 cup of almonds, finely chopped
- For the vinaigrette:
- 4 Tbsp olive oil
- 2 Tbsp lemon juice (freshly squeezed)
- 1 - 2 Tbsp of mayonnaise
- Salt and black pepper to taste

Directions:

1. Rinse and chop lettuce, peel avocado and carrot, and place all together in a large salad bowl.
2. In a bowl, whisk all ingredients for dressing.
3. Sprinkle almonds over salad.
4. Pour dressing and toss to combine well.
5. Serve immediately.

Nutritional Value:

Calories: 223 Carbohydrates: 8.7g Proteins: 3.8g Fat: 19.5g Fiber: 6g

136. Homemade Spicy Harissa Paste

Serves: 6

Preparation: 15 minutes
Cooking: 10 minutes

Ingredients

- 5 red chili peppers
- 2 Tbsp of extra-virgin olive oil
- 4 cloves of garlic, sliced
- 2 tsp cumin seeds
- 2 tsp coriander seeds
- 2 Tbsp of white wine
- 3 Tbsp of chopped fresh parsley
- Salt to taste

Directions:

1. Heat the oil in a non-stick skillet, and fry the chili peppers for 2-3 minutes.
2. Put peppers in a bowl, cover with aluminum foil and allow it to cool.
3. In a skillet roast the cumin and coriander seeds for two minutes.
4. When the peppers cooled down completely, remove the peel with gloves and cut them in the middle to remove the seeds.
5. Place cleaned peppers in mortar along with garlic, cumin and coriander seeds; beat until you get a smooth mixture.
6. Stir in the wine, add a little bit of oil and beat until you get a smooth paste.
7. Add chopped parsley and season the salt.
8. Serve or keep refrigerated.

Nutritional Value:

Calories: 27 Carbohydrates: 4g Proteins: 1.1g Fat: 1g Fiber: 1g

137. Keto Canary Island Red Sauce

Serves: 6
Preparation: 10 minutes
Cooking:

Ingredients

- 2 large red bell peppers cut into chunks
- 1 bunch fresh cilantro
- 3 cloves garlic
- 1 Tbsp ground sweet paprika
- 1/4 cup olive oil
- 1 chili pepper
- 2 Tbsp ground almonds

Directions:

1. Combine all ingredients in a blender; blend until finely smooth.
2. Place in a glass jar and refrigerate for one hour.
3. Serve.

Nutritional Value:

Calories: 101 Carbohydrates: 4.2g Proteins: 0.8g Fat: 9.2g Fiber: 1.4g

138. Keto Hollandaise Sauce

Serves: 4
Preparation: 5 minutes
Cooking: 10 minutes

Ingredients

- 3 egg yolks from free-range chickens
- 1/4 cup water
- 2 Tbsp of lemon juice , freshly squeezed
- 1/2 cup cold butter, cut into 8 pieces
- 1/8 tsp cayenne pepper
- 1/8 tsp paprika
- Salt to taste

Directions:

1. Separate the eggs. Heat the egg yolks, water and lemon juice in a small saucepan over low heat.
2. Cook, stirring constantly, until the mixture begins to bubble.
3. Add the butter, and stir until melted and sauce is thickened.
4. Add the paprika and cayenne pepper, and season with the salt to taste.
5. Remove from heat and allow it to cool.
6. Serve. Keep refrigerated.

Nutritional Value:

Calories: 246 Carbohydrates: 1g Proteins: 2.3g Fat: 26.4g Fiber: 0.1g

139. Nutty Sauce for Roast

Serves: 6
Preparation: 5 minutes

Cooking: 2 hours

Ingredients

- 1 cup bone broth (preferable homemade)
- 1 cup water
- 1 cup red wine
- 1 Tbsp fresh parsley finely chopped
- 1 Tbsp fresh basil finely chopped
- 1/3 cup ground almonds
- 1 Tbsp fresh butter
- Lemon juice, to taste
- Salt and freshly ground white pepper to taste

Directions:

1. Add all ingredients to the inner pot in the Crock Pot.
2. Cover and cook on LOW setting for 1 - 2 hours.
3. Serve warm or cold.
4. Keep refrigerated.

Nutritional Value:

Calories: 39 Carbohydrates: 1.5g Proteins: 1.5g Fat: 8g Fiber: 1g

140. Keto Mock Hollandaise Sauce

Serves: 6
Preparation: 5 minutes
Cooking: 10 minutes

Ingredients

- 2 egg whites from free-range chickens
- 1 cup mayonnaise
- 2 Tbsp lemon juice (freshly squeezed)
- 1/2 tsp dry mustard
- Salt to taste

Directions:

1. Separate the eggs.
2. In a saucepan, beat slightly the egg whites.
3. Add mayonnaise, lemon juice, dry mustard, and salt; beat until combined well.
4. Place the saucepan over medium-low heat and stirring constantly, cook the sauce until thick, but do not boil.
5. Remove the saucepan from the heat and let it cool.
6. Serve or keep refrigerated.

Nutritional Value:

Calories: 34 Carbohydrates: 3.2g Proteins: 1.3g Fat: 1g Fiber: 0.1g

141. Marinated Olives

Serves: 4
Preparation: 5 minutes
Cooking:

Ingredients

- 24 large olives, black and green
- 2 Tbsp of extra-virgin olive oil
- 2 Tbsp red wine
- 2 cloves garlic, thinly sliced
- 2 tsp coriander seeds, crushed
- 1/2 tsp crushed red pepper
- 1 tsp dried thyme
- 1 tsp dried rosemary, crushed

Directions:

1. Place olives and all remaining ingredients in a large container or bag, and shake to combine well.
2. Cover (if in container), and refrigerate to marinate overnight.
3. Serve.

Nutritional Value:

Calories: 102 Carbohydrates: 2.7g Proteins: 0.5g Fat: 10g Fiber: 1.5g

142. Mornay Sauce for Seafood

Serves: 4
Preparation: 5 minutes
Cooking: 10 minutes

Ingredients

- 3 egg yolks from free-range chickens
- 1 cup Béchamel classic sauce
- 1/4 cup whipped cream
- 1 tsp of lemon juice, freshly squeezed
- 1/4 cup Parmesan cheese

Directions:

1. In a saucepan, whisk eggs yolks with the cream.
2. Add the Béchamel sauce mix and simmer over low heat; stir to avoid sauce burning.
3. Remove from heat and stir ground cheese. Serve.

Nutritional Value:

Calories: 134 Carbohydrates: 2.2g Proteins: 5.g Fat: 12g Fiber: 0.02g

143. Mushrooms and Wine Steak Sauce

Serves: 8
Preparation: 5 minutes
Cooking: 15 minutes

Ingredients

- 3 Tbsp of fresh butter grass-fed
- 4 oz fresh button mushrooms, rinsed
- 1/4 cup onion, finely chopped
- 1 clove garlic, minced
- 1 cup bone broth (preferable homemade)
- 1 1/2 Tbsp of grated tomato
- 1/8 tsp ground black pepper, freshly ground
- 2 tsp almond flour
- 1 Tbsp of water
- 2 Tbsp dry red wine

Directions:

1. Heat butter in a saucepan over medium heat. Add mushrooms, onion and garlic; sauté for about 3 - 4 minutes.
2. Stir in bone broth, tomato paste and black pepper. Bring to the boil; reduce heat to low and simmer, covered, for 5 minutes.
3. Blend the almond flour with water. Add some of the hot mushroom sauce into almond mixture and return to saucepan.
4. Pour wine and stir sauce until thickened.
5. Serve hot or cold.
6. Keep refrigerated.

Nutritional Value:

Calories: 55 Carbohydrates: 1.4g Proteins: 5.g Fat: 5.5g Fiber: 0.4g

144. Provençal Black Olive Paste

Serves: 4
Preparation: 5 minutes

Ingredients

- 1/2 lb black olives pitted
- 4 Tbsp capers
- 2 cloves garlic finely chopped
- 2 Tbsp of mustard
- 1/2 cup of olive oil
- Freshly ground black pepper
- Fresh thyme (optional)

Directions:

1. Place all ingredients in a high-speed blender and blend until smooth.
2. Place in a glass jar or container and refrigerate for 2 hours.
3. Serve.

Nutritional Value:

Calories: 125 Carbohydrates: 6.2g Proteins: 1.5g Fat: 11g Fiber: 4g

145. Roasted Radicchio Salad

Serves: 4
Preparation: 10 minutes
Cooking: 20 minutes

Ingredients

- 1 lb radicchio (cut in wedges)
- 1/4 cup olive oil
- 1 Tbsp fresh thyme, chopped
- 2 Tbsp lemon juice (freshly squeezed)
- Salt and pepper to taste

Directions:

1. Preheat oven to 450°F.
2. Cut radicchio into wedges and rinse in cold water; gently shake off excess water.
3. Place radicchio in large bowl; drizzle with olive oil, sprinkle with thyme, salt, and pepper and toss to coat.
4. Arrange radicchio wedges on rimmed baking sheet.

5. Roast for about 10 - 13 minutes.
6. Stir and bake for further 6 - 7 minutes.
7. Arrange radicchio on platter, sprinkle with a pinch of salt and pepper, drizzle generously with lemon juice and serve.

Nutritional Value:

Calories: 153 Carbohydrates: 5.4g Proteins: 2g Fat: 15g Fiber: 1.2g

146. Romaine Lettuce with Roquefort Dressing

Serves: 8
Preparation: 15 minutes

Ingredients

- 1 lbs Romaine lettuce
- 3 cherry tomatoes, chopped
- 1 green onion, sliced thin rings
- 1/2 cup white mushrooms, well cleaned, and thinly sliced
- 1/4 cup of extra-virgin olive oil
- 1/2 cup cream cheese (full-fat)
- 1/3 cup Roquefort cheese
- Freshly-ground black pepper, to taste

Directions:

1. Rinse and clean the lettuce and place in a salad bowl.
2. Add cherry tomatoes, green onion and mushrooms; toss to combine.
3. In a bowl, whisk the olive oil, cream cheese, ground pepper and Roquefort cheese. Pour the dressing over salad and toss to combine well.
4. Serve.

Nutritional Value:

Calories: 101 Carbohydrates: 5.11g Proteins: 7g Fat: 6.5g Fiber: 2.5g

147. Savory and Sweet Rhubarb Puree

Serves: 4
Preparation: 15 minutes
Cooking: 15 minutes

Ingredients

- 1 lb of rhubarb, cut into slices
- 2 Tbsp of olive oil
- 2 Tbsp of water
- 1 piece of fresh ginger, peeled, finely shredded
- 1/4 cup stevia sweetener, granulated
- 1 cinnamon stick
- 2 Tbsp of mustard (Dijon, English, ground stone)

Directions:

1. Clean and cut rhubarb into slices.
2. Place the rhubarb into a saucepan with water, ginger, stevia sweetener and the cinnamon stick.
3. Simmer over low heat about 10 - 12 minutes or until the rhubarb is tender.
4. Remove the cinnamon stick and ginger, and transfer the rhubarb mixture in a blender or food processor.
5. Blend on high to create a smooth puree.
6. Add mustard and stir for 20 - 30 seconds.
7. Serve.

Nutritional Value:

Calories: 39 Carbohydrates: 6.2g Proteins: 1.5g Fat: 5g Fiber: 4.5g

148. Tangy Lemon and Dill Vinaigrette

Serves: 4
Preparation: 10 minutes
Cooking:

Ingredients

- 4 Tbsp of white wine vinegar
- 4 Tbsp of Dijon mustard
- 4 Tbsp of fresh dill, chopped
- 2 tsp finely chopped garlic
- 2 fresh lemon juice, or to taste
- 1/3 cup extra-virgin olive oil
- Salt and freshly ground black pepper to taste

Directions:

1. Stir vinegar and mustard together in a small bowl until smooth.
2. Stir the dill, chopped garlic, and lemon juice into vinegar mixture.

3. Slowly, pour the olive oil into the mixture while whisking continuously until the dressing is creamy and smooth.
4. Season with the salt and ground black pepper.
5. Ready!

Nutritional Value:

Calories: 181 Carbohydrates: 3.7g Proteins: 1g Fat: 19g Fiber: 0.5g

149. Slow-Roasted Cherry Tomatoes with Parmesan

Preparation Time: 25 minutes
Servings 4)

Nutritional Value:247 Calories; 19.8g Fat; 5.3g Carbs; 11g Protein; 2.2g Sugars

Ingredients

- 1 ½ pounds cherry tomatoes, halved
- 1/4 cup olive oil
- 1 tablespoon Worcestershire sauce
- 1 tablespoon white wine vinegar
- 1 teaspoon garlic, minced
- Sea salt and freshly ground black pepper, to taste
- 1 spring of fresh rosemary, chopped
- 2 sprigs of fresh thyme, chopped
- 1 cup Parmesan cheese,freshly grated

Directions

1. Preheat the oven to 400 degrees F.
2. Place the tomatoes in a broiler-proof ceramic baking dish. Drizzle the tomatoes with olive oil Worcestershire sauce, and vinegar.
3. Sprinkle with the garlic, salt, pepper, rosemary and thyme. Top with Parmesan cheese.
4. Roast for 20 to 22 minutes, until the tomatoes begin to caramelizebut not split. Bon appétit!

150. Buttered Savoy Cabbage with Scallions

Preparation Time: 20 minutes
Servings 4)

Nutritional Value:142 Calories; 11.6g Fat; 5.7g Carbs; 2g Protein; 2.4g Sugars

Ingredients

1. 1/2 stick butter, melted
2. 1 bunch scallions, chopped
3. 1 garlic clove, minced
4. 1 pound Savoy cabbage, outer leaves discarded, cored and shredded
5. 1 large-sized carrot, thinly sliced
6. 1/4 teaspoon fresh ginger root,grated
7. 1/2 teaspoon sea salt
8. 1/2 teaspoon mixed peppercorns, freshly cracked
9. 1/4 cup chicken stock
10. 1 tablespoon dry white wine
11. 1/3 teaspoon mustard seeds
12. A pinch of nutmeg

Directions

1. Melt the butter in a pan over a medium-high flame. Now, sauté the scallions and garlic until they're just tender and fragrant.
2. Stir in the cabbage, carrots, and ginger; cook for 10 minutes, stirring occasionally.
3. Add the remaining ingredients and cook an additional 5 minutes.Test to check if Savoy cabbage is done to your liking. Enjoy!

151. Cabbage with Ham and Fried Eggs

Preparation Time: 15 minutes
Servings 4

Nutritional Value:173 Calories; 10.6g Fat; 5.6g Carbs; 14.2g Protein; 2.1g Sugars

Ingredients

- 2 tablespoons bacon fat
- 1 cup spring onions, minced
- 1 garlic clove, minced
- 2 cups red cabbage, shredded
- 1 bay leaf
- 1/2 teaspoon salt
- 1/2 teaspoon ground black pepper
- 4 rashers of ham, chopped

- 2 teaspoons dry red wine
- 4 eggs

Directions

1. Heat 1 tablespoon of bacon fat in a nonstick skillet over a moderate flame. Now, sauté the onions and garlic until just tender.
2. Then, add the cabbage and cook, stirring continuously, until tender or about 5 minutes. Add the bay leaf, salt, pepper and chopped ham. Add the wine and cook an additional 3 minutes.
3. Heat the remaining 1 tablespoon of bacon fat in another skillet. Crack the eggs into another skillet and cook to desired doneness.
4. Divide prepared cabbage among four serving plates; top with fried egg and serve immediately.

152. Colorful Vegetable and Broccoli Rice

Preparation Time: 20 minutes
Servings 4

Nutritional Value:126 Calories; 11.6g Fat; 5.4g Carbs; 1.3g Protein; 2.5g Sugars

Ingredients

- 1 head broccoli, broken into florets
- 1/2 stick butter
- 1/2 yellow onion, chopped
- 1 garlic clove, minced
- 1 red bell pepper, chopped
- 1 Aji Fantasy chili pepper, minced
- 1/2 celery stalk, chopped
- Salt and ground black pepper, to taste

Directions

1. Blitz the broccoli in your food processor until it has reached a rice-like texture.
2. Now, melt the butter in a sauté pan over a moderate heat. Sweat yellow onion for 2 to 3 minutes; stir in the garlic and cook until slightly browned and fragrant.
3. After that, add the peppers and celery; cook an additional 4 minutes or until they're just tender. Add broccoli "rice" and season with salt and pepper.
4. Cook for a further 5 minutes, stirring periodically. Serve warm and enjoy!

153. Bok Choy with Shrimp

Preparation Time: 15 minutes
Servings 4

Nutritional Value:171 Calories; 8.4g Fat; 5.8g Carbs; 18.9g Protein; 2.1g Sugars

Ingredients

- 2 tablespoons sesame oil
- 2 garlic cloves, crushed
- 1 ½ pounds Bok choy, trimmed and thinly sliced
- 1 (1/2-inch) piece ginger, freshly grated
- 1 tablespoon oyster sauce
- Salt and ground black pepper, to taste
- 1 teaspoon cayenne pepper
- 10 ounces shrimp, peeled and deveined

Directions

1. Heat 1 tablespoon of sesame oil in a sauté pan over a moderate heat. Now, cook the garlic until it is just browned.
2. Stir in the Bok choy and ginger. Add the oyster sauce, salt, black pepper and cayenne pepper. Cook for 5 minutes, gently stirring. Transfer to a serving platter and reserve.
3. Now, heat the remaining tablespoon of sesame oil in a clean sauté pan. Cook the shrimp, stirring periodically, until they are just pink and opaque, about 3 minutes.
4. Serve with reserved Bok choy, garnished with lemon wedges.

154. Spring Artichoke Salad with Feta Cheese

Preparation Time: 25 minutes
Servings 6

Nutritional Value:146 Calories; 9.4g Fat; 6.1g Carbs; 5.8g Protein; 2.1g Sugars

Ingredients

- 2 tablespoons extra-virgin olive oil
- 3 artichoke hearts, defrosted

- 1 teaspoon coarse salt
- 1/2 teaspoon freshly ground black pepper
- 1 cup white onions, peeled and finely chopped
- 2 tablespoons lime juice,freshly squeezed
- 1 ½ teaspoons brown mustard
- 3 tablespoons champagne vinegar
- 1/2 pint grape tomatoes
- 1/3 cup baby green oak lettuce
- 1/3 cup red Swiss chard
- 1/3 cup arugula
- 1/3 cup butter lettuce
- 3 tablespoons capers, drained
- 1 roasted poblano pepper, sliced thin
- 1/2 teaspoon dried basil
- 2 ounces Kalamata olives, pitted and sliced
- 4 ounces feta cheese,crumbled

Directions

1. Start by preheating your oven to 350 degrees F. Line a baking sheet with parchment paper or a silicone mat.
2. Arrange artichoke hearts on the prepared sheet pan and drizzle with olive oil. Season your artichokes with the salt and pepper and roast for 18 to 23 minutes.
3. In the meantime, thoroughly combine the onions, lime juice, mustard and vinegar in a mixing dish; mix to combine well.
4. Transfer the cooled artichoke hearts to a serving bowl; dress with the prepared vinaigrette.
5. Toss with the remaining ingredients, except for feta cheese. Serve well chilled, garnished with crumbled feta. Enjoy!

155. Sautéed Chicory with Pistachios

Preparation Time: 10 minutes
Servings 4

Nutritional Value:65 Calories; 4.7g Fat; 5.7g Carbs; 2.1g Protein; 1g Sugars

Ingredients

- 2 heads chicory greens, outer ribs discarded and cut into pieces
- 3 teaspoons olive oil
- 1 teaspoon garlic cloves,minced
- 2 green onions,chopped
- Salt and pepper, to taste
- 1/2 teaspoon hot red pepper flakes
- 1/4 cup shelled pistachios

Directions

1. Cookchicory in a pot of boiling salted water about 5 minutes. Drain well.
2. Dry the pot and heat olive oil over moderately high heat until it shimmers. Add chicory, garlic and green onions.
3. Season with salt, black pepper and red pepper flakes; sauté until the leaves are wilted.
4. Serve garnished with pistachios. Bon appétit!

156. Two-Cheese, Mushroom and Cauliflower Casserole

Preparation Time: 35 minutes
Servings 4

Nutritional Value:275 Calories; 21.3g Fat; 5.3g Carbs; 14g Protein; 2.6g Sugars

Ingredients

- 2 tablespoons lard
- 1 cup chicken stock
- 4 eggs, lightly beaten
- 1/2 cup sour cream
- 1 cup chive & onion cream cheese
- 1 cup aged goat cheese
- 1 tablespoon Piri piri sauce
- 1 teaspoon yellow mustard
- 1/2 pound brown cremini mushrooms, thinly sliced
- 1 teaspoon fresh or dry rosemary, minced
- 1/2 teaspoon coarse salt
- 1/3 teaspoon freshly ground black pepper
- 1 large head cauliflower, cut into florets

Directions

1. Start by preheating your oven to 360 degrees F. Then, spritz a casserole dish with a nonstick cooking spray.
2. Next step, melt the lard in a pan that is preheated over a moderate heat. Cook the stock, eggs, sour cream, cheese, Piri piri sauce and mustard in the pan until heated through.
3. Layer cremini mushrooms and cauliflower on the bottom of your baking dish. Season with rosemary, salt, and black pepper.
4. Pour saucepan mixture over the top. Bake for 25 to 35 minutes and serve warm. Bon appétit!

157. Spinach and Cheddar Breakfast Muffins

Preparation Time: 30 minutes
Servings 6

Nutritional Value:252 Calories; 19.7g Fat; 3g Carbs; 16.1g Protein; 1.6g Sugars

Ingredients

- 1 cup full-fat milk
- 8 eggs
- 2 tablespoons vegetable oil
- 1/3 teaspoon salt
- 1/4 teaspoon ground black pepper, or more to the taste
- 1 cup spinach, chopped
- 1 ½ cups cheddar cheese, grated

Directions

1. Preheat your oven to 350 degrees F.
2. In a bowl, mix the milk, with eggs and oil. Add the remaining ingredients. Mix well to combine.
3. Add the mixture to a lightly greased muffin tin.
4. Bake for 25 minutes or until your muffins spring back when lightly pressed.

158. Gruyère Cheese and Kale Muffins

Preparation Time: 25 minutes
Servings 6

Nutritional Value:275 Calories; 15.8g Fat; 2.2g Carbs; 21.6g Protein; 0.4g Sugars

Ingredients

- 5 eggs
- 1/2 cup full-fat milk
- Sea salt, to taste
- 1/2 teaspoon dried basil
- 1 ½ cups Gruyère cheese,grated
- 10 ounces kale, cooked and drained
- 1/2 pound prosciutto, chopped

Directions

1. Start by preheating your oven to 360 degrees F. Spritz a muffin tin with a cooking spray.
2. Whisk the milk, salt, basil and cheese in a mixing bowl. Toss in kale and prosciutto. Spoon the batter into each muffin cup (3/4 full).
3. Bake for 20 to 25 minutes and serve with sour cream.

159. Family Pizza with Spring Vegetables

Preparation Time: 25 minutes
Servings 4

Nutritional Value:234 Calories; 16.1g Fat; 6.3g Carbs; 13.6g Protein; 3.5g Sugars

Ingredients

- For the Crust:
- A spray coating
- 1 pound cauliflower
- 1/2 cup Edam cheese
- 4 medium-sized eggs
- 1/4 cup heavy cream
- 1 tablespoon basil-infused oil
- Salt, to taste
- For the Topping:
- 1 cup spring mix
- 3/4 cup tomato sauce, sugar-free
- 2 tablespoons chives, finely chopped
- 1 tablespoon fresh sage
- 1/4 cup Kalamata olives, pitted and sliced

- 1 cup mozzarella cheese

Directions

1. Cook the cauliflower in a large pot of salted water until it is just tender; cut into florets and add the remaining ingredients for the crust.
2. Then, preheat your oven to 380 degrees F; add an oven rack to the middle of the oven. Lightly grease a baking pan with a thin layer of a spray coating.
3. Spread the crust mixture onto the bottom of the prepared baking pan. Bake for 15 minutes or until thecrust is firm and golden.
4. Remove from the oven and add the remaining ingredients, ending with mozzarella cheese; bake until the cheese has completely melted.
5. Add a few grinds of black pepper if desired and serve immediately.

160. Roasted Carrots with Green Peppercorn Sauce

Preparation Time: 40 minutes
Servings 6

Nutritional Value:183 Calories; 14.2g Fat; 6.5g Carbs; 2.6g Protein; 3.2g Sugars

Ingredients

- 1 ½ pounds carrots, trimmed and halved lengthwise
- 2 tablespoons butter, melted
- 1/4 teaspoon freshly grated nutmeg
- 1/2 teaspoon celery salt
- 1/4 teaspoon freshly ground black pepper
- 2 tablespoons apple cider vinegar
- 1 tablespoon green garlic, minced
- For the Sauce:
- 2 tablespoons butter
- 1/2 cup green onions, minced
- 3 tablespoons Cognac
- 1 ½ cups beef broth
- 1 cup whipping cream
- 2 tablespoons green peppercorns in brine, drained and crushed slightly

Directions

1. Preheat your oven to 425 degrees F.
2. Toss carrots with butter, nutmeg, celery salt, black pepper, vinegar and green garlic.
3. Roast, stirring once or twice, until carrots are softened, about 35 minutes.
4. Meanwhile, melt 2 tablespoons of butter in a pan over a moderately high flame. Sweat the onions for 2 minutes.
5. Add Cognac and bring it to a boil for 2 minutes. Pour in beef broth and let it boil another 4 minutes.
6. Lastly, stir in the cream and peppercorns; turn the heat to medium. Continue to simmer until the sauce is thickened and thoroughly warmed.
7. Serve with roasted carrots and enjoy!

161. Mushroom and Caciocavallo Stuffed Peppers

Preparation Time: 30 minutes
Servings 6

Nutritional Value:319 Calories; 18.8g Fat; 5.6g Carbs; 10.3g Protein; 2.5g Sugars

Ingredients

- 2 tablespoons avocado oil
- 1 shallot, chopped
- 1 teaspoon garlic, minced
- 3/4 pound button mushrooms, chopped
- 1 teaspoon Pimento
- 2 tablespoons fresh chives, chopped
- 1 teaspoon caraway seeds
- Salt to taste
- 6 bell peppers, seeds and tops removed
- 1/2 cup Caciocavallo cheese, grated
- 1⁄2 cup tomato sauce

Directions

1. Preheat your oven to 380 degrees F. Heat the oil in a pan that is preheated over moderately high heat.
2. Sauté the shallots and garlic until the shallot softens. Stir in the mushrooms and cook an additional 4 minutes or until the mushrooms are fragrant.

3. Add pimento, chives, caraway seeds and salt; stir until everything is heated through.
4. Place the peppers in a foil-lined roasting pan; fill them with the mushroom stuffing. Top each pepper with Caciocavallo cheese.
5. Afterwards, pour the tomato sauce over everything. Bake for 18 to 23 minutes or until cheese is lightly browned. Enjoy!

162. Baked Avocado with Bacon and Cottage Cheese

Preparation Time: 25 minutes
Servings 6

Nutritional Value:255 Calories; 21g Fat; 3.3g Carbs; 10.8g Protein; 0.4g Sugars

Ingredients

- 3 medium-sized ripe avocados, halved and pitted, skin on
- 2 eggs, beaten
- 3 ounces Cottage cheese
- 2 tablespoons fresh chives, chopped
- 3 ounce cooked bacon, crumbled
- Salt and pepper, to taste
- 1/4 teaspoon smoked paprika

Directions

1. Preheat your oven to 390 degrees F. Place avocado halves in shallow ramekins.
2. In a mixing bowl, thoroughly combine the other ingredients. Divide the mixture among avocado halves.
3. Bake for about 20 minutes and serve right away!

163. Cabbage "Noodles" with Turkey Sauce

Preparation Time: 20 minutes
Servings 4

Nutritional Value:236 Calories; 8.3g Fat; 5.1g Carbs; 29.9g Protein; 2g Sugars

Ingredients

- 1 pound white cabbage
- 2 slices bacon
- 1 yellow onion, chopped
- 1 garlic clove, minced
- 3/4 pound turkey meat, ground
- 1 Aleppo chili pepper, minced
- Sea salt and ground black pepper, to taste
- 1/2 teaspoon cayenne pepper
- 1/2 teaspoon dried oregano
- 1/2 teaspoon dried basil
- 1/4 teaspoon bay leaf, ground

Directions

1. Remove any loose outer leaves of your cabbage. Now, spiralize your cabbage and reserve.
2. Bring a pot of lightly salted water to a rolling boil; parboil cabbage for 3 minutes, until crisp-tender; drain.
3. Heat a nonstick skillet over a moderately high heat. Now, cook the bacon for 3 to 4 minutes, crumbling with a fork; reserve.
4. Now, cook onion and garlic in pan drippings until tender. Add turkey meat and chili pepper; cook until the meat is browned. Sprinkle with seasonings and stir to combine.
5. Then, add the cabbage and bacon back to the skillet. Serve warm and enjoy!

165. Keto Pasta with Alfredo Sauce

Preparation Time: 30 minutes
Servings 4

Nutritional Value:614 Calories; 55.9g Fat; 3.6g Carbs; 25.6g Protein; 0.3g Sugars

Ingredients

- 2 ounces cream cheese, room temperature
- 3 eggs, room temperature
- 1/2 teaspoon wheat gluten
- 1 stick butter
- 1 cup heavy cream
- 1 garlic clove, minced
- 2 cups Parmesan cheese, grated
- 1 teaspoon Italian seasoning

Directions

1. Start by preheating your oven to 320 degrees F. Line a baking sheet with a Silpat mat.
2. Blend the cream cheese, eggs, and gluten until uniform and creamy.
3. Press the batter into the pan, keeping it nice and thin. Bake in the preheated oven for 5 to 6 minutes.
4. Allow it to rest for 5 to 10 minutes before cutting into strips. Now, simmer the pasta in a lightly salted water for a couple of minutes or until it's done.
5. Then, melt the butter in a skillet. Now, add the cream and garlic, and cook over a moderate heat, stirring with wire whisk.
6. Stir in parmesan cheese and Italian seasonings; remove from heat. The sauce will thicken as it cools. Add warm pasta and serve immediately.

165. Ranch Brussels Sprouts

Preparation time: 10 minutes
Cooking time: 30 minutes
Servings: 4

Ingredients:

- 1 pound Brussels sprouts, halved
- 1 teaspoon oregano, dried
- 1 tablespoon olive oil
- 3 garlic cloves, minced
- ½ teaspoon hot paprika
- A pinch of salt and black pepper
- 2 tablespoons keto ranch dressing
- 1 tablespoon parmesan, grated

Directions:

1. Spread the sprouts on a lined baking sheet, add oregano, oil, garlic, paprika, salt and pepper, toss, bake them in the oven at 425 degrees F for 30 minutes, add parmesan and keto ranch dressing, toss well, divide between plates and serve as a side dish.
2. Enjoy!

Nutritional Value:calories 222, fat 4, fiber 6, carbs 12, protein 8

166. Fried Cauliflower Rice

Preparation time: 10 minutes
Cooking time: 15 minutes
Servings: 4

Ingredients:

- 1 tablespoon ghee, melted
- 1 small yellow onion, chopped
- 2 carrots, chopped
- 2 hot dogs, sliced
- 1 tablespoon avocado oil
- 1 garlic clove, minced
- 2 and ½ cups cauliflower rice, steamed
- 2 eggs, whisked
- 2 tablespoons coconut aminos
- 2 scallion, sliced

Directions:

1. Heat up a pan with the ghee over medium-high heat, add onion, carrots, garlic and hot dogs, stir and cook for 5 minutes.
2. Add cauliflower rice and avocado oil, stir and cook for 5 minutes more.
3. Add the eggs, toss everything, cook for 5 more minutes until the eggs are scrambled, add the aminos and the scallions, toss, divide between plates and serve as a side dish.
4. Enjoy!

Nutritional Value:calories 200, fat 3, fiber 5, carbs 13, protein 8

167. Baked Asparagus Dish

Preparation time: 10 minutes
Cooking time: 30 minutes
Servings: 6

Ingredients:

- 3 garlic cloves, minced
- ¾ cup coconut cream
- 2 pounds asparagus, trimmed
- 1 cup parmesan, grated
- A pinch of salt and black pepper
- 1 cup mozzarella, shredded

Directions:

1. In a baking dish, combine the asparagus with the garlic, cream, salt, pepper, mozzarella and top with the parmesan, introduce in the oven and bake at 400 degrees F for 30 minutes.
2. Divide between plates and serve as a side dish.
3. Enjoy!

Nutritional Value:calories 200, fat 3, fiber 6, carbs 12, protein 9

168. Creamy Carrots

Preparation time: 10 minutes
Cooking time: 20 minutes
Servings: 4

Ingredients:

- 2 and ½ pounds baby carrots
- 3 shallots, chopped
- 2 tablespoons olive oil
- 1 teaspoon thyme, chopped
- A pinch of salt and black pepper
- ¼ cup coconut cream

Directions:

1. In a baking dish, combine the carrots with the shallots, oil, thyme, salt, pepper and cream, toss, introduce in the oven and bake at 425 degrees F for 20 minutes.
2. Divide the mix between plates and serve as a side dish.
3. Enjoy!

Nutritional Value:calories 199, fat 2, fiber 5, carbs 9, protein 5

169. Carrots and Walnuts Mix

Preparation time: 10 minutes
Cooking time: 10 minutes
Servings: 4

Ingredients:

- 2 pounds baby carrots
- 2 tablespoons ghee, melted
- 3 ounces canned walnuts, chopped
- 1 teaspoon apple cider vinegar
- A pinch of salt and black pepper
- 1 tablespoon chives, chopped

Directions:

1. Put the carrots in a pot, add water to cover them, bring to a simmer over medium heat, cook for 8 minutes and drain them well.
2. Heat up a pan with the ghee over medium heat, add walnuts, vinegar, salt and pepper, stir and cook for 2 minutes.
3. Add the carrots, and the chives, stir, divide between plates and serve as a side dish.
4. Enjoy!

Nutritional Value:calories 210, fat 3, fiber 4, carbs 9, protein 6

170. Carrots and Capers Mix

Preparation time: 10 minutes
Cooking time: 13 minutes
Servings: 8

Ingredients:

- 3 pounds rainbow carrots, sliced
- 1 yellow onion, chopped
- 2 tablespoons olive oil
- ½ cup water
- 3 tablespoons raisins
- 3 tablespoons vinegar
- 1 tablespoon capers
- A pinch of salt and black pepper

Directions:

1. Heat up a pan with the oil over medium-high heat, add the onion, stir and cook for 5 minutes.
2. Add the carrots, water, raisins, vinegar, capers, salt and pepper, stir, cover the pan, cook the mix for 8 minutes, divide between plates and serve as a side dish.
3. Enjoy!

Nutritional Value:calories 199, fat 2, fiber 3, carbs 9, protein 11

171. Chipotle Rainbow Carrots

Preparation time: 10 minutes
Cooking time: 25 minutes
Servings: 8

Ingredients:

- 3 pounds rainbow carrots, halved lengthwise
- 3 tablespoons olive oil
- ½ teaspoon cumin, ground
- ¼ teaspoon chipotle powder
- A pinch of salt and black pepper
- 1 tablespoon cilantro, chopped

Directions:

1. Spread the carrots on a lined baking sheet, add the oil, cumin, chipotle powder, salt, pepper and cilantro, toss, introduce in the oven and bake at 425 degrees F for 25 minutes.
2. Divide between plates and serve as a side dish.
3. Enjoy!

Nutritional Value:calories 200, fat 2, fiber 4, carbs 9, protein 8

172. Simple Haricot Verts Mix

Preparation time: 10 minutes
Cooking time: 15 minutes
Servings: 4

Ingredients:

- 2 pounds haricot verts
- 4 ounces pancetta, chopped
- ½ cup dates, sliced
- A pinch of salt and black pepper

Directions:

1. Heat up a pan over medium-high heat, add the pancetta, stir and cook for 5 minutes.
2. Add haricot verts, dates, salt and pepper, toss, cook for 10 minutes, divide between plates and serve as a side dish.
3. Enjoy!

Nutritional Value:calories 181, fat 2, fiber 6, carbs 9, protein 8

173. Green Beans Mix

Preparation time: 10 minutes
Cooking time: 20 minutes
Servings: 4

Ingredients:

- 2 pounds green beans, halved
- 3 tablespoons olive oil
- A pinch of salt and black pepper
- ¼ cup cranberries, dried
- ¼ cup almonds, chopped

Directions:

1. Spread the green beans on a lined baking sheet, season with salt, pepper and the oil, toss, introduce in the oven and cook at 425 degrees F for 15 minutes.
2. Add the cranberries and the almonds, toss, cook for 5 minutes more, divide between plates and serve as a side dish.
3. Enjoy!

Nutritional Value:calories 181, fat 3, fiber 5, carbs 10, protein 6

174. Garlicky Green Beans

Preparation time: 10 minutes
Cooking time: 10 minutes
Servings: 4

Ingredients:

- 1 and ½ pounds green beans, trimmed
- 4 garlic cloves, minced
- ½ teaspoon red pepper flakes
- 3 tablespoons olive oil
- 2 tablespoons parmesan, grated

Directions:

1. Put the green beans in a pot, add water to cover them, bring to a simmer over medium-high heat, cook for 5 minutes, drain and put into a bowl.
2. Heat up a pan with the oil over medium-high heat, add the garlic, pepper flakes and the green beans, stir, cook for 6 minutes, divide between plates, sprinkle parmesan on top and serve as a side dish.
3. Enjoy!

Nutritional Value:calories 200, fat 3, fiber 6, carbs 11, protein 6

175. Easy Parmesan Zucchini

Preparation time: 10 minutes

Cooking time: 15 minutes
Servings: 4

Ingredients:

- Cooking spray
- 4 zucchinis, quartered lengthwise
- ½ teaspoon thyme, dried
- ½ cup parmesan, grated
- 2 tablespoons olive oil
- 2 tablespoons parsley, chopped
- ½ teaspoon basil, dried
- ¼ teaspoon garlic powder
- A pinch of salt and black pepper
- ½ teaspoon oregano, dried

Directions:

1. Grease a lined baking sheet with the cooking spray, spread zucchini quarters, add salt, pepper, thyme, oil, basil, garlic powder, oregano, parmesan and parsley, toss, introduce in the oven and cook at 350 degrees F for 15 minutes.
2. Divide between plates and serve as a side dish.
3. Enjoy!

Nutritional Value:calories 200, fat 2, fiber 4, carbs 11, protein 7

176. Baked Mushrooms Mix

Preparation time: 10 minutes
Cooking time: 15 minutes
Servings: 4

Ingredients:

- 3 tablespoons olive oil
- ¼ cup lemon juice
- Zest of 1 lemon, grated
- 1 and ½ pounds cremini mushrooms, sliced
- 3 garlic cloves, minced
- 2 teaspoons thyme, dried
- ¼ cup parmesan, grated
- A pinch of salt and black pepper

Directions:

1. Grease a baking dish with the oil, add the mushrooms, lemon juice, lemon zest, garlic, thyme, parmesan, salt and pepper, toss, introduce in the oven and cook at 375 degrees F for 15 minutes.
2. Divide between plates and serve as a side dish.
3. Enjoy!

Nutritional Value:calories 199, fat 2, fiber 7, carbs 12, protein 7

177. Green Beans Fries

Preparation time: 10 minutes
Cooking time: 15 minutes
Servings: 6

Ingredients:

- ½ cup parmesan, grated
- A pinch of salt and black pepper
- 1 and ½ pounds green beans
- ½ cup coconut flour
- 2 eggs, whisked
- A drizzle of olive oil

Directions:

1. In a bowl, combine the parmesan with salt and pepper and stir.
2. Dredge the green beans in flour, then in eggs and parmesan mix, arrange the fries on a lined baking sheet after you have greased it with a drizzle of oil, introduce in the oven and bake at 425 degrees F for 15 minutes.
3. Divide the green beans fries between plates and serve as a side dish.
4. Enjoy!

Nutritional Value:calories 188, fat 2, fiber 6, carbs 14, protein 5

178. Creamy Mushrooms Mix

Preparation time: 10 minutes
Cooking time: 15 minutes
Servings: 4

Ingredients:

- 3 garlic cloves, minced
- 2 tablespoons ghee, melted
- 15 ounces mushrooms, sliced
- 1/3 cup coconut cream

- ½ teaspoon oregano, dried
- A pinch of salt and black pepper
- 2 tablespoons parsley, chopped
- 2 tablespoons parmesan, grated

Directions:

1. Heat up a pan with the ghee over medium heat, add the garlic, stir and cook for 2 minutes.
2. Add the mushrooms, the cream, oregano, salt and pepper, stir and cook for 10 minutes more.
3. Add parsley and parmesan, toss, cook for 3 minutes more, divide between plates and serve as a side dish.
4. Enjoy!

Nutritional Value:calories 212, fat 4, fiber 7, carbs 14, protein 9

179. Savory Tomato Side Salad

Preparation time: 10 minutes
Cooking time: 0 minutes
Servings: 6

Ingredients:

- 2 tablespoons olive oil
- 2 tablespoons red vinegar
- 2 teaspoons stevia
- 2 teaspoons coconut aminos
- 3 tablespoons ginger, grated
- 1 garlic clove, minced
- ¼ teaspoon orange zest, grated
- 2 teaspoons black sesame seeds
- ½ teaspoon red pepper, crushed
- A pinch of salt and black pepper
- 1 and ½ pounds tomatoes, cut into wedges
- 2 dark plums, cut into wedges
- 1 cup scallions, chopped
- 1 cup cilantro, chopped

Directions:

1. In a bowl, combine the oil with the vinegar, stevia, aminos, ginger, garlic and orange zest and whisk well.
2. In a salad bowl, combine the tomatoes with the plums, scallions, cilantro, salt and pepper and toss.
3. Add the dressing and the sesame seeds, toss, divide between plates and serve as a side dish.
4. Enjoy!

Nutritional Value:calories 199, fat 3, fiber 3, carbs 11, protein 9

180. Tomato and Green Beans Mix

Preparation time: 10 minutes
Cooking time: 12 minutes
Servings: 8

Ingredients:

- 2 pounds green beans, trimmed and halved
- ½ cup cilantro, chopped
- 1 teaspoon cumin, ground
- A pinch of salt and black pepper
- 2 tablespoons jalapeno pepper, chopped
- ¼ cup olive oil
- 1 tablespoons lime juice
- 1 cup cherry tomatoes, halved
- 1 garlic clove, minced
- ½ cup cheddar cheese, shredded

Directions:

1. Put some water in a pot, bring to a boil over medium-high heat, add the green beans, cook them for 6 minutes, drain and put them in a baking dish.
2. Add cilantro, cumin, salt, pepper, jalapeno, oil, lime juice, cherry tomatoes and garlic and toss.
3. Sprinkle the cheese all over, introduce the dish in your preheated broiler over medium heat and cook the mix for 6 minutes more.
4. Divide the green beans mix between plates and serve as a side dish.
5. Enjoy!

Nutritional Value:calories 200, fat 3, fiber 4, carbs 14, protein 8

181. Tomato Gratin

Preparation time: 10 minutes
Cooking time: 50 minutes
Servings: 8

Ingredients:

- 3 tablespoons olive oil
- 3 garlic cloves, minced
- 1 tablespoon balsamic vinegar
- 1/3 cup coconut cream
- A pinch of salt and black pepper
- 2 tablespoons marjoram, chopped
- ½ cup parmesan, grated
- 3 pounds tomatoes, sliced
- Cooking spray

Directions:

1. Heat up a pan with the olive oil over medium heat, add the garlic, stir and cook for 2 minutes.
2. Add the vinegar, coconut cream, salt, pepper and marjoram, stir and cook for 3 minutes more.
3. Grease baking dish with cooking spray and arrange the tomato slices.
4. Pour the coconut cream mix all over, spread, sprinkle parmesan on top, introduce in the oven and bake at 400 degrees F for 45 minutes.
5. Divide the gratin between plates and serve as a side dish.
6. Enjoy!

Nutritional Value:calories 251, fat 3, fiber 7, carbs 12, protein 9

182. Simple Tomato and Onion Side Salad

Preparation time: 10 minutes
Cooking time: 0 minutes
Servings: 6

Ingredients:

- 3 tablespoons white vinegar
- 1 tablespoon olive oil
- 1 teaspoon stevia
- 2 cucumbers, sliced
- 4 tomatoes, cut into wedges
- 1 sweet onion, sliced
- 2 tablespoons parsley, chopped
- 2 tablespoons chives, chopped
- A pinch of salt and black pepper

Directions:

1. In a bowl, combine the tomatoes with the cucumbers, onion, parsley, chives, salt, pepper, stevia, oil and vinegar, toss, divide between plates and serve as a side dish.
2. Enjoy!

Nutritional Value:calories 171, fat 2, fiber 1, carbs 8, protein 7

183. Tex Mex Avocado Side Dish

Preparation time: 10 minutes
Cooking time: 0 minutes
Servings: 4

Ingredients:

- 2 avocados, peeled, pitted and sliced
- 1 tablespoon avocado oil
- 1 plum tomato, sliced
- A pinch of salt and black pepper
- 2 tablespoons cilantro, chopped
- ½ teaspoon chili powder
- 1 tablespoon lime juice
- 2 tablespoons feta cheese, crumbled

Directions:

1. In a salad bowl, combine the avocado slices with the tomato, oil, salt, pepper, cilantro, chili powder and lime juice and toss.
2. Sprinkle feta cheese, divide between plates and serve as a side salad.
3. Enjoy!

Nutritional Value:calories 200, fat 2, fiber 3, carbs 12, protein 9

SEAFOOD

184. Tossed Sardine Salad

Preparation Time: 10 MIN
Serve: 1

Ingredients:

- 5 oz canned sardines in oil
- 1 tbsp lemon juice
- 1 small cucumber, chopped
- ½ tbsp mustard
- Salt and black pepper to taste

Directions:

1. Drain sardines, put them in a bowl, and mash with a fork.
2. Add all remaining ingredients, stir well, and serve cold.
3. Enjoy!

Nutritional Value:

Calories 200
Total Fats 20g
Carbs: 0g
Protein 20g
Fiber: 1g

185. Family Style Clams

Preparation Time: 20 MIN
Serve: 6

Ingredients:

- ½ cup ghee
- 36 clams, scrubbed clean
- 1 tsp red pepper flakes, crushed
- 1 tsp parsley, chopped
- 5 garlic cloves, minced
- 1 tbsp oregano, dried
- 2 cups white wine

Directions:

1. Heat the ghee in a pan over medium heat, add garlic, and cook for 1 minute.
2. Add parsley, oregano, wine, and pepper flakes. Stir well.
3. Add in the clams, cover the pan, and cook for 10 minutes.
4. Discard any unopened clams, and serve in bowls.
5. Enjoy!

Nutritional Value:

Calories 224
Total Fats 15g
Carbs: 3g
Protein 4g
Fiber: 2g

186. Grilled Salmon Skewers

Preparation Time: 20 MIN
Serve: 2

Ingredients:

- 2 lemons, sliced
- 1 lb wild salmon, skinless and cubed
- ¼ cup balsamic vinegar
- ¼ cup orange juice
- 1 tsp coconut oil
- 1/3 cup orange marmalade, no sugar added

Directions:

1. Heat a pot over medium heat, pour in vinegar, orange juice, and marmalade. Stir well, and bring to a simmer for 1 minute. Reduce temperature, and cook until it thickens a bit and take off heat.
2. Arrange salmon cubes and lemon slices on skewers, and brush them on one side with the orange glaze.
3. Brush your kitchen grill with coconut oil, and heat to medium heat.
4. Place salmon kebabs on grill, glazed side down, and cook for 4 minutes.
5. Flip kebabs, brush them with the remaining orange glaze, and cook for 4 minutes more.
6. Serve immediately.
7. Enjoy!

Nutritional Value:

Calories 160
Total Fats 3g
Carbs: 1g
Protein 8g
Fiber: 2g

187. Spicy Tuna Over Arugula

Preparation Time: 15 MIN
Serve: 4

Ingredients:

- ½ cup cilantro, chopped
- 1/3 cup olive oil
- 2 tbsp olive oil
- 1 small red onion, chopped
- 3 tbsp balsamic vinegar
- 2 tbsp parsley, chopped
- 2 tbsp basil, chopped
- 1 jalapeno pepper, chopped
- 1 lb sushi grade tuna steak
- Salt and black pepper to taste
- 1 tsp red pepper flakes
- 1 tsp thyme, chopped
- A pinch of cayenne pepper
- 3 garlic cloves, minced
- 2 avocados, pitted and sliced
- 6 oz baby arugula

Directions:

1. In a bowl, mix the 1/3 cup oil with jalapeno, vinegar, onion, cilantro, basil, garlic, parsley, pepper flakes, thyme, cayenne, salt and pepper. Leave aside for later.
2. Heat a pan on medium high heat with the second amount of olive oil. Add tuna, season with salt and pepper, and cook for 2 minutes on each side. Transfer the tuna to a cutting board and slice into strips.
3. Mix arugula with half of the olive oil mix you have made and toss together to coat.
4. Divide arugula onto plates, top with tuna slices, and drizzle the rest of the sauce over the top. Serve with avocado slices on the side.
5. Enjoy!

Nutritional Value:

Calories 186
Total Fats 3g
Carbs: 4g
Protein 20g
Fiber: 1g

188. Salmon in Spicy Garlic Dipping Sauce

Preparation Time: 25 MIN
Serve: 6

Ingredients:

For the Salmon

- 1 ¼ cups coconut, desiccated and unsweetened
- 1 lb salmon, cubed
- 1 egg
- ½ tsp Salt
- ½ tsp black pepper
- 1 tbsp water
- 1/3 cup coconut flour
- 3 tbsp olive oil

For the sauce:

- ¼ tsp agar agar
- 3 garlic cloves, chopped
- ¾ cup water
- 4 Thai red chilis, chopped
- ¼ cup balsamic vinegar
- ½ cup stevia
- A pinch of salt

Directions:

1. In a bowl, mix together coconut flour with salt and pepper.
2. In another bowl, whisk the egg and 1 tablespoon water. Put the desiccated coconut in a third bowl.
3. Dip salmon cubes in flour, then egg, and then in coconut and place them on a plate until all the salmon is coated.
4. Heat up a pan with the olive oil on medium high heat, and cook the salmon for 3 minutes on each side. Transfer them to paper towels.
5. Heat up a new pan with ¾ cup water

over high heat, sprinkle in agar agar, and bring to a boil.

6. Cook for 3 minutes and take off the heat.
7. In a blender, combine garlic with chilis, vinegar, stevia, a pinch of salt.
8. Transfer this mix to a small pan, and heat up over medium high heat.
9. Add the agar mix to the sauce, and cook for 3 minutes.
10. Serve your salmon with chili sauce on the side.
11. Enjoy!

Nutritional Value:

Calories 50
Total Fats 2g
Carbs: 4g
Protein 2g
Fiber: 0g

189. Sweet Apple Clams

Preparation Time: 20 MIN
Serve: 4

Ingredients:

- 2 lb clams, scrubbed
- 3 oz pancetta
- 1 tbsp olive oil
- 3 tbsp ghee
- 2 garlic cloves, minced
- 1 small shallot, diced
- 1 bottle infused cider
- Salt and black pepper to taste
- Juice of ½ a lemon
- 1 small green apple, chopped
- 2 thyme springs, chopped

Directions:

1. Heat olive oil in a pan over medium high heat, add pancetta, and brown for 3 minutes. Reduce temperature to medium.
2. Add in ghee, garlic, salt, pepper, and shallot. Stir and cook for 3 minutes.
3. Increase heat to high, and add cider. Stir well, and cook for 1 minute.
4. Add clams and thyme sprigs. Cover the pan, and simmer for 5 minutes.
5. Discard unopened clams, add the lemon juice and apple pieces, and then divide into bowls.
6. Serve hot.
7. Enjoy!

Nutritional Value:

Calories 100
Total Fats 2g
Carbs: 1g
Protein 20g
Fiber: 1g

190. Zesty Scallops for Two

Preparation Time: 20 MIN
Serve: 2

Ingredients:

- 8 scallops
- ½ tsp Salt
- ¼ tsp black pepper
- 1 fennel, trimmed, leaves chopped, and bulbs cut into wedges
- Juice of ½ a lime
- Zest from 1 lime
- 1 egg yolk
- 3 tbsp ghee, melted and heated up
- ½ tbsp avocado oil
- 1 lime, cut into wedges

Directions:

1. Season scallops with salt and pepper, put in a bowl, and mix with half of the lime juice and half of the zest. Toss well to coat.
2. In a separate bowl, mix egg yolk with some salt and pepper, the rest of the lime juice, and the rest of the lime zest.
3. Add melted ghee to the egg mixture, and stir very well. Fold in the fennel leaves only.
4. Brush fennel wedges with oil, place on heated grill over medium high heat, and cook for 2 minutes. Flip the wedges, and cook for 2 minutes more.
5. Add scallops to the grill, and cook for 2 minutes per side.
6. Divide the grilled fennel and scallops on

plates, drizzle the ghee mix over everything, and serve with lime wedges on the side.

7. Enjoy!

Nutritional Value:

Calories 400
Total Fats 24g
Carbs: 12g
Protein 25g
Fiber: 4g

191. Spanish Oysters

Preparation Time: 20 MIN
Serve: 6

Ingredients:

- 18 oysters, scrubbed clean
- ¼ cup cilantro, chopped
- 2 tomatoes, chopped
- 1 jalapeno pepper, chopped
- ¼ cup red onion, finely chopped
- Salt and black pepper to taste
- ½ cup Monterey Jack cheese, shredded
- Juice from 1 lime
- 2 limes, cut into wedges

Directions:

1. In a bowl, mix together onion, jalapeno, cilantro, tomatoes, salt, pepper, lime juice, and stir well.
2. Place oysters on a preheated grill over medium high heat, cover, and cook for 7 minutes until the oysters open.
3. Transfer opened oysters to a baking dish, and discard unopened ones.
4. Top oysters with cheese, and place under a preheated broiler for 1 minute.
5. Arrange oysters on a platter, top each with the salsa mix you made earlier, and serve with lime wedges on the side.
6. Enjoy!

Nutritional Value:

Calories 70
Total Fats 2g
Carbs: 1g
Protein 1g
Fiber: 0g

192. Mexican Inspired Grilled Squid

Preparation Time: 20 MIN
Serve: 2

Ingredients:

For the Squid

- 2 medium squids, tentacles separated, and tubes scored lengthwise
- A drizzle of olive oil
- Juice from 1 lime
- Salt and black pepper to taste

For the guacamole:

- 2 avocados, pitted and chopped
- ¼ tsp ground coriander
- 2 red chilies, chopped
- 1 tomato, chopped
- 1 red onion, chopped
- Juice from 2 limes

Directions:

- Season squid and squid tentacles with salt and pepper. Drizzle some olive oil and massage well.
- Place squid on a preheated grill over medium high heat, score side down, and cook for 2 minutes.
- Flip the tentacles, and cook for 2 minutes more. Transfer to a bowl.
- Squeeze juice from 1 lime over the bowl, and toss to coat.
- Use a fork to mash the avocado in a new bowl.
- Add the remaining ingredients to the avocado, and stir everything.
- Divide squid onto plates, top with guacamole, and serve.
- Enjoy!

Nutritional Value:

Calories 500
Total Fats 43g
Carbs: 7g
Protein 20g

Fiber: 6g

193. Bacon and Shrimp Over Cauliflower Grits

Preparation Time: 25 MIN
Serve: 2

Ingredients:

- 1 tbsp ghee
- 1 cauliflower head, florets separated
- 1 lb shrimp, peeled and deveined
- ¼ cup coconut milk
- 8 oz mushrooms, roughly chopped
- ¼ tsp red pepper flakes
- Salt and black pepper to taste
- 2 garlic cloves, minced
- 4 bacon slices
- ½ cup beef stock
- 1 tbsp parsley, finely chopped
- 1 tbsp chives, chopped

Directions:

1. Cook the bacon in a pan on medium-high heat until it's crispy. Transfer to paper towels and leave aside.
2. Heat up another pan with 1 tablespoon of the bacon fat over medium high heat, add shrimp, and cook for 2 minutes on each side. Transfer to a bowl.
3. Heat up the same pan again over medium heat, add mushrooms, and cook for 3-4 minutes.
4. Add garlic and pepper flakes, and cook for 1 minute.
5. Pour in beef stock, salt, pepper, and return the shrimp to pan as well.
6. Cook until the liquid thickens a bit, then take off heat and keep warm.
7. Meanwhile, put cauliflower in your food processor and mince it finely.
8. Place the minced cauliflower into a heated pan over medium high heat, and cook for 5 minutes.
9. Add ghee to the cauliflower. Then, blend into grits using an immersion blender.
10. Add salt and pepper to the taste, stir and divide the grits into bowls.
11. Top with the shrimp, and serve with parsley and chives sprinkled all over.
12. Enjoy!

Nutritional Value:

Calories 245
Total Fats 7g
Carbs: 6g
Protein 20g
Fiber: 4g

194. Shrimp Stuffed Salmon

Preparation Time: 35 MIN
Serve: 2

Ingredients:

- 2 salmon fillets
- 1 tbsp olive oil
- 5 oz tiger shrimp, peeled, deveined and chopped
- 6 mushrooms, chopped
- 3 green onions, chopped
- 2 cups spinach
- ¼ cup macadamia nuts, toasted and chopped
- Salt and black pepper to taste
- ¼ tsp nutmeg
- ¼ cup mayonnaise

Directions:

1. Heat up a pan with the olive oil on medium high heat. Add mushrooms, onions, salt, and pepper, and cook for 4 minutes.
2. Add in the macadamia nuts, and cook for another 2 minutes.
3. Add spinach, and cook for 1 minute.
4. Finally, add the shrimp, stir, and cook for 1 minute.
5. Take the pan off the heat, and stir in mayo and nutmeg.
6. Make an incision lengthwise on each salmon fillet, sprinkle salt and pepper inside, and divide spinach and shrimp mix into incisions.
7. Heat up a pan with an extra drizzle of oil over medium high heat, place the stuffed salmon, skin side down, and cook for 1

minutes. Reduce the temperature, cover the pan, and cook for 8 minutes.

8. Broil the pan in the oven for 3 minutes, divide between plates, and serve.
9. Enjoy!

Nutritional Value:

Calories 430
Total Fats 30g
Carbs: 7g
Protein 50g
Fiber: 3g

195. Calamari with Sriracha Sauce

Preparation Time: 30 MIN
Serve: 2

Ingredients:

- 1 squid, cut into medium rings
- ¼ tsp cayenne pepper
- 1 egg, whisked
- 2 tbsp coconut flour
- Salt and black pepper to taste
- Coconut oil, for frying
- 1 tbsp lemon juice
- 4 tbsp mayo
- 1 tsp sriracha sauce

Directions:

1. Season squid rings with salt, pepper, and cayenne, and put themin a bowl.
2. In a separate bowl, whisk the egg with salt, pepper and coconut flour.
3. Dredge calamari rings in the egg mix.
4. Heat a pan with enough coconut oil to cover the surface over medium heat. Fry the calamari rings until they become gold on both sides.
5. Transfer to paper towels, drain grease, and put in a bowl.
6. In another bowl, mix mayonnaise with lemon juice and sriracha sauce, and serve your calamari rings with this sauce on the side.
7. Enjoy!

Nutritional Value:

Calories 345
Total Fats 32g
Carbs: 3g
Protein 13g
Fiber: 3g

196. Shrimp and Calamari Dippers

Preparation Time: 30 MIN
Serve: 1

Ingredients:

- 8 oz calamari, cut into medium rings
- 7 oz shrimp, peeled and deveined
- 1 egg
- 3 tbsp coconut flour
- 1 tbsp coconut oil
- 2 tbsp avocado, chopped
- 1 tsp tomato paste
- 1 tbsp mayonnaise
- ¼ tsp Worcestershire sauce
- 1 tsp lemon juice
- 2 lemon slices
- Salt and black pepper to taste
- ½ tsp turmeric

Directions:

1. In a bowl, whisk the egg with coconut oil.
2. Toss the calamari and shrimp in the bowl to coat them.
3. In a new bowl, mix the flour with salt, pepper, and turmeric.
4. Dredge the calamari and shrimp in this flour mix, place everything on a lined baking sheet, and bake in the oven a,,,,,,t 400 degrees F for 10 minutes.
5. Flip calamari and shrimp to their other side, and bake for 10 minutes more.
6. Meanwhile, in a bowl, mash avocado with mayo and tomato paste using a fork.
7. Add Worcestershire sauce, lemon juice, salt and pepper to the avocado bowl.
8. Divide baked calamari and shrimp onto plates, and serve with the sauce and lemon slices on the side.
9. Enjoy!

Nutritional Value:

Calories 368
Total Fats 23g
Carbs: 10g
Protein 34g
Fiber: 3g

197. Fresh Salad with Octopus

Preparation Time: 50 MIN
Serve: 2

Ingredients:

- 21 oz octopus, rinsed
- Juice of 1 lemon
- 4 celery stalks, chopped
- 3 oz olive oil
- Salt and black pepper to taste
- 4 tbsp parsley, chopped

Directions:

1. Place the octopus in a pot, add water until it's covered, and bring to a boil over medium heat. Cook for 40 minutes, covered, drain, and leave aside to cool down when done.
2. Chop cooled octopus, and put it in a salad bowl.
3. Add celery stalks, parsley, olive oil and lemon juice, and toss everything together well.
4. Season with salt and pepper, toss once more, and serve.
5. Enjoy!

Nutritional Value:

Calories 140
Total Fats 10g
Carbs: 6g
Protein 23g
Fiber: 3g

198. Classic Clam Chowder Soup

Preparation Time: 2 HR 10 MIN
Serve: 4

Ingredients:

- 1 cup celery stalks, chopped
- Salt and black pepper to taste
- 1 tsp dried thyme
- 2 cups chicken stock
- 14 oz canned baby clams
- 2 cups heavy cream
- 1 cup onion, chopped
- 13 bacon slices, chopped

Directions:

1. Brown bacon in a pan over medium high heat, and transfer the cooked pieces to a bowl. Save the grease in the pan.
2. Heat up the same pan over medium heat, add celery and onion, and cook for 5 minutes.
3. Transfer cooked and remaining ingredients to a slow cooker, and cook on high heat for 2 hours.
4. Divide into bowls and serve.
5. Enjoy!

Nutritional Value:

Calories 420
Total Fats 22g
Carbs: 5g
Protein 25g
Fiber: 0g

199. Flounder with Seafood Étouffée

Preparation Time: 30 MIN
Serve: 4

Ingredients:

For the seasoning:

- 2 tsp onion powder
- 2 tsp thyme, dried
- 2 tsp sweet paprika
- 2 tsp garlic powder
- Salt and black pepper to taste
- ½ tsp allspice, ground
- 1 tsp oregano, dried
- A pinch of cayenne pepper
- ¼ tsp nutmeg, ground
- ¼ tsp cloves
- A pinch of cinnamon powder

For the etouffee:

- 2 shallots, chopped
- 1 tbsp ghee
- 8 oz bacon, sliced
- 1 green bell pepper, chopped
- 1 celery stick, chopped
- 2 tbsp coconut flour
- 1 tomato, chopped
- 4 garlic cloves, minced
- 8 oz shrimp, peeled, deveined and chopped
- 2 cups chicken stock
- 1 tbsp coconut milk
- A handful parsley, chopped
- 1 tsp Tabasco sauce
- Salt and black pepper to taste

For the flounder:

- 4 flounder fillets
- 2 tbsp ghee

Directions:

1. For the seasoning, combine all spices in a bowl and mix together.
2. Reserve 2 tablespoons of this mix, and rub the flounder with the rest.
3. Heat up a pot over medium heat, and cook the bacon for 6 minutes.
4. Add celery, bell pepper, shallots and 1 tablespoon ghee to the pot, and cook for 4 minutes.
5. Add tomato and garlic, and cook for 4 minutes.
6. Add coconut flour and reserved seasoning, stir, and cook for an additional 2 minutes.
7. Pour in chicken stock and bring the pot to a simmer.
8. Meanwhile, heat up a pan with 2 tablespoons ghee over medium high heat, add the flounder, and cook for 2 minutes on each side. Set this pan aside.
9. Add shrimp to the pot of stock, stir, and cook for 2 minutes.
10. Add parsley, salt, pepper, coconut milk and Tabasco sauce to the pot, then take off heat.
11. Divide fish onto plates, top with the shrimp sauce, and serve.
12. Enjoy!

Nutritional Value:

Calories 200
Total Fats 5g
Carbs: 4g
Protein 20g
Fiber: 7g

200. Chopped Shrimp Tarragon Salad

Preparation Time: 20 MIN
Serve: 4

Ingredients:

- 2 tbsp olive oil
- 1 lb shrimp, peeled and deveined
- Salt and black pepper to taste
- 2 tbsp lime juice
- 3 endives, leaves separated
- 3 tbsp parsley, chopped
- 2 tsp mint, chopped
- 1 tbsp tarragon, chopped
- 1 tbsp lemon juice
- 2 tbsp mayonnaise
- 1 tsp lime zest
- ½ cup sour cream

Directions:

1. In a bowl, mix the shrimp with salt, pepper, and olive oil. Toss to coat, and then spread the shrimp on a lined baking sheet.
2. Place the shrimp in the oven at 400 degrees F, and bake for 10 minutes.
3. After baking, squeeze on lime juice, toss to coat the shrimp again, and leave aside for now.
4. In a new bowl, mix mayo with sour cream, lime zest, lemon juice, salt, pepper, tarragon, mint and parsley.
5. Chop the shrimp, add to salad dressing, and toss to coat everything. Spoon the salad into endive leaves.
6. Serve right away.
7. Enjoy!

Nutritional Value:

Calories 200
Total Fats 11g
Carbs: 1g
Protein 13g
Fiber: 2g

201. Spicy Saucy Oysters

Preparation Time: 10 MIN
Serve: 4

Ingredients:

- 12 oysters, shucked
- Juice of 1 lemon
- Juice from 1 orange
- Zest from 1 orange
- Juice from 1 lime
- Zest from 1 lime
- 2 tbsp ketchup
- 1 Serrano chili pepper, chopped
- 1 cup tomato juice
- ½ tsp ginger, grated
- ¼ tsp garlic, minced
- Salt to taste
- ¼ cup olive oil
- ¼ cup cilantro, chopped
- ¼ cup scallions, chopped

Directions:

1. In a bowl, combine all ingredients, except for oysters, with a whisk.
2. Spoon this mixture into oysters, and serve them immediately.
3. Enjoy!

Nutritional Value:

Calories 100
Total Fats 1g
Carbs: 2g
Protein 5g
Fiber: 0g

202. Creamy Lobster Soup

Preparation Time: 1 HR 10 MIN
Serve: 4

Ingredients:

- 4 garlic cloves, minced
- 1 small red onion, chopped
- 24 oz lobster chunks, pre-cooked
- Salt and black pepper to taste
- ½ cup tomato paste
- 2 carrots, finely chopped
- 4 celery stalks, chopped
- 1 quart seafood stock
- 1 tbsp olive oil
- 1 cup heavy cream
- 3 bay leaves
- 1 tsp thyme, dried
- 1 tsp peppercorns
- 1 tsp paprika
- 1 tsp xanthan gum
- ¼ cup parsley, chopped
- 1 tbsp lemon juice

Directions:

1. Heat up a large pot with the olive oil over medium heat, add onion, and cook for 4 minutes.
2. Add garlic, stir, and cook for 1 minute.
3. Add celery and carrot, stir, and cook for another minute.
4. Add tomato paste and stock to the pot.
5. Add bay leaves, salt, pepper, peppercorns, paprika, thyme and xanthan gum. Stir the ingredients, and simmer over medium heat for 1 hour.
6. Discard bay leaves, pour in cream, and bring to a simmer.
7. Use an immersion blender to combine the ingredients, and add lobster chunks.
8. Cook for a few minutes more.
9. Stir in lemon juice, divide into bowls, and sprinkle parsley on top.
10. Enjoy!

Nutritional Value:

Calories 200
Total Fats 12g
Carbs: 6g
Protein 12g
Fiber: 7g

203. Salmon Nori Rolls

Preparation Time: 10 MIN
Serve: 12

Ingredients:

- 2 nori sheets
- 1 small avocado, pitted and finely chopped
- 6 oz smoked salmon. Sliced
- 4 oz cream cheese
- 1 cucumber, sliced
- 1 tsp wasabi paste
- Pickled ginger for serving

Directions:

1. Place nori sheets flat on a sushi mat.
2. Divide salmon slices among the sheets. Then divide the avocado and cucumber slices.
3. In a bowl, mix the cream cheese with wasabi paste and stir well to combine.
4. Spread the mix over cucumber slices, and roll your nori sheets. Slice each sheet into 6 pieces, and serve with pickled ginger.
5. Enjoy!

Nutritional Value:

Calories 80
Total Fats 6g
Carbs: 2g
Protein 4g
Fiber: 1g

204. Citrus Pepper and Salmon Skewers

Preparation Time: 18 MIN
Serve: 4

Ingredients:

- 12 oz salmon fillet, cubed
- 1 red onion, cut into chunks
- ½ red bell pepper, cut in chunks
- ½ green bell pepper, cut in chunks
- ½ orange bell pepper, cut in chunks
- Juice from 1 lemon
- Salt and black pepper to taste
- 1 tbsp olive oil

Directions:

1. Thread skewers with onion, the bell pepper, and salmon cubes evenly.
2. Season the skewers with salt and pepper. Drizzle olive oil and lemon juice over them, and place them on preheated grill on medium high heat.
3. Cook for 4 minutes on each side, divide between plates, and serve.
4. Enjoy!

Nutritional Value:

Calories 150
Total Fats 3g
Carbs: 3g
Protein 8g
Fiber: 6g

205. Swordfish Steaks with Salsa

Preparation Time: 16 MIN
Serve: 2

Ingredients:

- 2 medium swordfish steaks
- Salt and black pepper to taste
- 2 tsp avocado oil
- 1 tbsp cilantro, chopped
- 1 mango, chopped
- 1 avocado, pitted, and chopped
- ¼ tsp cumin
- ¼ tsp onion powder
- ¼ tsp garlic powder
- 1 orange, peeled and sliced
- ½ tbsp balsamic vinegar

Directions:

1. Season the swordfish steaks with salt, pepper, garlic powder, onion powder and cumin on each side.
2. Heat a pan with half of the olive oil over medium high heat, add fish steaks, and cook them for 3 minutes on each side.
3. Meanwhile, in a clean bowl, mix the avocado with mango, cilantro, balsamic vinegar, salt, pepper and the rest of the olive oil.
4. Divide fish on two plates, top with mango salsa, and serve with orange slices on the side.

5. Enjoy!

Nutritional Value:

Calories 160
Total Fats 3g
Carbs: 4g
Protein 8g
Fiber: 2g

206. Tuna and Cauliflower Salad

Preparation Time: 17 MIN
Serve: 4

Ingredients:

For the Tuna

- 1 ahi tuna steak
- 2 tbsp coconut oil
- 1 cauliflower head, florets separated
- 2 tbsp green onions, chopped
- 1 avocado, pitted and chopped
- 1 cucumber, grated
- 1 nori sheet, torn

For the salad dressing:

1. 1 tbsp sesame oil
2. 2 tbsp coconut aminos
3. 1 tbsp apple cider vinegar
4. A pinch of salt
5. 1 tsp stevia

Directions:

1. Put cauliflower florets in your food processor, and pulse until you obtain a cauliflower "rice".
2. Fill a pot with water, add a steamer basket inside, and put the cauliflower rice inside. Bring the water to a boil over medium heat, cover, steam for a few minutes, drain, and transfer "rice" to a bowl.
3. Heat a pan with the coconut oil over medium high heat, and add the tuna steak. Cook for 1 minute on each side, and transfer to a cutting board.
4. Divide cauliflower rice into bowls, top with nori pieces, cucumber, green onions and avocado.
5. For the dressing, in a bowl, mix all ingredients with a whisk.
6. Drizzle this over cauliflower rice and mixed veggies, top with tuna pieces and serve.
7. Enjoy!

Nutritional Value:

Calories 300
Total Fats 12g
Carbs: 6g
Protein 15g
Fiber: 6g

207. Savory Seasoned Swordfish

Preparation Time: 3 HR 20 MIN
Serve: 4

Ingredients:

- 1 tbsp parsley, chopped
- 1 lemon, cut into wedges
- 4 swordfish steaks
- 3 garlic cloves, minced
- 1/3 cup chicken stock
- 3 tbsp olive oil
- ¼ cup lemon juice
- Salt and black pepper to taste
- ½ tsp rosemary, dried
- ½ tsp sage, dried
- ½ tsp marjoram, dried

Directions:

1. In a bowl, whisk together the chicken stock with garlic, lemon juice, olive oil, salt, pepper, sage, marjoram and rosemary.
2. Add swordfish steaks to the bowl, toss to coat, and keep in the fridge to marinate for 3 hours.
3. Place marinated fish steaks on preheated grill over medium high heat, and cook for 5 minutes on each side.
4. Serve on plates with parsley and lemon wedges on the side.
5. Enjoy!

Nutritional Value:

Calories 136
Total Fats 5g
Carbs: 1g

Protein 20g
Fiber: 0g

208. Classic Crab Cakes

Preparation Time: 22 MIN
Serve: 6

Ingredients:

- 1 lb crabmeat
- ¼ cup parsley, chopped
- Salt and black pepper to taste
- 2 green onions, chopped
- ¼ cup cilantro, chopped
- 1 tsp jalapeno pepper, minced
- 1 tsp lemon juice
- 1 tsp Worcestershire sauce
- 1 tsp old bay seasoning
- ½ tsp mustard powder
- ½ cup mayonnaise
- 1 egg
- 2 tbsp olive oil

Directions:

1. In a large bowl, mix the crab meat with salt, pepper, parsley, green onions, cilantro, jalapeno, lemon juice, old bay seasoning, mustard powder and Worcestershire sauce with a large spoon or spatula.
2. In another bowl, mix egg wit mayo with a whisk.
3. Combine this mix with the crabmeat mix, and stir everything.
4. Shape 6 patties from this mix with your hands, and place them on a plate.
5. Heat a large pan with the olive oil over medium high heat, and add 3 crab cakes. Cook for 3 minutes per side, and transfer them to paper towels.
6. Repeat with the other 3 crab cakes, drain excess grease, and serve immediately.
7. Enjoy!

Nutritional Value:

Calories 254
Total Fats 17g
Carbs: 1g
Protein 20g
Fiber: 1g

209. Paprika-Rubbed Jumbo Shrimp

Preparation Time: 15 min
Serves: 3

Nutrition Value:Calories 112; Net Carbs 1g; Fat 5g; Protein 15g

Ingredients

- 1 lb jumbo shrimp
- Salt to taste
- ¼ tsp old bay seasoning
- ⅓ tsp smoked paprika
- ¼ tsp cayenne pepper
- 1 tbsp olive oil

Directions

1. Preheat the Air Fryer to 390°F.
2. In a bowl, add the shrimp, paprika, oil, salt, old bay seasoning, and cayenne pepper. Combine well.
3. Place the shrimp in the fryer basket, close the Air Fryer, and cook for 5 minutes.
4. Remove the shrimp onto a serving plate.

210. Fennel Trout en Papillote with Herbs

Preparation Time: 30 min
Serves: 2

Nutrition Value:Calories 305; Net Carbs 8.9g; Fat 21.1g; Protein 9.6g

Ingredients

- ¾ lb whole trout, scaled and cleaned
- ¼ bulb fennel, sliced
- ½ brown onion, sliced
- 3 tbsp chopped parsley
- 3 tbsp chopped dill
- 2 tbsp olive oil
- 1 lemon, sliced
- Salt and black pepper to taste

Directions

1. In a bowl, add the onion, parsley, dill, fennel, and garlic. Mix and drizzle the

olive oil over it.

2. Preheat the Air Fryer to 350°F.
3. Open the cavity of the fish and fill with the fennel mixture. Wrap the fish thoroughly in parchment paper and then in foil. Place the fish in the fryer basket and cook for 10 minutes.
4. Remove the paper and foil and top with lemon slices. Serve with a side of cooked mushrooms.

211. Simple Pomfret Fish Fry

Preparation Time: 15 min

Serves: 5

Nutrition Value:Calories 463; Net Carbs 3.4g; Fat 23g; Protein 55g

Ingredients

- 3 lb silver pomfret
- 1 tbsp turmeric powder
- 3 pinches of red chili powder
- ¾ tbsp ginger
- 3 pinches of cumin powder
- 2 tbsp lemon juice
- 2 tbsp olive oil
- Salt and black pepper, to taste

Directions

1. Wash the fish and soak in lemon juice to remove any unpleasant smell.
2. After 30 minutes, remove and wash the fish. Draw diagonal shaped slits on the fish. Combine black pepper, salt, garlic paste, lemon juice, and the turmeric powder.
3. Rub the mixture above and inside the fish and refrigerate for 30 minutes.
4. Arrange the fish in the basket of the Air Fryer and pour 2 tbsp of oil. Cook it for 12 minutes at 340°F.

212. Herb Crusted Halibut

Preparation Time: 30 min

Serves: 4

Nutrition Value:Calories 287; Net Carbs 1.3g; Fat 18g; Protein 22g

Ingredients

- ¾ cup pork rinds, crushed
- 4 halibut fillets
- ½ cup fresh parsley, chopped
- ¼ cup fresh dill, chopped
- ¼ cup fresh chives, chopped
- 1 tbsp extra virgin olive oil
- 1 tbsp finely grated lemon zest
- Sea salt and black pepper to taste

Directions

1. Preheat the Air Fryer to 390°F.
2. In a large bowl, mix the pork rinds, the parsley, the dill, the chives, the olive oil, the lemon zest, the sea salt, and black pepper.
3. Rinse the halibut fillets and dry them on a paper towel. Arrange the halibut fillets on a baking sheet.
4. Spoon the rinds on the fish. Lightly press the crumb mixture on the fillet. Cook the fillets in a preheated Air Fryer's basket for 30 minutes.

213. Fried Spinach Fish

Preparation Time: 10 min

Serves: 2

Nutrition Value:Calories 173; Net Carbs 0.5g; Fat 18g; Protein 4g

Ingredients

- 4 oz spinach leaves
- 2 cups almond flour
- A pinch of salt
- 2 tbsp oil
- 1 large beaten egg

Directions

1. In a deep bowl, add beaten egg, wheat flour, salt, and spinach leaves. Marinate the fish. Cook in the Air Fryer for 12 minutes at 370°F. Serve with lemon slices.

214. Easy Bacon Wrapped Shrimp

Preparation Time: 15 min

Serves: 4

Nutrition Value:Calories 95; Net Carbs 3.2g; Fat

7g; Protein 6g

Ingredients

- 2 pounds king shrimp
- 16 bacon strips, cooked
- Barbecue sauce, to serve

Directions

1. Wrap the shrimp with bacon strips, then secure with toothpicks. Cook at 390°F for 5 minutes. Shake the basket from time to time. Serve the shrimp with the BBQ sauce.

215. Mediterranean Halibut

Preparation Time: 35 min
Serves: 6

Nutrition Value:Calories 432; Net Carbs 7.1g; Fat 32g; Protein 27g

Ingredients

- 2 lb halibut fillets, cut in 6 pieces
- Salt and black pepper
- 3-4 chopped green onions
- ½ cup mayonnaise
- ½ cup sour cream
- 1 tbsp dried dill weed

Directions

2. Preheat the Air Fryer to 390°F. Season the halibut with salt and pepper.
3. In a bowl, mix onions, mayonnaise, sour cream, and dill. Spread this mixture over the fish. Cook for 20 minutes.

216. Lemon-Zest Salmon

Preparation Time: 20 min
Serves: 2

Nutrition Value:Calories 421; Net Carbs 1.3g; Fat 17g; Protein 64g

Ingredients

- 2 salmon fillets
- Pink salt to taste
- Zest of 1 lemon
- Directions
- Spray the fillets with cooking spray. Rub them with salt and lemon zest.
- Line baking paper in your air fryer's basket to avoid sticking. Cook the fillets for 10 minutes at 360°F, turning once halfway through cooking. Serve with steamed asparagus and a drizzle of lemon juice.

217. Crispy Fish Strips

Preparation Time: 20 min
Serves: 4

Nutrition Value:Calories 183; Net Carbs 2.6g; Fat 6.7g; Protein 24g

Ingredients

- 2 fresh white fish fillets, cut into 4 fingers each
- 1 egg, beaten
- ½ cup buttermilk
- 1 cup pork rinds, crushed
- Salt and black pepper to taste

Directions

1. In a bowl, mix egg and buttermilk. On a plate, mix pork rinds, salt and black pepper.
2. Dip each finger into the egg mixture, then roll it up in the pork rinds, and grease with cooking spray. Arrange them in the air fryer and cook for 10 minutes at 340°F, turning once halfway through cooking. Serve with garlic mayo and lemon wedges.

218. Garlic & Chili Prawns

Preparation Time: 12 min
Serves: 1

Nutrition Value:Calories 151; Net Carbs 3.2g; Fat 2g; Protein 23g

Ingredients

- 8 prawns, cleaned
- Salt and black pepper to taste
- ½ tsp ground cayenne pepper
- ½ tsp chili flakes
- ½ tsp ground cumin
- ½ tsp garlic powder

Directions

1. In a bowl, season the prawns with salt and black pepper. Sprinkle cayenne, flakes, cumin and garlic and stir to coat. Grease the air fryer's basket and arrange the prawns in an even layer. Cook for 8 minutes at 340°F, turning once halfway through cooking.

219. Chinese Fish with Mushrooms

Preparation Time: 12 min
Serves: 4

Nutrition Value:Calories 267; Net Carbs 3.5g; Fat 8g; Protein 39g

Ingredients

- 2 lb white fish fillets
- ½ tbsp salt
- 4 mushrooms, sliced
- 1 tbsp liquid stevia
- 2 onions, sliced
- 4 tbsp soy sauce
- 2 tbsp red chili powder
- 2 tbsp vinegar
- 2 tbsp Chinese winter pickle

Directions

1. Fill the fish with the pickle and mushrooms. Spread the onion on the fish. In a bowl, combine the vinegar, soy sauce, stevia, and salt. Sprinkle over the fish, and cook in the Fryer for 10 minutes at 350°F.

220. Restaurant-Style Dragon Shrimp

Preparation Time: 10 min
Serves: 2

Nutrition Value:Calories 405; Net Carbs 5.2g; Fat 27g; Protein 31g

Ingredients

- ½ lb shrimp
- ½ cup soy sauce
- 2 eggs
- 2 tbsp olive oil
- 1 cup onions, chopped
- A pinch of ginger, grated
- ¼ cup almond flour

Directions

1. Boil the shrimps for around 5 minutes.
2. Prepare a paste made of ginger and onion. Beat the eggs and add ginger, onion, soya sauce, almond flour and mix them very well. Add shrimps to the mixture and cook them for 10 minutes, at 390°F. Remove from the Air Fryer and serve with keto mayo.

221. Ginger Cedar Planked Salmon

Preparation Time: 35 min
Serves: 6

Nutrition Value:Calories 476; Net Carbs 4.1g; Fat 38g; Protein 33g

Ingredients

- 4 untreated cedar planks
- ½ cup vegetable oil
- 1½ tbsp rice vinegar
- 1 tbsp sesame oil
- ½ cup soy sauce
- ¼ cup green onions, chopped
- 1 tbsp fresh ginger root, grated
- 1 tbsp garlic, grated
- 2 lb salmon fillets, skin removed

Directions

1. Start by soaking the cedar planks for 2 hours.
2. Take a shallow dish and stir in the vegetable oil, the rice vinegar, the sesame oil, the soy sauce, the green onions, and ginger. Put the salmon fillets in the prepared marinade for at least 20 minutes.
3. Place the planks in the basket of the Air Fryer. Cook for 15 minutes at 360°F.

222. Delicious Octopus with Green Chilies

Preparation Time: 35 min
Serves: 3

Nutrition Value:Calories 195; Net Carbs 4.2g; Fat 7g; Protein 25g

Ingredients

- 3 roots coriander, washed
- 7 medium green chilies
- 2 cloves garlic
- A pinch of salt
- 2 drops liquid stevia
- 2 small limes
- 1 tbsp olive oil
- 1 lb clean octopus
- 1 tsp fish sauce

Directions

1. Mash the washed roots of coriander in the mortar.
2. Add the green chilies, the 2 cloves of garlic, a pinch of salt, stevia, 1 teaspoon of fish sauce, the juice of 2 limes and a teaspoon of olive oil. Put the dipping sauce in a bowl. Cut the octopus into tentacles.
3. Arrange the tentacles of the octopus in the Air Fryer basket and set the heat to 370°F. Cook them for 4 minutes on each side. Serve with the dipping sauce.

223. Quick Tuna Sandwich with Mozzarella

Preparation Time: 10 min
Serves: 2

Nutrition Value:Calories 451; Net Carbs 7.2g; Fat 17g; Protein 61g

Ingredients

- 4 slices zero carb bread
- 2 small tins of tuna, drained
- ½ onion, finely chopped
- 2 tbsp mayonnaise
- 1 cup mozzarella cheese, shredded

Directions

1. Lay your zero carb bread out onto a board.
2. In a small bowl, mix tuna, onion, mayonnaise. Spoon the mixture over 2 bread slices.
3. Top with cheese and put the other piece of bread on top.
4. Spray with cooking spray each side and arrange the sandwiches into the air fryer.
5. Cook at 360°F for 6 minutes, turning once halfway through cooking.

224. Hot Crab Cakes with Green Onions

Preparation Time: 20 min
Serves: 8

Nutrition Value:Calories 121; Net Carbs 1.5g; Fat 5.5g; Protein 14g

Ingredients

- 1 lb crab meat, shredded
- 2 eggs, beaten
- ½ cup pork rinds, crushed
- ⅓ cup green onions, chopped
- ¼ cup parsley, chopped
- 1 tbsp mayonnaise
- 1 tsp chili sauce
- ½ tsp paprika
- Salt and black pepper to taste

Directions

1. In a bowl, add meat, eggs, pork rinds, green onion, parsley, mayo, chili sauce, paprika, salt and black pepper and mix well with hands.
2. Shape into 8 cakes and grease them lightly with cooking spray.
3. Arrange the cakes into the fryer, without overcrowding. Cook for 8 minutes at 400°F, turning once halfway through cooking.

225. Mixed Seafood with Yogurt

Preparation Time: 15 min
Serves: 4

Nutrition Value:Calories 211; Net Carbs 5.2g; Fat 8.1g; Protein 24g

Ingredients

- 1 lb of mixed seafood
- 2 eggs, lightly beaten

- Salt and black pepper to taste
- 1 cup pork rinds, crushed mixed with the zest of 1 lemon
- Yogurt, for dipping

Directions

1. Clean the seafood as needed. Dip each piece into the egg. Season with salt and pepper.
2. Coat in the pork rinds and spray with oil. Arrange into your air fryer and cook for 6 minutes at 400°F, turning once halfway through cooking.

226. Pork Rind & Almond-Coated Scallops

Preparation Time: 5 min
Serves: 6

Nutrition Value:Calories 105; Net Carbs 2.7g; Fat 3.4g; Protein 14g

Ingredients

12 fresh scallops
3 tbsp almond flour
Salt and black pepper to taste
1 egg, lightly beaten
1 cup pork rinds, crushed

Directions

- Coat the scallops with almond flour. Dip into the egg, then into the pork rinds. Spray them with cooking spray and arrange them in the air.
- Cook for 6 minutes at 360°F, turning once halfway through cooking.

227. Lime Salmon with Broccoli

Preparation Time: 25 min
Serves: 2

Nutrition Value:Calories 511; Net Carbs 7.2g; Fat 21g; Protein 64g

Ingredients

- 2 salmon fillets
- 1 tsp olive oil
- Juice of 1 lime
- 1 tsp chili flakes

7.

- Salt and black pepper to taste
- 1 head of broccoli, cut into florets
- 1 tsp olive oil
- 1 tbsp soy sauce, sugar-free

Directions

1. In a bowl, add oil, lime juice, flakes, salt and black pepper.
2. Rub the mixture onto fillets. Lay the florets into your air fryer and drizzle with oil. Arrange the fillets around or on top and cook for 10 minutes at 340°F.
3. Drizzle the florets with soy sauce to serve.

228. Crispy Fish & Turnip Chips

Preparation Time: 25 min
Serves: 4

Nutrition Value:Calories 265; Net Carbs 3.3g; Fat 10.3g; Protein 34g

Ingredients

- 2 turnips, cut into thin slices chips
- Salt and black pepper to taste
- 4 white fish fillets
- 2 tbsp almond flour
- 1 egg, beaten
- 1 cup pork rinds, crushed
- Salt and black pepper to taste

Directions

1. Grease the turnip chips with cooking spray and season with salt and black pepper.
2. Places them in the air fryer, and cook for 20 minutes at 400°F.
3. Meanwhile, spread almond flour on a plate and coat the fish.
4. Dip them in the egg, then into the pork rinds and season with salt and black pepper.
5. At the 10 minutes' mark, add the fish to the fryer and cook with the chips.
6. Cook until crispy. Serve with lemon slices.

229. Jalapeno Chicken Casserole

Preparation Time: 1 HR 15 MIN
Serve: 6

Ingredients:

- 6 Bacon slices
- 12 oz Cream cheese
- 4 oz Cheddar cheese, shredded
- ¼ cup hot sauce
- 6 Chicken thighs
- 3 Jalapenos, seeds removed
- ¼ cup Mayonnaise
- 2 oz Mozzarella cheese, shredded
- Salt
- Black pepper

Directions:

1. Remove bones from thighs and set the oven to 400 F. Use pepper and salt to season chicken and line a baking sheet with foil.
2. Place chicken onto a baking sheet and bake for 40 minutes.
3. Chop bacon, heat skillet and cook bacon for 4-5 minutes until crisp; add peppers to bacon and cook for 3 minutes until softened.
4. Add hot sauce, mayo and cream cheese to pot; season with pepper and salt to taste and mix together.
5. Take chicken from oven, cool and remove skin. Transfer chicken to a baking dish and top with cream cheese mixture. Sprinkle mozzarella and cheddar all over casserole.
6. Bake for 15 minutes and broil for 5 minutes.
7. Serve.

Nutritional Value:

Calories 740
Total Fats 61.2g
Net Carbs: 2.5g
Protein 31.8g
Fiber 0.2g

230. Roasted Turkey Legs

Preparation Time: 1 HR 5 MIN
Serve: 4

Ingredients:

- 2 lbs Turkey legs
- 2 tsp Salt
- ¼ tsp Cayenne pepper
- ½ tsp Garlic powder
- ½ tsp Ancho chili powder
- 1 tsp Worcestershire sauce
- 2 tbsp Duck fat
- ½ tsp Black pepper
- ½ tsp Onion powder
- ½ tsp Thyme, dried
- 1 tsp Liquid smoke

Directions:

1. Add all dry spices to a bowl and combine then add wet ingredients and combine thoroughly.
2. Combine dry spices, pat turkey legs and use seasoning to rub turkey legs.
3. Set oven to 350 F. Heat a cast iron pan and heat fat until it gets smoky then add turkey legs and sear for 2 minutes on each side.
4. Transfer cast iron pot to oven and roast for 60 minutes. Turning halfway through cooking time.
5. Serve.

Nutritional Value:

Calories 382
Total Fats 22.5g
Net Carbs: 0.8g
Protein 44g

231. Asian Grilled Chicken

Preparation Time: 55 MIN
Serve: 4

Ingredients:

- 1 tbsp Olive oil
- 1 tbsp Rice wine vinegar
- 1 tsp Garlic, diced
- ¼ tsp Xanthan gum
- 1 tsp Red pepper flakes
- 6 Chicken thighs, with skin and bones
- 1 tbsp Ketchup, low sugar
- 2 tsp Sriracha
- 1 tsp Ginger, diced
- 4 cups Spinach
- Salt
- Black pepper

Directions:

1. Set oven to 425 F.
2. Rinse chicken and use hand towels to dry chicken and season with black pepper and salt.
3. Combine all ingredients for sauce and coat chicken in sauce. Line a baking sheet with foil and place a wire rack onto a baking sheet.
4. Add chicken and bake for 50 minutes until skin is slightly charred and crisp.
5. Take chicken from oven and put aside.
6. Add spinach, salt, pepper and red pepper flakes to fat on a baking tray.
7. Mix together and serve with chicken.

Nutritional Value:

Calories 606
Total Fats 53.5g
Net Carbs: 1.5g
Protein 28.8g
Fiber 0.8g

232. Fettuccine Chicken Alfredo

Preparation Time: 25 MIN
Serve: 2

Ingredients:

- For Alfredo sauce:
- 2 Tbsp Butter
- 4 Tbsp Parmesan cheese (grated
- 2 Garlic Cloves
- ½ Cup Heavy cream
- ½ Tsp Basil (dried
- For Noodles and Chicken:
- 2 Chicken thighs (skinless and boneless
- Salt
- 1 Tbsp Olive oil
- 1 pack Shirataki Miracle Fettuccine Noodles
- Black pepper

Directions:

1. Melt butter in a skillet and sauté garlic for 2 minutes.
2. Add cream to the pot and cook for 2 minutes then add parmesan cheese and stir.
3. Add basil, pepper, and salt and cook for an additional 5 minutes over a low flame.
4. Pound chicken thighs and season with pepper and salt.
5. Heat oil in a skillet and fry chicken for 7 minutes per side and remove from pot. Use forks to shred chicken.
6. Prepare noodles as directed on package.
7. Drain and add chicken and noodles to Alfredo sauce. Heat for 2 minutes and toss.
8. Serve.

Nutritional Value:

Calories 585
Total Fats 51g
Net Carbs: 1g
Protein 25g
Fiber 2g

233. Ethiopian Doro Watt

Preparation Time: 8 HR 10 MIN
Serve: 8

Ingredients:

- 1 Garlic clove (diced
- 4 Tbsp Ethiopian Berbere
- 1 Chicken (separated
- 2 Onions (diced
- ½ Cup Butter
- 2 Tsp Salt
- 8 Eggs (hard boiled

Directions:

1. Add chopped onions, butter, garlic, salt and Berbere to a slow cooker.
2. Set cooker on low and cook for 8 hours or more.
3. Add chicken to slow cooker and cook for an additional 8 minutes until chicken is tender.
4. Serve with boiled eggs.

Nutritional Value:

Calories 315
Total Fats 25g
Net Carbs: 4g
Protein 19g
Fiber 0.8g

234. Buffalo Chicken

Preparation Time: 6 HR 5 MIN
Serve: 4

Ingredients:

- 3 Tbsp butter
- 6 frozen chicken breasts
- 1 bottle of your favorite cayenne peppers sauce
- 1 cup of your favorite garlic sauce

Directions:

1. Put the chicken in the bottom of your Slow Cooker. Pour the hot sauce over chicken and sprinkle ranch over top
2. Cover the lid and cook on LOW for 6 hours.
3. Once ready, add butter, and cook on LOW uncovered for one hour more. Serve hot.

Nutritional Value:

Calories 517
Total Fats 18g
Net Carbs: 2.2g
Protein 80g
Fiber 0.3g

235. Curried Coconut Chicken Fingers

Preparation Time: 45 MIN
Serve: 5

Ingredients:

- 24 oz Chicken thighs, boneless with skin
- ½ cup Pork rinds, crushed
- 2 tsp Curry powder
- ¼ tsp Garlic powder
- Salt
- Black pepper
- 1 Egg
- ½ cup Coconut, shredded, unsweetened
- ½ tsp Coriander
- ¼ tsp Onion powder

For Dipping Sauce:

- ¼ cup Sour cream
- 1 ½ tsp Mango extract
- ½ tsp Garlic powder
- ¼ tsp Cayenne powder
- ¼ cup Mayonnaise
- 2 tbsp Ketchup, sugar-free
- 1 ½ tsp Red pepper flakes
- ½ tsp Ground ginger
- 7 drops Liquid Stevia

Directions:

1. Set oven to 400 F.
2. Beat egg in a bowl and slice chicken into strips.
3. Combine spices, pork rind, and coconut in another bowl. Coat with egg and then in the dry mix.
4. Place onto a lined baking sheet and bake for 15 minutes and turn over; bake for an additional 20 minutes.
5. Combine all ingredients for dipping sauce in a bowl and serve with chicken.

Nutritional Value:

Calories 494
Total Fats 39.4g
Net Carbs: 2.1g
Protein 29.4g
Fiber 1.2g

236. Greek Chicken

Preparation Time: 7 HR 10 MIN
Serve: 4

Ingredients:

- 4 pcs boneless chicken thighs
- 3 cloves of garlic, minced
- 3 tbsp lemon juice
- 1 ½ cups hot water
- 2 cubes chicken bouillon
- 3 tbsp Greek Rub

Directions:

1. Coat the slow cooker with cooking spray
2. Season the chicken with the Greek rub followed by the minced garlic.
3. Transfer the chicken to the slow cooker and sprinkle with lemon juice on top.
4. Crumble the chicken cubes and put in the slow cooker. Pour the water and stir.
5. Cover and cook on low for 6-7 hours.

Nutritional Value:

Calories 140
Total Fats 5.7g
Net Carbs: 2.2g
Protein 18.6g

237. Roasted Wrapped Chicken

Preparation Time: 1 HR 25 MIN
Serve: 6

Ingredients:

- 1 whole dressed chicken
- 10 strips of bacon
- 3 sprigs fresh thyme
- 2 pcs lime
- Salt and pepper to taste

Directions:

1. Set the oven at 500 F.
2. Thoroughly rinse the chicken and stuff it with the lime and thyme sprigs.
3. Season the chicken with salt and pepper and then wrap the chicken with the bacon.
4. Season again with salt and pepper and then place on a roasting tray on top of a baking sheet (make sure to catch the juices and place in the oven to roast for 15 minutes.
5. Lower the temperature to 350 F and then roast for another 45 minutes.
6. Remove the chicken from the oven, cover with foil and set aside for 15 minutes.
7. Take the juices from the tray and place in a saucepan. Bring to a boil over high heat and use an immersion blending to mix all the "good stuff" from the juice.
8. Serve the chicken with the sauce on the side.

Nutritional Value:

Calories 375
Total Fats 29.8g
Net Carbs: 2.4g
Protein 24.5g |Fiber: 0.9g

238. Chicken Satay

Preparation Time: 25 MIN
Serve: 3

Ingredients:

- 1 lb. ground chicken
- 4 tbsp low-sodium soy sauce
- 3 tbsp all-natural peanut butter
- 1 tbsp lime juice
- ¼ tsp cayenne pepper
- ¼ tsp smoked paprika
- 1 tbsp rice vinegar
- 1 tbsp liquid stevia
- 2 tsp chili paste
- 1 clove of garlic minced
- 2 tsp sesame oil
- 2 green onions, chopped
- 1/3 bell pepper, chopped

Directions:

1. Drizzle with the sesame oil on a pan over the medium-high fire.
2. Add the ground chicken and the rest of the ingredients and mix well. Cook until the chicken is done.
3. Serve with the green onions and bell pepper on top.

Nutritional Value:

Calories 393
Total Fats 23g

Net Carbs: 3.7g
Protein 35g | Fiber: 7g

239. Sage and Orange Glazed Duck

Preparation Time: 25 MIN
Serve: 1

Ingredients:

- 2 tbsp Butter
- 1 tbsp Swerve
- ¼ tsp Sage
- 6 oz Duck breast
- 1 tbsp Heavy cream
- ½ tsp Orange extract
- 1 cup Spinach

Directions:

1. Use a knife to score the skin of the duck and season with black pepper and salt.
2. Add Swerve and butter to a pot and cook until slightly golden then add extract and sage. Cook until butter has darkened.
3. In another pot, place chicken breast with skin side down and place over a medium flame and cook until skin is crisp.
4. Flip over and add cream to sage mixture and pour over duck. Cook until duck is done.
5. Add spinach to the pot and cook until wilted.
6. Serve.

Nutritional Value:

Calories 798
Total Fats 71g
Net Carbs: 0g
Protein 36g
Fiber 1g

240. Chicken Pot Pie

Preparation Time: 30 MIN
Serve: 8

Ingredients:

For filling:

- 5 Bacon, slices
- 1 tsp Garlic powder
- 8 oz Cream cheese
- 6 cups Spinach
- Salt
- 6 Chicken thighs, boneless and skinless
- 1 tsp Onion powder
- ¾ tsp Celery seed
- 4 oz Cheddar cheese
- ¼ cup Chicken broth

For crust:

- 3 tbsp Psyllium Husk Powder
- 1 Egg
- ¼ cup Cheddar cheese
- ¼ tsp Garlic powder
- Salt
- 1/3 cup Almond Flour
- 3 tbsp Butter
- ¼ cup Cream cheese
- ½ tsp Paprika
- ¼ tsp Onion powder
- Black pepper

Directions:

1. Cube chicken and season with black pepper and salt.
2. Set oven to 375 F.
3. Use spices to season chicken and place into an oven proof skillet and place on fire and cook until golden on the outside. Add bacon to pan and cook until golden.
4. Add broth to the pan along with cheeses and stir to combine. Put in spinach in the pan and cook until wilted.
5. Combine dry ingredients for crust in a bowl and add cheddar and cream cheese to a microwave safe dish and then add cheese and combine. Add mixture to dry ingredients and mix together.
6. Form crust, stir ingredients in pot and top with crust and use fork to pierce crust all over.
7. Bake for 15 minutes, take from oven and cool.
8. Serve.

Nutritional Value:

Calories 434

Total Fats 35.6g
Net Carbs: 3.4g
Protein 20.4g
Fiber: 3.6 g

241. Chicken Parmesan

Preparation Time: 25 MIN
Serve: 4

Ingredients:

For Chicken:

- 3 Chicken breasts
- 1 cup Mozzarella cheese
- Salt
- Black pepper

For coating:

- ¼ cup Flaxseed meal
- 1 tsp Oregano
- ½ tsp Black pepper
- ½ tsp Garlic powder
- 1 Egg
- oz Pork rinds
- ½ cup Parmesan cheese
- ½ tsp Salt
- ¼ tsp Red pepper flakes
- 2 tsp Paprika
- 1 ½ tsp Chicken broth

For Sauce:

- 1 cup Tomato sauce, low carb
- 2 Garlic Cloves
- Salt
- ½ cup Olive oil
- ½ tsp Oregano
- Black pepper

Directions:

1. Add flax meal, spices, pork rinds and parmesan cheese in a processor and grind until combined.
2. Pound chicken breast and whisk egg with broth in a container. Add all ingredients for the sauce to a pan, stir and put over a low flame to cook.
3. Dip chicken in egg and then coat with dry mixture.
4. Heat oil in a pan and fry chicken then transfer to a casserole dish. Top with sauce and mozzarella and bake for 10 minutes.
5. Serve.

Nutritional Value:

Calories 646
Total Fats 46.8g
Net Carbs: 4g
Protein 49.3g
Fiber 2.8g

242. Pad Thai

Preparation Time: 30 MIN
Serve: 4

Ingredients:

- 3 pcs boneless and skinless chicken thighs
- 2 packs konjac yam noodles (Shirataki
- 2 organic eggs
- ¼ cup cilantro, chopped
- ½ cup mung bean sprouts
- 3 pcs green onions, chopped
- 2 tbsp peanuts, chopped
- 4 tbsp melted coconut oil
- For the sauce:
- 4 tbsp lime juice
- 2 cloves of garlic, minced
- 1 tbsp all-natural peanut butter
- ½ tsp Worcestershire sauce
- 1½ tbsp low-sugar ketchup
- 3 tbsp fish sauce
- 1 ½ tbsp sambal oelek
- 1 tsp rice wine vinegar
- 7 drops liquid stevia

Directions:

1. Whisk all the ingredients of the sauce in the bowl. Set aside.
2. Drain the noodles in boiling water for 5 times and then dry using a clean towel cloth.
3. Heat the coconut oil in a pan over medium-high. When the pan is hot, sear

the chicken on both sides. Set aside and allow the chicken to rest for a few minutes.

4. Using the same pan throw in the noodles and fry for 6-8 minutes. Crack the eggs on top and scramble with the noodles.
5. Add the sauce to the pan along with the cilantro, mung bean sprouts, and green onions and cook for another 7-10 mins.
6. Garnish with the chopped peanuts on top.

Nutritional Value:

Calories 310
Total Fats 14.9g
Net Carbs: 3.8g
Protein 39.3g
Fiber: 0.7g

243. Creamy Tarragon Chicken

Preparation Time: 25 MIN
Serve: 1

Ingredients:

- 5 oz Chicken breast
- ¼ Onion, sliced
- ½ cup Chicken broth
- 1 tsp Grain mustard
- Salt
- 1 tbsp Olive oil
- 3 oz Mushrooms
- ¼ cup Heavy cream
- ½ tsp Tarragon, dried
- Black pepper

Directions:

1. Cube chicken and season with pepper and salt.
2. Heat oil in a pan and sauté chicken for 6 minutes until golden all over. Take from pan and put aside.
3. Add mushrooms and cook for 3 minutes until golden then add onion and cook for 3 minutes until soft and translucent.
4. Add broth and bring to a boil for 4 minutes then add remaining ingredients and adjust black pepper and salt to taste.
5. Return chicken to sauce in the pan and cook for 5 minutes.
6. Serve.

Nutritional Value:

Calories 490
Total Fats 40g
Net Carbs: 5g
Protein 32g
Fiber 1g

244. Chicken & Endive Casserole

Preparation Time: 40 MIN
Serve: 6

Ingredients:

- 1 endive head, cut into wide strips
- 1 1/2 lbs. skinless boneless chicken thighs
- 1 Tbsp dried oregano
- 2 cups chopped onions
- 4 celery stalks, chopped
- 4 garlic cloves, chopped
- 1 cup diced tomatoes in juice
- 2 Tbsp olive oil
- 8 cups water

Directions:

1. In a large saucepan heat oil over medium-high heat.
2. Sprinkle the chicken with salt, pepper, and oregano. Add chicken in a saucepan. Mix in onions, celery, and garlic. Sauté until vegetables begin to soften, about 4-5minutes.
3. Stir in tomatoes. Add broth; bring to boil. Reduce heat to medium; simmer until vegetables and chicken are tender, about 15 minutes.
4. Add endive hearts; simmer until wilted, about 3 minutes. Season with salt and pepper.
5. Ladle into bowls and serve hot.

Nutritional Value:

Calories 144
Total Fats 7g
Net Carbs: 9g
Protein 9.8g

Fiber 2.5g

245. Creamy Smoked Turkey Salad with Almonds

Preparation Time: 10 MIN
Serve: 4

Ingredients:

Salad ingredients:

- 2 cups diced, cooked smoked turkey breast
- 1/4 cup sliced almonds
- 1/2 cup diced celery
- 1/4 cup sliced green onions
- 1/4 cup shredded cabbage

Dressing ingredients:

- 4 oz. mayonnaise
- 2 oz. sour cream
- 2 drops sweet liquid Splenda
- 1 tsp curry powder
- Salt and pepper to taste

Directions:

1. In a bowl, combine sour cream and mayonnaise and whisk until smooth.
2. Add the spices and continue to whisk until smooth.
3. In a big bowl, combine all salad ingredients and the dressing and toss well.
4. Serve and enjoy.

Nutritional Value:

Calories 235
Total Fats 17g
Net Carbs: 10.9g
Protein 9.8g
Fiber 1.6g

246. Creamy Chicken Salad

Preparation Time: 10 MIN
Serve: 4

Ingredients:

Salad ingredients

- 2 cups diced, cooked chicken
- 1/2 cup sliced green onion
- 1/4 cup parsley, chopped
- 1/2 cup diced celery

Dressing ingredients

- 4 oz. mayonnaise
- 2 oz. blue cream cheese softened
- 1 tsp dried tarragon
- 1/2 tsp dried thyme
- Salt and pepper to taste

Directions:

1. In a bowl, whisk cream cheese and mayonnaise until smooth.
2. Add the spices and continue to whisk.
3. Combine the salad ingredients and add dressing to taste, mixing to coat all the ingredients.
4. Serve immediately.

Nutritional Value:

Calories 250
Total Fats 12g
Net Carbs: 9.7g
Protein 24g
Fiber 0.7g

247. Duck Breast with Balsamic Vinegar

Preparation Time: 3 HR 25 MIN
Serve: 4

Ingredients:

- 1 lb. duck breasts
- 4 Tbsp duck fat (or lark
- 4 green onions (chopped
- 1 tsp fresh ginger grated
- 1/2 Tbsp lime juice
- Marjoram to taste
- 2 Tbsp coconut oil
- 2 Tbsp apple cider vinegar
- Salt and freshly ground pepper to taste

Directions:

1. In a frying pan add 1 tbsp coconut oil and add the duck breast. Sauté it at high heat about 3-4 minutes.
2. In a deep saucepan add the duck fat, and add the duck meat. Cook for 3 hours

about. Add the chopped green onions in the last 30 minutes of the cooking process.

3. Remove green onion and duck breast from the heat, and place them in a separate dish to cool down. Sprinkle the marjoram, balsamic vinegar, and the lime juice. Serve hot.

Nutritional Value:

Calories 471
Total Fats 46g
Net Carbs: 2.7g
Protein 10g
Fiber 0.4g

248. Zesty Herbed Chicken

Preparation Time: 20 MIN
Serve: 2

Ingredients:

- 2 pcs boneless chicken thighs
- 2 tbsp fresh parsley, chopped
- ½ tsp dried oregano
- 4 tbsp lemon juice
- 1 tbsp olive oil
- Salt and pepper to taste

Directions:

1. Sprinkle the lemon juice on the chicken and season with salt and pepper.
2. Heat the olive oil in a cast iron skillet over medium-high heat and then add the chicken thighs. Cook for 4-5 minutes on each side.
3. Season with oregano and turn of the heat.
4. Transfer the chicken to a serving plate and garnish with fresh parsley on top.

Nutritional Value:

Calories 469
Total Fats 22.9g
Net Carbs: 1.2g
Protein 61.1g

249. Chicken Pesto Salad

Preparation Time: 10 MIN
Serve: 6

Ingredients:

- 2 cups cooked chicken, chopped
- 2 tbsp organic pesto sauce
- ¼ cup mayonnaise
- 1 pc celery, chopped
- ½ onion, chopped
- 2 tbsp fresh parsley, chopped
- Salt and pepper to taste

Directions:

1. Combine the chicken and the pesto sauce and mayonnaise in a bowl. Stir well.
2. Throw in the celery, onion, parsley, season with salt and pepper, and mix well.
3. Serve with fresh lettuce.

Nutritional Value:

Calories 406
Total Fats 20.6g
Net Carbs: 10.8g
Protein 42.7g
Fiber 1.0g

250. Hot Peri-Peri Chicken on Green Salad

Preparation Time: 15 MIN
Serve: 1

Ingredients:

- 2 cups baby spinach
- ½ boneless chicken thighs cut into strips
- 1 tbsp hot peri-peri sauce
- ½ ripe avocado, sliced thin
- 1 strip of bacon, cooked and crumbled

Directions:

1. Cook the bacon first and then use the same pan to cook the bacon to fry the chicken. Place the chicken on the pan and cook for 1 minute on one side and then cook the other side for 5-6 minutes.
2. Place the baby spinach in a salad bowl and then top with the avocado and cooked chicken strips.
3. Sprinkle with the bacon crumbles and drizzle with the hot peri-peri sauce.

Nutritional Value:

Calories 325
Total Fats 22g
Net Carbs: 10.8g
Protein 23.9g | Fiber: 8.1g

251. Mediterranean Chicken

Preparation Time: 1 HR 10 MIN
Serve: 2

Ingredients:

- 1 whole free-range chicken, chopped into pieces
- 1 tsp capers, chopped
- 4 ripe tomatoes, chopped
- ½ cup olives, chopped
- ½ tsp red pepper flakes
- Salt and pepper to taste
- 2 tbsp olive oil

Directions:

1. Set the oven at 350 F.
2. In a large baking dish combine the capers, tomatoes, olives, pepper flakes and olive oil. Season with salt and pepper and stir.
3. Add the chicken at the center and place in the oven to cook for an hour.
4. Serve warm.

Nutritional Value:

Calories 205
Total Fats 18.2g
Net Carbs: 12g
Protein 2.5g | Fiber: 4.2g

252. Turkey Meatballs

Preparation Time: 40 MIN
Serve: 2

Ingredients:

- 1 lbs. turkey, ground
- 1 pc organic egg
- 3 oz mozzarella cheese, cubed
- 1 pc green onion, chopped
- 2 pcs sun-dried tomatoes, chopped
- 2 pcs clove of garlic, minced
- 1tbsp fresh cilantro, chopped
- ½ tsp cumin powder
- 1 pc shallot, chopped
- Salt and pepper to taste

Directions:

1. Set the oven 350 F.
2. In a bowl, combine the ground turkey green onions, sun-dried tomatoes, minced garlic, cilantro, cumin, and shallots. Season with salt and pepper. Combine the ingredients using your hands.
3. Form the mixture into meatballs and flatten them to create patties. Place a mozzarella cub at the center of the patty and form again into a bowl.
4. Transfer the meatballs to a baking sheet lined with parchment paper and place in the oven to bake for 30 minutes.
5. Serve warm.

Nutritional Value:

Calories 509
Total Fats 19.1g
Net Carbs: 1.8g
Protein 78.7g

253. Roast Chicken and Pepper Salad

Preparation Time: 40 MIN
Serve: 4

Ingredients:

- lbs. boneless chicken thighs
- 1 onion, roughly chopped
- 1 large bell pepper, cut in half and seeded
- ¼ cup cilantro leaves
- 1 romaine lettuce
- For the dressing
- 1 tbsp lime juice
- ¼ cup mayonnaise
- ¼ cup sour cream
- 2 tbsp olive oil
- Salt and pepper to taste

Directions:

1. Set oven to 350 F.
2. Lay the chicken thighs and onions on a baking sheet lined with foil and greased.
3. Drizzle with the chicken with olive oil and season with salt and pepper.
4. Place the chicken in the oven to bake for 20 minutes. When done baking, remove from the oven and let it sit for 10 minutes.
5. Char the bell peppers while waiting for the chicken to bake. Slice into strips when done the grilling.
6. In a salad bowl, whisk together the ingredients for the dressing. Add the lettuce into the bowl.
7. Top the salad with the cubed baked chicken with onions, and bell pepper on top.
8. Serve immediately.

Nutritional Value:

Calories 349
Total Fats 16g
Net Carbs: 7g
Protein 42g
Fiber 3g

254. Turkey & Mushroom Bake

Preparation Time: 55 minutes
Serves: 8

Ingredients

- 4 cups mushrooms, sliced
- 1 egg, whisked
- 3 cups green cabbage, shredded
- 3 cups turkey meat, cooked and chopped
- ½ cup chicken stock
- ½ cup cream cheese
- 1 tsp poultry seasoning
- 2 cup cheddar cheese, grated
- ½ cup Parmesan cheese, grated
- Salt and ground black pepper, to taste
- ¼ tsp garlic powder

Directions

1. Set a pan over medium-low heat. Stir in chicken broth, egg, Parmesan cheese, pepper, garlic powder, poultry seasoning, cheddar cheese, cream cheese, and salt, and simmer.
2. Place in the cabbage and turkey meat, and set away from the heat.
3. Add the mushrooms, pepper, turkey mixture and salt in a baking dish and spread. Place aluminum foil to cover, set in an oven at 390°F, and bake for 35 minutes. Allow cooling and enjoy.

Nutritional Value: Calories 245, Fat 15g, Net Carbs 3g, Protein 25g

255. Pancetta & Chicken Casserole

Preparation Time: 40 minutes
Serves: 3

Ingredients

- 8 pancetta strips, chopped
- ⅓ cup Dijon mustard
- Salt and black pepper, to taste
- 1 onion, chopped
- 1 tbsp olive oil
- 1½ cups chicken stock
- 3 chicken breasts, skinless and boneless
- ¼ tsp sweet paprika

Directions

1. Using a bowl, combine the paprika, pepper, salt, and mustard. Sprinkle this on chicken breasts and massage. Set a pan over medium-high heat, stir in the pancetta, cook until it browns, and remove to a plate. Place oil in the same pan and heat over medium-high heat, add in the chicken breasts, cook for each side for 2 minutes and set aside.
2. Place in the stock, and bring to a simmer. Stir in pepper, pancetta, salt, and onions. Return the chicken to the pan as well, stir gently, and simmer for 20 minutes over medium heat, turning the meat halfway through. Split the chicken on serving plates, sprinkle the sauce over it to serve.

Nutritional Value: Calories 313, Fat 18g, Net Carbs 3g, Protein 26g

256. Quattro Formaggi Chicken

Preparation Time: 40 minutes
Serves: 8

Ingredients

- 3 pounds chicken breasts
- 2 ounces mozzarella cheese, cubed
- 2 ounces mascarpone cheese
- 4 ounces cheddar cheese, cubed
- 2 ounces provolone cheese, cubed
- 1 zucchini, shredded
- Salt and ground black pepper, to taste
- 1 tsp garlic, minced
- ½ cup pancetta, cooked and crumbled

Directions

1. Sprinkle pepper and salt to the zucchini, squeeze well, and place to a bowl. Stir in the pancetta, mascarpone, cheddar cheese, provolone cheese, mozzarella, pepper, garlic, and cream cheese.
2. Cut slits into chicken breasts, apply pepper and salt, and stuff with the zucchini and cheese mixture. Set on a lined baking sheet, place in the oven at 400°F, and bake for 45 minutes.

Nutritional Value: Calories 565, Fat 37g, Net Carbs 2g, Protein 51g

257. Chicken Stroganoff

Preparation Time: 4 hours 15 minutes
Serves: 4

Ingredients

- 2 garlic cloves, minced
- 8 oz mushrooms, chopped
- ¼ tsp celery seeds, ground
- 1 cup chicken stock
- 1 cup sour cream
- 1 cup leeks, chopped
- 1 pound chicken breasts
- 1½ tsp dried thyme
- 2 tbsp fresh parsley, chopped
- Salt and black pepper, to taste
- 4 zucchinis, spiralized

Directions

1. Place the chicken in a slow cooker. Place in the salt, leeks, sour cream, half of the parsley, celery seeds, garlic, pepper, mushrooms, stock, and thyme. Cook on high for 4 hours while covered.
2. Uncover the pot, add more pepper and salt if desired, and the rest of the parsley. Heat a pan with water over medium heat, place in some salt, bring to a boil, stir in the zucchini pasta, cook for 1 minute, and drain. Place in serving bowls, top with the chicken mixture, and serve.

Nutritional Value: Calories 365, Fat 22g, Net Carbs 4g, Protein 26g

258. Chicken in White Wine Sauce

Preparation Time: 50 minutes
Serves: 4

Ingredients

- 8 chicken thighs
- Salt and black pepper, to taste
- 1 onion, peeled and chopped
- 1 tbsp coconut oil
- 4 pancetta strips, chopped
- 4 garlic cloves, minced
- 10 oz white mushrooms, halved
- 2 cups white wine
- 1 cup whipping cream
- ½ cup fresh parsley, chopped

Directions

1. Set a pan over medium heat and warm oil, cook the pancetta until crispy, about 4-5 minutes and remove to paper towels. To the pancetta fat, add the chicken, sprinkle with pepper and salt, cook until brown, and remove to paper towels too.
2. In the same pan, sauté the onions and garlic for 4 minutes. Then, mix in the mushrooms and cook for another 5 minutes. Return the pancetta and browned chicken to the pan.
3. Stir in the wine and bring to a boil, reduce the heat, and simmer for 20 minutes. Pour in the whipping cream and

warm without boiling. Split among serving bowls and enjoy. Scatter over the parsley and serve with steamed green beans.

Nutritional Value: Calories 345, Fat 12g, Net Carbs 4g, Protein 24g

259. Chicken and Zucchini Bake

Preparation Time: 45 minutes
Serves: 4

Ingredients

- zucchini, chopped
- Salt and black pepper, to taste
- 1 tsp garlic powder
- 1 tbsp avocado oil
- 2 chicken breasts, skinless, boneless, sliced
- 1 tomato, cored and chopped
- ½ tsp dried oregano
- ½ tsp dried basil
- ½ cup mozzarella cheese, shredded

1

Directions

1. Apply pepper, garlic powder and salt to the chicken. Set a pan over medium heat and warm avocado oil, add in the chicken slices, cook until golden; remove to a baking dish. To the same pan add the zucchini, tomato, pepper, basil, oregano, and salt, cook for 2 minutes, and spread over chicken.
2. Bake in the oven at 330°F for 20 minutes. Sprinkle the mozzarella over the chicken, return to the oven, and bake for 5 minutes until the cheese is melted and bubbling. Serve with green salad.

Nutritional Value: Calories 235, Fat 11g, Net Carbs 2g, Protein 35g

260. Almond-Crusted Chicken Breasts

Preparation Time: 60 minutes
Serves: 4

Ingredients

- 4 bacon slices, cooked and crumbled
- 4 chicken breasts
- 1 tbsp water
- ½ cup olive oil
- 1 egg, whisked
- Salt and black pepper, to taste
- 1 cup asiago cheese, shredded
- ¼ tsp garlic powder
- 1 cup ground almonds

Directions

1. Using a bowl, combine the ground almonds with pepper, salt, and garlic. Place the whisked egg in a separate bowl and combine with water. Apply a seasoning of pepper and salt to the chicken, and dip each piece into the egg, and then into almond mixture.
2. Set a pan over medium-high heat and warm oil, add in the chicken breasts, cook until are golden-brown, and remove to a baking pan. Bake in the oven at 360°F for 20 minutes. Scatter with Asiago cheese and bacon and return to the oven. Roast for a few minutes until the cheese melts.

Nutritional Value: Calories 485, Fat 32g, Net Carbs 1g, Protein 41g

261. Chicken with Asparagus & Root Vegetables

Preparation Time: 35 minutes
Serves: 4

Ingredients

- 2 cups whipping cream
- 3 chicken breasts, boneless, skinless, chopped
- 3 tbsp butter
- ½ cup onion, chopped
- ¾ cup carrot, chopped
- 5 cups chicken stock
- Salt and black pepper, to taste
- 1 bay leaf
- 1 turnip, chopped
- 1 parsnip, chopped

- 17 ounces asparagus, trimmed
- 3 tsp fresh thyme, chopped

Directions

1. Set a pan over medium heat and add whipping cream, allow simmering, and cook until it's reduced by half for about 7 minutes. Set another pan over medium heat and warm butter, sauté the onion for 3 minutes. Pour in the chicken stock, carrots, turnip, and parsnip, chicken, and bay leaf, bring to a boil, and simmer for 20 minutes.
2. Add in the asparagus and cook for 7 minutes. Discard the bay leaf, stir in the reduced whipping cream, adjust the seasoning and ladle the stew into serving bowls. Scatter with fresh thyme.

Nutritional Value: Calories 497, Fat 31g, Net Carbs 7.4g, Protein 37g

262. Chicken Gumbo

Preparation Time: 40 minutes
Serves: 5

Ingredients

- 2 sausages, sliced
- 3 chicken breasts, cubed
- 1 cup celery, chopped
- 2 tbsp dried oregano
- 2 bell peppers, seeded and chopped
- 1 onion, peeled and chopped
- 2 cups tomatoes, chopped
- 4 cups chicken broth
- 3 tbsp dried thyme
- 2 tbsp garlic powder
- 2 tbsp dry mustard
- 1 tsp cayenne powder
- 1 tbsp chili powder
- Salt and black pepper, to taste
- 6 tbsp cajun seasoning
- 3 tbsp olive oil

Directions

1. In a pot over medium heat warm olive oil. Add the sausages, chicken, pepper, onion, dry mustard, chili, tomatoes, thyme, bell peppers, salt, oregano, garlic powder, cayenne, and cajun seasoning.
2. Cook for 10 minutes. Add the remaining ingredients and bring to a boil. Reduce the heat and simmer for 20 minutes covered. Serve hot divided between bowls.

Nutritional Value: Calories 361, Fat 22g, Net Carbs 6g, Protein 26g

263. Stuffed Mushrooms with Chicken

Preparation Time: 40 minutes
Serves: 5

Ingredients

- 3 cups cauliflower florets
- Salt and black pepper, to taste
- 1 onion, chopped
- 1½ pounds ground chicken
- 3 tsp fajita seasoning
- 2 tbsp butter
- 10 portobello mushrooms, stems removed
- ½ cup vegetable broth

Directions

1. In a food processor, add the cauliflower florets, pepper and salt, blend for a few times, and transfer to a plate. Set a pan over medium heat and warm butter, stir in onion and cook for 3 minutes. Add in the cauliflower rice, and cook for 3 minutes.
2. Stir in the seasoning, pepper, chicken, broth, and salt and cook for a further 2 minutes. Arrange the mushrooms on a lined baking sheet, stuff each one with chicken mixture, put in the oven at 350°F, and bake for 30 minutes. Serve in serving plates and enjoy.

Nutritional Value: Calories 261, Fat 16g, Net Carbs 6g, Protein 14g

264.bBaked Chicken with Acorn Squash and Goat's Cheese

Preparation Time: 1 hour 15 minutes
Serves: 6

Ingredients

- 6 chicken breasts, skinless and boneless
- 1 lb acorn squash, peeled and sliced
- Salt and ground black pepper, to taste
- 1 cup goat's cheese, shredded
- Cooking spray

Directions

1. Take cooking oil and spray on a baking dish, add in chicken breasts, pepper, squash, and salt and drizzle with olive. Transfer in the oven set at 420°F, and bake for 1 hour. Scatter goat's cheese, and bake for 15 minutes. Remove to a serving plate and enjoy.

Nutritional Value: Calories 235, Fat 16g, Net Carbs 5g, Protein 12g

265. Baked Pecorino Toscano Chicken

Preparation Time: 60 minutes
Serves: 4

Ingredients

- 4 chicken breasts, skinless and boneless
- ½ cup mayonnaise
- ½ cup buttermilk
- Salt and ground black pepper, to taste
- ¾ cup pecorino toscano cheese, grated
- Cooking spray
- 8 mozzarella cheese slices
- 1 tsp garlic powder

Directions

1. Spray a baking dish, add in the chicken breasts, and top 2 mozzarella cheese slices to each piece. Using a bowl, combine the Pecorino cheese, pepper, buttermilk, mayonnaise, salt, and garlic. Sprinkle this over the chicken, set the dish in the oven at 370°F, and bake for 1 hour.

Nutritional Value: Calories 346, Fat 24g, Net Carbs 6g, Protein 20g

266. Habanero Chicken Wings

Preparation Time: 65 minutes
Serves: 4

Ingredients

- 2 pounds chicken wings
- Salt and black pepper, to taste
- 3 tbsp coconut aminos
- 2 tsp white vinegar
- 3 tbsp rice vinegar
- 3 tbsp stevia
- ¼ cup chives, chopped
- ½ tsp xanthan gum
- 5 dried habanero peppers, chopped

Directions

1. Spread the chicken wings on a lined baking sheet, sprinkle with pepper and salt, set in an oven at 370°F, and bake for 45 minutes. Put a small pan over medium heat, add in the white vinegar, coconut aminos, chives, stevia, rice vinegar, xanthan gum, and habanero peppers, bring the mixture to a boil, cook for 2 minutes, and remove from heat.
2. Dip the chicken wings into this sauce, lay them all on the baking sheet again, and bake for 10 more minutes. Serve warm.

Nutritional Value: Calories 416, Fat 25g, Net Carbs 2g, Protein 26g

267. Chicken with Green Sauce

Preparation Time: 35 minutes
Serves: 4

Ingredients

- 2 tbsp butter
- 4 scallions, chopped
- 4 chicken breasts, skinless and boneless
- Salt and black pepper, to taste
- 6 ounces sour cream
- 2 tbsp fresh dill, chopped

Directions

1. Heat a pan with the butter over medium-high heat, add in the chicken, season with pepper and salt, and fry for 2-3 per side

until golden. Transfer to a baking dish and cook in the oven for 15 minutes at 390°F, until no longer pink.
2. To the pan add scallions, and cook for 2 minutes. Pour in the sour cream, warm through without boil. Slice the chicken and serve on a platter with green sauce spooned over.

Nutritional Value: Calories 236, Fat 9g, Net Carbs 2.3g, Protein 18g

268. Chicken and Green Cabbage Casserole

Preparation Time: 55 minutes
Serves: 4

Ingredients

- 3 cups cheddar cheese, grated
- 10 ounces green cabbage, shredded
- 3 chicken breasts, skinless, boneless, cooked, cubed
- 1 cup mayonnaise
- 1 tbsp coconut oil, melted
- ⅓ cup chicken stock
- Salt and ground black pepper, to taste
- Juice of 1 lemon

Directions

1. Apply oil to a baking dish, and set chicken pieces to the bottom. Spread green cabbage, followed by half of the cheese. Using a bowl, combine the mayonnaise with pepper, stock, lemon juice, and salt.
2. Pour this mixture over the chicken, spread the rest of the cheese, cover with aluminum foil, and bake for 30 minutes in the oven at 350°F. Open the aluminum foil, and cook for 20 more minutes.

Nutritional Value: Calories 231, Fat 15g, Net Carbs 6g, Protein 25g

269. Coconut Chicken Soup

Preparation Time: 30 minutes
Serves: 4

Ingredients

- 3 tbsp butter
- 4 ounces cream cheese
- 2 chicken breasts, diced
- 4 cups chicken stock
- Salt and black pepper, to taste
- ½ cup coconut cream
- ¼ cup celery, chopped

Directions

1. In the blender, combine stock, butter, coconut cream, salt, cream cheese, and pepper. Remove to a pot, heat over medium heat, and stir in the chicken and celery. Simmer for 15 minutes, separate into bowls, and enjoy.

Nutritional Value: Calories 387, Fat 23g, Net Carbs 5g, Protein 31g

270. Chicken Breasts with Cheddar & Pepperoni

Preparation Time: 40 minutes
Serves: 4

Ingredients

- 12 oz canned tomato sauce
- 1 tbsp olive oil
- 4 chicken breast halves, skinless and boneless
- Salt and ground black pepper, to taste
- 1 tsp dried oregano
- 4 oz cheddar cheese, sliced
- 1 tsp garlic powder
- 2 oz pepperoni, sliced

Directions

- Preheat your oven to 390°F. Using a bowl, combine chicken with oregano, salt, garlic, and pepper.
- Heat a pan with the olive oil over medium-high heat, add in the chicken, cook each side for 2 minutes, and remove to a baking dish. Top with the cheddar cheese slices spread the sauce, then cover with pepperoni slices. Bake for 30 minutes. Serve warm garnished with fresh oregano if desired

Nutritional Value: Calories 387, Fat 21g, Net Carbs 4.5g, Protein 32g

271. Chicken, Eggplant and Gruyere Gratin

Preparation Time: 55 minutes
Serves: 4

Ingredients

- 3 tbsp butter
- 1 eggplant, chopped
- 2 tbsp gruyere cheese, grated
- Salt and black pepper, to taste
- 2 garlic cloves, minced
- 6 chicken thighs

Directions

1. Set a pan over medium heat and warm 1 tablespoon butter, place in the chicken thighs, season with pepper and salt, cook each side for 3 minutes and lay them in a baking dish. In the same pan melt the rest of the butter and cook the garlic for 1 minute.
2. Stir in the eggplant, pepper, and salt, and cook for 10 minutes. Ladle this mixture over the chicken, spread with the cheese, set in the oven at 350°F, and bake for 30 minutes. Turn on the oven's broiler, and broil everything for 2 minutes. Split among serving plates and enjoy.

Nutritional Value: Calories 412, Fat 37g, Net Carbs 5g, Protein 34g

272. Homemade Chicken Pizza Calzone

Preparation Time: 60 minutes
Serves: 4

Ingredients

- 2 eggs
- 1 low carb pizza crust
- ½ cup Pecorino cheese, grated
- 1 lb chicken breasts, skinless, boneless, halved
- ½ cup sugar-free marinara sauce
- 1 tsp Italian seasoning
- 1 tsp onion powder
- 1 tsp garlic powder
- Salt and black pepper, to taste
- ¼ cup flax seed, ground
- 6 ounces provolone cheese

Directions

1. Using a bowl, combine the Italian seasoning with onion powder, salt, Pecorino cheese, pepper, garlic powder, and flaxseed. In a separate bowl, combine the eggs with pepper and salt.
2. Dip the chicken pieces in eggs, and then in seasoning mixture, lay all parts on a lined baking sheet, and bake for 25 minutes in the oven at 390° F.
3. Place the pizza crust dough on a lined baking sheet and spread half of the provolone cheese on half. Remove chicken from oven, chop it, and scatter it over the provolone cheese. Spread over the marinara sauce and top with the remaining cheese.
4. Cover with the other half of the dough and shape the pizza in a calzone. Seal the edges, set in the oven and bake for 20 minutes. Allow the calzone to cool down before slicing and enjoy.

Nutritional Value: Calories 425, Fat 15g, Net Carbs 4.6g, Protein 28g

273. Red Wine Chicken

Preparation Time: 30 minutes
Serves: 4

Ingredients

- 3 tbsp coconut oil
- 2 lb chicken breast halves, skinless and boneless
- 3 garlic cloves, minced
- Salt and black pepper, to taste
- 1 cup chicken stock
- 3 tbsp stevia
- ½ cup red wine
- 2 tomatoes, sliced
- 6 mozzarella slices
- Fresh basil, chopped, for serving

Directions

1. Set a pan over medium-high heat and warm oil, add the chicken, season with

pepper and salt, cook until brown. Stir in the stevia, garlic, stock, and red wine, and cook for 10 minutes.

2. Remove to a lined baking sheet and arrange mozzarella cheese slices on top. Broil in the oven over medium heat until cheese melts and lay tomato slices over chicken pieces.
3. Sprinkle with chopped basil to serve.

Nutritional Value: Calories 314, Fat 12g, Net Carbs 4g, Protein 27g

274. Spinach & Ricotta Stuffed Chicken Breasts

Preparation Time: 25 minutes
Serves: 3

Ingredients

- 1 cup spinach, cooked and chopped
- 3 chicken breasts
- Salt and ground black pepper, to taste
- 4 ounces cream cheese, softened
- 1/2 cup ricotta cheese, crumbled
- 1 garlic clove, peeled and minced
- 1 tbsp coconut oil
- ½ cup white wine

Directions

1. Using a bowl, combine the ricotta cheese with cream cheese, salt, garlic, pepper, and spinach. Add the chicken breasts on a working surface, cut a pocket in each, stuff them with the spinach mixture, and add more pepper and salt.
2. Set a pan over medium-high heat and warm oil, add the stuffed chicken, cook each side for 5 minutes. Put in a baking tray, drizzle with white wine and 2 tablespoons of water and then place in the oven at 420°F. Bake for 10 minutes, arrange on a serving plate and serve.

Nutritional Value: Calories 305, Fat 12g, Net Carbs 4g, Protein 23g

275. Oven Baked "Buffalo" Turkey Wings

Serves: 6
Preparation: 10 minutes
Cooking: 1 hour and 10 minutes

Ingredients

- 3 1/2 lbs turkey wings, cut in half
- 3/4 cup almond flour
- 1/2 tsp salt to taste
- 1 tsp cayenne pepper
- Olive oil for frying
- 1/4 cup almond butter melted
- 2 Tbsp of white vinegar
- 2 Tbsp hot red pepper sauce
- 2 Tbsp of fresh celery chopped

Directions:

1. Preheat the oven on 375 F/180 C.
2. Combine the almond flour, salt and cayenne pepper on a plate. Dust wings in almond flour mixture, shaking off excess.
3. Heat olive oil in a large heavy skillet over medium heat. Fry chicken for 10 minutes, turning once. Remove from heat, and drain on kitchen paper towels.
4. Combine the almond butter, vinegar and hot pepper sauce in a small bowl. Place wings in a large baking pan; drizzle sauce over wings.
5. Bake wings for 1 hour, turning once.
6. Serve hot with fresh chopped celery.

Nutritional Value:

Calories: 549 Carbohydrates: 2.5g Proteins: 63g Fat: 31g Fiber: 1.2g

276. Oven Baked Creamy Chicken Thighs

Serves: 6
Preparation: 10 minutes
Cooking: 40 minutes

Ingredients

- 3/4 cup mayonnaise
- 1/4 cup yellow mustard
- 1/2 cup Parmesan cheese freshly grated
- 1 tsp Italian seasoning
- 1/4 tsp of coriander
- 1/4 tsp of marjoram

- 2 lbs chicken thighs (boneless and skinless
- 1/2 tsp salt and ground black pepper

Directions:

1. Preheat oven to 400 F/200 C.
2. Oil one 8-inch square baking dish.
3. In a bowl combine together the mayonnaise, mustard, Parmesan cheese, coriander, marjoram and Italian seasoning.
4. Season generously chicken thigh with salt and pepper and place in a prepared baking dish.
5. Spread with mayo-mustard sauce and bake for 35 - 40 minutes. Serve warm.

Nutritional Value:

Calories: 335 Carbohydrates: 7g Proteins: 34g
Fat: 18g Fiber: 0.3g

277. Roasted Turkey - Mushrooms Loaf

Serves: 6
Preparation: 15 minutes
Cooking: 1 hour

Ingredients

- 1/2 cup ground almonds
- 1 Tbsp of dried parsley
- 1/4 tsp ground allspice
- 1/2 tsp dried thyme leaves
- 1/2 tsp salt and pepper to taste
- 1 1/2 lb ground turkey
- 8 oz turkey ham cut into 1/4-inch cubes
- 1/2 lb mushrooms coarsely chopped
- 1/2 cup spring onion chopped
- 2 cloves garlic minced
- 1 large egg beaten
- Olive oil cooking spray

Directions:

1. Preheat the oven to 350 F/175 C.
2. In large bowl combine ground almonds, parsley, allspice, thyme, salt and pepper.
3. Add ground turkey, turkey ham, mushrooms, spring onions, garlic and beaten egg; knead with your hands to get a compact mixture.
4. Coat one 9-inch pie plate with olive oil cooking spray, shape turkey mixture into round loaf.
5. Bake for 50 to 60 minutes or until inserted thermometer reaches 160 degrees F.
6. Serve hot.

Nutritional Value:

Calories: 310 Carbohydrates: 5.5g Proteins: 34g
Fat: 18g Fiber: 2g

278. Chicken - Artichokes Casserole

Serves: 4
Preparation: 10 minutes
Cooking: 25 minutes

Ingredients

- 2 Tbsp butter
- 1 can (11 oz) of artichoke hearts, drained
- 2 green onions, green and white parts included, chopped
- 1 chicken breast cut in cubes
- 1/2 cup dry white wine
- 1 Tbsp almond flour
- 1/2 cup bone broth (or water)
- 1/2 cup cream
- 1 tsp salt and ground black pepper
- 1/4 tsp tarragon leaves
- 2 Tbsp chopped parsley for serving

Directions:

1. Preheat oven to 350 F/175 C.
2. Grease one deep casserole dish with the butter.
3. Cut artichokes and place on the bottom of casserole dish.
4. Add the green onion, and the chicken cubes over the artichokes.
5. In a bowl, combine together wine, bone broth, cream and almond flour; stir until almond flour is completely dissolved.
6. Pour the mixture evenly in a casserole dish.

7. Place in the oven and bake for 20 - 25 minutes. Serve hot.

Nutritional Value:

Calories: 101 Carbohydrates: 8.5g Proteins: 22g Fat: 29g Fiber: 6g

279. Chicken Liver and Pancetta Casserole

Serves: 4
Preparation: 5 minutes
Cooking: 50 minutes

Ingredients

- 1/4 cup of olive oil
- 1 onion finely chopped
- 2 cloves of garlic
- 1 1/2 lb of chicken liver
- 1/2 tsp smoked red ground pepper
- 7 oz of pancetta (cut into strips)
- 1 tsp of dried thyme
- 1/2 cup of red wine
- 1 bunch of parsley finely chopped
- Salt and freshly ground black pepper

Directions:

1. Preheat oven to 350 F/175 C.
2. Grease a casserole with olive oil; set aside.
3. Heat the olive oil in a skillet over medium-high heat.
4. Sauté the onion and the garlic for 3 - 4 minutes,
5. Add chopped pancetta and stir for 1 - 2 minutes.
6. Add chicken liver, smoked pepper, thyme, salt and pepper and cook for 3-4 minutes.
7. Pour the red wine, and add chopped parsley; stir.
8. Transfer the mixture in a prepared casserole dish.
9. Bake for 35 - 45 minutes. Serve hot.

Nutritional Value:

Calories: 340 Carbohydrates: 4g Proteins: 29g Fat: 22g Fiber: 1g

280. Chicken Pandemonio Casserole

Serves: 6
Preparation: 15 minutes
Cooking: 35 minutes

Ingredients

- 1 Tbsp of chicken fat
- 2 lb of chicken, cubed
- Salt and ground pepper to taste
- 12 oz of frozen or fresh spinach
- 1/4 cup bacon crumbled
- 1 cup of cream cheese softened
- 1/2 cup of mayonnaise
- 1 tsp garlic powder
- 1 cup grated parmesan cheese

Directions:

1. Preheat oven to 350F/ 175 C
2. Grease one 9 x13 baking dish with chicken fat.
3. Season the chicken generously with the salt and pepper, and place into baking dish.
4. Add the spinach over chicken, and sprinkle with crumbled bacon.
5. In a bowl, combine together the cream cheese, mayo, garlic, and grated parmesan cheese.
6. Pour the mixture in a casserole.
7. Place in oven and bake for 30 - 35 minutes.
8. Serve hot.

Nutritional Value:

Calories: 374 Carbohydrates: 8.5g Proteins: 15g Fat: 32g Fiber: 2g

281. Chicken with Curry and Coriander Casserole

Serves: 4
Preparation: 10 minutes
Cooking: 25 minutes

Ingredients

- 1 lb of chicken breast cut in cubes
- 1 Tbsp of chicken fat

- 1 onion finely sliced
- 1 carrot
- 2 tsp of curry powder
- 1 pinch of saffron
- 1/2 cup of wine
- 1/2 cup of bone broth
- 1 Tbsp of fresh coriander
- Salt to taste

Directions:

1. Cut the chicken breasts into large cubes.
2. Heat the chicken fat in a casserole and sauté the onion.
3. Add the chicken cubes and brown them on all sides; stir for 2 - 3 minutes.
4. Sprinkle with curry and saffron, stir in the carrots and stir well.
5. Pour the wine and bone broth and stir.
6. Season with the salt, cover and let simmer for 20 minutes.
7. Sprinkle with fresh chopped coriander leaves and serve.

Nutritional Value:

Calories: 186 Carbohydrates: 6g Proteins: 26g Fat: 8g Fiber: 2g

282. Asiago Chicken Wings

Serves: 6
Preparation: 10 minutes
Cooking: 20 minutes

Ingredients

- 2 Tbsp olive oil
- 20 frozen chicken wings
- 1 tsp salt
- 1/2 Tbsp garlic powder
- 2 tsp dried oregano
- 1 cup of grated Asiago cheese (or Parmesan)
- 1/2 can water

Directions:

1. Pour the oil to the inner stainless steel pot in the Instant Pot.
2. Season frozen chicken legs with salt, garlic powder and oregano.
3. Place the seasoned chicken wings in your Instant Pot and pour water.
4. Lock lid into place and set on the POULTRY setting for 20 minutes.
5. Use Quick Release - turn the valve from sealing to venting to release the pressure.
6. Transfer chicken wings to serving platter and generously sprinkle with grated cheese.
7. Let rest for 10 minutes and serve.

Nutritional Value:

Calories: 438 Carbohydrates: 2g Proteins: 37g Fat: 35g Fiber: 0.5g

283. Chicken Cilantro Wraps

Serves: 4
Preparation: 10 minutes
Cooking: 12 minutes

Ingredients

- 2 chicken breasts boneless, skinless
- 1 cup bone broth (or water)
- Juice of 1 lemon freshly squeezed
- 1 green onion finely chopped
- 1 cup cilantro, chopped
- 1 tsp chili powder
- 1 tsp cumin
- 1 tsp garlic powder
- Sea salt and pepper to taste
- 12 lettuce leaves

Directions:

1. Season chicken breast with the salt and pepper and place in your Instant Pot.
2. Add all remaining ingredients (except lettuce leaves; lock lid into place and set on the POULTRY setting for 12 minutes.
3. When the timer beeps, press "Cancel" and carefully flip the Quick Release valve to let the pressure out.
4. Open lid and transfer chicken in a bowl; Shred chicken with two forks.
5. Combine shredded chicken with juices from Instant Pot.
6. Add one spoon of shredded chicken in each lettuce leaf and wrap. Serve

immediately.

Nutritional Value:

Calories: 7163 Carbohydrates: 4g Proteins: 34g Fat: 5g Fiber: 1g

284. Perfect Braised Turkey Breast

Serves: 8
Preparation: 10 minutes
Cooking: 30 minutes

Ingredients

- 2 Tbsp butter softened on room temperature
- 4 lbs turkey breast boneless
- 1 cup water
- 1/2 cup coconut aminos (from coconut sap)
- 1/2 tsp fresh rosemary, finely chopped
- 1/2 tsp fresh sage, finely chopped
- 1/2 tsp fresh rosemary finely chopped
- 1 tsp salt and ground red pepper to taste

Directions:

1. Season turkey breasts with salt and pepper.
2. Press SAUTÉ button on your Instant Pot.
3. When the word "hot" appears on the display, add butter and sear turkey breasts for 3 minutes.
4. Pour water and coconut aminos and stir for 2 minutes.
5. Sprinkle with herbs, and the salt and pepper and stir again. Turn off the SAUTÉ button.
6. Lock lid into place and set on the MANUAL high pressure setting for 28 - 30 minutes (turkey meat is ready when meat thermometer shows 161 F/80 C).
7. When the timer beeps, press "Cancel" and carefully flip the Natural Release for 15 minutes.
8. Remove turkey breast on a plate, and allow it to cool for 10 minutes.
9. Slice and serve.

Nutritional Value:

Calories: 357 Carbohydrates: 1.5g Proteins: 62g Fat: 10g Fiber: 0.5g

285. Roasted Whole Chicken

Serves: 6
Preparation: 10 minutes
Cooking: 35 minutes

Ingredients

- 2 cups water
- 4 lb whole chickens
- 1/4 cup olive oil
- Seasoned salt and black ground pepper to taste
- 1/4 tsp dry thyme
- 1/4 tsp dry rosemary
- 1/4 tsp dry marjoram
- 1/4 tsp of dry sage

Directions:

1. Pour water to the inner stainless steel pot in the Instant Pot, and place the trivet inside (steam rack or a steamer basket).
2. Rinse well the turkey and pat dry. Rub with olive oil and season to taste with salt and pepper, thyme, rosemary, marjoram and sage.
3. Put the turkey on the trivet into Instant Pot.
4. Press MANUAL mode and set time for 35 minutes.
5. Use Natural Release - it takes 15 - 20 minutes to depressurize naturally.
6. Remove the chicken on a serving plate and allow cool for 15 minutes before serving.

Nutritional Value:

Calories: 589 Carbohydrates: 0.1g Proteins: 54g Fat: 47g Fiber: 1g

286. Serrano Chicken Stir Fry

Serves: 6
Preparation: 10 minutes
Cooking: 15 minutes

Ingredients

- 2 lbs chicken breasts cut small pieces

- 1 tsp sea salt
- 1 Tbsp sesame oil
- 1 Tbsp ginger, minced
- 1 Tbsp lemon juice
- 2 Tbsp coconut oil
- 1 green onion, minced
- 2 cloves garlic, minced
- 8 Serrano peppers cut in half
- 1 cup water

Directions:

1. In a bowl, whisk the salt, sesame oil, ginger and lemon juice.
2. Season chicken breast with the mixture.
3. Turn on the Instant Pot and press SAUTÉ button.
4. When the word "hot" appears on the display, add the coconut oil and sauté the green onion and garlic about 3 minutes. Add halved peppers and sauté for about 2 minutes.
5. Turn off SAUTÉ button; add seasoned chicken, pour water and stir.
6. Lock lid into place and set on the POULTRY setting on HIGH pressure for 10 minutes.
7. When the timer beeps, press "Cancel" and carefully flip the Quick Release valve to let the pressure out. Serve hot.

Nutritional Value:

Calories: 359.55 Carbohydrates: 2.5g Proteins: 48g Fat: 17g Fiber: 1g

287. Tasty Chicken Curry (Instant Pot)

Serves: 4
Preparation: 10 minutes
Cooking: 10 minutes

Ingredients

- 2 Tbsp olive oil
- 1 lb chicken breast boneless, skinless, cut in small cubes
- Salt and ground black pepper
- 1/2 tsp onion powder
- 1/2 tsp garlic powder
- 1 tsp of curry powder
- 1 1/2 cup coconut cream
- 1/2 cup water
- 1 Tbsp of chopped parsley for serving

Directions:

1. Pour the oil to the inner stainless steel pot in the Instant Pot.
2. Season salt and pepper the chicken breast and place in Instant Pot.
3. In a bowl, combine together all remaining ingredients and pour over chicken.
4. Lock lid into place and set on the MANUAL setting for 10 minutes.
5. Use Natural Release for 15 minutes.
6. Serve hot with chopped parsley.

Nutritional Value:

Calories: 304 Carbohydrates: 2g Proteins: 25g Fat: 22g Fiber: 0.3g

288. Chicken Thighs in Coconut Sauce

Serves: 6
Preparation: 10 minutes
Cooking: 4 hours and 20 minutes

Ingredients

- 1 1/2 lbs of chicken thighs boneless and skinless
- 1 red bell pepper finely chopped
- 1 green onion chopped
- 1 chili pepper (peeled and finely chopped)
- 2 cloves garlic (minced)
- 1 cup of bone broth
- 1/2 cup of coconut flakes
- 2 Tbsp of curry powder
- Salt and ground pepper to taste
- 1/4 tsp of ground cinnamon
- 1/2 cup of coconut milk unsweetened
- 1 Tbsp of coconut flour
- Fresh cilantro for serving

Directions:

1. Place the chicken thighs, bell pepper,

onions, chili pepper and garlic in Crock Pot.
2. Pour broth, and add the coconut flakes, curry powder, salt and pepper, and cinnamon.
3. Cover and cook on LOW for 8 - 9 hours or HIGH for 4 hours.
4. In a small bowl, dissolve the coconut flour in coconut milk.
5. Open lid and pour the coconut mixture; stir.
6. Cover again and cook on HIGH for further 20 minutes.
7. Serve hot with fresh chopped cilantro.

Nutritional Value:

Calories: 359 Carbohydrates: 5g Proteins: 24g Fat: 28g Fiber: 1.5g

289. Delicious Chicken Breast with Turmeric

Serves: 4
Preparation: 15 minutes
Cooking: 4 hours

Ingredients

- 1/2 cup chicken fat
- 4 chicken breasts, boneless, skinless
- Table salt and ground white pepper to taste
- 4 cloves garlic, finely sliced
- 1 Tbsp ground turmeric
- 1 cup of bone broth

Directions:

1. Season the salt and pepper chicken breast and cut into pieces.
2. Add tallow in inner pot of your Slow Cooker, and place the chicken breasts.
3. Add the turmeric, garlic and chicken broth.
4. Cover and cook on LOW for 3 - 4 hours.
5. Transfer the chicken breasts on a serving plate.
6. Serve hot with cooking juice.

Nutritional Value:

Calories: 488 Carbohydrates: 2.5g Proteins: 52g Fat: 32g Fiber: 0.5g

290. Chicken Cutlets with Spinach Stir-Fry

Serves: 4
Preparation: 5 minutes
Cooking: 15 minutes

Ingredients

- 2 Tbsp chicken fat
- 1 spring onion (only green parts), finely chopped
- 2 medium cloves garlic, thinly sliced
- 8 boneless, skinless, chicken breast cutlets cut in pieces
- Salt and freshly ground black pepper
- 3 Tbsp capers, rinsed and chopped
- 1 lb of fresh spinach, steamed
- 1/2 cup water
- 2 Tbsp fresh lemon juice

Directions:

1. Heat the chicken fat in a deep pot, and sauté spring onion and garlic for 3 - 4 minutes.
2. Add chicken cutlets, and stir for 4 - 5 minutes.
3. Season with the salt and pepper,
4. Reduce the heat to medium and add the capers and spinach leaves. Cook stirring, until the spinach softens, about 3 minutes.
5. Pour water and lemon juice, and cook for further 2 - 3 minutes.
6. Serve hot.

Nutritional Value:

Calories: 347 Carbohydrates: 5g Proteins: 57g Fat: 15g Fiber: 3g

291. Chicken with Zucchini Spaghetti Stir Fry

Serves: 4
Preparation: 15 minutes
Cooking: 7 - 10 minutes

Ingredients

- 1 lb chicken breasts, boneless, skinless, cut in slices
- 2 Tbsp of chicken fat

- 2 cups zucchini, spiralized (or made into ribbons with a vegetable peeler)
- Marinade
- 1 spring onion finely chopped
- 2 cloves garlic, minced
- 1 cup water
- 1 cup fresh lemon juice
- 1/3 cup coconut aminos
- 1/3 cup olive oil
- 4 green onion, sliced
- 1" piece of ginger, grated
- Salt and ground black pepper to taste

Directions:

1. Place the chicken slices in a container and season with the salt and pepper.
2. In a deep bowl, combine all ingredients for marinade; stir until well combined.
3. Pour the marinade evenly over the chicken; cover and refrigerate for 2 hours.
4. Heat the chicken fat in a large and deep frying skillet over medium-high heat.
5. Add the chicken to the skillet and stir-fry about 5 - 7 minutes. Toss in the zucchini ribbons and cook only for 2 minutes. Serve hot.

Nutritional Value:

Calories: 327 Carbohydrates: 6g Proteins: 27g Fat: 22g Fiber: 2g

292. Hungarian Chicken Fillet Stir-fry

Serves: 4
Preparation: 5 minutes
Cooking: 30 minutes

Ingredients

- 1 Tbsp of chicken fat
- 1 lb of chicken fillet cut in strips
- 2 - 3 spring onions, finely chopped
- 2 cloves garlic
- 1 green pepper, chopped
- 1 tomato grated
- Salt and black ground pepper to taste
- 1 Tbsp of fresh parsley, chopped
- 1 egg, beaten

Directions:

1. Heat the chicken fat in a large pan.
2. Sauté the onion and garlic with a pinch of salt for 4 - 5 minutes.
3. Add chicken strips and stir for 5 - 6 minutes.
4. Add chopped pepper and grated tomato; season with the salt and pepper.
5. Cover and cook for 12 - 15 minutes over low-medium heat.
6. Crack one egg in a pan and stir well.
7. Sprinkle with fresh parsley and serve hot.

Nutritional Value:

Calories: 67 Carbohydrates: 6.5g Proteins: 6g Fat: 3g Fiber: 2g

293. Serrano Pepper - Chicken Stir-Fry

Serves: 4
Preparation: 10 minutes
Cooking: 20 minutes

Ingredients

- 2 lbs chicken breasts, boneless skinless, cut in pieces
- 1 tsp sea salt
- 2 cloves garlic, minced
- 1 Tbsp almond flour
- 1 cup water
- 1 Tbsp sesame oil
- 1 Tbsp ginger, minced
- 4 - 5 Serrano peppers, sliced
- 3 Tbsp olive oil
- 2 green onions cut into thin slices

Directions:

1. Place chicken in a large container, and rub with the mixture of salt, garlic, sesame oil, ginger, almond flour and water.
2. Refrigerate for 1 hour.
3. Heat the olive oil in a large skillet over a high heat.
4. Add Serrano peppers and fry for about 2

minutes.

5. Add the chicken, stir, reduce the heat and stir-fry for 5 - 6 minutes.
6. Add chopped green onion, some water, and cook for further 6-7 minutes.
7. Adjust salt, stir and serve hot.

Nutritional Value:

Calories: 388 Carbohydrates: 2g Proteins: 48g Fat: 20g Fiber: 0.5g

294. Shredded Turkey with Asparagus Stir-fry

Serves: 4
Preparation: 5 minutes
Cooking: 30 minutes

Ingredients

- 2 Tbsp of chicken fat
- 2 spring onions, diced
- 1 tsp minced garlic
- 1 red pepper finely chopped
- 1/4 lb button mushrooms sliced thin
- 1 cup cooked asparagus cut into small pieces
- 1/2 tsp dried rosemary
- Salt and ground black pepper to taste
- 1 1/2 lbs turkey breast meat, boneless, shredded
- 1 cup bone broth

Directions:

1. In a large frying skillet heat the chicken fat over medium-high heat.
2. Sauté the onion, garlic and red pepper with a little salt for 4 to 5 minutes.
3. Add mushrooms and asparagus; sauté for 2 - 3 minutes.
4. Stir in rosemary, pepper, and season with the salt to taste.
5. Add shredded turkey meat, and stir well.
6. Pour the bone broth, cover and cook for 13 -15 minutes over medium heat.
7. Taste and adjust seasonings. Serve hot.

Nutritional Value:

Calories: 210 Carbohydrates: 8g Proteins: 35g Fat: 4g Fiber: 2.5g

295. Squash Spaghetti and Chicken Mince Stir-fry

Serves: 4
Preparation: 5 minutes
Cooking: 25 minutes

Ingredients

- 1/4 cup olive oil
- 1 1/4 lb squash, spiralized
- 1 lb chicken mince
- 1 Tbsp fresh lemon juice (about 2 lemons)
- 1/2 Tbsp fresh herbs mixture (tarragon, marjoram, oregano)
- Salt and freshly ground pepper to taste
- 1/2 cup shredded Mozzarella cheese for garnish

Directions:

1. Heat the olive oil in a skillet over medium-high heat.
2. Sauté the squash spaghetti with a pinch of salt for about 8 minutes.
3. Add the ground chicken, fresh lemon juice, fresh herbs and season salt and pepper to taste.
4. Stir, and stir-fry for 8 - 10 minutes over medium heat.
5. Taste and adjust seasonings; cook for further 5 minutes; gently stir.
6. Serve hot with shredded cheese.

Nutritional Value:

Calories: 338 Carbohydrates: 6g Proteins: 32g Fat: 21g Fiber: 2g

296. Yurkey Mince and Green Beans Stir-fry

Serves: 4
Preparation: 5 minutes
Cooking: 15 minutes

Ingredients

- 1 Tbsp chicken fat
- 1 lb turkey mince
- 2 cloves garlic, minced
- 2 spring onions, sliced

- 1 piece ginger, finely grated
- 1/2 lb of green beans, boiled
- 2 zucchini, cut into slices
- 2 Tbsp yellow mustard
- 1/2 cup fresh basil leaves
- Salt and ground black pepper

Directions:

1. Heat the chicken fat in a large frying pan.
2. Add turkey mince and stir-fry for 2 - 3 minutes,
3. Stir the garlic, spring onions and ginger; season with the salt and pepper and stir-fry for 3 -4 minutes.
4. Add green beans and zucchini, and stir-fry for 3 minutes; stir well.
5. At the end, add mustard and gently toss.
6. Serve hot with fresh basil leaves.

Nutritional Value:

Calories: 193 Carbohydrates: 9g Proteins: 23g Fat: 6g Fiber: 4g

297.bOne Pan Chicken Mix

Preparation time: 10 minutes
Cooking time: 16 minutes
Servings: 4

Ingredients:

- 1 and ½ pounds chicken thighs, boneless and skinless
- 2 teaspoons thyme, chopped
- A pinch of salt and black pepper
- 1 tablespoon olive oil
- 12 ounces Brussels sprouts, halved
- 1 red onion, sliced
- 1 garlic clove, minced
- 2 teaspoons stevia
- 2 tablespoons balsamic vinegar
- 1/3 cup walnuts, chopped

Directions:

1. Heat up a pan with the oil over medium-high heat, add chicken pieces, season with salt, pepper and thyme, cook for 5 minutes on each side and transfer to a plate.
2. Heat up the same pan over medium-high heat, add Brussels sprouts, garlic and onion, stir and cook for 6 minutes.
3. Add stevia and vinegar, stir and take off heat.
4. Divide the chicken between plates, add Brussels sprouts in the side and sprinkle walnuts on top.
5. Enjoy!

Nutritional Value:calories 231, fat 4, fiber 7, carbs 12, protein 25

298. Chicken Chili

Preparation time: 10 minutes
Cooking time: 20 minutes
Servings: 6

Ingredients:

- 1 pound chicken, ground
- 2 garlic cloves, minced
- 1 yellow onion, chopped
- 1 and ½ tablespoon olive oil
- 1 tablespoon chili powder
- 7 ounces canned green chilies, chopped
- 28 ounces canned tomatoes, chopped
- 3 cups butternut squash, peeled and cubed
- 14 ounces chicken stock
- A pinch of salt and black pepper

Directions:

1. Heat up a pot with the oil over medium-high heat, add chicken, garlic and onion, stir and cook for 6 minutes.
2. Add chili powder, chilies, tomatoes, squash, stock, salt and pepper, stir, cover the pot, simmer for 15 minutes, divide into bowls and serve.
3. Enjoy!

Nutritional Value:calories 211, fat 3, fiber 4, carbs 13, protein 7

299. Chipotle Chicken

Preparation time: 10 minutes
Cooking time: 12 minutes
Servings: 4

Ingredients:

- 1 pound chicken breast, skinless, boneless and cut into strips
- 1 teaspoon chili powder
- 1 teaspoon cumin, ground
- A pinch of salt and black pepper
- 1 tablespoon olive oil
- 1 red bell pepper, sliced
- 1 cup mushrooms, sliced
- 1 yellow onion, chopped
- 1 tablespoon chipotles in adobo sauce, chopped
- 3 garlic cloves, minced
- 1 and ½ tablespoons lime juice

Directions:

1. Heat up a pan with the oil over medium-high heat, add chicken strips, chili powder, cumin, salt and pepper, stir and cook for 6 minutes.
2. Add bell pepper, mushrooms, onion, chipotles, garlic and lime juice, stir, cook for 6 minutes more, divide into bowls and serve.
3. Enjoy!

Nutritional Value:calories 212, fat 3, fiber 6, carbs 15, protein 18

300. Chicken and Tomatoes

Preparation time: 10 minutes
Cooking time: 16 minutes
Servings: 4

Ingredients:

- 4 chicken breast fillets, skinless and boneless
- A pinch of salt and black pepper
- 1 tablespoon olive oil
- ¼ cup parmesan, grated
- 1 tablespoon parsley, chopped
- 1 garlic clove, minced
- 1 pound cherry tomatoes, halved

Directions:

1. Grease a baking dish with the oil, add chicken fillets, tomatoes and garlic, season with salt and pepper, sprinkle parmesan and parsley, introduce in the oven and cook for 16 minutes at 450 degrees F.
2. Divide everything between plates and serve.
3. Enjoy!

Nutritional Value:calories 251, fat 3, fiber 6, carbs 11, protein 13

301. Chicken, Squash and Apples

Preparation time: 10 minutes
Cooking time: 40 minutes
Servings: 3

Ingredients:

- 1 butternut squash, peeled and cubed
- 2 tablespoons olive oil
- 1 apple, cored and cubed
- 2 chicken breasts, skinless and boneless
- 1 tablespoon cilantro, chopped
- A pinch of salt and pepper

Directions:

1. In a bowl, mix squash with apples, cilantro, salt, pepper and 1 tablespoon oil and toss.
2. Heat up a pan with the rest of the oil over medium heat, add chicken, salt and pepper and cook for 5 minutes on each side.
3. Add apple and squash mix, stir, introduce everything in the oven at 425 degrees F and bake for 20 minutes.
4. Shred the meat, divide everything between plates and serve.
5. Enjoy!

Nutritional Value:calories 210, fat 14, fiber 3, carbs 11, protein 15

302. Chicken and Pineapple Mix

Preparation time: 10 minutes
Cooking time: 13 minutes
Servings: 4

Ingredients:

- 20 ounces canned pineapple, cubed

- 1 tablespoon olive oil
- A pinch of salt and black pepper
- 3 cups chicken thighs, boneless, skinless and cut into medium pieces
- 1 tablespoon sweet paprika
- 1 tablespoon cilantro, chopped

Directions:

1. Heat up a pan with the oil over medium-high heat, add chicken, salt, pepper and paprika, toss, cook for 10 minutes, add pineapple and cilantro, cook for 3 minutes more, divide everything between plates and serve.

Nutritional Value:calories 220, fat 3, fiber 7, carbs 8, protein 12

303. Chicken and Mango Chutney

Preparation time: 10 minutes
Cooking time: 10 minutes
Servings: 4

Ingredients:

- 4 chicken breast halves, skinless and boneless
- 1 tablespoon coconut aminos
- 2 tablespoons lime juice
- 2 tablespoons olive oil
- 2 tablespoons mango chutney
- 1 cup mango, peeled and chopped
- 1 avocado, peeled, pitted and chopped
- A pinch of salt and black pepper

Directions:

1. In a bowl, mix the chicken with oil, chutney, lime juice, and coconut aminos and toss to coat.
2. Heat up your kitchen grill over medium-high heat, add chicken, reserve 1 tablespoon chutney mix, cook for 4 minutes on each side, cut into thin strips, put in a salad bowl, add mango, avocado and reserved chutney, toss and serve.
3. Enjoy!

Nutritional Value:calories 210, fat 3, fiber 4, carbs 8, protein 15

304. Chicken and Cucumber Mix

Preparation time: 10 minutes
Cooking time: 0 minutes
Servings: 4

Ingredients:

- 2 chicken breast halves, cooked and shredded
- 2 cucumbers, cubed
- 4 green onions, chopped
- A pinch of salt and black pepper
- 3 tablespoons mustard
- ¼ cup mint, chopped
- 2 cups baby spinach

Directions:

1. In a bowl, mix chicken with cucumbers, onions, mint, spinach, mustard, salt and pepper, toss and serve.
2. Enjoy!

Nutritional Value:calories 230, fat 4, fiber 4, carbs 8, protein 15

305. Chicken and Parsnips

Preparation time: 10 minutes
Cooking time: 40 minutes
Servings: 6

Ingredients:

- 1 whole chicken, cut into medium pieces
- 3 tablespoons olive oil
- Salt and black pepper to the taste
- 1 yellow onion, chopped
- 1 tablespoon black peppercorns, crushed
- 4 parsnips, sliced
- 1 cup celery, chopped
- 1 cup chicken stock
- 2 tablespoons parsley, chopped
- 4 carrots, sliced

Directions:

1. Heat up a pot with the oil over medium-high heat, add the chicken, brown it for 5 minutes on each side and transfer to a bowl.
2. Heat up the same pan over medium-high

heat, add the onion, peppercorns, parsnips, celery and carrots, stir and cook for 5 minutes more.
3. Return the chicken pieces, also add the stock, cover and cook everything for 25 minutes more.
4. Add parsley, divide everything between plates and serve. And serve.
5. Enjoy!

Nutritional Value: calories 250, fat 7, fiber 3, carbs 12, protein 9

306. Chicken and Leeks Mix

Preparation time: 10 minutes
Cooking time: 1 hour and 30 minutes
Servings: 4

Ingredients:

- 1 whole chicken
- A pinch of salt and black pepper
- 1 cup veggie stock
- 1 cup tomato sauce
- 1 leek, sliced
- 1 carrot, sliced
- 3 tablespoons olive oil
- 2 cups yellow onion, chopped
- ½ cup lemon juice

Directions:

1. Grease a baking dish with the oil, add chicken, season with a pinch of salt and black pepper, add leek, carrots, onion, lemon juice, veggie stock and tomato sauce, toss, introduce in the oven and bake at 400 degrees F for 1 hour and 30 minutes.
2. Carve the chicken, divide it and the veggies between plates and serve with cooking juices on top.
3. Enjoy!

Nutritional Value: calories 219, fat 3, fiber 5, carbs 6, protein 20

307. Indian Chicken Soup

Preparation time: 10 minutes
Cooking time: 2 hours
Servings: 5

Ingredients:

- 1 whole chicken, cut into medium pieces
- 1 yellow onion, chopped
- 3 and ½ quarts veggie stock
- 4 carrots, chopped
- 4 celery ribs, chopped
- 1 garlic clove, minced
- 1 teaspoon black peppercorns
- 6 parsley springs
- A pinch of salt and black pepper
- ¼ cup olive oil
- 2 tomatoes, chopped
- 2 tablespoons ginger, grated
- 1 tablespoon tomato paste
- 1 cup coconut milk
- 1 green banana, chopped
- 2 tablespoons cilantro, chopped

Directions:

1. Put chicken in a pot, add the stock, onion and carrots, stir and bring to a simmer over medium heat.
2. Add peppercorns, garlic and parsley springs, stir, cover and simmer for 1 hour and 30 minutes.
3. Meanwhile, heat up a pan with the oil over medium-high heat, add tomatoes, ginger, tomato paste and curry powder, stir and cook for 7 minutes.
4. Add banana and coconut milk, stir, and pour everything over the soup, cook for 30 minutes more, ladle into bowls, sprinkle cilantro on top and serve.
5. Enjoy!

Nutritional Value: calories 219, fat 9, fiber 5, carbs 10, protein 9

308. Chicken and Almond Butter Stew

Preparation time: 10 minutes
Cooking time: 40 minutes
Servings: 4

Ingredients:

- 1 cup chicken stock
- 1 garlic clove, minced

- ½ yellow onion, chopped
- 8 ounces chicken breast skinless, boneless and chopped
- 1 cup collard greens, chopped
- ½ cup soft almond butter
- Salt and black pepper to the taste
- 2 tablespoons ginger, grated

Directions:

1. Put the stock in a pot, add garlic, chicken and onion, stir, bring to a boil over medium heat and simmer for 20 minutes.
2. In a bowl, mix almond butter with 1 tablespoon soup, stir well, and pour over the mix in the pot.
3. Add collard greens, salt, pepper and ginger, stir and cook for 5 more minutes.
4. Divide into bowls and serve.
5. Enjoy!

Nutritional Value: calories 209, fat 5, fiber 5, carbs 8, protein 11

309. Chinese Chicken Soup

Preparation time: 15 minutes
Cooking time: 15 minutes
Servings: 4

Ingredients:

- 1 and ½ tablespoon five spice powder
- 3 chicken thighs boneless, skinless and cut into small pieces
- A pinch of salt and black pepper
- 2 tablespoons olive oil
- 1 chili pepper, chopped
- 2 garlic cloves
- 1 head bok choy, chopped
- 2 tablespoons coconut aminos
- ½ cup cilantro, chopped
- 3 cups chicken stock

Directions:

1. Put chicken in a bowl, season with salt, pepper and five spice powder and rub.
2. Heat up a pot with the oil over medium heat, add garlic and chili pepper, stir and cook for 3 minutes.
3. Add chicken, bok choy, aminos and stock, stir, cook for 12 minutes, divide into bowls and serve with chopped cilantro on top.
4. Enjoy!

Nutritional Value: calories 227, fat 4, fiber 5, carbs 10, protein 9

310. Chicken and Bacon Soup

Preparation time: 10 minutes
Cooking time: 30 minutes
Servings: 4

Ingredients:

- 12 ounces chicken thighs, skinless, boneless and cubed
- 3 smoked bacon slices, chopped
- 1 cup tomato, chopped
- ½ cup yellow onion, chopped
- 1 garlic clove, minced
- 2 tablespoon oregano, chopped
- Salt and black pepper to the taste
- 3 cups veggie stock
- 2 tablespoons cilantro, chopped

Directions:

1. Heat up a pot over medium-high heat, add bacon, stir, cook for 7 minutes, take off heat and transfer to a bowl
2. Heat up the same pot over medium heat, add chicken, cook for 6 minutes, and put in the same bowl with the bacon.
3. Return the pot to medium heat one more time, add garlic and onion, stir and cook for 4 minutes.
4. Add tomato, salt, pepper, oregano, bacon, chicken and stock, stir, bring to a boil, cook for 6 minutes more, add parsley, stir, ladle into soup bowls and serve.
5. Enjoy!

Nutritional Value: calories 205, fat 4, fiber 5, carbs 12, protein 26

MEAT

311. Baked Pork Meatballs in Pasta Sauce

Preparation Time: 40 minutes
Serves: 6

Ingredients

- 2 lb ground pork
- 1 tbsp olive oil
- 1 cup pork rinds, crushed
- 3 cloves garlic, minced
- ½ cup coconut milk
- 2 eggs, beaten
- ½ cup grated Parmesan cheese
- ½ cup grated asiago cheese
- Salt and black pepper to taste
- ¼ cup chopped parsley
- 2 jars sugar-free marinara sauce
- ½ tsp Italian seasoning
- 1 cup Italian blend kinds of cheeses
- Chopped basil to garnish
- Cooking spray

Directions

1. Preheat the oven to 400°F, line the cast iron pan with foil and oil it with cooking spray. Set aside.
2. Combine the coconut milk and pork rinds in a bowl. Mix in the ground pork, garlic, Asiago cheese, Parmesan cheese, eggs, salt, and pepper, just until combined. Form balls of the mixture and place them in the prepared pan. Bake in the oven for 20 minutes at a reduced temperature of 370°F.
3. Transfer the meatballs to a plate. Remove the foil and pour in half of the marinara sauce. Place the meatballs back in the pan and pour the remaining marinara sauce all over them. Sprinkle all over with the Italian blend cheeses, drizzle the olive oil on them, and then sprinkle with Italian seasoning.
4. Cover the pan with foil and put it back in the oven to bake for 10 minutes. After, remove the foil, and continue cooking for 5 minutes. Once ready, take out the pan and garnish with basil. Serve on a bed of squash spaghetti.

Nutritional Value: Calories 590, Fat 46.8g, Net Carbs 4.1g, Protein 46.2g

312. Grilled Pork Loin Chops with Barbecue Sauce

Preparation Time: 1 hour 47 minutes
Serves: 4

Ingredients

- 4 (6 oz) thick-cut pork loin chops, boneless
- ½ cup sugar-free BBQ sauce
- 1 tsp black pepper
- 1 tbsp erythritol
- ½ tsp ginger powder
- 2 tsp sweet paprika

Directions

1. In a bowl, mix the black pepper, erythritol, ginger powder, and sweet paprika, and rub the pork chops on all sides with the mixture. Then, cover the pork chops with plastic wraps and place it in the refrigerator to marinate for 1 hour 30 minutes.
2. Preheat the grill to 450°F. Unwrap the meat, place on the grill grate, and cook for 2 minutes per side. Reduce the heat and brush the BBQ sauce on the meat, cover the lid, and grill them for 5 minutes.
3. Open the lid, turn the meat and brush again with barbecue sauce. Continue cooking covered for 5 minutes. Remove the meat to a serving platter and serve with mixed steamed vegetables.

Nutritional Value: Calories 363, Fat 26.6g, Net Carbs 0g, Protein 34.1g

313. Pork Sausage Bake

Preparation Time: 50 minutes
Serves: 4

Ingredients

- 12 pork sausages
- 5 large tomatoes, cut in rings
- 1 red bell pepper, seeded and sliced
- 1 yellow bell pepper, seeded and sliced
- 1 green bell pepper, seeded and sliced
- 1 sprig thyme, chopped
- 1 sprig rosemary, chopped
- 4 cloves garlic, minced
- 2 bay leaves
- 1 tbsp olive oil
- 2 tbsp balsamic vinegar

Directions

1. Preheat the oven to 350°F.
2. In the cast iron pan, add the tomatoes, bell peppers, thyme, rosemary, garlic, bay leaves, sausages, olive oil, and balsamic vinegar. Toss everything and arrange the sausages on top of the veggies.
3. Put the pan in the oven and bake for 20 minutes. After, remove the pan shake it a bit and turn the sausages over with a spoon. Continue cooking them for 25 minutes or until the sausages have browned to your desired color. Serve with the veggie and cooking sauce with cauli rice.

Nutritional Value: Calories 465, Fat 41.6g, Net Carbs 4.4g, Protein 15.1g

314. Charred Tenderloin with Lemon Chimichurri

Preparation Time: 64 minutes
Serves: 4

Ingredients

- Lemon Chimichurri
- 1 lemon, juiced
- ¼ cup chopped mint leaves
- ¼ cup chopped oregano leaves
- 2 cloves garlic, minced
- ¼ cup olive oil
- Salt to taste
- Pork
- 1 (4 lb) pork tenderloin
- Salt and black pepper to season
- Olive oil for rubbing

Directions

1. Make the lemon chimichurri to have the flavors incorporate while the pork cooks.
2. In a bowl, mix the mint, oregano, and garlic. Then, add the lemon juice, olive oil, and salt, and combine well. Set the sauce aside in room temperature.
3. Preheat the charcoal grill to 450°F in medium-high heat creating a direct heat area and indirect heat area. Rub the pork with olive oil, season with salt and pepper. Place the meat over direct heat and sear for 3 minutes on each side, after which, move to the indirect heat area.
4. Close the lid and cook for 25 minutes on one side, then open, turn the meat, and grill closed for 20 minutes on the other side. Remove the pork from the grill and let it sit for 5 minutes before slicing. Spoon lemon chimichurri over the pork and serve with a fresh salad.

Nutritional Value: Calories 388, Fat 18g, Net Carbs 2.1g, Protein 28g

315. Balsamic Grilled Pork Chops

Preparation Time: 2 hours 20 minutes
Serves: 6

Ingredients

- 6 pork loin chops, boneless
- 2 tbsp erythritol
- ¼ cup balsamic vinegar
- 3 cloves garlic, minced
- ¼ cup olive oil
- ⅓ tsp salt
- Black pepper to taste

Directions

1. Put the pork in the plastic bag. In a bowl, mix the erythritol, balsamic vinegar, garlic, olive oil, salt, pepper, and pour the sauce over the pork. Seal the bag, shake it, and place in the refrigerator.
2. Marinate the pork for 1 to 2 hours. Preheat the grill on medium-high heat,

remove the pork when ready, and grill covered for 10 to 12 minutes on each side. Remove the pork chops, let them sit for 4 minutes, and serve with a syrupy parsnip sauté.

Nutritional Value: Calories 418, Fat 26.8g, Net Carbs 1.5g, Protein 38.1g

316. Herb Pork Chops with Raspberry Sauce

Preparation Time: 17 minutes
Serves: 4

Ingredients

- 1 tbsp olive oil + extra for brushing
- 2 lb pork chops
- Pink salt and black pepper to taste
- 2 cups raspberries
- ¼ cup water
- 1 ½ tbsp Italian Herb mix
- 3 tbsp balsamic vinegar
- 2 tsp sugar-free Worcestershire sauce

Directions

1. Heat oil in a skillet over medium heat, season the pork with salt and black pepper and cook for 5 minutes on each side. Put on serving plates and reserve the pork drippings.
2. Mash the raspberries with a fork in a bowl until jam-like. Pour into a saucepan, add the water, and herb mix. Bring to boil on low heat for 4 minutes. Stir in pork drippings, vinegar, and Worcestershire sauce. Simmer for 1 minute. Spoon sauce over the pork chops and serve with braised rapini.

Nutritional Value: Calories 413, Fat 32.5g, Net Carbs 1.1g, Protein 26.3g

317. Pork Nachos

Preparation Time: 15 minutes
Serves: 4

Ingredients

- 1 bag low carb tortilla chips
- 2 cups leftover pulled pork
- 1 red bell pepper, seeded and chopped
- 1 red onion, diced
- 2 cups shredded Monterey Jack cheese

Directions

1. Preheat oven to 350°F. Arrange the chips in a medium cast iron pan, scatter pork over, followed by red bell pepper, and onion, and sprinkle with cheese. Place the pan in the oven and cook for 10 minutes until the cheese has melted. Allow cooling for 3 minutes and serve.

Nutritional Value: Calories 452, Fat 25g, Net Carbs 9.3g, Protein 22g

318. Zoodle, Bacon, Spinach, and Halloumi Gratin

Preparation Time: 35 minutes
Serves: 4

Ingredients

- 2 large zucchinis, spiralized
- 4 slices bacon, chopped
- 2 cups baby spinach
- 4 oz halloumi cheese, cut into cubes
- 2 cloves garlic, minced
- 1 cup heavy cream
- ½ cup sugar-free tomato sauce
- 1/6 cup water
- 1 cup grated mozzarella cheese
- ½ tsp dried Italian mixed herbs
- Salt and black pepper to taste

Directions

1. Preheat the oven to 350°F. Place the cast iron pan over medium heat and fry the bacon for 4 minutes, then add garlic and cook for 1 minute.
2. In a bowl, mix the heavy cream, tomato sauce, and water, and add it to the pan. Stir in the zucchini, spinach, halloumi, Italian herbs, salt, and pepper to taste.
3. Turn the heat off, sprinkle the mozzarella cheese on top, and transfer the pan to the oven. Bake for 20 minutes or until the cheese is golden.
4. When ready, remove the pan and serve

the gratin warm with a low carb baguette.

Nutritional Value: Calories 350, Fat 27g, Net Carbs 5.3g, Protein 16g

319. Pork Osso Bucco

Preparation Time: 1 hour 55 minutes
Serves: 6

Ingredients

- 4 tbsp butter, softened
- 6 (16 oz) pork shanks
- 2 tbsp olive oil
- 3 cloves garlic, minced
- 1 cup diced tomatoes
- Salt and black pepper to taste
- ½ cup chopped onions
- ½ cup chopped celery
- ½ cup chopped carrots
- 2 cups Cabernet Sauvignon
- 5 cups beef broth
- ½ cup chopped parsley + extra to garnish
- 2 tsp lemon zest

Directions

1. Melt the butter in a large saucepan over medium heat. Season the pork with salt and pepper and brown it for 12 minutes; remove to a plate.
2. In the same pan, sauté 2 cloves of garlic and onions for 3 minutes then return the pork shanks. Stir in the Cabernet, carrots, celery, tomatoes, and beef broth with a season of salt and pepper. Cover the pan and let it simmer on low heat for 1 ½ hours basting the pork every 15 minutes with the sauce.
3. In a bowl, mix the remaining garlic, parsley, and lemon zest to make a gremolata, and stir the mixture into the sauce when it is ready. Turn the heat off and dish the Osso Bucco. Garnish with parsley and serve with a creamy turnip mash.

Nutritional Value: Calories 590, Fat 40g, Net Carbs 6.1g, Protein 34g

320. BBQ Pork Pizza with Goat Cheese

Preparation Time: 30 minutes
Serves: 4

Ingredients

- 1 low carb pizza bread
- Olive oil for brushing
- 1 cup grated manchego cheese
- 2 cups leftover pulled pork
- ½ cup sugar-free BBQ sauce
- 1 cup crumbled goat cheese

Directions

1. Preheat oven to 400°F and put pizza bread on a pizza pan. Brush with olive oil and sprinkle the manchego cheese all over. Mix the pork with BBQ sauce and spread on the cheese. Drop goat cheese on top and bake for 25 minutes until the cheese has melted and golden brown on top. Slice the pizza with a cutter and serve warm.

Nutritional Value: Calories 344, Fat 24g, Net Carbs 6,5g, Protein 18g

321. Lemon Pork Chops with Buttered Brussels Sprouts

Preparation Time: 27 minutes
Serves: 6

Ingredients

- 3 tbsp lemon juice
- 3 cloves garlic, pureed
- 1 tbsp olive oil
- 6 pork loin chops
- 1 tbsp butter
- 1 lb brussels sprouts, trimmed and halved
- 2 tbsp white wine
- Salt and black pepper to taste

Directions

1. Preheat broiler to 400°F and mix the lemon juice, garlic, salt, pepper, and oil in a bowl.
2. Brush the pork with the mixture, place in a baking sheet, and cook for 6 minutes

on each side until browned. Share into 6 plates and make the side dish.

3. Melt butter in a small wok or pan and cook in brussels sprouts for 5 minutes until tender. Drizzle with white wine, sprinkle with salt and black pepper and cook for another 5 minutes.
4. Ladle brussels sprouts to the side of the chops and serve with a hot sauce.

Nutritional Value: Calories 549, Fat 48g, Net Carbs 2g, Protein 26g

322. Peanut Butter Pork Stir-Fry

Preparation Time: 23 minutes
Serves: 4

Ingredients

- 1 ½ tbsp ghee
- 2 lb pork loin, cut into strips
- Pink salt and chili pepper to taste
- 2 tsp ginger- garlic paste
- ¼ cup chicken broth
- 5 tbsp peanut butter
- 2 cups mixed stir-fry vegetables

Directions

1. Melt the ghee in a wok and mix the pork with salt, chili pepper, and ginger-garlic paste. Pour the pork into the wok and cook for 6 minutes until no longer pink.
2. Mix the peanut butter with some broth to be smooth, add to the pork and stir; cook for 2 minutes. Pour in the remaining broth, cook for 4 minutes, and add the mixed veggies. Simmer for 5 minutes.
3. Adjust the taste with salt and black pepper, and spoon the stir-fry to a side of cilantro cauli rice.

Nutritional Value: Calories 571, Fat 49g, Net Carbs 1g, Protein 22.5g

323. Pork Burgers with Caramelized Onion Rings

Preparation Time: 20 minutes
Serves: 6

Ingredients

- 2 lb ground pork
- Pink salt and chili pepper to taste
- 3 tbsp olive oil
- 1 tbsp butter
- 1 white onion, sliced into rings
- 1 tbsp balsamic vinegar
- 3 drops liquid stevia
- 6 low carb burger buns, halved
- 2 firm tomatoes, sliced into rings

Directions

1. Combine the pork, salt and chili pepper in a bowl and mold out 6 patties.
2. Heat the olive oil in a skillet over medium heat and fry the patties for 4 to 5 minutes on each side until golden brown on the outside. Remove onto a plate and sit for 3 minutes.
3. Meanwhile, melt butter in a skillet over medium heat, sauté the onions for 2 minutes to be soft, and stir in the balsamic vinegar and liquid stevia.
4. Cook for 30 seconds stirring once or twice until caramelized. In each bun, place a patty, top with some onion rings and 2 tomato rings. Serve the burgers with cheddar cheese dip.

Nutritional Value: Calories 445, Fat 32g, Net Carbs 7.6g, Protein 26g

324. Spicy Mesquite Ribs

Preparation Time: 8 hours 45 minutes
Serves: 6

Ingredients

- 3 racks pork ribs, silver lining removed
- 2 cups sugar-free BBQ sauce
- 2 tbsp erythritol
- 2 tsp chili powder
- 2 tsp cumin powder
- 2 tsp onion powder
- 2 tsp smoked paprika
- 2 tsp garlic powder
- Salt and pepper to taste
- 1 tsp mustard powder

Directions

1. Preheat the smoker to 400°F using mesquite wood to create flavor in the smoker.
2. In a bowl, mix the erythritol, chili powder, cumin powder, black pepper, onion powder, smoked paprika, garlic powder, salt, and mustard powder. Rub the ribs and let marinate for 30 minutes.
3. Place on the grill grate, and cook at reduced heat of 225°F for 4 hours. Flip the ribs after and continue cooking for 4 hours. Brush the ribs with bbq sauce on both sides and sear them in increased heat for 3 minutes per side. Remove the ribs and let sit for 4 minutes before slicing. Serve with red cabbage coleslaw.

Nutritional Value: Calories 580, Fat 36.6g, Net Carbs 0g, Protein 44.5g

325. Sweet Chipotle Grilled Ribs

Preparation Time: 32 minutes
Serves: 4

Ingredients

- 2 tbsp erythritol
- Pink salt and black pepper to taste
- 1 tbsp olive oil
- 3 tsp chipotle powder
- 1 tsp garlic powder
- 1 lb spare ribs
- 4 tbsp sugar-free BBQ sauce + extra for serving

Directions

1. Mix the erythritol, salt, pepper, oil, chipotle, and garlic powder. Brush on the meaty sides of the ribs and wrap in foil. Sit for 30 minutes to marinate.
2. Preheat oven to 400°F, place wrapped ribs on a baking sheet, and cook for 40 minutes to be cooked through. Remove ribs and aluminium foil, brush with BBQ sauce, and brown under the broiler for 10 minutes on both sides. Slice and serve with extra BBQ sauce and lettuce tomato salad.

Nutritional Value: Calories 395, Fat 33g, Net Carbs 3g, Protein 21g

326. Beef Mushroom Meatloaf

Preparation Time: 1 hour and 15 minutes
Serves: 12

Ingredients

- 3 pounds ground beef
- ½ cup chopped onions
- ½ cup almond flour
- 2 garlic cloves, minced
- 1 cup sliced mushrooms
- 3 eggs
- ¼ tsp pepper
- 2 tbsp chopped parsley
- ¼ cup chopped bell peppers
- ⅓ cup grated Parmesan cheese
- 1 tsp balsamic vinegar
- 1 tsp salt
- Glaze:
- 2 cups balsamic vinegar
- 1 tbsp sweetener
- 2 tbsp sugar-free ketchup

Directions

1. Combine all meatloaf ingredients in a large bowl. Press this mixture into 2 greased loaf pans. Bake at 370°F for about 30 minutes.
2. Meanwhile, make the glaze by combining all ingredients in a saucepan over medium heat. Simmer for 20 minutes, until the glaze is thickened. Pour ¼ cup of the glaze over the meatloaf. Save the extra for future use. Put the meatloaf back in the oven and cook for 20 more minutes.

Nutritional Value: Calories 294, Fat: 19g, Net Carbs: 6g, Protein: 23g

327. Pork Lettuce Cups

Preparation Time: 20 minutes
Serves: 6

Ingredients

- 2 lb ground pork
- 1 tbsp ginger- garlic paste
- Pink salt and chili pepper to taste
- 1 tsp ghee

- 1 head Iceberg lettuce
- 2 sprigs green onion, chopped
- 1 red bell pepper, seeded and chopped
- ½ cucumber, finely chopped

Directions

1. Put the pork with ginger-garlic paste, salt, and chili pepper seasoning in a saucepan. Cook for 10 minutes over medium heat while breaking any lumps until the pork is no longer pink. Drain liquid and add the ghee, melt and brown the meat for 4 minutes, continuously stirring. Turn the heat off.
2. Pat the lettuce dry with paper towel and in each leaf spoon two to three tablespoons of pork, top with green onions, bell pepper, and cucumber. Serve with soy drizzling sauce.

Nutritional Value: Calories 311, Fat 24.3g, Net Carbs 1g, Protein 19g

328. Zucchini Boats with Beef and Pimiento Rojo

Preparation Time: 25 minutes
Serves: 4

Ingredients

- 4 zucchinis
- 2 tbsp olive oil
- 1 ½ lb ground beef
- 1 medium red onion, chopped
- 2 tbsp chopped pimiento
- Pink salt and black pepper to taste
- 1 cup grated yellow cheddar cheese

Directions

1. Preheat oven to 350°F.
2. Lay the zucchinis on a flat surface, trim off the ends and cut in half lengthwise. Scoop out pulp from each half with a spoon to make shells. Chop the pulp.
3. Heat oil in a skillet; add the ground beef, red onion, pimiento, and zucchini pulp, and season with salt and black pepper. Cook for 6 minutes while stirring to break up lumps until beef is no longer pink. Turn the heat off. Spoon the beef into the boats and sprinkle with cheddar cheese.
4. Place on a greased baking sheet and cook to melt the cheese for 15 minutes until zucchini boats are tender. Take out, cool for 2 minutes, and serve warm with a mixed green salad.

Nutritional Value: Calories 335, Fat 24g, Net Carbs 7g, Protein 18g

329. Beef Cauliflower Curry

Preparation Time: 26 minutes
Serves: 6

Ingredients

- 1 tbsp olive oil
- 1 ½ lb ground beef
- 1 tbsp ginger-garlic paste
- 1 tsp garam masala
- 1 (7 oz) can whole tomatoes
- 1 head cauliflower, cut into florets
- Pink salt and chili pepper to taste
- ¼ cup water

Directions

1. Heat oil in a saucepan over medium heat, add the beef, ginger-garlic paste and season with garam masala. Cook for 5 minutes while breaking any lumps.
2. Stir in the tomatoes and cauliflower, season with salt and chili pepper, and cook covered for 6 minutes. Add the water and bring to a boil over medium heat for 10 minutes or until the water has reduced by half. Adjust taste with salt.
3. Spoon the curry into serving bowls and serve with shirataki rice.

Nutritional Value: Calories 374, Fat 33g, Net Carbs 2g, Protein 22g

330. Pork Pie with Cauliflower

Preparation Time: 1 hour and 40 minutes
Serves: 8

Ingredients

- Crust:
- 1 egg

- ¼ cup butter
- 2 cups almond flour
- ¼ tsp xanthan gum
- ¼ cup shredded mozzarella
- A pinch of salt
- Filling:
- 2 pounds ground pork
- ½ cup water
- ⅓ cup pureed onion
- ¾ tsp allspice
- 1 cup cooked and mashed cauliflower
- 1 tbsp ground sage
- 2 tbsp butter

Directions

1. Preheat your oven to 350°F.
2. Whisk together all crust ingredients in a bowl. Make two balls out of the mixture and refrigerate for 10 minutes. Combine the water, meat, and salt, in a pot over medium heat. Cook for about 15 minutes, place the meat along with the other ingredients in a bowl. Mix with your hands to combine.
3. Roll out the pie crusts and place one at the bottom of a greased pie pan. Spread the filling over the crust. Top with the other coat. Bake in the oven for 50 minutes then serve.

Nutritional Value: Calories 485, Fat: 41g, Net Carbs: 4g, Protein: 29g

331. Easy Zucchini Beef Lasagna

Preparation Time: 1 hour 15 minutes
Serves: 4

Ingredients

- 1 lb ground beef
- 2 large zucchinis, sliced lengthwise
- 3 cloves garlic
- 1 medium white onion, finely chopped
- 3 tomatoes, chopped
- Salt and black pepper to taste
- 2 tsp sweet paprika
- 1 tsp dried thyme
- 1 tsp dried basil
- 1 cup shredded mozzarella cheese
- 1 tbsp olive oil
- Cooking spray

Directions

1. Preheat the oven to 370°F and lightly grease a baking dish with cooking spray.
2. Lay the zucchini slices on a paper towel and sprinkle with salt. Set aside.
3. Heat the olive oil in a skillet and cook the beef for 4 minutes while breaking any lumps as you stir. Top with onion, garlic, tomatoes, salt, paprika, and pepper. Stir and continue cooking for 5 minutes.
4. Then, back to the zucchinis, use a paper towel to blot out any liquid on it and lay ⅓ of the slices in the baking dish. Top with ⅓ of the beef mixture and repeat the layering process two more times with the same quantities.
5. Finally, sprinkle the mozzarella cheese on top and tuck the baking dish in the oven. Bake for 35 minutes. Remove the lasagna and let it rest for 10 minutes before serving.

Nutritional Value: Calories 344, Fat 17.8g, Net Carbs 2.9g, Protein 40.4g

332. Pork Casserole

Preparation Time: 38 minutes
Serves: 4

Ingredients

- 1 lb ground pork
- 1 large yellow squash, thinly sliced
- Salt and black pepper to taste
- 1 clove garlic, minced
- 4 green onions, chopped
- 1 cup chopped cremini mushrooms
- 1 (15 oz) can diced tomatoes
- ½ cup pork rinds, crushed
- ¼ cup chopped parsley
- 1 cup cottage cheese
- 1 cup Mexican cheese blend
- 3 tbsp olive oil

- ⅓ cup water

Directions

1. Preheat the oven to 370°F.
2. Heat the olive oil in a skillet over medium heat, add the pork, season it with salt and pepper, and cook for 3 minutes or until no longer pink. Stir occasionally while breaking any lumps apart.
3. Add the garlic, half of the green onions, mushrooms, and 2 tablespoons of pork rinds. Continue cooking for 3 minutes. Stir in the tomatoes, half of the parsley, and water. Cook further for 3 minutes, and then turn the heat off.
4. Mix the remaining parsley, cottage cheese, and Mexican cheese blend. Set aside. Sprinkle the bottom of a baking dish with 3 tablespoons of pork rinds; top with half of the squash and a season of salt, 2/3 of the pork mixture, and the cheese mixture. Repeat the layering process a second time to exhaust the ingredients.
5. Cover the baking dish with foil and put in the oven to bake for 20 minutes. After, remove the foil and brown the top of the casserole with the broiler side of the oven for 2 minutes. Remove the dish when ready and serve the casserole warm.

Nutritional Value: Calories 495, Fat 29g, Net Carbs 2.7g, Protein 36.5g

333. Spicy Spinach Pinwheel Steaks

Preparation Time: 42 minutes
Serves: 6

Ingredients

- Cooking spray
- 1 ½ lb flank steak
- Pink salt and black pepper to season
- 1 cup crumbled feta cheese
- ½ loose cup baby spinach
- 1 jalapeño, chopped
- ¼ cup chopped basil leaves

Directions

1. Preheat oven to 400°F and grease a baking sheet with cooking spray.
2. Wrap the steak in plastic wrap, place on a flat surface, and gently run a rolling pin over to flatten. Take off the wraps. Sprinkle with half of the feta cheese, top with spinach, jalapeno, basil leaves, and the remaining cheese. Roll the steak over on the stuffing and secure with toothpicks.
3. Place in the greased baking sheet and cook for 30 minutes, flipping once until nicely browned on the outside and the cheese melted within. Cool for 3 minutes, slice into pinwheels and serve with thyme sautéed mixed veggies.

Nutritional Value: Calories 490, Fat 41g, Net Carbs 2g, Protein 28g

334. Grilled Lamb on Lemony Sauce

Preparation Time: 25 minutes
Serves: 4

Ingredients

- 8 lamb chops
- 2 tbsp favorite spice mix
- 1 tsp olive oil
- Sauce:
- ¼ cup olive oil
- 1 tsp red pepper flakes
- 2 tbsp lemon juice
- 2 tbsp fresh mint
- 3 garlic cloves, pressed
- 2 tbsp lemon zest
- ¼ cup parsley
- ½ tsp smoked paprika

Directions

1. Rub the lamb with the oil and sprinkle with the seasoning. Preheat the grill to medium. Grill the lamb chops for about 3 minutes per side. Whisk together the sauce ingredients. Serve the lamb chops with the sauce.

Nutritional Value: Calories 392, Fat: 31g, Net Carbs: 1g, Protein: 29g

335. White Wine Lamb Chops

Preparation Time: 1 hour and 25 minutes
Serves: 6

Ingredients

- 6 lamb chops
- 1 tbsp sage
- 1 tsp thyme
- 1 onion, sliced
- 3 garlic cloves, minced
- 2 tbsp olive oil
- ½ cup white wine
- Salt and black pepper, to taste

Directions

1. Heat the olive oil in a pan. Add onion and garlic and cook for 3 minutes, until soft. Rub the sage and thyme over the lamb chops. Cook the lamb for about 3 minutes per side. Set aside.
2. Pour the white wine and 1 cup of water into the pan, bring the mixture to a boil. Cook until the liquid is reduced by half. Add the chops in the pan, reduce the heat, and let simmer for 1 hour.

Nutritional Value: Calories 397, Fat: 30g, Net Carbs: 4.3g, Protein: 16g

336. Parsley Beef Burgers

Preparation Time: 25 minutes
Serves: 6

Ingredients

- 2 pounds ground beef
- 1 tbsp onion flakes
- ¾ almond flour
- ¼ cup beef broth
- 1 tbsp chopped parsley
- 1 tbsp Worcestershire sauce

Directions

1. Combine all ingredients in a bowl. Mix well with your hands and make 6 patties out of the mixture. Arrange on a lined baking sheet. Bake at 370°F, for about 18 minutes, until nice and crispy.

Nutritional Value: Calories 354, Fat: 28g, Net Carbs: 2.5g, Protein: 27g

337. Crusted Pork Loin

Preparation time: 10 minutes
Cooking time: 1 hour and 10 minutes
Servings: 8

Ingredients:

- 3 tablespoons mustard
- 2 tablespoons ghee, melted
- 1 tablespoon stevia
- ¼ cup dill, chopped
- 3 green onions, chopped
- 1 tablespoon lemon peel, grated
- A pinch of salt and black pepper
- 1 pork loin, boneless

Directions:

1. In a bowl, combine the ghee with the mustard and stevia and whisk.
2. In another bowl, mix the lemon peel with the dill and spring onions and stir.
3. Season the pork loin with salt and pepper, brush with the mustard mix and spread the spring onions all over.
4. Place the pork loin in a roasting pan, introduce in the oven and cook at 375 degrees F for 1 hour and 10 minutes.
5. Slice, divide between plates and serve with a side salad.
6. Enjoy!

Nutritional Value:calories 221, fat 3, fiber 5, carbs 14, protein 20

338. Glazed Pork Chops

Preparation time: 10 minutes
Cooking time: 12 minutes
Servings: 4

Ingredients:

- 4 pork chops, bone-in
- 2 tablespoons stevia
- 1 tablespoon balsamic vinegar
- 4 tablespoons ghee, melted
- 4 ounces baby spinach

Directions:

1. Heat up a pan with the ghee over medium-high heat, add pork chops, stevia and vinegar, toss, cook for 1 minute, introduce in preheated broiler and cook over medium-high heat for 4 minutes on each side.
2. Divide the pork chops between plates, heat up the pan with the glaze over medium heat, add spinach, cook for about 3 minutes, divide between plates and serve.
3. Enjoy!

Nutritional Value:calories 321, fat 13, fiber 3, carbs 12, protein 20

339. Pork Meatballs

Preparation time: 10 minutes
Cooking time: 12 minutes
Servings: 4

Ingredients:

- ½ cup carrots, grated
- ¼ cup mint, chopped
- 3 garlic cloves, minced
- 1 shallot, chopped
- 1 lemongrass stalk, chopped
- 1 pound pork, ground
- 1 teaspoon hot sauce
- 1 tablespoon cilantro, chopped
- 2 tablespoons olive oil

Directions:

1. In a bowl, combine the carrots with mint, garlic, shallots, lemongrass, pork, hot sauce and cilantro, stir and shape medium meatballs out of this mix.
2. Heat up a pan with the oil over medium-high heat, add the meatballs, cook them for 6 minutes on each side, divide between plates and serve with a side salad.
3. Enjoy!

Nutritional Value:calories 261, fat 13, fiber 7, carbs 13, protein 14

340. Pork and Asparagus

Preparation time: 10 minutes
Cooking time: 20 minutes
Servings: 4

Ingredients:

- 4 pork loin chops, boneless
- 2 tablespoons tarragon, chopped
- A pinch of salt and black pepper
- 1 pound asparagus, trimmed and halved
- 2 tablespoons olive oil
- 1 bunch green onions, chopped
- ½ cup veggie stock

1 tablespoon mustard

Directions:

1. Heat up a pan with the oil over medium-high heat, add pork loin chops, season with salt and pepper, sprinkle tarragon, cook for 4 minutes on each side and transfer to a bowl.
2. Heat up the same pan over medium heat, add the asparagus and green onions, stir and cook for 3 minutes.
3. Add mustard and stock, stir and cook for 2 minutes more.
4. Return the pork to the pan, cook for 4 minutes more, divide between plates and serve.
5. Enjoy!

Nutritional Value:calories 300, fat 9, fiber 2, carbs 14, protein 20

341. Easy Pulled Pork

Preparation time: 10 minutes
Cooking time: 2 hours and 30 minutes
Servings: 4

Ingredients:

1 pound pork tenderloin, sliced

- 2 tablespoons chili powder
- ½ cup tomato paste
- 2 tablespoons mustard
- 2 tablespoons olive oil
- 2 tablespoon balsamic vinegar

A pinch of salt and black pepper

Directions:

1. Grease a roasting pan with the oil and add pork tenderloin slices inside.
2. Add chili powder, tomato paste, mustard, oil, vinegar, salt and pepper, toss well, cover the dish, introduce in the oven and cook at 350 degrees F for 2 hours and 30 minutes.
3. Shred the meat, divide it between plates and serve with a side salad.
4. Enjoy!

Nutritional Value:calories 264, fat 11, fiber 8, carbs 12, protein 20

342. Delicious Pork Tenderloin

Preparation time: 10 minutes
Cooking time: 37 minutes
Servings: 6

Ingredients:

- 2 pounds pork tenderloin
- 2 lemons, sliced
- 4 teaspoons olive oil
- A pinch of salt and black pepper
- 2 garlic cloves, minced
- 2 bunches Swiss chard, chopped

Directions:

1. Arrange pork tenderloin on a lined baking sheet, add the oil, salt, pepper, garlic and lemon slices, toss everything, introduce in the oven and cook at 450 degrees F for 30 minutes.
2. Add the Swiss chard, toss, introduce in the oven, cook for 7 minutes, slice the pork loin, divide everything between plates and serve.
3. Enjoy!

Nutritional Value:calories 312, fat 11, fiber 5, carbs 15, protein 18

343. Slow Cooked Ribs

Preparation time: 10 minutes
Cooking time: 4 hours
Servings: 4

Ingredients:

- 2 pounds baby back ribs
- A pinch of salt and black pepper
- 1 cup tomato sauce
- 1 tablespoon balsamic vinegar
- 2 garlic cloves, minced
- 1 teaspoon sesame seeds

Directions:

1. In your slow cooker, combine the ribs with salt, pepper, tomato sauce, vinegar and garlic, toss, cover and cook on High for 4 hours.
2. Divide the ribs between plates, sprinkle sesame seeds all over and serve.
3. Enjoy!

Nutritional Value:calories 294, fat 11, fiber 2, carbs 16, protein 30

344. Pork Chops and Apricot Sauce

Preparation time: 10 minutes
Cooking time: 15 minutes
Servings: 4

Ingredients:

- 4 pork chops, bone-in
- 1 tablespoon olive oil
- ½ cup veggie stock
- ¼ cup keto apricot jam
- 3 tablespoons mustard
- A pinch of salt and black pepper

Directions:

1. Heat up a pan with the oil over medium-high heat, add pork chops, cook them for 6 minutes on each side and divide between plates.
2. Heat up the same pan over medium heat, add the stock, jam, mustard, salt and pepper, stir, cook for 3 minutes, drizzle over the pork chops and serve.
3. Enjoy!

Nutritional Value:calories 321, fat 7, fiber 5, carbs 14, protein 20

345. Vietnamese Salad

Preparation time: 10 minutes
Cooking time: 10 minutes

Servings: 4

Ingredients:

- 3 tablespoons coconut aminos
- 2 tablespoons stevia
- 2 tablespoons white vinegar
- 1 tablespoon olive oil
- 1 pound pork, ground
- 1 jalapeno, chopped
- 1 romaine lettuce heart, sliced
- ¼ cup mint, chopped
- 3 garlic cloves, minced

Directions:

1. Heat up a pan with the oil over medium-high heat, add the pork, stir and cook for 5 minutes.
2. Add the coconut aminos, stevia, vinegar, jalapeno, mint and garlic, stir and cook for 5 minutes more.
3. Put the lettuce in a bowl; add the pork mix, toss and serve.
4. Enjoy!

Nutritional Value:calories 342, fat 12, fiber 4, carbs 13, protein 28

346. Grilled Pork and Mango Salsa

Preparation time: 10 minutes
Cooking time: 6 minutes
Servings: 4

Ingredients:

- 4 pork loin chops, boneless
- 2 tablespoons olive oil
- 1 teaspoon chili powder
- A pinch of salt and black pepper
- 1 mango, peeled and chopped
- 1 tomato, cubed
- 1 teaspoon balsamic vinegar

Directions:

1. Heat up a pan with half of the oil over medium-high heat, add pork chops, season with salt, pepper and chili powder, cook them for 3 minutes on each side and divide between plates.
2. In a bowl, combine the mango with the tomato and vinegar, toss, divide next to the pork and serve.
3. Enjoy!

Nutritional Value:calories 290, fat 12, fiber 4, carbs 14, protein 8

347. Pork Roast and Cabbage

Preparation time: 10 minutes
Cooking time: 32 minutes
Servings: 4

Ingredients:

- 2 tablespoons olive oil
- 1 pork tenderloin
- ¼ cup tomato sauce
- 1 red cabbage head, shredded
- 4 green onions, chopped
- 2 tablespoons balsamic vinegar
- 1 jalapeno, chopped

Directions:

1. Heat up a pan with half of the oil over medium-high heat, add pork and brown for 3 minutes on each side.
2. Transfer to a roasting pan, brush with the tomato sauce, introduce in the oven, roast at 450 degrees F for 17 minutes, slice and divide between plates.
3. Heat up a pan over medium-high heat, add the cabbage, green onions, jalapeno and vinegar, toss, cook for 9-10 minutes, divide next to the pork roast and serve.
4. Enjoy!

Nutritional Value:calories 300, fat 12, fiber 9, carbs 18, protein 30

348. Pork and Apples

Preparation time: 10 minutes
Cooking time: 1 hour and 10 minutes
Servings: 8

Ingredients:

- 1 pork loin, boneless
- 1 and ½ teaspoon red pepper, crushed
- 2 tablespoons olive oil
- 3 apples, cored and cut into wedges

- 2 yellow onions, cut into wedges
- 2 tablespoons ghee, melted
- ¼ cup apple vinegar
- 2 teaspoons cinnamon powder
- 3 star anise
- 5 garlic slices, chopped
- 1 tablespoon parsley, chopped

Directions:

1. Put the pork in a roasting pan, add red pepper, oil, apples, onions, ghee, vinegar, cinnamon, star anise, garlic and parsley, toss, introduce in the oven and cook at 400 degrees F for 1 hour and 10 minutes.
2. Slice the roast, divide between plates, add apples mix on the side and serve.
3. Enjoy!

Nutritional Value:calories 321, fat 10, fiber 4, carbs 13, protein 20

349. Fried Pork Chops

Preparation time: 10 minutes
Cooking time: 10 minutes
Servings: 4

Ingredients:

- 1 cup olive oil
- 1 pound pork chops, boneless
- A pinch of salt and black pepper
- ½ cup coconut flour

Directions:

1. Season pork chops with salt and pepper and dredge in coconut flour.
2. Heat up a pan with the oil over medium-high heat, add pork chops and cook them for 5 minutes on each side.
3. Divide between plates and serve with a side salad.
4. Enjoy!

Nutritional Value:calories 299, fat 4, fiber 6, carbs 14, protein 18

350. Pork Chops and Arugula Mix

Preparation time: 10 minutes
Cooking time: 12 minutes
Servings: 4

Ingredients:

- 4 pork chops, bone-in
- A pinch of salt and black pepper
- ¼ cup capers
- 3 garlic cloves, minced
- 1 cup basil, chopped
- 1 cup parsley, chopped
- 5 cups baby arugula
- 1 cup olive oil+ 1 tablespoon
- Juice of 1 lemon

Directions:

1. In a blender, combine the capers with garlic, basil, parsley and 1-cup arugula and pulse well.
2. Spread this over the pork chops, heat up a pan with 1-cup oil over medium-high heat, add pork chops, cook them for 6 minutes on each side and divide between plates.
3. In a bowl, combine the rest of the rest of the arugula with the remaining oil and lemon juice, toss, add next to the pork chops and serve.
4. Enjoy!

Nutritional Value:calories 311, fat 4, fiber 8, carbs 12, protein 7

351. Meatball Soup

Preparation time: 10 minutes
Cooking time: 10 minutes
Servings: 4

Ingredients:

- 1 pound pork, ground
- 3 garlic cloves, minced
- 2 green onions, chopped
- 1-inch ginger, grated
- 1-quart chicken stock
- 1 cup spinach, torn
- A pinch of salt and black pepper

Directions:

1. In a bowl, combine the pork with garlic, green onions, ginger, salt and pepper, stir, shape medium meatballs out of this mix, introduce them in preheated broiler and

cook for 5 minutes.

2. Heat up a pot with the stock over medium-high heat, add the meatballs, salt, pepper and the spinach, toss, cook for 5 minutes more, ladle into bowls and serve.
3. Enjoy!

Nutritional Value:calories 300, fat 3, fiber 7, carbs 12, protein 14

352. Pork Chops and Peperonata

Preparation time: 10 minutes
Cooking time: 10 minutes
Servings: 4

Ingredients:

- 5 teaspoons olive oil
- 4 pork loin chops, bone-in
- A pinch of salt and black pepper
- 1 cup red onion, chopped
- 4 garlic cloves, minced
- 1 poblano chili, chopped
- 1 red bell pepper, chopped
- 1 yellow bell pepper, chopped
- 3 tablespoons parsley, chopped
- 2 tablespoons capers
- 3 tablespoons red vinegar
- ¼ teaspoon red pepper, crushed

Directions:

1. Heat up a pan with half of the oil over medium-high heat, add pork chops, season with salt and pepper, cook for 3 minutes on each side and divide between plates.
2. Heat up the same pan with the rest of the oil over medium-high heat, add poblano, onion, garlic and bell peppers and cook them for 4 minutes.
3. Add capers, vinegar, parsley and crushed red pepper, stir, cook for 1 minute more, divide next to the pork chops and serve.
4. Enjoy!

Nutritional Value:calories 265, fat 11, fiber 4, carbs 14, protein 20

353. Pork Tenderloin and Pears

Preparation time: 10 minutes
Cooking time: 28 minutes
Servings: 4

Ingredients:

- 3 tablespoons olive oil
- 2 garlic cloves, minced
- 1 tablespoon thyme, chopped
- 1 and ½ pounds pork tenderloin
- 3 shallots, cut into medium wedges
- 3 pears, cored and quartered
- 4 tablespoons ghee, melted
- 1 and ½ cups chicken stock
- ¾ cup pear juice, unsweetened

Directions:

1. In a bowl, mix the pears, shallots, oil, garlic, thyme, and toss.
2. Heat up a pan over medium-high heat, add the shallots and the tenderloin, brown for 7 minutes and transfer them to a baking dish.
3. Heat up the same pan over medium-high heat, add pears, stir, cook for 4 minutes and transfer to the baking dish as well.
4. Introduce in the oven, cook at 425 degrees F for 10 minutes and divide between plates.
5. Put the ghee in the same pan, heat it up, add stock and pear juice, stir, cook for 7 minutes, drizzle over the pork, shallots and pears and serve.
6. Enjoy!

Nutritional Value:calories 351, fat 3, fiber 6, carbs 15, protein 20

354. Lamb Cutlets with Garlic Sauce

Preparation Time: 40 MIN
Serve: 10

Ingredients:

- 4 lbs. lamb cutlets
- 1 small head of garlic, cloves peeled
- 2 Tbsp apple cider vinegar
- 1/2 cup water
- 1/4 cup extra-virgin olive oil

- Pinch salt and black ground pepper to taste

Directions:

1. Crush the garlic cloves thoroughly in a mortar. In a bowl, add the vinegar and water and mix it well with the crushed garlic. Set aside.
2. In a large frying pan, pour the olive oil and fry the lamb cutlets until nicely brown.
3. Add the garlic mixture and let it cook gently for about 10 minutes.
4. Shake the frying pan to spread the garlic mixture evenly over the lamb.
5. Season with salt and black pepper to taste. Serve.

Nutritional Value:

Calories 416
Total Fats 28g
Net Carbs: 0.16g
Protein 36g
Fiber: 0.1g

355. Hot Mexican Meatballs

Preparation Time: 35 MIN
Serve: 6

Ingredients:

- 1 lb. ground beef (92% lean
- 4 oz. white onion, minced
- 4 oz. Monterey Jack cheese with spicy peppers
- 1 Tbsp butter
- 3 cloves garlic
- 1 1 tsp chili powder
- 1 tsp ground cumin
- 1 tsp ground coriander
- 1 egg
- Sea salt and freshly ground pepper to taste

Directions:

1. Preheat oven to 350 degrees F.
2. In a frying pan, sauté onions in butter until translucent. Set aside
3. Shred and mince the Monterey Jack cheese with spicy peppers. Set aside.
4. In a mixing bowl, whisk the egg with ricotta cheese. Add the spices, salt, and pepper and mix.
5. Add onions and minced Monterey Jack cheese with spicy peppers. Mix well.
6. Add beef and mix until all ingredients are combined.
7. Roll the meat mixture into a ball.
8. Place the meatballs on a cookie sheet, and bake about 20 minutes.
9. Serve hot.

Nutritional Value:

Calories 321
Total Fats 25g
Net Carbs: 2.9g
Protein 19g
Fiber: 0.9g

356. Baked Cheesy Meatballs

Preparation Time: 35 MIN
Serve: 6

Ingredients:

- 1 lb. ground beef (lean
- 2 white onion
- 1 cup grated Cheddar cheese
- 4 oz. Gruyere cheese
- 1 egg
    - tsp nutmeg
    - tsp allspice
- Sea salt and freshly black pepper to taste
- Butter for greasing

Directions:

1. Preheat oven to 350 F.
2. In a greased frying pan, sauté onions until translucent. Remove from heat, and let cool.
3. In a food processor mince the Gruyere cheese. Set aside.
4. In a mixing bowl, whisk the egg with grated Cheddar cheese. Add the spices, salt, and pepper and mix.
5. Add in onions and Gruyere cheese. Mix well until smooth.
6. Add the beef and mix until all ingredients

are combined well.

7. Divide meat mixture and roll each piece into a ball.
8. Place the meatballs on a cookie sheet, and bake in preheated oven about 20 minutes. Serve hot.

Nutritional Value:

Calories 385
Total Fats 29g
Net Carbs: 4.7g
Protein 25g
Fiber 0.9g

357. Tangy Asian Short Ribs

Preparation Time: 20 MIN
Serve: 3

Ingredients:

- 1 ½ lb. short ribs

For the rub:

- 1 tsp ginger, grated
- 1 clove of garlic, minced
- ½ tsp onion powder
- ½ tsp red pepper flakes
- ¼ tsp cardamom
- ½ tsp sesame seed
- 1 tsp salt

For the marinade:

- ¼ low-sodium soy sauce
- 2 tbsp fish sauce
- 2 tbsp rice vinegar

Directions:

1. Whisk all the ingredients for the marinade and pour it over the ribs. Allow the ribs to marinate for an hour.
2. Mix all the ingredients for the rubbing
3. Roll marinated ribs in the rubbing and making sure to evenly coat.
4. Heat the grill and cook for 4-5 minutes on each side.

Nutritional Value:

Calories 417
Total Fats 31.8g
Net Carbs: 0.9g
Protein 29.5g

358. Beanless Chili con Carne

Preparation Time: 60 MIN
Serve: 5

Ingredients:

- 1 lb Ground beef
- 1 Green pepper, chopped
- 1 Onion, chopped
- 2 tbsp Curry powder
- 2 tbsp Cumin
- 1 tbsp Coconut oil
- 1 tsp Onion powder
- 1 tsp Black pepper
- 1 lb Italian sausage, spicy
- 1 Yellow pepper, chopped
- 16 oz Tomato sauce
- 2 tbsp Chili powder
- 1 tbsp Garlic, diced
- 1 tbsp Butter
- 1 tsp Salt

Directions:

1. Heat oil and butter in a pan, heat thoroughly and add garlic, onions and bell peppers. Cook for 3 minutes then add beef and sausage.
2. Cook for 5 minutes until browned then add onion and chili powder. Stir to combine and add tomato sauce. Lower flame and cook for 20 minutes.
3. Add cumin and curry, stir and cook for 45 minutes or until chili thickens to your liking.
4. Serve.

Nutritional Value:

Calories 415
Total Fats 25g
Net Carbs: 6g
Protein 146g
Fiber 51

359. Delicious Meaty Meatloaf

Preparation Time: 1 HR 20 MIN
Serve: 4

Ingredients:

- 7 oz prosciutto, sliced thin

- 7 oz provolone, sliced thin
- 2 cups baby spinach
- 1 cup tomato sauce
- ½ cup tomato paste
- 1 tbsp apple cider vinegar
- 4 tbsp stevia
- 1 lb. ground pork
- ½ onion, chopped
- ½ cup bell pepper, chopped
- 2 cloves of garlic, minced
- ¼ cup parmesan cheese, grated
- 2 organic eggs
- 1 tsp oregano, dried
- 1 tsp basil, dried
- Salt and pepper to taste
- 1 tbsp butter

Directions:

1. Set the oven at 350 F.
2. Melt the butter in a pan over medium fire. Throw in the baby spinach and season with salt and pepper. Cook until the leaves wilt.
3. In a bowl combine the tomato sauce and paste, along with the apple cider and stevia. Stir and set aside.
4. In another bowl, combine the pork, onion, bell pepper, garlic, parmesan, and herbs. Mix well.
5. Lay a parchment paper about 10 inches and spread the meat on top. Arrange the prosciutto on top followed by the spinach and provolone to create a meatloaf. Seal sides.
6. Place the meatloaf in a loaf pan lined with foil and pour the tomato sauce on top.
7. Bake in the oven for a little over an hour or until the inner temperature reaches 165 F.

Nutritional Value:

Calories 516
Total Fats 37g
Net Carbs: 8g
Protein 37g

360. Pulled Pork Shoulder

Preparation Time: 5 HR 10 MIN
Serve: 4

Ingredients:

- 2 lbs. whole pork shoulder
- 2 tsp paprika
- 1 tsp salt
- 1 tsp pepper
- ½ tsp cumin
- ¼ tsp cinnamon

Directions:

1. Set the oven at 450 F.
2. Score the skin of the pork with a sharp knife.
3. Combine all of the ingredients of the rub and then smother it over the pork.
4. Place in a baking dish and cook in the oven for 30 mins.
5. Take off from the oven and cover the dish with a foil.
6. Lower the heat to 350 F and place the covered dish in the oven to cook for another 4 hours and 30 mins.
7. Take the pork out of the oven and pull using forks. Serve with a low-carb BBQ sauce.

Nutritional Value:

Calories 534
Total Fats 39g
Net Carbs: 0.9g
Protein 42.4g | Fiber: 0.5g

361. Slow Roast Lamb

Preparation Time: 7 HR 15 MIN
Serve: 3

Ingredients:

- 1 lb. leg of lamb
- 2 tbsp Dijon mustard
- 3 cloves of garlic
- 3 sprigs of thyme
- ½ tsp rosemary, dried
- 3 pcs mint leaves
- 1 tbsp liquid stevia

- ¼ cup olive oil
- Salt and pepper to taste

Directions:

1. Cut large slits on the leg of lamb and place in a slow cooker.
2. Combine the mustard, olive oil and stevia and then rub over the lamb. Season with salt and pepper.
3. Inset the garlic and rosemary of the slits.
4. Cover and cook on low for 7 hours.
5. Add the mint leaves and thyme after 7 hours and cook for another hour.

Nutritional Value:

Calories 413
Total Fats 35.2g
Net Carbs: 0.5g
Protein 26g

362. Lamb Curry & Spinach

Preparation Time: 8 HR 25 MIN
Serve: 5

Ingredients:

- 1/3 cup Coconut or olive oil
- 3 chopped yellow onions
- 4 cloves garlic, peeled and minced
- 2cm piece of ginger, peeled and grated
- 2 tsp Ground cumin
- 1 ½ tsp Cayenne pepper
- 1½ tsp Ground turmeric
- 2 cups Beef stock, high quality
- 53 oz Leg of lamb cut into 2cm cubes
- Salt
- 6 cups Baby spinach
- 1 1/5 cups Plain full-fat yogurt

Directions:

1. Place oil into a large skillet over medium to high heat.
2. Add chopped onions and garlic into the skillet and sauté until brown, 4 - 5 minutes.
3. Then add ginger, cayenne pepper, turmeric, and cumin to the skillet. Stir and let the flavor develop for 30 seconds.
4. Pour in beef stock and scrape the browned bits off the bottom of the skillet.
5. Once the stock comes to a boil, take the skillet off the heat.
6. Place the lamb in your slow cooker. Add the contents of skillet and 1 tbsp of salt.
7. Cover the slow cooker with the lid and cook on high for 4 hours or low for 8 hours.
8. 5 minutes before the slow cooker is done, stir the spinach into the dish wait for it to wilt.
9. Before serving, stir in the yogurt.
10. Serve and enjoy.

Nutritional Value:

Calories 304
Total Fats 16.32g
Net Carbs: 5.5g
Protein 32.85g

363. Cheeseburger Casserole

Preparation Time: 45 MIN
Serve: 6

Ingredients:

- 3 Bacon slices
- 1 ¼ cups Cauliflower
- ½ tsp Garlic powder
- 2 tbsp Ketchup, no sugar
- 2 tbsp Mayonnaise
- 4 oz Cheddar cheese
- 1 lb Ground beef
- ½ cup Almond Flour
- 1 tbsp Psyllium Husk Powder
- ½ tsp Onion powder
- 1 tbsp Dijon mustard
- 3 Eggs
- Salt

Black pepper

Directions:

1. Set oven to 350 F.
2. Place cauliflower into a processor and pulse until fine like rice. Add remaining dry ingredients except for cheese.
3. Add beef and bacon in processor until

combined and pasty.

4. Heat skillet and cook meat for 8 minutes then add to dry ingredients in a bowl along with half of cheese. Stir to combine and line a baking dish with parchment paper.
5. Press mixture into dish and top with leftover cheese. Bake for 30 minutes on top rack.
6. Take from heat, cool and slice.
7. Serve.

Nutritional Value:

Calories 478
Total Fats 35.5g
Net Carbs: 3.6g
Protein 32.2g
Fiber 3.3g

364. Leftover Meat Salad

Preparation Time: 10 MIN
Serve: 1

Ingredients:

- 1 cup left-over meat (chicken or pork, shredded
- 2 cups iceberg lettuce
- 1 tbsp mayonnaise
- 2 tbsp sour cream
- Salt and pepper to taste

Directions:

1. Whisk the mayo and sour cream in a salad bowl.
2. Add the lettuce to the bowl along with the shredded meat.
3. Season with salt and pepper and toss.
4. Serve immediately.

Nutritional Value:

Calories 252
Total Fats 53.6g
Net Carbs: 6.4g
Protein 15g | Fiber: 1.2g

365. Asian-Flavored Steak

Preparation Time: 55 MIN
Serve: 4

Ingredients:

- 4 pcs steak
- For the glaze marinade:
- ½ tsp sesame oil
- ½ tsp chili flakes
- 1 tsp ginger, grated
- ½ cup low-sodium soy sauce
- 2 pcs green onions

Directions:

1. Combine all the ingredients for the marinade in a large bowl and whisk well.
2. Place the steaks in the bowl and marinate for at least 45 minutes.
3. Heat the grill on high and cook the steaks for 5 minutes on each side, or depending on your liking.

Nutritional Value:

Calories 531
Total Fats 13.7g
Net Carbs: 4.7g
Protein 94.4g

366. Stir Fried Beef

Preparation Time: 25 MIN
Serve: 2

Ingredients:

- 1 tbsp olive oil
- 12 oz sirloin steak, cut into strips
- 1 onion, chopped
- 2 cloves of garlic, crushed
- 1 cup cherry tomatoes, quartered
- 1 red bell pepper chopped
- 2 tsp ginger, grated
- 4 tbsp organic apple cider vinegar
- Salt and pepper to taste

Directions:

1. Drizzle the olive oil on a non-stick pan and heat over medium fire.
2. Season the sirloin with salt and pepper and sear in the hot oil for 4 minutes on each side.
3. While waiting, whisk the ginger and apple cider together and pour over the steak in the pan.

4. Add the chopped onion, garlic, bell pepper, and cherry tomatoes with the beef and reduce the fire to low.
5. Cover the pan and allow to simmer for 5 minutes.
6. Turn off the heat and then allow the beef to rest for 5 minutes before serving.

Nutritional Value:

Calories 359
Total Fats 19g
Net Carbs: 10g
Protein 39

367. Pizza on Lettuce Rolls

Preparation Time: 15 MIN
Serve: 2

Ingredients:

- 6 pcs Romaine lettuce leaves
- 3 tbsp mayonnaise
- 6 slices of provolone cheese
- 6 slices salami
- 6 slices pepperoni
- 6 slice ham

Directions:

1. Lay the lettuce leaves on a serving plate.
2. Spread the mayonnaise on top of the leaves and layer with the cheese, salami, pepperoni, and ham.
3. Carefully roll the leaves and secure with a toothpick.
4. Serve and immediately.

Nutritional Value:

Calories 592
Total Fats 46g
Net Carbs: 6g
Protein 37g
Fiber: 1.1g

368. Spicy Bacon-Wrapped Dogs

Preparation Time: 15 MIN
Serve: 2

Ingredients:

- 1 tbsp ghee
- 1 onion, chopped
- 1 red bell pepper, chopped
- 1 pc jalapeno, seeds removed and chopped
- 4 pcs beef hot dogs
- 4 bacon strips
- 3 cheddar cheese slices

Directions:

1. Heat the ghee in a non-stick pan over medium fire.
2. Add the onions, bell peppers, and chopped jalapeno and sauté for 4 minutes. Remove from the pan and set aside
3. Wrap the hotdog with bacon strips and secure with a toothpick. And cook in the same pan where the peppers were cooked.
4. Fry the dogs for 5 minutes or until crispy on both sides.
5. Lay the cheese slices on top of the cooking hotdogs and cover for 30 seconds to cook, or until the cheese melts.
6. Serve the hot dogs with the sautéed peppers on the side.

Nutritional Value:

Calories 349
Total Fats 29g
Net Carbs: 8g
Protein 14g

369. Savoury Mince

Preparation Time: 25 MIN
Serve: 10

Ingredients:

- 4 tbsp coconut oil
    - lbs beef
- 2 onions finely diced
- 4 cups mixed Vegetables
- 4 carrots finely grated
- 1 packet gluten-free gravy
- ½ cup tomato paste
- 1 cup chicken stock

Directions:

1. Heat coconut oil in a pan and fry chopped onion, beef mince with and tomato paste and fry.
2. Add chopped vegetables and grated carrot to the cooked mince.
3. Continue to cook on a low heat until the vegetables are well cooked.
4. If your mixture seems to be drying out, keep adding chicken stock to keep at the right consistency.
5. The longer you cook this mixture, the more the flavors will infuse through the mince.
6. Add gluten-free gravy.

Nutritional Value:

Calories 298
Total Fats 12.1g
Net Carbs: 14g
Protein 32.7g
Fiber: 5.3g

370. Spring Roll in a Bowl

Preparation Time: 25 MIN
Serve: 12

Ingredients:

- lbs pork mince
- cups cabbage, shredded finely
- cup grated carrot
- 2 cups grated baby marrows
- 1 cup mushrooms
- tbsp coconut oil
- 1/2 cup soya sauce
- 1 cup chicken stock
- 2 tsp vinegar
- cloves garlic, minced
- 4 tsp grated ginger
- 4 finely sliced spring onions
- ½ cup toasted sesame seeds
- 1 hard-boiled egg, chopped

Directions:

1. Heat the coconut oil and fry the garlic, spring onions, ginger.
2. Add the pork mince and brown.
3. Add the cabbage and carrot to the pot and toss to combine. Stir in the soy sauce.
4. Cover and cook until the vegetables are soft, about 15 minutes.
5. Dish up, add chopped hard-boiled egg over each of the bowls.
6. Garnish with sesame seeds once you have dished up.

Nutritional Value:

Calories 219
Total Fats 9.7g
Net Carbs: 32.6g
Protein 3.2g

371. Homemade Meatballs

Preparation Time: 25 MIN
Serve: 12

Ingredients:

- lbs ground beef
- 1 whole egg
- ½ cup almond flour
- cloves of garlic, minced
- 1 tsp oregano, dried
- 1 tsp thyme, dried
- 1 cup mozzarella cheese, shredded
- Salt and pepper to taste
- ½ cup homemade marinara sauce

Directions:

1. Preheat oven to 450 F.
2. In a large bowl, place the ground beef, egg, almond flour, garlic, oregano, thyme, and season with salt and pepper. Also, add the cheese.
3. Using your hands, mix all the ingredients together; making sure that everything is well combined.
4. Create 25 pcs of meatballs and lay them on a baking sheet lined with parchment paper.
5. Cook in the oven to cook for 15 minutes or until golden brown.
6. Serve the meatballs with marinara sauce.

Nutritional Value:

Calories 117

Total Fats 9.3g
Net Carbs: 0.9g
Protein 7g

372. Beef Shred Salad

Preparation Time: 10 MIN
Serve: 2

Ingredients:

- cups beef, shredded
- 1 yellow pepper, sliced thinly lengthwise
- 1 white onion, sliced lengthwise
- butter lettuce
- 2 tsp mayo
- 1/8 tsp chili flakes

Directions:

1. Place the butter lettuce on a serving plate. Spread mayo on the lettuce and top with the shredded beef.
2. Place pepper slices and onions on top and season with chili flakes.
3. Serve as it is or rolled.

Nutritional Value:

Calories 338
Total Fats 25g
Net Carbs: 2.4g
Protein 24g

373. Cheesy Hotdog Pockets

Preparation Time: 50 MIN
Serve: 2

Ingredients:

- 2 beef hot dogs
- 2 thick sticks of quick-melt cheese (or mozzarella
- slices of bacon
- 1/8 tsp garlic powder
- 1/8 tsp onion powder
- Salt and pepper to taste

Directions:

1. Preheat oven to 400 F.
2. Cut the hotdogs lengthwise to create slits.
3. Insert the cheese sticks in the hotdog and then wrap the bacon around the beef hot dog. Secure the bacon using a toothpick.
4. Transfer the hotdogs on a baking sheet lined with foil and flavor with garlic and onion powder.
5. Place in the oven to cook for 40 minutes or until the hotdogs turns golden brown and the cheese is melted.
6. Serve with a veggie salad on the side.

Nutritional Value:

Calories 378
Total Fats 35g
Net Carbs: 0.3g
Protein 17g

374. Cheese Steak Salad

Preparation Time: 35 MIN
Serve: 2

Ingredients:

- For steaks:
- ¼ Tsp Salt
- 2 Tbsp Ghee
- oz Ribeye steak
- For salad:
- 2 ½ oz onions (sliced
- 1 Green pepper (sliced
- ½ Cup Cheddar cheese (grated
- Salt
- 1 Tbsp Ghee
- 1 Garlic clove (diced
- 1 Red pepper (sliced
- oz. Mixed greens
- Fresh herbs

Directions:

1. Let steaks sit at room temperature for 15 minutes. Pat dry with paper towel and melt ghee. Coat with ghee, pepper, and salt.
2. Heat a cast iron pot and sear steaks for 4 minutes until browned all over. Lower heat and cook steak until desired doneness have been achieved.
3. Take steaks from pots and put aside to rest for 7 minutes then slice.
4. Slice vegetables and add ghee to skillet

and melt. Cook for 5 minutes until veggies are crisp.
5. Add lettuce to bowl and top with cooked veggies, steak, and top with cheese.
6. Serve warm.

Nutritional Value:

Calories 622
Total Fats 47.1g
Net Carbs: 12.3g
Protein 38.1g
Fiber 4g

375. Sausage and Cheese Balls

Preparation Time: 20 MIN
Serve: 12

Ingredients:

- 12 Cubes Cheddar cheese
- oz. Cheddar cheese (shredded
- 12 oz. Ground sausage

Directions:

1. Combine sausage and cheese in a bowl.
2. Divide mixture into 12 parts.
3. Place cheese in middle of sausage mixture and form into balls/
4. Place on a try and put into the freezer.
5. Heat oil in a deep pot and fry for 5 minutes.
6. Serve warm.

Nutritional Value:

Calories 173
Total Fats 14g
Net Carbs: 1g
Protein 10g |Fiber: 0g

376. Bunless Bacon and Almond Butter Burger

Preparation Time: 50 MIN
Serve: 4

Ingredients:

For Almond Sauce:

- 1 cup water
- 4 Thai chilis
- 1 tsp swerve
- 1 cup almond butter
- 4 garlic cloves
- tbsp coconut amino
- 1 tbsp rice vinegar

For Burger:

- 4 pepper jack cheese slices
- 1 red onion, sliced
- Salt
- 1 ½ lbs ground beef
- bacon slices
- romaine lettuce leaves
- Black pepper

Directions:

1. Prepare almond butter sauce by adding water and almond butter to a saucepan.
2. Heat mixture until it starts to thicken, stirring occasionally then add coconut aminos.
3. Add garlic, vinegar, Swerve and peppers, pulse until thoroughly combined.
4. Transfer pepper mixture to butter sauce in pot and mix together.
5. Put aside until needed.
6. Prepare burgers by seasoning beef with pepper and salt. Shape into patties and make an indent in each.
7. Place patties on baking sheet and put into the broiler for 7 minutes until golden. Flip patties and broil for an additional 7 minutes.
8. Top with cheese and bake for 5 minutes until melted.
9. Slice onions and cook bacon.
10. Arrange burgers by placing patties onto lettuce and topping with almond sauce, onion and bacon.
11. Serve.

Nutritional Value:

Calories 890
Total Fats 68g
Net Carbs: 8g
Protein 54.4g |Fiber: 10g

377. Pigs in a Blanket

Preparation Time: 40 MIN
Serve: 36

Ingredients:

- oz cheddar cheese
- 1 tbsp Psyllium Husk powder
- 1 egg
- ½ tsp black pepper
- 37 mini hot dogs
- 3/ cup almond flour
- 3 tbsp cream cheese
- ½ tsp salt
- ½ tsp black pepper

Directions:

1. Place mozzarella in a microwave safe dish and heat until cheese melts and is bubbling.
2. Add flour, salt, pepper and husk powder to cheese and mix together until dough is formed.
3. Spread dough on a plate and place into refrigerator for 20 minutes until firm.
4. Set oven to 400 F.
5. Transfer chilled dough to a piece of foil and slice into 37 strips.
6. Wrap each hot dog and place onto baking sheet. Bake for 15 minutes and broil for 2 minutes.
7. Serve warm.

Nutritional Value:

Calories 72
Total Fats 5.9g
Net Carbs: 0.6g
Protein 3.8g | Fiber: 0.4g

378. Cheese Stuffed Hot Dogs wrapped in Bacon

Preparation Time: 45 MIN
Serve: 6

Ingredients:

- 6 Hot dogs
- 2 oz cheddar cheese
- ½ tsp onion powder
- 12 bacon slices
- ½ tsp garlic powder
- Salt
- Black pepper

Directions:

1. Set oven to 400 F.
2. Slice each hot dog open and fill with cheese slices.
3. Use 2 slices of bacon to wrap each hot dog and use toothpicks to hold in place.
4. Place a wire rack on top of a baking sheet and add wrapped hot dogs. Season with garlic and onion powder.
5. Bake for 40 minutes.
6. Serve warm.

Nutritional Value:

- Calories 380
- Total Fats 34.5g
- Net Carbs: 0.3g
- Protein 16.8g
- Cheesy Crust Pizza
- Preparation Time: 35 MIN
- Serve: 12

Ingredients:

- ½ lb ground beef
- 2 eggs
- 1 tsp garlic powder
- ¼ tsp basil
- ¼ tsp turmeric
- oz cream cheese
- 1 chorizo sausage
- ¼ cup parmesan cheese, grated
- ½ tsp cumin
- ½ tsp Italian seasoning
- Salt
- Black pepper

Directions:

- Set oven to 375 F.
- Add parmesan cheese, pepper, garlic, cream cheese and eggs to a bowl and use a hand mixer to combine until smooth.
- Coat baking pan with cooking spray and spread mixture in pan; bake for 15 minutes.
- While crust bakes heat a skillet and

season beef with basil, salt, pepper, cumin, Italian seasoning, and turmeric; cook for 10 minutes.

- Remove crust from oven and cool for 10 minutes. Top crust with tomato sauce and cheese along with the meat.
- Bake for an additional 10 minutes and broil for 5 minutes.
- Cool, slice and serve.

Nutritional Value:

Calories 145
Total Fats 11.3g
Net Carbs: 1.2g
Protein 8.2g

379. No-Bread Cheeseburger

Preparation Time: 20 MIN
Serve: 2

Ingredients:

- ½ lb. ground beef
- ½ onion, chopped
- 1 tsp salt
- 1 tsp pepper
- 4 slices American cheddar
- 4 bacon strips, cooked and chopped
- 4 pcs butter or romaine lettuce leaves
- 4 tbsp mayonnaise

Directions:

1. Heat a cast iron skillet over medium heat. Add the ground beef and sauté with the onions. Cook until the beef is no longer pink.
2. Season the beef with the garlic powder, salt, and pepper.
3. Reduce the heat to low and then top the beef with the slices of cheese. Cover and cook for 3 minutes, or until the cheese has melted
4. Scoop the cooked "burger patties" on the top of the lettuce leaves and dollop mayonnaise on top.
5. Serve immediately.

Nutritional Value:

Calories 224
Total Fats 7.1g
Net Carbs: 3.2g
Protein 34.8g
Fiber 0.9g

380. Ham and Cheese Stromboli

Preparation Time: 35 MIN
Serve: 4

Ingredients:

- 1 ¼ cups mozzarella cheese
- 3 tbsp coconut flour
- 1 tsp Italian seasoning
- 3 ½ oz cheddar cheese
- 4 tbsp almond flour
- 1 egg
- 4 oz ham
- Salt
- Black pepper

Directions:

1. Preheat oven to 400 F. Place mozzarella into a microwave safe dish and melt for 1 minute, stirring occasionally.
2. Mix flour and seasoning together in a bowl then add melted cheese and combine thoroughly.
3. Cool for a minute then add egg and mix together.
4. Place parchment paper on a baking sheet and place mozzarella dough onto paper, top with another paper and use a rolling pin to flatten.
5. Use a knife to slice dough diagonally from edge to middle of the dough, leaving 4 inches of dough unsliced.
6. Place ham and cheese on unsliced section of dough and cover with sliced section
7. Bake for 15-20 minutes until the top is browned. Serve warm.

Nutritional Value:

Calories 306
Total Fats 21.8g
Net Carbs: 4.7g
Protein 25.6g
Fiber: 3.8g

381. Keto Aubergines Bourgeoises

Serves: 6
Preparation: 10 minutes
Cooking: 40 minutes

Directions:

- 2 scallions finely chopped
- 2 Tbsp of olive oil
- 1 cup of small white mushrooms
- 2 eggplants cut into slices
- 3 cloves garlic
- 2 Tbsp of almond flour
- 2 Tbsp tomato puree
- 1 1/2 cups of red wine
- 1 cup of water
- 1 cup of bone broth
- 1/4 cup of fresh thyme finely chopped
- Salt and ground pepper to taste

Directions:

1. Heat the olive oil in a skillet. Sauté scallions and mushrooms for 2 - 3 minutes.
2. Add the eggplant and sauté for 2-3 minutes until golden.
3. Add sliced garlic and stir for 2 - 3 minutes.
4. Sprinkle with the almond flour and stir with a wooden spoon.
5. Add the tomato paste and stir again. Pour wine, water and bone broth and stir well.
6. Cover and cook for 30-35 minutes at medium - low temperature
7. Add chopped thyme, stir and cook for 5 minutes.
8. Adjust salt and pepper and serve hot.

Nutritional Value:

Calories: 110 Carbohydrates: 8.2g Proteins: 3.5g Fat: 5.4g Fiber: 7g

382. Cauliflower Mash in Red Sauce

Serves: 6
Preparation: 10 minutes
Cooking: 15 minutes

Ingredients

- 2 Tbsp of olive oil
- 1 medium head of cauliflower cut in florets
- 1 medium onion, finely chopped
- 2 garlic cloves, finely sliced
- 1/2 cup of chopped chives
- Chopped parsley to taste
- 1 Tbsp of coconut aminos
- 2 cups of water
- 1 pinch of turmeric
- 1 pinch of black pepper powder
- Salt to taste

Directions:

1. Heat the oil in a large pot at medium-high heat.
2. Sauté the onion and the garlic until soft.
3. Add the coconut aminos and sauté for 2 minutes at low heat.
4. Pour water and add all remaining ingredients.
5. Cook for 10 - 12 minutes; stir.
6. Transfer the cauliflower mixture in a blender and blend for 30 - 45 seconds.
7. Return it in a pot, drizzle with olive oil, adjust seasonings and serve.

Nutritional Value:

Calories: 96 Carbohydrates: 5.3g Proteins: 2.5g Fat: 8g Fiber: 2.5g

383. Roasted Brussels sprouts with Bacon

Serves: 4
Preparation: 10 minutes
Cooking: 30 minutes

Ingredients

- 1 ½ lbs of Brussels sprouts
- 2 Tbsp of olive oil
- Salt and pepper to taste
- 6 slices bacon cut into pieces

Directions:

1. Preheat oven to 400 F/200 C.
2. Clean and cut the Brussels sprouts.
3. Place Brussels sprouts in a large baking dish and drizzle with olive oil.
4. Season with the salt and pepper.
5. Sprinkle chopped bacon evenly over Brussels sprouts.
6. Bake for 20-30 minutes. Serve hot.

Nutritional Value:

Calories: 395 Carbohydrates: 11g Proteins: 12.5g Fat: 33g Fiber: 4.1g

384. Boosting Kale, Cucumber and Avocado Smoothie

Serves: 6
Preparation: 10 minutes

Ingredients

- 1 cup fresh kale leaves, finely chopped
- 1 cup cucumber, chopped
- 1/3 cup avocado cut in cubes
- 1/2 cup celery, chopped
- 2 Tbsp of fresh mint leaves
- 1 cup water
- 1 cup ice cubes, or as needed

Directions:

1. Place all ingredients in your fast-speed blender.
2. Blend until smooth.
3. Serve in chilled glasses and drink.

Nutritional Value:

Calories: 31 Carbohydrates: 2g Proteins: 1g Fat: 2g Fiber: 1.5g

385. Crispy Cheddar Kale Chips

Serves: 4
Preparation: 15 minutes
Cooking: 10 minutes

Ingredients

- 1/4 cup garlic-infused olive oil
- Sea salt and ground black pepper to taste
- 1/2 cup Cheddar cheese grated
- 1 lb Kale roughly chopped soft stems

Directions:

1. Preheat oven to 400 F/200C.
2. Rinse and place the kale on a few sheets of kitchen paper towel to dry.
3. Clean and break kale into small pieces.
4. Pour the olive oil and season salt and pepper to taste. Toss to coat.
5. Line a baking dish with parchment paper.
6. Spread kale pieces in a single layer in a baking dish and sprinkle with grated Cheddar cheese.
7. Bake for about 10 minutes, or until the kale pieces become crispy.
8. Serve.

Nutritional Value:

Calories: 114 Carbohydrates: 9g Proteins: 7g Fat: 6g Fiber: 2g

386. Green Beans Soup with Red Pepper Flakes

Serves: 8
Preparation: 5 minutes
Cooking: 45 minutes

Ingredients

- 2 Tbsp of olive oil
- 1 green onion, diced
- 2 clove garlic, minced
- 1 lb fresh green beans
- 1/2 cup fresh cilantro, chopped
- 1 carrot finely sliced
- 2 cup water
- 1 cup bone broth (or water)
- 1 tsp crushed red pepper flakes
- 1/4 tsp chili powder
- 1 tsp cumin
- Salt and ground pepper to taste

Directions:

1. Heat the oil in a large pot and sauté the onion and garlic with a pinch of salt until

soft.

2. Add the green beans and cilantro and stir for further 2 minutes.
3. Add all remaining ingredients and give a good stir.
4. Cover and cook for 30 - 35 minutes or until green beans are soft.
5. Adjust salt and pepper and serve hot.

Nutritional Value:

Calories: 127 Carbohydrates: 8.5g Proteins: 11g Fat: 9g Fiber: 2g

387. Green Keto Puree

Serves: 6
Preparation: 10 minutes
Cooking: 20 minutes

Ingredients

- 1 scallion, chopped
- 2 Tbsp extra virgin olive oil
- 1 lb fresh spinach leaves
- 1/2 lb Swiss chard, tough stems removed
- 3 cups water
- 1/4 cup coconut milk
- Sea salt and black ground pepper to taste

Directions:

1. Heat the olive oil in a skillet and sauté the scallion for about 2-3 minutes.
2. Add the Swish chard and spinach leaves, water and salt and pepper to taste; stir.
3. Bring to the boil and let it simmer for 15 minutes.
4. Transfer spinach mixture in a food processor along with the coconut milk and blend until creamy.
5. Adjust salt and pepper and serve.

Nutritional Value:

Calories: 85 Carbohydrates: 4.5g Proteins: 3g Fat: 7g Fiber: 2.5g

388. Hearty Asparagus Salad with Creamy Dressing

Serves: 4
Preparation: 10 minutes

Ingredients

- 10 ounces frozen cut asparagus, thawed
- 1/2 avocado, chopped
- 2 small spring onions finely chopped
- Sea salt to taste
- 1/2 cup Greek yogurt
- 3 Tbsp of grated Parmesan cheese
- 1 Tbsp mustard (Dijon, English, ground stone)
- 2 Tbsp extra virgin olive oil

Directions:

1. In a salad bowl, combine the asparagus, avocado, and onions; sprinkle with a pinch of the salt, and set aside.
2. In a separate bowl, whisk together Greek yogurt, Parmesan cheese and mustard.
3. Add to the asparagus mixture and toss until well coated.
4. Drizzle with little olive oil and serve immediately or refrigerate until serving.

Nutritional Value:

Calories: 143 Carbohydrates: 6g Proteins: 5g Fat: 12g Fiber: 2.4g

389. Heavy - Creamy Spinach Puree

Serves: 4
Preparation: 10 minutes
Cooking: 15 minutes

Ingredients

- 1 Tbsp tallow
- 1 lb of frozen spinach drained
- 2 clove garlic, minced
- Salt and fresh-ground black pepper to taste
- 1/2 cup water
- 1 cup heavy cream
- 3/4 cup grated parmesan cheese

Directions:

1. Thaw (about two hours) and drain the spinach in a colander.
2. Heat the tallow in a large pot and sauté garlic, spinach with a pinch of salt and pepper.

3. Pour water, cover and boil for three minutes or until spinach begins to wilt.
4. Transfer spinach in a blender along with cream and parmesan cheese; blend for 25 - 35 seconds or until combined well.
5. Taste and adjust salt and ground pepper.
6. Serve.

Nutritional Value:

Calories: 327 Carbohydrates: 8g Proteins: 13g Fat: 28g Fiber: 4g

390. Mayo- Mustard Asparagus and Mushrooms Salad

Serves: 4
Preparation: 15 minutes
Cooking: 15 minutes

Ingredients

- 20 large spears of asparagus
- 2 cups mushrooms
- 1/2 cup of mayonnaise
- 2 Tbsp yellow mustard
- 1 lemon juice
- Salt and ground pepper to taste

Directions:

1. Cut the woody part of the asparagus, rinse, and place in pot with salted water.
2. Boil asparagus for 10 minutes over medium-high heat. Remove asparagus in colander, allow it to cool, and cut into pieces.
3. Place the asparagus pieces in a large salad bowl.
4. Rinse the mushrooms and cut them into thin slices. Put them in a bowl with asparagus
5. Season with the salt and pepper to taste, add the mayonnaise and mustard and stir; pour lemon juice to taste, stir and serve.

Nutritional Value:

Calories: 101 Carbohydrates: 4g Proteins: 4g Fat: 6g Fiber: 3g

391. Oriental Spiced Cucumber and Fennel Salad

Serves: 4
Preparation: 10 minutes
Cooking: 20 minutes

Ingredients

- 1 lb cucumber cut into pieces
- 2 fennel bulb thinly sliced
- 3 hot peppers
- 3 cloves garlic (peeled and left whole)
- 1 Tbsp of coriander seeds
- 1 cinnamon sticks (broken into several pieces)
- 2 cups white vinegar
- 1/2 tsp red pepper flakes
- 1 cup water
- 3 Tbsp of stevia sweetener granulated
- 2 Tbsp of kosher salt
- 1 bay leaf
- 1 tsp black peppercorns
- Olive oil for serving

Directions:

1. Place all ingredients in a large and deep pot. Cook covered for about 15 - 20 minutes over medium heat.
2. Transfer mixture in colander to drain.
3. Remove all ingredients from colander in a salad bowl, drizzle with olive oil and serve.

Nutritional Value:

Calories: 148 Carbohydrates: 8g Proteins: 7g Fat: 14g Fiber: 4.5g

392. Steamed "Italiano" Broccoli

Serves: 5
Preparation: 10 minutes
Cooking: 10 minutes

Ingredients

- 1 1/2 lb of fresh broccoli florets (or thawed frozen)
- 1/2 cup Italian salad dressing

Directions:

1. Place broccoli florets in steamer basket above 2 inches boiling water.
2. Cover and steam for about 4 minutes or until broccoli is soft.

3. Remove from the steam, drain and place broccoli in serving plate.
4. Drizzle with Italian dressing and toss to coat. Serve.

Nutritional Value:

Calories: 60 Carbohydrates: 6g Proteins: 14g Fat: 11g Fiber: 2g

393. Warm Avocado - Zucchini Salad

Serves: 5
Preparation: 5 minutes
Cooking: 20 minutes

Ingredients

- 2 Tbsp olive oil
- 1 spring onion finely chopped
- 2 cloves of garlic
- 3 zucchini
- 1 large avocado
- 1 Tbsp of fresh thyme finely chopped
- Salt and black ground pepper to taste
- 1 lemon (zest and juice)

Directions:

1. Heat the olive oil in a frying skillet over medium-high heat.
2. Sauté the onion and garlic with a pinch of salt until soft, for about 4 - 5 minutes.
3. Add the zucchini and cook for about 2 - 3 minutes.
4. Add the lemon zest, thyme, and season with the salt and pepper; stir well.
5. Add avocado and lemon juice and cook for further 3 - 4 minutes.
6. Remove from the heat; let cool for 10 minutes and serve.

Nutritional Value:

Calories: 171 Carbohydrates: 7g Proteins: 7g Fat: 19g Fiber: 5g

394. Wild Greens, Asparagus with Cheese Sauce

Serves: 6
Preparation: 10 minutes
Cooking: 25 minutes

Ingredients

- 1 1/4 lb mustard greens or amaranth cut coarsely
- 1 bunch of asparagus green (about 10 -12 pieces), cleaned, and cut 4 pieces
- Salt and ground black pepper to taste
- For the cheese sauce
- 1/2 cup of olive oil
- 1 clove of garlic, cleaned finely minced
- 1 Tbsp rosemary leaves, finely chopped
- 1 tsp hot dried paprika
- 1 cup cream cheese (full-fat)

Directions:

1. salted water in a saucepan with plenty of salted boiling water.
2. Boil the greens and asparagus for about 7 to 10 minutes.
3. Drain well and put in a salad bowl.
4. Boil

Cheese sauce:

1. In a frying pan heat the olive oil and heat the garlic over medium heat.
2. Add the cheese, rosemary leaves, and hot dried paprika, salt and freshly ground pepper; stir well.
3. Stir for 15 - 20 seconds and remove from the heat.
4. Pour hot cheese salad over the greens and asparagus. Serve.

Nutritional Value:

Calories: 261 Carbohydrates: 7g Proteins: 10g Fat: 22g Fiber: 5.5g

395. Creamy Broccoli and Bacon Casserole

Serves: 4
Preparation: 15 minutes
Cooking: 35 minutes

Ingredients

- 1 Tbsp of olive oil
- 2 cups of broccoli florets, cooked
- 8 eggs
- 1/4 cup water
- 1 cup of Cottage cheese

- 1 tsp of fresh thyme
- Salt and ground black pepper to taste
- 3 ounces of bacon, crumbled
- 2 Tbsp of Feta cheese, crumbled

Directions:

1. Preheat the oven to 380 F/190 C.
2. Coat the casserole dish with olive oil.
3. Place the broccoli florets (cooked) on a bottom of casserole dish; sprinkle with the pinch of salt and pepper.
4. Add the Cottage cheese and fresh thyme over the broccoli.
5. In a bowl, whisk the eggs with 1/4 cup of water; season with the salt and pepper.
6. Pour the egg mixture over the broccoli, and sprinkle with crumbled bacon and crumbled feta cheese.
7. Place the casserole in the oven, and bake for 35 minutes.
8. Let rest for 10 minutes before slicing and serving.

Nutritional Value:

Calories: 325 Carbohydrates: 5g Proteins: 22g Fat: 24g Fiber: 0.2g

396. Delicious Spinach - Bacon Casserole

Serves: 5
Preparation: 15 minutes
Cooking: 15 minutes

Ingredients

- 1 tsp of tallow
- 8 slices bacon (pancetta)
- 3/4 lb fresh spinach chopped
- 8 eggs from free-range chickens
- 1 cup Parmesan cheese grated
- 2 pinch salt and pepper

Directions:

1. Preheat the oven to 400 F/200 C.
2. Grease one casserole dish with the tallow.
3. Lay the bacon slices on the bottom of casserole dish.
4. Sprinkle chopped spinach leaves over the bacon, and sprinkle with little salt.
5. In a bowl, whisk the eggs along with Parmesan cheese and the pinch of salt and pepper.
6. Pour the egg mixture over the spinach evenly.
7. Place in oven and cook for 20 minutes.
8. Turn off the oven but leave the casserole for 10 - 15 minutes inside.
9. Serve hot.

Nutritional Value:

Calories: 502 Carbohydrates: 4.5g Proteins: 27g Fat: 42g Fiber: 1.5g

397. Steak Strips and Zucchini Omelet Casserole

Serves: 5
Preparation: 10 minutes
Cooking: 30 minutes

Ingredients

- 1 Tbsp lard
- 1 lb bacon, cut into strips
- 1 spring onion, finely diced
- 3 large sized zucchinis, grated
- 1 tsp of sea salt and ground black pepper
- 6 free range eggs
- 1/2 can of feta cheese, crumbled

Directions:

1. Preheat oven to 350 F/175 C.
2. Grease one large casserole dish with the lard.
3. Place the bacon strips in a casserole dish, and cover with sliced green onion and zucchini rings.
4. Season with the salt and pepper.
5. Beat the eggs in a bowl with a pinch of salt and crumbled feta cheese.
6. Pour the egg mixture in a casserole dish.
7. Bake for 30 minutes or until the eggs are cooked.
8. Serve hot.

Nutritional Value:

Calories: 496 Carbohydrates: 5g Proteins: 19g Fat: 48g Fiber: 1.5g

398. Zucchini Noodles with

Parmesan

Serves: 4
Preparation: 15 minutes
Cooking: 5 minutes

Ingredients

- 2 cups zucchini noodles (zoodles)
- Salt and fresh cracked pepper to taste
- 2 Tbsp olive oil
- 2 cloves garlic, minced
- 1 Tbsp green pepper chopped
- 3 Tbsp fresh basil (chopped)
- 1 tsp red pepper flakes
- 1 cup water
- 1/4 cup Parmesan cheese

Directions:

1. Pour oil to the inner stainless steel pot in the Instant Pot.
2. Cut zucchini into thin, noodle-like strips with a mandolin. Season zucchini noodles with the salt and pepper.
3. Place zucchini in Instant Pot, and add minced garlic, green pepper, fresh basil, red pepper flakes and water over zucchini.
4. Lock lid into place and set on the MANUAL setting for 5 minutes.
5. When the timer beeps, press "Cancel" and carefully flip the Quick Release valve to let the pressure out.
6. Remove zucchini noodles on a serving plate, sprinkle with Parmesan and serve.
7. **Nutritional Value:**

Calories: 113 Carbohydrates: 4g Proteins: 7g Fat: 10g Fiber: 3g

399. Brown Cremini Mushrooms Gravy

Serves: 8
Preparation: 5 minutes
Cooking: 4 hours

Ingredients

- 1 lb of Cremini mushrooms (or white mushrooms, shiitake mushrooms)
- 1 medium onion finely chopped
- 1 cup of cream
- 1 cup of almond milk (unsweetened)
- 1/4 cup white dry wine
- 1 Tbsp butter
- Salt and red ground pepper to taste

Directions:

1. Place mushrooms along with all ingredients in Slow Cooker; stir gently to combine.
2. Cover and cook on HIGH for 1 - 2 hours or on LOW for 3 - 4 hours.
3. Open lid, stir well, adjust salt and pepper and allow to cool.
4. Store in glass jar and keep refrigerated.

Nutritional Value:

Calories: 150 Carbohydrates: 4g Proteins: 3g Fat: 14g Fiber: 0.2g

400. Creamed Portobello Mushrooms

Serves: 4
Preparation: 10 minutes
Cooking: 3 hour and 30 minutes

Ingredients

- 1 1/2 lbs of Portobello mushrooms, halved
- Salt and ground white pepper
- 1 Tbsp of butter
- 1/2 cup of bone broth
- 2 Tbsp of brandy
- 1 Tbsp of almond flour
- 3/4 cup of fresh cream
- 2 Tbsp of chopped fresh parsley

Directions:

1. Place mushrooms in your Slow Cooker along with salt and pepper, butter, bone broth, brandy and almond flour.
2. Cover and cook on HIGH for 3 hours.
3. Open lid and stir cream; cover and cook on HIGH for further 25 - 30 minutes.
4. Serve hot with chopped parsley.

Nutritional Value:

Calories: 236 Carbohydrates: 5g Proteins: 7g Fat:

21g Fiber: 2g

401. Dense Green Squash Puree

Serves: 6
Preparation: 5 minutes
Cooking: 9 hours

Ingredients

- 2 Tbsp garlic-infused olive oil
- 1 lb green squash, sliced
- 2 cups green olives, pitted and chopped
- 1 grated tomato
- 2 tsp capers
- 1 Tbsp fresh basil finely chopped
- Salt and pepper, to taste
- 2 Tbsp sesame seeds toasted (for serving)

Directions:

1. Add all ingredients from the list in your Slow Cooker and stir well.
2. Cover and cook on LOW 7 - 9 hours.
3. Transfer the mixture into blender or food processor and blend it until smooth.
4. Taste and adjust salt and pepper to taste.
5. Sprinkle with toasted sesame and serve.

Nutritional Value:

Calories: 152 Carbohydrates: 6g Proteins: 2.5g Fat: 14g Fiber: 4g

402. Easy Cauliflower Mousse with Sesame

Serves: 4
Preparation: 10 minutes
Cooking: 4 hours

Ingredients

- 1 lb cauliflower florets
- 1 Tbsp fresh butter
- 1 small onion, chopped small
- 1 cup cooking cream
- Salt and pepper to taste
- 1/2 cup toasted sesame
- Fresh parsley leaves, for garnish (or cilantro)

Directions:

1. Add the cauliflower florets together with all ingredients in your Slow Cooker.
2. Cover and cook on LOW for 6 hours or on HIGH for 4 hours.
3. Taste and adjust salt; stir well.
4. Serve with chopped parsley.

Nutritional Value:

Calories: 180 Carbohydrates: 8g Proteins: 6g Fat: 14g Fiber: 4g

403. Savory Zucchini Cream with Nuts

Serves: 6
Preparation: 10 minutes
Cooking: 3 hours

Ingredients

- 6 medium zucchini
- 4 Tbsp of ground almonds
- 1 cup almond milk
- Seasoned salt and ground white pepper
- 1/3 cup of garlic-infused olive oil

Directions:

1. Rinse, clean and cut zucchini in slices.
2. Place all ingredients in your Slow Cooker.
3. Cover and cook on HIGH for 3 hours.
4. Transfer zucchini mixture in a blender; blend for 25 - 30 seconds or until smooth.
5. Adjust salt and pepper and blend again.
6. Serve immediately or keep refrigerated.

Nutritional Value:

Calories: 72 Carbohydrates: 5g Proteins: 4g Fat: 7g Fiber: 3g

404. Bok Choy Stir-Fry

Serves: 2
Preparation: 10 minutes
Cooking: 15 minutes

Ingredients

- 20 oz Bok choy, fresh
- 2 Tbsp garlic-infused olive oil
- 2 green onions finely chopped
- 2 cloves garlic minced

- 1 Tbsp of oyster sauce (made with stevia sweetener)
- Salt to taste
- 1 tsp almond flour
- 4 Tbsp water

Directions:

1. Rinse your Bok Choy and drain well.
2. Heat the oil in a skillet and sauté the onion and garlic for 3 - 4 minutes.
3. Add Bok Choy and stir for approximately 2 - 3 minutes.
4. In a bowl, whisk the oyster sauce, salt, almond flour and water.
5. Pour the mixture over Bok Choy, turn off the heat, stir, and let sit for 5 minutes.
6. Serve hot.

Nutritional Value:

Calories: 134 Carbohydrates: 2.5g Proteins: 1g Fat: 14g Fiber: 0.5g

405. Genoa Salami and Vegetable Frittata

Preparation Time: 25 minutes
Servings 4)

Nutritional Value:310 Calories; 26.2g Fat; 3.9g Carbs; 15.4g Protein; 1.9g Sugars

Ingredients

- **1/2 stick butter, at room temperature**
- 1/2 cup scallions, chopped
- 2 garlic cloves, minced
- 1 serrano pepper, chopped
- 1 carrot, chopped
- 8 Genoa salami slices
- 8 eggs, whisked
- Salt and black pepper, to taste
- 1/2 teaspoon dried dill weed

Directions

1. Melt the butter in a pan that is preheated over a moderately high heat. Now, sauté the scallions for 4 minutes, stirring periodically.
2. Add garlic and cook for 1 minute or until it is fragrant. Add serrano pepper and carrot. Cook an additional 4 minutes.
3. Transfer the mixture to a baking pan that is lightly greased with a nonstick cooking spray. Top with salami slices.
4. Pour the eggs over vegetables and salami; season with salt, pepper, and dill. Bake approximately 18 minutes. Eat warm with a dollop of full-fat Greek yogurt.

406. Two Cheese Omelet with Pimenta and Chervil

Preparation Time: 15 minutes
Servings 2)

Nutritional Value:490 Calories; 44.6g Fat; 4.5g Carbs; 22.7g Protein; 2.7g Sugars

Ingredients

- 2 tablespoons avocado oil
- 4 eggs, beaten
- Salt and black pepper, to taste
- 1/4 teaspoon Pimenta, ground
- 1/4 teaspoon cayenne pepper
- 1/2 cup Asiago cheese
- 1/2 cup Boursin cheese
- 2 tablespoons fresh chervil, roughly chopped

Directions

1. Heat the oil in a pan that is preheated over a moderately high heat.
2. Season the eggs with salt, black pepper, ground Pimenta, and cayenne pepper. Add the seasoned eggs to the pan; tilt the pan to spread the eggs out evenly.
3. Once set, top your eggs with cheese. Slice the omelet into two halves.
4. Serve garnish with fresh chervil. Bon appétit!

407. Asiago and Sausage Egg Cups

Preparation Time: 10 minutes
Servings 3

Nutritional Value:423 Calories; 34.1g Fat; 2.2g Carbs; 26.5g Protein; 0.9g Sugars

Ingredients

- 1 teaspoon butter, melted
- 6 eggs, separated into yolks and whites
- Coarse salt and freshly ground black pepper, to taste
- 1/2 teaspoon smoked paprika
- 1/2 teaspoon dried sage
- 1 cup Asiago cheese, freshly grated
- 3 beef sausages, chopped

Directions

1. **Begin by preheating your oven to 420 degrees F. Lightly grease a muffin pan with melted butter.**

2. Now, beat the egg whites with an electric mixer until stiff peaks form. Add seasonings, cheese, and sausage.
3. Pour into muffin cups and bake for 4 minutes.
4. Now, add an egg to each cup. Bake for 4 more minutes.Leave the cups to cool down for a few minutes before serving time. Bon appétit!

408. Madras and Asparagus Cheesy Frittata

Preparation Time: 20 minutes
Servings 4
Nutritional Value:248 Calories; 17.1g Fat; 6.2g Carbs; 17.6g Protein; 1.1g Sugars

Ingredients

2 tablespoons avocado oil
1/2 cup shallots, chopped
1 cup asparagus tips
8 eggs, beaten
1/2 teaspoon jalapeno pepper, minced
1 teaspoon Madras curry paste
Salt and red pepper, to your liking
3/4 cup Colby cheese, grated

- 1/4 cup fresh cilantro, to serve

Directions

1. In an ovenproof frying pan, heat avocado oil over a medium flame. Now, sauté the shallots until they are caramelized.
2. Add the asparagus tips and cook until they're just tender.
3. Stir in the eggs, jalapeno pepper and Madras curry paste; season with salt and pepper. Now, cook until the eggs are nearly set.
4. Scatter the cheese over the top of your frittata. Cook in the preheated oven at 375 degrees F for about 12 minutes, until your frittata is set in the middle.
5. Cut into wedges and serve garnished with fresh cilantro.

409. Colby Cheese and Sausage Gofres

Preparation Time: 30 minutes
Servings 6

Nutritional Value:316 Calories; 25g Fat; 1.5g Carbs; 20.2g Protein; 1.2g Sugars

Ingredients

- 6 eggs
- 6 tablespoons whole milk
- 1 teaspoon Spanish spice mix
- Sea salt and ground black pepper, to taste
- 3 fully-cooked breakfast sausage links, chopped
- 1 cup Colby cheese, shredded
- Nonstick cooking spray

Directions

1. In a mixing bowl, beat the eggs, milk, Spanish spice mix, salt, and black pepper.
2. Now, stir in chopped sausage and shredded cheese.
3. Spritz a waffle iron with a nonstick cooking spray.
4. Cook the egg mixture about 5 minutes, until it is golden. Serve immediately with a homemade sugar-free tomato ketchup. Enjoy!

410. Mushroom, Cheese and Tomato Rolls

Preparation Time: 20 minutes
Servings 4

Nutritional Value:172 Calories; 14g Fat; 3.4g Carbs; 9.5g Protein; 2.3g Sugars

Ingredients

For the Wraps:

- 6 eggs, separated into yolks and whites
- 2 tablespoons full-fat milk
- 1 tablespoon olive oil
- Sea salt, to taste

For the Filling:

- 1 teaspoon olive oil
- 1 cup button mushrooms, chopped
- Salt and black pepper, to taste
- 1/2 teaspoon cayenne pepper
- 6-8 fresh lettuce leaves
- 4 slices of Swiss cheese
- 2 small-sized Roma tomatoes, thinly

sliced

Directions

1. Thoroughly combine all ingredients for the wraps.
2. Preheat a frying pan. Pour 1/4 of the mixture into the pan; cook over medium-low heat until thoroughly heated, 4 minutes per side.
3. Repeat three more times and set your wraps aside, keeping them warm.
4. In another pan, heat 1 teaspoon of olive oil over a moderately high flame. Now, cook the mushrooms until they are softened, about 5 minutes; season with salt, black pepper and cayenne pepper.
5. Lay 1-2 lettuce leaves onto each wrap. Divide the mushrooms among prepared wraps. Top with cheese and tomatoes. Enjoy!

411. Eggs with Crabmeat and Sour Cream Sauce

Preparation Time: 15 minutes
Servings 3

Nutritional Value:334 Calories; 26.2g Fat; 4.4g Carbs; 21.1g Protein; 1.2g Sugars

Ingredients

1 tablespoon olive oil

- 6 eggs, whisked
- 1 can crabmeat, flaked
- 1 teaspoon Montreal seasoning

For the Sauce:

- 3/4 cup sour cream
- 1/2 cup scallions, white and green parts, chopped
- 1/2 teaspoon garlic powder
- Salt and black pepper to the taste
- 1/2 teaspoon fresh dill, chopped

Directions

1. Heat olive oil in a sauté pan that is preheated over a moderate flame. Now, add eggs and scramble them.
2. Add crabmeat and cook, stirring frequently, until everything is thoroughly cooked; sprinkle with Montreal seasoning.
3. In a mixing dish, gently whisk all the sauce ingredients.
4. Divide egg/crabmeat mixture among 4 plates; serve with the scallion/sour cream sauce on the side. Bon appétit!

412. Easy Breakfast Muffins

Preparation Time: 20 minutes
Servings 6

Nutritional Value:81 Calories; 3.5g Fat; 6.7g Carbs; 5.5g Protein; 4.4g Sugars

Ingredients

- 3/4 cream cheese
- 1/4 cup Greek-style yogurt
- 3 eggs, beaten
- 2 tablespoons hazelnuts, ground
- 4 tablespoons erythritol
- 1/2 teaspoon vanilla essence
- 1/3 teaspoon ground cinnamon
- 1 apple, cored and sliced

Directions

1. Preheat your oven to 360 degrees F. Treat a muffin pan with a nonstick cooking spray.
2. Then, thoroughly combine all of the above ingredients. Divide the batter among the muffin cups.
3. Bake for 12 to 15 minutes. Transfer to a wire rack to cool slightly before serving. Serve garnished with apples and enjoy!

413. Dill Pickle, Cheese, and Cauliflower Balls

Preparation Time: 3 hours 15 minutes
Servings 6

Nutritional Value:407 Calories; 26.8g Fat; 5.8g Carbs; 33.4g Protein; 1.5g Sugars

Ingredients

- 4 cups cauliflowerrice
- 1/2 pound pancetta, chopped
- 6 ounces Cottage cheese,curds, 2% fat
- 6 ounces Ricotta cheese
- 1 cup Colby cheese

- 1/2 cup dill pickles,chopped and thoroughly squeezed
- 2 cloves garlic, crushed
- 1 cup grated Parmesan cheese
- 1/2 teaspoon caraway seeds
- 1/4 teaspoon dried dill weed
- 1/2 teaspoon shallot powder
- Salt and black pepper, to taste
- 1 cup crushed pork rinds
- Cooking oil

Directions

1. Thoroughly combine cauliflower rice, pancetta, Cottage cheese, Ricotta cheese, Colby cheese, dill pickles, garlic, and 1/2 cup of grated Parmesan.
2. Stir until everything is well mixed and shape cauliflower mixture into even balls. Now, transfer to your refrigerator for 3 hours.
3. Now, in a mixing bowl, thoroughly combine the remaining 1/2 cup of Parmesan cheese, caraway seeds, dill, shallot powder, salt, black pepper and crushed pork rinds.
4. Roll cheese ball in Parmesan mixture until they are completely coated.
5. Then, heat about 1-inch of oil in a skillet over a moderately high flame. Fry cheeseballs until they are golden brown on all sides.
6. Transfer to a paper towel to soak up excess oil. Serve immediately or at room temperature. Enjoy!

414. Easy Two-Cheese Omelet

Preparation Time: 15 minutes
Servings 2

Nutritional Value:307 Calories; 25g Fat; 2.5g Carbs; 18.5g Protein; 1.6g Sugars

Ingredients

- 4 eggs
- Salt, to taste
- 1/4 teaspoon black peppercorns,crushed
- 1 tablespoon sesame oil
- 1/4 cup Blue Cheese, crumbled
- 1/4 cup Appenzeller cheese, shredded
- 1 tomato, thinly sliced

Directions

1. Whisk the eggs in a mixing bowl; season with salt and crushed peppercorns.
2. Heat the oil in a sauté pan over medium-low heat. Now, pour in the eggs and cook, using a spatula to swirl the eggs around the pan.
3. Cook the eggs until partially set. Top with cheese; fold your omelet in half to enclose filling.
4. Serve warm, garnished with tomato. Bon appétit!

415. Spicy Cheese Crisps

Preparation Time: 10 minutes
Servings 4

Nutritional Value:205 Calories; 15g Fat; 2.9g Carbs; 14.5g Protein; 0.7g Sugars

Ingredients

- 2 cups Swiss cheese, shredded
- 1/2 teaspoon garlic powder
- 1/4 teaspoon shallot powder
- 1 rosemary sprig, minced
- 1/2 teaspoon chili powder

Directions

1. Preheat an oven to 400 degrees F. Coat two baking sheets with parchment paper or Silpat mat.
2. Then, thoroughly combine Swiss cheese with seasonings.
3. Then, form 1 tablespoons of cheese mixture into small mounds on the baking sheets.
4. Bake for 6 minutes and let them cool before serving. Enjoy!

416. Three-Cheese Party Balls

Preparation Time: 10 minutes
Servings 10

Nutritional Value:105 Calories; 7.2g Fat; 2.8g Carbs; 7.5g Protein; 0.5g Sugars

Ingredients

- 1 ½ cups Ricotta cheese, at room temperature
- 3/4 cup Monterey Jack cheese,shredded
- 3/4 cup goat cheese, shredded
- 1/3 cup black olives, pitted and chopped
- 1 ½ tablespoons tomato paste
- 1 teaspoon cayenne pepper
- Salt and freshly ground black pepper
- 20 fresh basil leaves

Directions

1. In a bowl, thoroughly combine the cheese, olives, tomato paste, cayenne pepper, salt and black pepper. Then, shape the mixture into 20 balls.
2. Place 1 basil leaf on top of each ball and secure with a toothpick. Serve and enjoy!

417. Sriracha Egg Salad with Scallions

Preparation Time: 15 minutes
Servings 8

Nutritional Value:174 Calories; 13g Fat; 5.7g Carbs; 7.4g Protein; 2.4g Sugars

Ingredients

- 10 eggs
- 3/4 cup mayonnaise
- 1 teaspoon Sriracha
- 1 tablespoon whole grain mustard
- 1/2 cup scallions
- 1/2 stalk of celery, minced
- 1/2 teaspoon fresh lime juice
- 1/2 teaspoon sea salt
- 1/2 teaspoon ground black pepper, to taste
- 1 head Romaine lettuce, torn into pieces

Directions

1. Place the eggs in a pan and cover them with at least 1-inch of water; bring to a boil. Then, remove from heat, cover, and let them sit approximately 10 minutes.
2. Chop the eggs coarsely and add them to a salad bowl.
3. Add the remaining ingredients and gently stir until everything is well incorporated. Place in the refrigerator until ready to serve. Bon appétit!

418. Easy Vegetarian Cheese Tacos

Preparation Time: 10 minutes
Servings 6

Nutritional Value:370 Calories; 30g Fat; 4.9g Carbs; 19.5g Protein; 1.2g Sugars

Ingredients

- 1/2 pound Cheddar cheese, grated
- 1/2 pound Colby cheese, grated
- 1 teaspoon taco seasoning mix
- 1 ½ cups guacamole
- 1 cup sour cream
- A small-sized head of lettuce

Directions

1. Combine both types of cheese with taco seasoning mix.
2. Then, preheat a pan over a moderate flame.
3. Scatter the shredded cheese mixture all over the pan, covering the bottom. Fry for 4 to 5 minutes, turning once.
4. Top with guacamole,sour cream and lettuce, roll them up and serve immediately. Bon appétit!

419. Sopressata and Blue Cheese Waffles

Preparation Time: 20 minutes
Servings 2

Nutritional Value:470 Calories; 40.3g Fat; 2.9g Carbs; 24.4g Protein; 1.7g Sugars

Ingredients

- 2 tablespoons butter, melted
- Salt and black pepper, to your liking
- 1/2 teaspoon parsley flakes
- 1/2 teaspoon chili pepper flakes
- 4 eggs
- 1/2 cup blue cheese, crumbled
- 4 slices Sopressata, chopped

- 2 tablespoons fresh chives, chopped

Directions

1. Combine all ingredients, except forfresh chives, in a mixing bowl. Preheat your waffle iron and grease with a cooking spray.
2. Add the omelet mixture and close the lid.
3. Fry about 5 minutes or until desired consistency is reached. Repeat with the remaining batter. Serve garnished with fresh chives and eat warm.

420. Festive Eggs with Cheese and Aioli

Preparation Time: 20 minutes
Servings 8

Nutritional Value:285 Calories; 22.5g Fat; 1.8g Carbs; 19.5g Protein; 1g Sugars

Ingredients

- 8 eggs, hard-boiled
- 2 cans tuna in brine, drained
- 1/2 cup Bibb lettuces, torn into pieces
- 1/2 cup red onions, finely chopped
- 1/2 goat cheese,crumbled
- 1/3 cup sour cream
- 1/2 tablespoon yellow mustard
- For Aioli:
- 1 egg
- 2 medium cloves garlic, minced
- 1 tablespoon lemon juice
- 1/2 cup olive oil
- Salt and black pepper, to taste

Directions

1. Peel and chop the eggs; transfer them to a serving bowl. Add tuna, lettuce, onion, cheese, sour cream and yellow mustard.
2. To make aioli, beat the egg, garlic, and lemon juice with an immersion blender. Add oil, salt and pepper, and blend again until everything is well mixed.
3. Add prepared aioli to the bowl and gently stir until everything is well incorporated.
4. Serve with pickles or bell peppers. Bon appétit!

421. Kid-Friendly Avocado Boats

Preparation Time: 20 minutes
Servings 4

Nutritional Value:342 Calories; 30.4g Fat; 6.5g Carbs; 11.1g Protein; 0.8g Sugars

Ingredients

- 2 avocados, halved and pitted, skin on
- 2 ounces blue cheese,crumbled
- 2 ounces Colby cheese, grated
- 2 eggs, beaten
- Salt and pepper, to taste
- 1 tablespoon fresh cilantro, chopped

Directions

1. Preheat your oven to 360 degrees F.
2. Arrange avocado halves in an ovenproof dish.
3. In a mixing dish, combine both types of cheeses, eggs, salt and pepper. Divide the mixture among avocado halves.
4. Bake for 15 to 17 minutes or until everything is thoroughly baked. Serve garnished with fresh cilantro. Enjoy!

422. Cheesy Cauliflower Fritters

Preparation Time: 35 minutes
Servings 6

Nutritional Value:199 Calories; 13.8g Fat; 6.8g Carbs; 13g Protein; 2.1g Sugars

Ingredients

- 1 ½ tablespoons olive oil
- 1 shallot, chopped
- 1 garlic clove, minced
- 1 pound cauliflower, grated
- 6 tablespoons almond flour
- 1/2 cup Swiss cheese, shredded
- 1 cup parmesan cheese
- 2 eggs, beaten
- 1/2 teaspoon dried dill weed
- Sea salt and ground black pepper, to taste

Directions

1. Heat the oil in a cast iron skillet over medium heat. Cook the shallots and

garlic until they are aromatic.

2. Add grated cauliflower and stir with a spatula for another minute or so; set aside to cool to room temperature so you can handle it easily.
3. Add the remaining ingredients; shape the mixture into balls, then, press each ball to form burger patties.
4. Bake in the preheated oven at 400 degrees F for 20 minutes. Flip and bake for another 10 minutes or until golden brown on top. Bon appétit!

423. Parmesan and Mushroom Burger Patties

Preparation Time: 20 minutes
Servings 4

Nutritional Value:370 Calories; 30g Fat; 4.7g Carbs; 16.8g Protein; 1g Sugars

Ingredients

- 1/2 stick butter, softened
- 2 garlic cloves, minced
- 2 cups brown mushrooms, chopped
- 4 tablespoons blanched almond flour
- 4 tablespoons ground flax seeds
- 4 tablespoons hemp seeds
- 4 tablespoons sunflower seeds
- 1 tablespoon Cajun seasonings
- 1 teaspoon deli mustard
- 2 eggs, whisked
- 1⁄2 cup parmesan cheese

Directions

1. Melt 1 tablespoon of butter in a pan that is preheated over medium-high heat. Now, sauté the garlic and mushrooms until mushrooms lose their water.
2. Add almond flour,flax seeds, hemp seeds,sunflower seeds,Cajun seasonings, mustard, eggs and Parmesan cheese.
3. Form the mixture into 4 burger patties with lightly oiled hands.
4. Melt the remaining butter in a pan; fry your patties for 6 to 7 minutes. Then, carefully flip them over with a wide spatula. Cook another 6 minutes. Serve warm.

424. Tinga and Queso Manchego Frittata

Preparation Time: 25 minutes
Servings 6

Nutritional Value:225 Calories; 17g Fat; 5.1g Carbs; 13.2g Protein; 2.3g Sugars

Ingredients

- 10 eggs
- 1 teaspoon seasoned salt
- 1/4 teaspoon ground black pepper, or more to taste
- 1/3 cup chive & onion cream cheese, room temperature
- 1 heaping tablespoon lard, room temperature
- 1 leek, chopped
- 1 teaspoon garlic paste
- 1 red bell pepper, chopped
- 1/2 green bell pepper, chopped
- 1 teaspoon Mexican Tinga paste
- 1 ½ cups baby spinach
- 1/2 cup Queso Manchego, shredded

Directions

1. Begin by preheating the oven to 370 degrees F.
2. Whisk the eggs with salt, pepper and cream cheese.
3. Melt the lard in an oven-safe skillet over a moderately high heat. Sauté the leeks until they are aromatic.
4. Now, stir in garlic paste, bell peppers, and Tinga paste, and continue sautéing an additional 3 to 4 minute or until they are softened
5. Add baby spinach and cook for 1 to 2 minutes more. Stir in the egg/cheese mixture. Shake your skillet to distribute the mixture evenlyand transfer to the oven.
6. Bake about 8 minutes or until your frittata is golden brown on topbut still slightly wobbly in the middle.
7. Top withshredded Queso Manchego and

bake an additional 3 minutes or until the cheese melts completely
8. Cut into 6 wedges and serve warm. Enjoy!

425. Two-Minute Eggs in a Mug

Preparation Time: 5 minutes
Servings 2

Nutritional Value:197 Calories; 13.8g Fat; 2.7g Carbs; 15.7g Protein; 2.2g Sugars

Ingredients

- 4 eggs
- 1/4 cup full-fat milk
- 1/4 cup Asiago cheese, freshly grated

4.

- 1 garlic clove, minced
- 1/4 teaspoon dried basil
- 1/4 teaspoon turmeric powder
- Sea salt and red pepper flakes, to taste

Directions

1. In a mixing bowl, thoroughly combine the eggs, milk, cheese, garlic, salt and pepper.
2. Spritz 2 microwave-safe mugs with a nonstick spray. Pour in the egg mixture.
3. Now, microwave for 30 to 40 seconds. Stir with a spoon and microwave for 60 to 70 seconds more or until they're set.

426. Taco Soup

Servings: 8
Preparation: Time: 20 Minutes

- **Nutritional Values: Calories 386; Fats 28 Grams; Carbs 8 Grams; Proteins 27 Grams**

Ingredients

- Ground beef (2 pounds)
- Beef broth (32 oz.)
- Cream cheese (8 oz.)
- Garlic (4 cloves, chopped)
- Tomatoes (20 oz., with chili
- Onion flakes (1 tbsp, optional)
- Cumin (2 tbsp)
- Chili powder (2 tbsp)
- Half cup heavy cream
- Salt
- Pepper
- Toppings
- Sour cream
- Jalapeno peppers
- Cheddar
- Black olives

Directions:

- Put the ground beef inside Pressure cooker, as well as set to "Sauté".
- Add the onion flakes, chili powder, salt, pepper, garlic, cumin, tomatoes with chili and beef broth and stir them well.
- Since it's not recommendable to pressure cook milk products, you may want to add the cream cheese and high cream once the stress cooking is done.
- Set the stress cooker to "Soup" for 5 more minutes.
- Once it's done, let the pot release pressure using the closed valve for 10 mins. Then add the cream and cheese.
- Serve while hot and add the toppings (this really is optional).

427. Zucchini And Yellow Squash Soup

Servings: 6
Preparation: Time: 1 Hour And 30 Minutes

Nutritive Values: Calories 250; Fats 20 Grams; Carbs 15 Grams; Fats 4.9 Grams

INGREDIENTS

- Green and yellow squash (8 cups)
- Vegetable stock/chicken stock (6-8 cups)
- Butter (1 tbsp)
- Olive oil (2 tbsp)
- Onion (chopped)
- Garlic (minced)
- Italian herb blend (1 tbsp)
- Fresh rosemary (4 tbsp, chopped)
- Salt
- Black pepper
- Parmesan cheese

Directions:

1. Melt the butter as well as the extra virgin olive oil within the Pressure cooker and set it to "Sauté"; add the onion and cook till the it softens up a bit bit.
2. Add Italian Herb Blend, garlic and rosemary, and cook for 3-5 more minutes.
3. Meanwhile, chop the zucchini and yellow squash (you'll need 8 cups), cook it for the short while with all the herbs and garlic; add the vegetable or chicken stock towards the onion mix and permit it to simmer for 10 mins.
4. Release the stress while using quick-release method once some time in order to smoke has ended.
5. Blend a combination; simmer it again (it will gain your preferred thickness); you'll need about twenty minutes in "Sauté" setting.
6. Add salt and pepper by preference and

serve it while it's still hot with sprinkled Parmesan cheese on the top.

428. Cauliflower Soup

Servings: 6
Preparation: Time: 40 Minutes
Nutritional Value: Calories 325; Fats 23.9 Grams; Proteins 14.7 Grams; Carbs 8.9 Grams

Ingredients

1. Bacon (6 slices)
2. Chicken broth
3. Cauliflower (1, chopped)
4. Sour cream (¾ cup)
5. Onion (¼ cup, chopped)
6. Celery (1 piece, chopped)
7. Garlic (2 cloves)
8. 1 ½ cups Cheddar or Monterey Jack
9. Salt
10. Pepper

Directions:

1. Put the cut bacon in the Pressure cooker and hang up to "Sauté"; stir occasionally so it won't stick. Fry it until it's crispy. Put the cooked bacon on the paper towel and permit the fat drain
2. Put the onion and garlic, celery, salt, and pepper inside the cooker, and cook before
3. INGREDIENTS are soft (3-4 minutes).
4. Pour the chicken broth inside, and add the chopped cauliflower. Close and lock the lid (the vent should be sealed). Set the pot to manual function to high and allow it to go cook for five more minutes.
5. Once it's done, allow the pot to naturally release the stress for ten minutes; then open the vent and eliminate the lid.
6. Pour inside the sour cream then one cup of cheese; blend this mixture in a blender and make certain it's smooth before you pour it in a mixer or a big blender.
7. Top the soup using the rest of the bacon, onion, and cheese.

429. Carrot Soup

Servings: 3
Preparation: Time: 35 Minutes
Nutritional Value: Calories 169; Fats 4.2 Grams; Carbs 28.5 Grams; Proteins 6.5 Grams

Ingredients

- Potato (1, peeled and chopped)
- Vegetable broth (5 and a half cups)
- Olive oil (2 tbsp)
- Onion (2 cups)
- Carrots (1 pound)
- Garlic (2 cloves)
- Turmeric (2 tbsp)
- Curry powder (2 tbsp)
- Cumin (half teaspoon)
- Salt (half teaspoon)
- Apple juice (half cup)
- Lemon juice (1 tbsp)
- Pumpkin seeds (1/4 cup, toasted)
- Cilantro

Directions:

1. Add as well as heat the oil inside pressure cooker; put within the carrots, garlic, and onion (they should all be chopped) and stir well. Set to "Sauté" for 5 minutes.
2. Add and stir the cumin, turmeric, salt, and curry powder and cook it to get a minute then put inside vegetable broth, apple juice, and potatoes.
3. Close and secure the coverage; cook on ruthless for five minutes. Release the stress while using quick-release method.
4. Once it's cool blend the mixture until it can be smooth.
5. Add the freshly squeezed lemon juice and season with salt and pepper as needed.
6. Serve it while using pumpkin seeds and cilantro while it's still hot.

430. Vegetable Soup

Servings: 12
Preparation: Time: 10 Minutes

Nutritive Values: Calories 51; Carbs 10 Grams; Proteins 3 Grams; Fiber 3 Grams

Ingredients

- Turnip (chopped in cubes)
- Onion (chopped)

- Spinach (1 pound, chopped)
- Celery (6 pieces, chopped)
- Carrot (chopped)
- Green beans (1 pound)
- Water (2 cups)
- Pumpkin puree (15 oz.)
- Chicken or vegetable broth (64 oz.)
- Fresh basil (1 tbsp, chopped)
- Thyme leaves (¼ tbsp chopped)
- Dry sage (1 teaspoon)
- Salt

Directions:

1. Put all of the
2. INGREDIENTS (except the spinach) within the Pressure cooker, cover the lid, and hang it in order to smoke on high pressure for 10 minutes.
3. Afterward, let it naturally release pressure for one more 10 mins. Open the pot and add the spinach, and stir well. Cover the lid and let the spinach sit for five more minutes.
4. Serve while it's still hot.

431. Chicken Soup With Poblano Peppers

Servings: 4

Preparation: Time: 45 Minutes

Nutritional Value: Calories 198; Fats 5 Grams; Carbs 13 Grams; Proteins 22 Grams

Ingredients

Water (2.5 cups)

- Navy beans (1/2 cup, soaked in water for 60 Minutes
- Chicken breast (chopped, 1.5 pounds)
- Onion (1 cup, chopped)
- Poblano peppers (3 pieces, chopped)
- Cauliflower (1 cup, diced)
- Garlic (5 cloves)
- Cilantro (¼ cup, chopped)
- Cumin (1 tbsp)
- Coriander (1 teaspoon)
- Salt (1-2 tbsp)
- Cream cheese for topping (2 oz.)

Directions:

1. Add everything in the pressure cooker (except the cream cheese) and cook for quarter-hour, on questionable. Release pressure naturally for 10 minutes (then manually release the rest).
2. Remove the chicken pieces aside; add the vegetables and also the liquid in a very blender and blend until smooth.
3. Set the pressure cooker to "Sauté" and put the soup in once it boils. Afterward, add the cream cheese. Stir before the cheese melts completely.
4. Bring back the shredded chicken and allow it to warm up inside liquid. Blend the chicken using the rest of the

INGREDIENTS if which is how you want your soups.

432. Goulash Soup

Servings: 4

Preparation: Time: 1 And A Half Hour)

Nutritive Values: Calories 289; Fats 7.8 Grams; Carbs 23.6 Grams; Proteins 31 Grams

Ingredients

- Ground beef (1 1/2 – 2 lbs)
- Red bell pepper (1, cut in little strips, no seeds or stem)
- Beef stock (homemade or canned, 14 oz.)
- Olive oil (3 tbsp)
- Onion (chopped)
- Garlic (chopped, 1 tbsp)
- Sweet paprika (2 tbsp)
- Hot paprika (half teaspoon)
- Fresh tomatoes (14 oz.)
- Sour cream for topping (by preference)

Directions:

1. Set your cooker "Saute" and add 2 tablespoons essential olive oil. Then cook the bottom beef inside hot oil. Break the meat in pieces with a fork before putting it into the pressure cooker.
2. Once the beef is semi-cooked (it should get brownish color), put it in a bowl and

allow it to drain from your grease.

3. Meanwhile cut the stem and get rid of the seeds from the red bell pepper and make the grade in strips. Cut the onion in strips (get them to even using the pepper strips).
4. Add the 3rd tablespoon essential olive oil in the cooker, atart exercising . the pepper and the onion and cook for more 3-4 minutes.
5. Add the garlic, sweet and hot paprika and cook for any couple of more minutes. Make sure you stir and so the paprika cooks well.
6. Pour inside the beef stock and also the tomatoes, and then add the floor beef. Close and lock the lid and hang up the cooker to "Soup", for 15 minutes. If you use a manual pressure cooker, then be sure you cook to low pressure.
7. Once it's cooked, release pressure to succeed manually for a couple minutes, then make use of the quick-release method and release all of the pressure.
8. Serve while it's hot with sour cream (this is an optional topping)

433. Chinese Hot And Sour Soup

Servings: 4

Preparation: Time: 20 Minutes

Nutritional Value: Calories 158; Fats 5 Grams; Carbs 5 Grams; Proteins 20 Grams

Ingredients

- 5 cups chicken broth (be sure it's low sodium)
- Thin slices of pork loin (1 pound)
- Mushrooms (1 cup)
- White vinegar (3 tbsp)
- Soy sauce (3 tbsp)
- Water (3 tbsp)
- Pepper (by taste)
- For as soon as the soup is cooked
- Tofu (1 pound)
- Eggs (4)

Directions:

1. Everything except the eggs and also the tofu goes within the pressure cooker; the choice is yours to "Soup" for 10 minutes. After it's done, release the pressure naturally for fifteen minutes; quick-release the remainder of the pressure.
2. Set pressure cooker to "Sauté" so the soup is able to keep the temperature.
3. Take out your mushrooms and cut them in thin pieces, and then return then in the soup.
4. Now it's some time to add the tofu (work in pieces) and stir well; beat the eggs and pour them in the soup. Stir and cover the pot therefore the eggs might have time in order to cook in the hot soup (about 60 seconds or so).
5. Serve and luxuriate in.

434. Leek And Cauliflower Soup

Servings: 8

Preparation: Time: 40-45 Minutes

Nutritive Values: Calories 201; Fats 19 Grams; Carbs 5 Grams; Proteins 2 Grams

Ingredients

- Leek (2, chopped by 50 %-inch pieces)
- Cauliflower (1 large head, cut in small pieces)
- Chicken broth (8 cups)
- Butter (3 tbsp)
- Heavy cream (1 cup)
- Olive oil (2 tbsp)
- Garlic (1 tbsp, peeled and minced)
- Onion
- Bacon
- Salt
- Pepper

Directions:

1. Add the butter and extra virgin olive oil inside the pressure cooker and set it to "Sauté"; add the chopped leeks, garlic, and cauliflower and cook for ten minutes.
2. Afterward, pour inside the chicken broth and stir. Close the lid and seal it; set the stress cooker to "Soup" and hang time to

thirty minutes.

3. When enough time has ended, release the pressure (either manually or naturally); get rid of the lid and blend the soup until eveything is smooth.
4. Add salt and pepper and also the heavy cream, then blend more.
5. Serve the soup with onions and bacon (this really is optional).

435. uick Chicken Soup

Servings: 4
Preparation: Time: 5 Minutes

Nutritional Value: Calories 215; Fats 4 Grams; Carbs 4 Grams; Proteins 36 Grams

Ingredients

- Chicken stock or broth (2 cups)
- Chicken (shredded, 8 oz.)
- Celery (10 pieces, chopped)
- Zucchini (2, cut in thin slices)
- Baby carrots (2 cups)
- Onion (half head, chopped)
- Red bell pepper (half piece, chopped)
- Garlic powder (1 tbsp)
- Dry rosemary (half tbsp)
- Salt (half teaspoon)
- Pepper (by taste)

Directions:

1. **All the ingredients walk into the pressure cooker; close the lid and seal it as well as set it to "High pressure" for 5 minutes.**
2. Once you hear the timer sound, the soup is cooked and it's time to produce the stress naturally.
3. Remove the lid, add salt and pepper along with the soup is ready for serving.

436. Coconut Soup

Preparation Time: 15 minutes
Cooking time: 35 minutes
Servings: 6

Ingredients:

1½ cups coconut milk
4 cups chicken stock
1 tsp fried lemongrass

- 3 lime leaves
- 4 Thai chilies, dried and chopped
- 1-inch fresh ginger, peeled and grated
- 1 cup fresh cilantro, chopped
- Salt and ground black pepper to taste
- 1 tbsp fish sauce
- 1 tbsp coconut oil
- 2 tbsp mushrooms, chopped
- 4 oz shrimp, peeled and deveined
- 2 tbsp onion, chopped
- 1 tbsp fresh cilantro, chopped
- Juice from 1 lime

Directions:

1. In medium pot, combine coconut milk, chicken stock, lemongrass and lime leaves.
2. Preheat pot on medium heat.
3. Add Thai chilies, ginger, cilantro, salt and pepper, stir and bring to simmer. Cook for 20 minutes.
4. Strain soup and return liquid to pot.
5. Heat up soup over medium heat.
6. Add fish sauce, coconut oil, mushrooms, shrimp, and onion. Stir well. Cook for 10 minutes.
7. Add cilantro and lime juice, stir. Set aside for 10 minutes.
8. Serve.

Nutritional Value: Calories - 448, Carbs – 7.9g, Fat – 33.8g, Protein – 11.8g

437. Broccoli Soup

Preparation Time: 12 minutes
Cooking time: 35 minutes
Servings: 4

Ingredients:

- 2 cloves garlic
- 1 medium white onion
- 1 tbsp butter
- 2 cups water
- 2 cups vegetable stock
- 1 cup heavy cream

- Salt and ground black pepper to taste
- ½ tsp paprika
- 1½ cups broccoli, divided into florets
- 1 cup cheddar cheese

Directions:

1. Peel and mince garlic. Peel and chop onion.
2. Preheat pot on medium heat, add butter and melt it.
3. Add garlic and onion and sauté for 5 minutes, stirring occasionally.
4. Pour in water, vegetable stock, heavy cream and add pepper, salt and paprika.
5. Stir and bring to boil.
6. Add broccoli and simmer for 25 minutes.
7. After that, transfer soup mixture to food processor and blend well.
8. Grate cheddar cheese and add to food processor, blend again.
9. Serve soup hot.

Nutritional Value: Calories - 348, Carbs – 6.8g, Fat – 33.8g, Protein – 10.9g

438. Simple Tomato Soup

Preparation Time: 15 minutes
Cooking time: 10 minutes
Servings: 6

Ingredients:

- 4 cups canned tomato soup
- 2 tbsp apple cider vinegar
- 1 tsp dried oregano
- 4 tbsp butter
- 2 tsp turmeric
- 2 oz red hot sauce
- Salt and ground black pepper to taste
- 4 tbsp olive oil
- 8 bacon strips, cooked and crumbled
- 4 oz fresh basil leaves, chopped
- 4 oz green onions, chopped

Directions:

1. Pour tomato soup in pot and preheat on medium heat. Bring to boil.
2. Add vinegar, oregano, butter, turmeric, hot sauce, salt, black pepper and olive oil. Stir well.
3. Simmer soup for 5 minutes.
4. Serve soup topped with crumbled bacon, green onion and basil.

Nutritional Value: Calories - 397, Carbs – 9.8g, Fat – 33.8, Protein – 11.7g

439. Green Soup

Preparation Time: 12 minutes
Cooking time: 15 minutes
Servings: 6

Ingredients:

- 2 cloves garlic
- 1 white onion
- 1 cauliflower head
- 2 oz butter
- 1 bay leaf, crushed
- 1 cup spinach leaves
- ½ cup watercress
- 4 cups vegetable stock
- Salt and ground black pepper to taste
- 1 cup coconut milk
- ½ cup parsley, for serving

Directions:

1. Peel and mince garlic. Peel and dice onion.
2. Divide cauliflower into florets.
3. Preheat pot on medium high heat, add butter and melt it.
4. Add onion and garlic, stir and sauté for 4 minutes.
5. Add cauliflower and bay leaf, stir and cook for 5 minutes.
6. Add spinach and watercress, stir and cook for another 3 minutes.
7. Pour in vegetable stock. Season with salt and black pepper. Stir and bring to boil.
8. Pour in coconut milk and stir well. Take off heat.
9. Use an immersion blender to blend well.
10. Top with parsley and serve hot.

Nutritional Value: Calories - 227, Carbs – 4.89g, Fat – 35.1, Protein – 6.97g

440. Sausage and Peppers Soup

Preparation Time: 15 minutes
Cooking time: 1 hour 15 minutes
Servings: 6

Ingredients:

- 1 tbsp avocado oil
- 2 lbs pork sausage meat
- Salt and ground black pepper to taste
- 1 green bell pepper, seeded and chopped
- 5 oz canned jalapeños, chopped
- 5 oz canned tomatoes, chopped
- 1¼ cup spinach
- 4 cups beef stock
- 1 tsp Italian seasoning
- 1 tbsp cumin
- 1 tsp onion powder
- 1 tsp garlic powder
- 1 tbsp chili powder

Directions:

1. Preheat pot with avocado oil on medium heat.
2. Put sausage meat in pot and brown for 3 minutes on all sides.
3. Add salt, black pepper and green bell pepper and continue to cook for 3 minutes.
4. Add jalapeños and tomatoes, stir well and cook for 2 minutes more.
5. Toss spinach and stir again, close lid and cook for 7 minutes.
6. Pour in beef stock, Italian seasoning, cumin, onion powder, chili powder, garlic powder, salt and black pepper, stir well. Close lid again. Cook for 30 minutes.
7. When time is up, uncover pot and simmer for 15 minutes more.
8. Serve hot.

Nutritional Value: Calories - 531, Carbs – 3.99g, Fat – 44.5g, Protein – 25.8g

441. Avocado Soup

Preparation Time: 12 minutes
Cooking time: 15 minutes
Servings: 4

Ingredients:

- 2 tbsp butter
- 2 scallions, chopped
- 3 cups chicken stock
- 2 avocados, pitted, peeled, and chopped
- Salt and ground black pepper to taste
- ⅔ cup heavy cream

Directions:

1. Preheat pot on medium heat, add butter and melt it.
2. Toss scallions, stir and sauté for 2 minutes.
3. Pour in 2 ½ cups stock and bring to simmer. Cook for 3 minutes.
4. Meanwhile, peel and chop avocados.
5. Place avocado, ½ cup of stock, cream, salt and pepper in blender and blend well.
6. Add avocado mixture to pot and mix well. Cook for 2 minutes.
7. Sprinkle with more salt and pepper, stir.
8. Serve hot.

Nutritional Value: Calories - 329, Carbs – 5.9g, Fat – 22.9g, Protein – 5.8g

442. ocado and Bacon Soup

Preparation Time: 15 minutes
Cooking time: 15 minutes
Servings: 6

Ingredients:

- 1 quart chicken stock
- 2 avocados, pitted
- ⅓ cup fresh cilantro, chopped
- 1 tsp garlic powder
- Salt and ground black pepper to taste
- Juice of ½ lime
- ½ lb bacon, cooked and chopped

Directions:

1. Pour chicken stock in pot and bring to boil over medium high heat.
2. Meanwhile, peeled and chopped avocados.
3. Place avocados, cilantro, garlic powder, salt, black pepper and lime juice in blender or food processor and blend

well.

4. Add avocado mixture in boiling stock and stir well.
5. Add bacon and season with salt and pepper to taste.
6. Stir and simmer for 3-4 minutes on medium heat.
7. Serve hot.

Nutritional Value: Calories - 298, Carbs – 5.98g, Fat – 22.8g, Protein – 16.8g

443. Roasted Bell Peppers Soup

Preparation Time: 15 minutes
Cooking time: 20 minutes
Servings: 6

Ingredients:

- 1 medium white onion
- 2 cloves garlic
- 2 celery stalks
- 12 oz roasted bell peppers, seeded
- 2 tbsp olive oil
- Salt and ground black pepper to taste
- 1 quart chicken stock
- 2/3 cup water
- ¼ cup Parmesan cheese, grated
- ⅔ cup heavy cream

Directions:

1. Peel and chop onion and garlic. Chop celery and bell pepper.
2. Preheat pot with oil on medium heat.
3. Put garlic, onion, celery, salt and pepper in pot, stir and sauté for 8 minutes.
4. Pour in chicken stock and water. Add bell peppers and stir.
5. Bring to boil, close lid and simmer for 5 minutes. Reduce heat if needed.
6. When time is up, blend soup using immersion blender.
7. Add cream and season with salt and pepper to taste. Take off heat.
8. Serve hot with grated cheese.

Nutritional Value: Calories - 180, Carbs – 3.9g, Fat – 12.9g, Protein – 5.9g

444. Spicy Bacon Soup

Preparation Time: 15 minutes
Cooking time: 30 minutes
Servings: 6

Ingredients:

- 10 oz bacon, chopped
- Salt to taste
- 1 tbsp olive oil
- 2/3 cup cauliflower, divided into florets
- 4 oz green bell pepper, seeded and chopped
- 1 jalapeno pepper, seeded and chopped
- 4 cups chicken stock
- 2 tbsp full-fat cream
- 1 tsp ground black pepper
- 1 tsp chili pepper

Directions:

1. In bowl, combine bacon with salt.
2. Heat up pan over medium heat and cook bacon for 5 minutes, stirring constantly.
3. Remove bacon from pan and set aside.
4. Pour olive oil in pan and add cauliflower, bell pepper and jalapeno.
5. Cook veggies on high heat for 1 minute, stirring occasionally.
6. In saucepan, mix bacon with vegetables. Pour in chicken stock. Stir.
7. Close lid and cook for 20-25 minutes.
8. Open lid and add cream, stir.
9. Season with salt, black pepper and chili pepper. Stir and cook for 5 minutes more.
10. Serve.

Nutritional Value: Calories - 301, Carbs – 3.9g, Fat - 23g, Protein - 19g

445. Italian Sausage Soup

Preparation Time: 15 minutes
Cooking time: 35 minutes
Servings: 10

Ingredients:

- 1 tsp avocado oil
- 2 cloves garlic
- 1 medium white onion

- 1½ lbs hot pork sausage, chopped
- 8 cups chicken stock
- 1 lb radishes, chopped
- 10 oz spinach
- 1 cup heavy cream
- 6 bacon slices, chopped
- Salt and ground black pepper to taste
- A pinch of red pepper flakes

Directions:

- Preheat pot on medium high heat and add oil.
- Peel and chop garlic and onion.
- Put garlic, onion and sausage in pot and stir.
- Cook for few minutes until browned.
- Pour in chicken stock; add radishes and spinach, stir.
- Bring mixture to simmer and add cream, bacon, black pepper, salt and red pepper flakes, stir well.
- Simmer for 20 minutes.
- Serve hot.

Nutritional Value: Calories - 289, Carbs – 3.8g, Fat – 21.8g, Protein – 18.1g

446. Cabbage Soup with Chorizo Sausages

Preparation Time: 20 minutes
Cooking time: 25 minutes
Servings: 5

Ingredients:

- ½ tbsp olive oil
- 10 oz chorizo sausages, sliced
- ½ tsp oregano
- ½ tsp cayenne pepper
- 1 tsp onion powder
- 1 tsp cilantro
- ½ tsp ground black pepper
- 1 tsp kosher salt
- 11 oz white cabbage, chopped
- 1 medium white onion, peeled and diced
- 5 cloves garlic, peeled and sliced
- 4 cups water
- 1 green bell pepper, seeded and diced

Directions:

1. Heat up pan over medium heat and add oil.
2. Add sausages and brown them for 2 minutes, stirring constantly.
3. In medium bowl, mix together oregano, cayenne pepper, onion powder, cilantro, black pepper and salt.
4. In another bowl, combine cabbage, onion, and garlic.
5. Season vegetables with spice mixture and stir.
6. Pour water into saucepan and bring to boil over high heat.
7. Add bell pepper and cabbage mixture.
8. Cook for 10 minutes on medium heat.
9. Add sausages and cook for another 10 minutes on low heat.
10. When time is up, take off heat and leave soup for 5-10 minutes.
11. Serve hot.

Nutritional Value: Calories - 299, Carbs – 10.1g, Fat – 23.2g, Protein – 14.9g

447. Vegetable Stew

Preparation Time: 17 minutes
Cooking time: 30 minutes
Servings: 5

Ingredients:

- 3 cups chicken stock
- oz eggplants, peeled and chopped
- oz cauliflower, divided into florets
- 1 tsp kosher salt
- 1 tsp oregano
- 1 tsp basil
- 1 tsp olive oil
- ¼ cup white onion, peeled and chopped
- 1 cup green bell pepper, seeded and chopped
- 3 tbsp butter
- ½ cup spinach, chopped roughly

Directions:

1. Sprinkle eggplants and cauliflower with salt to get rid of bitterness.
2. In small bowl, combine oregano and basil.
3. Preheat pan with olive oil on medium heat.
4. Add chopped onion and sauté for 2 minutes.
5. Then add eggplants and cook them for 5 minutes, stirring constantly.
6. Add cauliflower and fry for another 2 minutes.
7. Transfer fried veggies to saucepan.
8. Add spice mixture.
9. Add green bell pepper and 2 tablespoon of butter.
10. Pour in stock, close lid and simmer for 10 minutes on medium heat.
11. Heat up pan again over medium heat and add 1 tablespoon of butter, melt it.
12. Toss spinach on pan and cook for 2 minutes.
13. Then add spinach to saucepan with vegetables, stir and cook for 15 minutes more.
14. When time is up, stir and serve hot.

Nutritional Value: Calories - 99, Carbs - 7g, Fat - 8.65g, Protein - 2g

448. Spinach Soup

Preparation Time: 15 minutes
Cooking time: 20 minutes
Servings: 6

Ingredients:

- 1 medium white onion
- 2½ cups spinach
- 2 tbsp butter
- 1 tsp garlic, minced
- 5½ cups chicken stock
- 2 cups heavy cream
- ½ tsp ground nutmeg
- Salt and ground black pepper to taste

Directions:

1. Peel and chop onion. Chop spinach.
2. Preheat pot with butter on medium heat.
3. Add onion and sauté for 4 minutes, stirring frequently.
4. Toss garlic, stir and sauté for 1 minute more.
5. Pour in chicken stock and add spinach, stir and cook for 5 minutes.
6. With immersion blender, blend soup well.
7. Heat up soup again; add cream, nutmeg, pepper and salt.
8. Simmer for 5 minutes.
9. Serve hot.

Nutritional Value: Calories - 239, Carbs – 3.98g, Fat – 23.9g, Protein – 5.98g

449. Mediterranean Salad

Preparation Time: 10 minutes
Serves: 4

Ingredients

- 3 tomatoes, sliced
- 1 large avocado, sliced
- 8 kalamata olives
- ¼ lb buffalo mozzarella cheese, sliced
- 2 tbsp pesto sauce
- 2 tbsp olive oil

Directions

1. Arrange the tomato slices on a serving platter and place the avocado slices in the middle. Arrange the olives around the avocado slices and drop pieces of mozzarella on the platter. Drizzle the pesto sauce all over, and drizzle olive oil as well.

Nutritional Value: Calories 290, Fat: 25g, Net Carbs: 4.3g, Protein: 9g

450. Lobster Salad with Mayo Dressing

Preparation Time: 1 hour 10 minutes
Serves: 4

Ingredients

- 1 small head cauliflower, cut into florets
- ⅓ cup diced celery
- ½ cup sliced black olives

- 2 cups cooked large shrimp
- 1 tbsp dill, chopped

Dressing:

- ½ cup mayonnaise
- 1 tsp apple cider vinegar
- ¼ tsp celery seeds
- A pinch of black pepper
- 2 tbsp lemon juice
- 2 tsp swerve
- Salt to taste

Directions

1. Combine the cauliflower, celery, shrimp, and dill in a large bowl. Whisk together the mayonnaise, vinegar, celery seeds, sweetener, and lemon juice in another bowl. Season with salt to taste.
2. Pour the dressing over and gently toss to combine; refrigerate for 1 hour. Top with olives to serve.

Nutritional Value: Calories 182, Fat: 15g, Net Carbs: 2g, Protein: 12g

451. Power Green Soup

Preparation Time: 30 minutes
Serves: 6

Ingredients

- 1 broccoli head, chopped
- 1 cup spinach
- 1 onion, chopped
- 2 garlic cloves, minced
- ½ cup watercress
- 5 cups veggie stock
- 1 cup coconut milk
- 1 tsp salt
- 1 tbsp ghee
- 1 bay leaf
- Salt and black pepper, to taste

Directions

1. Melt the ghee in a large pot over medium heat. Add onion and cook for 3 minutes. Add garlic and cook for another minute. Add broccoli and cook for an additional 5 minutes.
2. Pour the stock over and add the bay leaf. Close the lid, bring to a boil, and reduce the heat. Simmer for about 3 minutes.
3. In the end, add spinach and watercress, and cook for 3 more minutes. Stir in the coconut cream, salt and pepper. Discard the bay leaf, and blend the soup with a hand blender.

Nutritional Value: Calories 392, Fat: 37.6g, Net Carbs: 5.8g, Protein: 4.9g

452. Green Salad with Bacon and Blue Cheese

Preparation Time: 15 minutes
Serves: 4

Ingredients

- 2 (8 oz) pack mixed salad greens
- 8 strips bacon
- 1 ½ cups crumbled blue cheese
- 1 tbsp white wine vinegar
- 3 tbsp extra virgin olive oil
- Salt and black pepper to taste

Directions

1. Pour the salad greens in a salad bowl; set aside. Fry bacon strips in a skillet over medium heat for 6 minutes, until browned and crispy. Chop the bacon and scatter over the salad. Add in half of the cheese, toss and set aside.
2. In a small bowl, whisk the white wine vinegar, olive oil, salt, and black pepper until dressing is well combined. Drizzle half of the dressing over the salad, toss, and top with remaining cheese. Divide salad into four plates and serve with crusted chicken fries along with remaining dressing.

Nutritional Value: Calories 205, Fat 20g, Net Carbs 2g, Protein 4g

453. Warm Baby Artichoke Salad

Preparation Time: 35 minutes
Serves: 4

Ingredients

- 6 baby artichokes
- 6 cups water
- 1 tbsp lemon juice
- ¼ cup cherry peppers, halved
- ¼ cup pitted olives, sliced
- ¼ cup olive oil
- ¼ tsp lemon zest
- 2 tsp balsamic vinegar, sugar-free
- 1 tbsp chopped dill
- ½ tsp salt
- ¼ tsp black pepper
- 1 tbsp capers
- ¼ tsp caper brine

Directions

1. Combine the water and salt in a pot over medium heat. Trim and halve the artichokes; add to the pot. Bring to a boil, lower the heat, and let simmer for 20 minutes until tender.
2. Combine the rest of the ingredients, except the olives in a bowl. Drain and place the artichokes in a serving plate. Pour the prepared mixture over; toss to combine well. Serve topped with the olives.

Nutritional Value: Calories 170, Fat: 13g, Net Carbs: 5g, Protein: 1g

454. Brazilian Moqueca (Shrimp Stew)

Preparation Time: 25 minutes
Serves: 6

Ingredients

- 1 cup coconut milk
- 2 tbsp lime juice
- ¼ cup diced roasted peppers
- 1 ½ pounds shrimp, peeled and deveined
- ¼ cup olive oil
- 1 garlic clove, minced
- 14 ounces diced tomatoes
- 2 tbsp sriracha sauce
- 1 chopped onion
- ¼ cup chopped cilantro
- Fresh dill, chopped to garnish
- Salt and black pepper, to taste

Directions

1. Heat the olive oil in a pot over medium heat. Add onion and cook for 3 minutes or until translucent. Add the garlic and cook for another minute, until soft. Add tomatoes, shrimp, and cilantro. Cook until the shrimp becomes opaque, about 3-4 minutes.
2. Stir in sriracha sauce and coconut milk, and cook for 2 minutes. Do not bring to a boil. Stir in the lime juice and season with salt and pepper. Spoon the stew in bowls, garnish with fresh dill to serve.

Nutritional Value: Calories 324, Fat: 21g, Net Carbs: 5g, Protein: 23.1g

455. Caesar Salad with Smoked Salmon and Poached Eggs

Preparation Time: 15 minutes
Serves: 4

Ingredients

- 3 cups water
- 8 eggs
- 2 cups torn romaine lettuce
- ½ cup chopped smoked salmon
- 6 slices bacon
- 2 tbsp heinz low carb caesar dressing

Directions

1. Boil the water in a pot over medium heat for 5 minutes and bring to simmer. Crack each egg into a small bowl and gently slide into the water. Poach for 2 to 3 minutes, remove with a perforated spoon, transfer to a paper towel to dry, and plate. Poach the remaining 7 eggs.
2. Put the bacon in a skillet and fry over medium heat until browned and crispy, about 6 minutes, turning once. Remove, allow cooling, and chop in small pieces.
3. Toss the lettuce, smoked salmon, bacon, and caesar dressing in a salad bowl. Divide the salad into 4 plates, top with two eggs each, and serve immediately or

chilled.

Nutritional Value: Calories 260, Fat 21g, Net Carbs 5g, Protein 8g

456. Brussels Sprouts Salad with Pecorino Romano

Preparation Time: 35 minutes
Serves: 6

Ingredients

- 2 lb Brussels sprouts, halved
- 3 tbsp olive oil
- Salt and black pepper to taste
- 2 ½ tbsp balsamic vinegar
- ¼ red cabbage, shredded
- 1 tbsp Dijon mustard
- 1 cup grated pecorino romano

Directions

1. Preheat oven to 400°F and line a baking sheet with foil. Toss the brussels sprouts with olive oil, a little salt, black pepper, and balsamic vinegar, in a bowl, and spread on the baking sheet in an even layer. Bake until tender on the inside and crispy on the outside, about 20 to 25 minutes.
2. Transfer to a salad bowl and add the red cabbage, Dijon mustard and half of the cheese. Mix until well combined. Sprinkle with the remaining cheese, share the salad onto serving plates, and serve with syrup-grilled salmon.

Nutritional Value: Calories 210, Fat 18g, Net Carbs 6g, Protein 4g

457. Slow Cooker Beer Soup with Cheddar & Sausage

Preparation Time: 8 hr
Serves: 8

Ingredients

- 1 cup heavy cream
- 10 ounces sausages, sliced
- 1 cup chopped celery
- 1 cup chopped carrots
- 4 garlic cloves, minced
- 8 ounces cream cheese
- 1 tsp red pepper flakes
- 6 ounces beer
- 16 ounces beef stock
- 1 onion, diced
- 1 cup cheddar cheese
- Salt and black pepper, to taste
- Fresh cilantro, chopped, to garnish

Directions

1. Turn on the slow cooker. Add broth, beer, sausage, carrots, onion, celery, salt, red pepper flakes, salt, and pepper, and stir to combine. Pour in enough water to cover all the ingredients by roughly 2 inches. Close the lid and cook for 6 hours on Low.
2. Open the lid and stir in the heavy cream, cheddar, and cream cheese, and cook for 2 more hours. Ladle the soup into bowls and garnish with cilantro before serving. Yummy!

Nutritional Value: Calories 244, Fat: 17g, Net Carbs: 4g, Protein: 5g

458. Beef Reuben Soup

Preparation Time: 20 minutes
Serves: 6

Ingredients

- 1 onion, diced
- 6 cups beef stock
- 1 tsp caraway seeds
- 2 celery stalks, diced
- 2 garlic cloves, minced
- ¾ tsp black pepper
- 2 cups heavy cream
- 1 cup sauerkraut
- 1 pound corned beef, chopped
- 3 tbsp butter
- 1 ½ cup swiss cheese
- Salt and black pepper, to taste

Directions

1. Melt the butter in a large pot. Add onion and celery, and fry for 3 minutes until

tender. Add garlic and cook for another minute.

2. Pour the broth over and stir in sauerkraut, salt, caraway seeds, and add a pinch of pepper. Bring to a boil. Reduce the heat to low, and add the corned beef. Cook for about 15 minutes, adjust the seasoning. Stir in heavy cream and cheese and cook for 1 minute.

Nutritional Value: Calories 450, Fat: 37g, Net Carbs: 8g, Protein: 23g

459. Pork Burger Salad with Yellow Cheddar

Preparation Time: 25 minutes
Serves: 4

Ingredients

- 1 lb ground pork
- Salt and black pepper to season
- 1 tbsp olive oil
- 2 hearts romaine lettuce, torn into pieces
- 2 firm tomatoes, sliced
- ¼ red onion, sliced
- 3 oz yellow cheddar cheese, shredded

Directions

1. Season the pork with salt and black pepper, mix and make medium-sized patties out of them.
2. Heat the oil in a skillet over medium heat and fry the patties on both sides for 10 minutes until browned and cook within. Transfer to a wire rack to drain oil. When cooled, cut into quarters.
3. Mix the lettuce, tomatoes, and onion in a salad bowl, season with a little oil, salt, and pepper. Toss and add the pork on top.
4. Melt the cheese in the microwave for about 90 seconds. Drizzle the cheese over the salad and serve.

Nutritional Value: Calories 310, Fat 23g, Net Carbs 2g, Protein 22g

460. Bacon and Spinach Salad

Preparation Time: 20 minutes
Serves: 4

Ingredients

- 2 large avocados, 1 chopped and 1 sliced
- 1 spring onion, sliced
- 4 cooked bacon slices, crumbled
- 2 cups spinach
- 2 small lettuce heads, chopped
- 2 hard-boiled eggs, chopped
- Vinaigrette:
- 3 tbsp olive oil
- 1 tsp Dijon mustard
- 1 tbsp apple cider vinegar

Directions

1. Combine the spinach, lettuce, eggs, chopped avocados, and spring onion, in a large bowl. Whisk together the vinaigrette ingredients in another bowl.
2. Pour the dressing over, toss to combine and top with the sliced avocado and bacon.

Nutritional Value: Calories 350, Fat: 33g, Net Carbs: 3.4g, Protein: 7g

461. Traditional Greek Salad

Preparation Time: 10 minutes
Serves: 4

Ingredients

- 5 tomatoes, chopped
- 1 large cucumber, chopped
- 1 green bell pepper, chopped
- 1 small red onion, chopped
- 16 kalamata olives, chopped
- 4 tbsp capers
- 1 cup feta cheese, chopped
- 1 tsp oregano, dried
- 4 tbsp olive oil
- Salt to taste

Directions

1. Place tomatoes, pepper, cucumber, onion, feta and olives in a bowl; mix to combine well. Season with salt. Combine capers, olive oil, and oregano, in a small

bowl. Drizzle with the dressing to serve.

Nutritional Value: Calories 323, Fat: 28g, Net Carbs: 8g, Protein: 9.3g

462. Broccoli Slaw Salad with Mustard-Mayo Dressing

Preparation Time: 10 minutes
Serves: 6

Ingredients

- 2 tbsp granulated swerve
- 1 tbsp Dijon mustard
- 1 tbsp olive oil
- 4 cups broccoli slaw
- ⅓ cup mayonnaise, sugar-free
- 1 tsp celery seeds
- 1 ½ tbsp apple cider vinegar
- Salt and black pepper, to taste

Directions

1. Whisk together all ingredients except the broccoli slaw. Place broccoli slaw in a large salad bowl. Pour the dressing over. Mix with your hands to combine well.

Nutritional Value: Calories 110, Fat: 10g, Net Carbs: 2g, Protein: 3g

463. Strawberry Salad with Spinach, Cheese & Almonds

Preparation Time: 20 minutes
Serves: 2

Ingredients

- 4 cups spinach
- 4 strawberries, sliced
- ½ cup flaked almonds
- 1 ½ cup grated hard goat cheese
- 4 tbsp raspberry vinaigrette
- Salt and black pepper, to taste

Directions

1. Preheat your oven to 400°F. Arrange the grated goat cheese in two circles on two pieces of parchment paper. Place in the oven and bake for 10 minutes.
2. Find two same bowls, place them upside down, and carefully put the parchment paper on top to give the cheese a bowl-like shape. Let cool that way for 15 minutes. Divide spinach among the bowls and drizzle with vinaigrette. Top with almonds and strawberries.

Nutritional Value: Calories 445, Fat: 34.2g, Net Carbs: 5.3g, Protein: 33g

464. Sriracha Egg Salad with Mustard Dressing

Preparation Time: 15 minutes
Serves: 8

Ingredients

- 10 eggs
- ¾ cup mayonnaise
- 1 tsp sriracha
- 1 tbsp mustard
- ½ cup scallions
- ½ stalk celery, minced
- ½ tsp fresh lemon juice
- ½ tsp sea salt
- ½ tsp black pepper, to taste
- 1 head romaine lettuce, torn into pieces

Directions

1. Add the eggs in a pan and cover with enough water and boil. Get them from the heat and allow to set for 10 minutes while covered. Chop the eggs and add to a salad bowl.
2. Stir in the remaining ingredients until everything is well combined. Refrigerate until ready to serve.

Nutritional Value: Calories 174; Fat 13g, Net Carbs 7.7g, Protein 7.4g

465. Chicken Creamy Soup

Preparation Time: 15 minutes
Serves: 4

Ingredients

- 2 cups cooked and shredded chicken
- 3 tbsp butter, melted
- 4 cups chicken broth
- 4 tbsp chopped cilantro

- ⅓ cup buffalo sauce
- ½ cup cream cheese
- Salt and black pepper, to taste

Directions

1. Blend the butter, buffalo sauce, and cream cheese, in a food processor, until smooth. Transfer to a pot, add the chicken broth and heat until hot but do not bring to a boil. Stir in chicken and cook until heated through. When ready, remove to soup bowls and serve garnished with cilantro.

Nutritional Value: Calories 406, Fat: 29.5g, Net Carbs: 5g, Protein: 26.5g

466. Salsa Verde Chicken Soup

Preparation Time: 15 minutes
Serves: 4

Ingredients

- ½ cup salsa verde
- 2 cups cooked and shredded chicken
- 2 cups chicken broth
- 1 cup shredded cheddar cheese
- 4 ounces cream cheese
- ½ tsp chili powder
- ½ tsp ground cumin
- ½ tsp fresh cilantro, chopped
- Salt and black pepper, to taste

Directions

1. Combine the cream cheese, salsa verde, and broth, in a food processor; pulse until smooth. Transfer the mixture to a pot and place over medium heat. Cook until hot, but do not bring to a boil.
2. Add chicken, chili powder, and cumin and cook for about 3-5 minutes, or until it is heated through.
3. Stir in Cheddar cheese and season with salt and pepper to taste. If it is very thick, add a few tablespoons of water and boil for 1-3 more minutes. Serve hot in bowls sprinkled with fresh cilantro.

Nutritional Value: Calories 346, Fat: 23g, Net Carbs: 3g, Protein: 25g

467. Green Mackerel Salad

Preparation Time: 25 minutes
Serves: 2

Ingredients

- 2 mackerel fillets
- 2 hard-boiled eggs, sliced
- 1 tbsp coconut oil
- 2 cups green beans
- 1 avocado, sliced
- 4 cups mixed salad greens
- 2 tbsp olive oil
- 2 tbsp lemon juice
- 1 tsp Dijon mustard
- Salt and black pepper, to taste

Directions

1. Fill a saucepan with water and add the green beans and salt. Cook over medium heat for about 3 minutes. Drain and set aside.
2. Melt the coconut oil in a pan over medium heat. Add the mackerel fillets and cook for about 4 minutes per side, or until opaque and crispy. Divide the green beans between two salad bowls. Top with mackerel, egg, and avocado slices.
3. In a bowl, whisk together the lemon juice, oil, mustard, salt, and pepper, and drizzle over the salad.

Nutritional Value: Calories 525, Fat: 41.9g, Net Carbs: 7.6g, Protein: 27.3g

468. Broccoli Cheese Soup

Preparation Time: 20 minutes
Serves: 4

Ingredients

- ¾ cup heavy cream
- 1 onion, diced
- 1 tsp minced garlic
- 4 cups chopped broccoli
- 4 cups veggie broth
- 2 tbsp butter
- 2 ¾ cups grated cheddar cheese
- ¼ cup cheddar cheese to garnish

- Salt and black pepper, to taste
- ½ bunch fresh mint, chopped

Directions

1. Melt the butter in a large pot over medium heat. Sauté onion and garlic for 3 minutes or until tender, stirring occasionally. Season with salt and pepper. Add the broth, broccoli and bring to a boil.
2. Reduce the heat and simmer for 10 minutes. Puree the soup with a hand blender until smooth. Add in the cheese and cook about 1 minute. Taste, season with salt and pepper. Stir in the heavy cream.Serve in bowls with the reserved grated Cheddar cheese and sprinkled with fresh mint.

Nutritional Value: Calories 561, Fat: 52.3g, Net Carbs: 7g, Protein: 23.8g

469. esar Salad with Chicken and Parmesan

Preparation Time: 1 hour and 30 minutes
Serves: 4

Ingredients

- 4 boneless, skinless chicken thighs
- ¼ cup lemon juice
- 2 garlic cloves, minced
- 4 tbsp olive oil
- ½ cup caesar salad dressing, sugar-free
- 12 bok choy leaves
- 3 Parmesan crisps
- Parmesan cheese, for garnishing

Directions

1. Combine the chicken, lemon juice, 2 tbsp of olive oil, and garlic in a Ziploc bag. Seal the bag, shake to combine, and refrigerate for 1 hour. Preheat the grill to medium heat and grill the chicken for about 4 minutes per side.
2. Cut the bok choy leaves lengthwise, and brush it with the remaining olive oil. Grill the bok choy for about 3 minutes. Place on a serving bowl. Top with the chicken and drizzle the caesar salad dressing over. Top with parmesan crisps and sprinkle the grated parmesan cheese over.

Nutritional Value: Calories 529, Fat: 39g, Net Carbs: 5g, Protein: 33g

470. Grilled Steak Salad with Pickled Peppers

Preparation Time: 15 minutes
Serves: 4

Ingredients

- 1 lb skirt steak, sliced
- Salt and black pepper to season
- 1 tsp olive oil
- 1 ½ cups mixed salad greens
- 3 chopped pickled peppers
- 2 tbsp red wine vinaigrette
- ½ cup crumbled queso fresco

Directions

1. Brush the steaks with olive oil and season with salt and pepper on both sides.
2. Heat frying pan over high heat and cook the steaks on each side to the desired doneness, for about 5-6 minutes. Remove to a bowl, cover and leave to rest while you make the salad.
3. Mix the salad greens, pickled peppers, and vinaigrette in a salad bowl. Add the beef and sprinkle with cheese. Serve the salad with roasted parsnips.

Nutritional Value: Calories 315, Fat 26g, Net Carbs 2g, Protein 18g

471. Winter Cabbage and Celery Soup

Serves: 6
Preparation: 5 minutes
Cooking: 30 minutes

Ingredients

- 2 Tbsp olive oil
- 2 cloves garlic, minced
- 1/2 head cabbage, shredded
- 2 stalks celery, chopped
- 1 grated tomato
- 3 cups bone broth (preferable

homemade)

- 3 cups water
- 1/2 tsp ground black pepper

Directions:

1. Heat the oil in a large pot over medium heat.
2. Sauté the garlic, celery and cabbage, stirring, for about 8 minutes.
3. Add grated tomato, and continue to cook for further 2 - 3 minutes.
4. Pour the broth and water. Bring to a boil, lower heat to low, cover and simmer for 20 minutes or until cabbage softened.
5. Sprinkle with ground black pepper, stir and serve.

Nutritional Value:

Calories: 85 Carbohydrates: 2g Proteins: 17g Fat: 11g Fiber: 1g

472. Spinach Soup with Shiitake mushrooms

Serves: 4
Preparation: 10 minutes
Cooking: 15 minutes

Ingredients

- 2 Tbsp of olive oil
- 1 medium onion, chopped
- 2 cloves garlic, minced
- 2 cups of water
- 1/2 bunch of spinach
- 2 cups shiitake mushrooms, chopped
- 2 Tbsp of almond flour
- 1 Tbsp of coconut aminos
- 1 tsp coriander dry
- 1/2 tsp of ground mustard
- Salt and ground black pepper to taste

Directions:

1. Heat the olive oil and sauté the garlic and onion until golden brown.
2. Add the coconut aminos and the mushrooms and stir for a few minutes.
3. Pour water, chopped spinach and all remaining ingredients.
4. Cover and cook for 5 - 6 minutes or until spinach is tender.
5. Taste and adjust salt and the pepper.
6. Stir for further 5 minutes and remove for the heat.
7. Serve hot.

Nutritional Value:

Calories: 175 Carbohydrates: 12g Proteins: 21g Fat: 8g Fiber: 4.3g

473. Vegan Artichoke Soup

Serves: 6
Preparation: 15 minutes
Cooking: 1 hour 5 minutes

Ingredients

- 1 Tbsp of butter
- 6 artichoke hearts, halved
- 2 cloves garlic, minced
- 1 small onion, chopped
- 1 cup bone broth
- 2 cups of water
- 2 Tbsp of almond flour
- Salt and ground black pepper to taste
- 2 Tbsp of olive oil
- Fresh chopped parsley to taste
- Fresh chopped fresh basil to taste

Directions:

1. Heat the butter in a large pot, and add artichoke hearts, garlic and chopped onion.
2. Stir and cook until artichoke hearts tender.
3. Add bone broth, water and almond flout: season with the salt and pepper.
4. Bring soup to boil, and cook for 2 minutes.
5. Add little olive oil, parsley and basil, stir and cook uncovered for 1 hour.
6. When ready, push the soup through sieve.
7. Taste and adjust salt and pepper.
8. Serve.

Nutritional Value:

Calories: 145 Carbohydrates: 6g Proteins: 7g Fat: 12g Fiber: 0.5%

474. Bouyambessa" Seafood Soup

Serves: 6
Preparation: 10 minutes
Cooking: 25 minutes

Ingredients

- 1/2 cup of olive oil
- 1 spring onion cut in cubes
- 2 Tbsp of fresh celery, chopped
- 2 cloves of garlic minced
- 1 tomato, peeled and grated
- 2 bay leaves
- 1 tsp of anise
- 6 large, raw shrimps
- 1 sea bass and 1 sea bream fillets cut in pieces; about 1 1/2 lbs
- 12 mussels, rinsed in plenty of cold water
- Salt and ground black pepper
- 3 Tbsp of chopped parsley for serving
- 6 cups of water

Directions:

1. Heat the olive oil in a large pot and sauté in the onion, garlic and celery for 4 -5 minutes over medium heat.
2. Add bay leaves, anise and grated tomato; stir and cook for further 5 minutes.
3. Add seafood and fish and pour 6 cups of water; season with little salt and pepper.
4. Cover and cook for 10 - 12 minutes on low heat. Serve hot with chopped parsley.

Nutritional Value:

Calories: 272.5 Carbohydrates: 2g Proteins: 19g Fat: 20g Fiber: 0.5g

475. "Classico" Beef Stew

Serves: 8
Preparation: 5 minutes
Cooking: 1 hour 35 minutes

Ingredients

- 1 1/2 lb beef filed, cut in cubes
- 1 green onion (white and green parts), chopped
- 2 cloves garlic, minced
- 1 small carrot
- 1 grated tomato
- 1 tsp fresh basil (chopped)
- 1 tsp fresh oregano chopped
- 3 cups bone broth (or water)
- 1/2 cup white vinegar
- 1 tsp salt
- 1 Tbsp lard

Directions:

1. Heat the lard in a large skillet and sauté beef meat with a pinch of salt.
2. Add the onion and garlic, and cook until soft.
3. Add grated tomato and the carrot and stir for further 2 minutes.
4. Add all the other ingredients cover and cook on very low heat for about 1 1/2 to 1 3/4 hours, until the beef is tender.
5. Serve hot.

Nutritional Value:

Calories: 498 Carbohydrates: 3g Proteins: 46g Fat: 42g Fiber: 1g

476. Chicken and Greens Soup

Serves: 8
Preparation: 12 minutes
Cooking: 1 hour 50 minutes

Ingredients

- 1/4 cup of olive oil
- 1 1/2 lbs chicken breast, boneless, cut into cube
- 1 spring onion, cut into cubes
- 1 clove of garlic, finely chopped
- 1 1/2 lettuce cos or romain, chopped
- 1 cup of fresh spinach finely chopped
- 1 bunch of dill finely chopped, without the thick stalks
- 1/2 Tbsp of sweet chill powder
- 1 tsp of fresh mint, chopped
- 1 tsp of fresh thyme, chopped
- Salt and freshly ground pepper
- 5 cups of water

Directions:

1. In a deep pot, heat the olive oil to a high heat and sauté the chicken for about 5 - 6 minutes.
2. Add the onion and sauté for about 3 minutes until softened.
3. Add the garlic, the lettuce, spinach, dill, mint, thyme and sauté for about 3-4 minutes, stirring with a wooden spoon.
4. Sprinkle with chili, salt, freshly ground pepper and pour 5 cups of water.
5. Bring to boil, and cook for 1 1/2 hours on low heat.
6. Serve hot.

Nutritional Value:

Calories: 181 Carbohydrates: 4.5g Proteins: 20g Fat: 10g Fiber: 3g

477. Chicken and Shredded Cabbage Stew

Serves: 4
Preparation: 10 minutes
Cooking: 50 minutes

Ingredients

- 2 Tbsp of chicken fat
- 1/2 cup of green onions, chopped
- 2 cloves garlic, sliced
- 2 chicken breast cut in pieces
- 1/2 tsp nutmeg
- 2 Tbsp of yellow mustard
- 1 3/4 cups water
- 1 cup white wine
- 1/4 cup apple cider vinegar
- 6 whole cloves
- 1 carrot, peeled, sliced
- 1/2 tsp salt
- 1/4 tsp pepper
- 1 cup shredded cabbage

Directions:

- Heat chicken fat in a large Dutch oven over medium high temperature.
- Add green onions, garlic chicken and cook about 5 - 6 minutes.
- Spread mustard over chicken pieces; stir nutmeg, salt and pepper, water, wine, vinegar, cloves and carrot; bring to a boil.
- Cover, reduce heat to low and cook 20 minutes.
- Add shredded cabbage, stir, cover and cook for about 10 - 12 minutes.
- Taste and adjust salt and pepper to taste.
- Serve hot in a bowls.

Nutritional Value:

Calories: 191 Carbohydrates: 6g Proteins: 26g Fat: 5g Fiber: 2g

478. Cold Cauliflower and Cilantro Soup

Serves: 4
Preparation: 5 minutes
Cooking: 25 minutes

Ingredients

- 1 1/2 lbs. cauliflower (previously steamed)
- 1 cup almond milk
- 1/2 tsp fresh ginger grated
- 3 bunches fresh cilantro
- 3 Tbsp garlic-infused olive oil
- 2 pinch of salt

Directions:

1. Heat water in a large pot until boiling. Place the steamer in a pot and put in the cauliflower.
2. Cover and steam cauliflower for 6 - 7 minutes.
3. Remove the cauliflower along with all ingredients from the list above in a high-speed blender.
4. Blend until smooth or until desired texture is achieved.
5. Pour the soup in a glass container, cover and refrigerate for 2 - 3 hours.
6. Serve cold.

Nutritional Value:

Calories: 132 Carbohydrates: 7.5g Proteins: 3.5g Fat: 11g Fiber: 3.5g

479. Creamy Broccoli Soup with Nutmeg

Serves: 6
Preparation: 15 minutes
Cooking: 20 minutes

Ingredients

- 2 Tbsp of olive oil
- 2 green onions finely chopped
- 1 lb broccoli floret, frozen or fresh
- 6 cups of bone broth (cold)
- 1 cup of cream
- Salt and ground pepper to taste
- 1 Tbsp of nutmeg

Directions:

1. Heat the olive oil in a pot over medium-high heat.
2. Add the onion in and sauté it until becomes translucent.
3. Add the broccoli, season with the salt and pepper, and bring to boil.
4. Cover the pot and cook for 6 - 8 minutes.
5. Transfer the broccoli mixture into blender, and blend until smooth.
6. Pour the cream, and blend for further 30 seconds.
7. Return the soup in a pot, and reheat it.
8. Adjust salt and pepper, and serve hot with grated nutmeg.

Nutritional Value:

Calories: 205 Carbohydrates: 5g Proteins: 35g
Fat: 18g Fiber: 0.4g

480. Creamy Mushroom Soup with Crumbled Bacon

Serves: 6
Preparation: 15 minutes
Cooking: 55 minutes

Ingredients

- 1 Tbsp of lard
- 2 lbs of white mushrooms
- 1/2 cup of water
- 3 1/2 cups of almond milk
- 2 green onions, finely sliced
- 3 sprigs of fresh rosemary
- 2 cloves garlic, finely chopped
- 6 slices of bacon, fried and crumbled
- Salt and ground black pepper

Directions:

1. Heat the lard in a large skillet and sauté green onions and garlic over medium-high heat.
2. Season with the salt and pepper, and rosemary; pour water and cook for 5 minutes.
3. Add the mushrooms and sauté for 1-2 minutes.
4. Pour the almond milk, stir, cover and simmer for 40 minutes over low heat.
5. Remove the rosemary, and transfer the soup in your blender; blend until creamy and soft.
6. Adjust salt, and if necessary, add some warm water.
7. Chop the bacon and fry in a hot pan until it becomes crisp.
8. Serve your soup in bowls and sprinkle with chopped bacon.

Nutritional Value:

Calories: 101 Carbohydrates: 5.5g Proteins: 8g
Fat: 6g Fiber: 2g

481. Delicious Pork Stew

Serves: 4
Preparation: 10 minutes
Cooking: 40 minutes

Ingredients

- 2 Tbsp lard
- 2 spring onions finely chopped
- 1 1/2 lb pork boneless, cut into cubes
- Sea salt and black ground pepper to taste
- 1 red bell pepper (cut into thin strips)
- 1/2 cup water
- 1/2 tsp of cumin
- 1/2 tsp caraway seeds

Directions:

1. Heat the lard in a large skillet over medium-high heat.
2. Sauté the spring onions for 3 - 4 minutes; stir.

3. Add the pork and simmer for about 5 minutes.
4. Add all remaining ingredients and stir well.
5. Lower heat, cover and cook for 25 minutes over low heat.
6. Taste and adjust salt and pepper to taste.
7. Serve hot.

Nutritional Value:

Calories: \380 Carbohydrates: 3g Proteins: 30g Fat: 27g Fiber: 1g

482. Fragrant "Greenery" Soup

Serves: 6
Preparation: 10 minutes
Cooking: 25 minutes

Ingredients

- 1/3 cup olive oil
- 1 leek, the white and tender green part, cut into slices
- 2 fresh onions, white and tender green part, finely chopped
- 1 lb of various greens (spinach, lettuce, chard, etc.), coarsely chopped
- Salt and ground pepper to taste
- 1/4 tsp of nutmeg
- 6 cups of water
- 1/2 cup of fresh dill, finely chopped

Directions:

1. Pout the oil in a pot, and sauté the leek, fresh onions and greens for 5 minutes; stir.
2. Season with the salt and pepper, grated nutmeg and pour water; bring to boil.
3. Cover and cook for 8 - 10 minutes over medium-low heat.
4. When the vegetables softened, transfer them in a blender; blend until soft.
5. Serve in a bowl, and sprinkle each serving with fresh dill and freshly ground pepper.

Nutritional Value:

Calories: 140 Carbohydrates: 6g Proteins: 4g Fat: 13g Fiber: 1g

483. Hungarian Tokany Turkey Stew (Keto adapted)

Serves: 6
Preparation: 15 minutes
Cooking: 1 hour 55 minutes

Ingredients

- 1/3 cup almond flour
- 1 tsp salt and ground pepper
- 2-1/2 lbs turkey thighs skinned & boned; cut into 1-inch cubes
- 2 Tbsp olive oil
- 1 cup green onions finely chopped
- 1/2 cup mushrooms sliced
- 1 grated tomato
- 1 cup dry white wine
- 1 Tbsp of ground paprika
- 1/2 tsp marjoram
- 1 cup water or bone broth
- 1/2 cup of fresh cream
- 3 slices of turkey bacon cooked and crumbled (optional)

Directions:

1. In plastic bag, combine almond flour, salt and pepper. Add the turkey meat in batches, and coat well with almond flour mixture.
2. Heat the oil in a large frying skillet and sauté turkey cubes for 4 - 5 minutes over medium heat; stir.
3. In Dutch oven, sauté green onions with a pinch of salt until translucent.
4. Add mushrooms, carrot, grated tomato and wine. Bring mixture to boil, reduce heat to low and simmer for 10 -12 minutes. Stir in paprika, marjoram, water or bone broth and turkey; bring mixture to boil.
5. Reduce heat, cover and simmer 1 1/2 hours or until turkey are totally tender.
6. Serve in a bowls with fresh cream and crumbled bacon.

Nutritional Value:

Calories: 315 Carbohydrates: 6g Proteins: 34g Fat: 13g Fiber: 2g

484. Light Grouper Soup with Celery

Ingredients

- 5 celery stalks, cut into three pieces each
- 1 Tbsp of dried oregano
- 7 -8 saffron fiber
- 1 carrot preferably organic, sliced
- 8 cups of water
- 2 small grouper fish, about 3 1/2 - 4 lbs, washed and cleaned
- 3/4 cup of olive oil
- 2 Tbsp of lemon juice
- Salt and ground black pepper

Directions:

1. Add celery and carrot in a large and wide pot, and sprinkle with oregano and saffron.
2. Place the fish pieces, and pour the olive oil.
3. Pour water and bring to boil over medium-high heat; cover and simmer for 15 minutes.
4. Season with the salt and pepper.
5. Remove the fish from the pot, and place on a large plate.
6. Strain the broth, return to pot, and cook for further 10 minutes.
7. Remove soup from heat and pour the lemon juice.
8. Taste and adjust salt to taste.
9. Clean carefully the fish and serve immediately with hot soup.

Nutritional Value:

Calories: 166 Carbohydrates: 3g Proteins: 27g Fat: 19g Fiber: 1g

485. Perfect Pork Stew

Serves: 6
Preparation: 15 minutes
Cooking: 1 hour 45 minutes

Ingredients

- 1/2 cup olive oil
- 2 lbs of pork [cut into cubes]
- 1 cup of red wine
- 1 small carrot, cut into slices
- 1 cup of white mushrooms, sliced
- 1 green onion, finely chopped
- 1 small grated tomato
- 1 cup of bone broth or water
- 1/2 tsp oregano
- 1 bay leaf
- Salt and ground black pepper to taste

Directions:

1. In a large pan, pour the oil and sauté the pork for 2 - 3 minutes.
2. Add the onion and sauté for 2 - 3 minutes; season with the salt and pepper.
3. Pour wine and stir for two minutes.
4. Add carrots, mushrooms, green onion, grated tomato, broth or water, oregano and bay leaf.
5. Bring to boil, lower heat, cover and cook for 1 1/2 hours on very low heat.
6. Taste and adjust salt and pepper to taste.
7. Serve hot.

Nutritional Value:

Calories: 695 Carbohydrates: 3g Proteins: 18g Fat: 73g Fiber: 1g

486. Spicy Ground Bison Meat Stew

Serves: 6
Preparation: 10 minutes
Cooking: 35 minutes

Ingredients

- 2 Tbsp of lard
- 1 1/2 lb grass-fed bison, ground
- 2 spring onions, finely chopped
- 2 cloves of garlic, minced
- 1 grated tomato
- 2 Tbsp mustard (Dijon, English, ground stone)
- 1 Tbsp chili powder
- 2 bay leaves
- 2 tsp cumin
- 1 tsp cinnamon
- 2 tsp salt and ground black pepper

- 1 1 cups bone broth
- Fresh cilantro and lime wedges to garnish

Directions:

1. Heat the lard in a large frying skillet over medium-high heat.
2. Add ground bison meat and sauté for 3 - 4 minutes; stir.
3. Add sliced onions and garlic and sauté until translucent.
4. Add grated tomato and tomato paste and cook for 5 minutes.
5. Add all remaining ingredients and bring to boil.
6. Cover, lower heat to low, and cook for 20 minutes.
7. Adjust seasonings and serve hot with fresh cilantro and a squeeze of lime.

Nutritional Value:

Calories: 282 Carbohydrates: 4g Proteins: 38g Fat: 16g Fiber: 2g

487. Swiss chard Soup with Fresh Herbs

Serves: 6
Preparation: 10 minutes
Cooking: 25 minutes

Ingredients

- 1/4 cup extra virgin olive oil
- 2 spring onions (only green parts finely chopped)
- 1 clove of garlic minced
- 2 lbs Swiss chard, tender stems and leaves cur into pieces
- 3 cups bone broth (or water)
- 1 Tbsp of fresh dill, parsley and thyme, chopped
- Salt and black ground pepper to taste

Directions:

1. Heat the oil in a large pot over medium-high heat.
2. Sauté the green parts of spring onions and garlic with a pinch of salt for 3 - 4 minutes.
3. Add chopped Swiss chard and bone broth; bring to the boil and let simmer for 10 minutes. Add chopped dill and parsley and cook for further 5 minutes.
4. Transfer your soup in a food processor. Blend into a very smooth soup.
5. Adjust seasonings and serve hot.

Nutritional Value:

Calories: 66 Carbohydrates: 6g Proteins: 6g Fat: 3g Fiber: 3g

488. Absolute Cacao Fat Bombs

Serves: 8

Preparation: 10 minutes

Ingredients

- 1/2 cup of coconut oil, melted
- 3/4 cup heavy cream
- 1/4 cup cacao dry powder, unsweetened
- 3 Tbsp of almond butter
- 1 tsp nutmeg (optional)
- 4 drops of natural sweeter stevia, or to taste

Directions

1. Melt the coconut oil in a microwave for 10 - 15 seconds.
2. Combine all ingredients in a bowl and stir well.
3. Pour the mixture in a cake moulds and freeze for two hours or until set.
4. Press out of molds and place on a plate or in a container.
5. Keep refrigerated.

Nutritional Value:

Calories: 239 Carbohydrates: 3.5g Proteins: 3g Fat: 26g Fiber: 2g

489. Zucchini Fat Bomb

Serves: 8

Preparation: 15 minutes

Ingredients

- 2 Tbsp almond butter
- 3 large zucchini shredded
- 1 cup fresh basil and chives finely chopped
- 1 cup shredded mozzarella
- 1/2 cup Cheddar cheese
- Pinch of salt (optional)

Directions

1. Peel zucchini, and shred in a food processor.
2. Line one baking sheet with parchment paper.
3. In a mixing bowl, combine all ingredients in a compact mixture.
4. For mixture into small balls, and place them on a prepared baking sheet.
5. Freeze for 2 - 3 hours in a freezer.
6. Serve. Keep refrigerated.

Nutritional Value:

Calories: 108 Carbohydrates: 3g Proteins: 8g Fat: 8g Fiber: 1g

490. Almonds Gale Fat Bombs

Serves: 12

Preparation: 10 minutes

Ingredients

- 1 cup coconut oil
- 1 cup almond butter (plain, unsalted)
- 1/4 cup ground almonds (without salt)
- 1 tsp vanilla extract
- 1/4 can natural sweetener such Stevia, Erythritol, Truvia,...etc.
- Pinch of salt

Directions

1. In a microwave safe bowl, softened the coconut butter.
2. Add all ingredients in your fast-speed blender.
3. Blend until thoroughly combined.
4. Make small balls and place on a plate lined with parchment paper.
5. Freeze for about 4 hours or overnight.
6. Serve.

Nutritional Value:

Calories: 301 Carbohydrates: 5g Proteins: 6g Fat: 30g Fiber: 2g

491. Bacon and Basil Fat Bombs

Serves: 8

Preparation: 15 minutes

Ingredients

- 2 cups of cream cheese from refrigerator
- 6 slices of bacon, finely chopped
- 1 small chili pepper, finely chopped
- 1 Tbsp fresh basil (chopped)
- 1/2 tsp onion powder
- 1/4 tsp garlic powder
- Salt and pepper to taste

Directions

1. Beat the cheese cream in a mixing bowl.
2. Add chopped bacon and stir well with the spoon.
3. Add all remaining ingredients and stir well to combine all ingredients.
4. Make small balls and place on a platter.
5. Refrigerate for 2 - 3 hours and serve.
6. Keep refrigerated.

Nutritional Value:

Calories: 265 Carbohydrates: 2g Proteins: 6g Fat: 27g Fiber: 0.03g

492. Berries and Maca Fat Bombs

Serves: 8
Preparation: 15 minutes

Ingredients

- 2 cups fresh cream
- 2 Tbsp fresh butter, softened
- 1/2 cup of natural granulated sweetener (Stevia, Erythritol...etc.)
- 1/2 cup frozen berries thawed (blueberries, bilberries, raspberries)
- 2 tsp Maca root powder
- 1 Tbsp arrowroot powder (or chia seeds as thickener)
- 1 tsp vanilla extract

Directions

1. Beat the cream with a hand mixer in a bowl until double in volume and stiff.
2. Add all remaining ingredients and continue to beat until combined completely.
3. Pour the berries mixture in ice cubes tray or in a muffin tray.
4. Freeze for at least 4 hours (preferably overnight).
5. Serve or Keep refrigerated.

Nutritional Value:

Calories: 152 Carbohydrates: 6g Proteins: 2g Fat: 15g Fiber: 0.5g

493. Chilly Tuna Fat Balls

Serves: 8
Preparation: 10 minutes

Ingredients

- 2 cans tuna, drained
- 1 medium avocado, cubed
- 2 Tbsp coconut butter
- 1/2 cup mayonnaise
- 2 Tbsp mustard
- 1 cup Parmesan cheese
- 1/3 cup ground almonds
- 1 tsp garlic powder
- Salt and pepper to taste

Directions

1. Cut medium avocado in half, remove the pit and skin, and cut the flesh in cubes.
2. Drain and add tuna in a large bawl along with all ingredients; stir well with the spoon.
3. Make the tuna mixture into small bowls
4. Place tuna balls on a plate lined with parchment paper, and refrigerate for 2 hours.
5. Serve or keep refrigerated.

Nutritional Value:

Calories: 197 Carbohydrates: 6g Proteins: 9g Fat: 17g Fiber: 2.2g

494. Choco - Peanut Butter Fat Balls

Serves: 12
Preparation: 15 minutes

Ingredients

- 1/2 cup fresh cream
- 1 cup of dark chocolate chips (60 - 69& cacao solid)
- 1/2 cup of peanut butter, softened

- 1/4 cup of coconut oil, softened
- 1/4 cup of fresh butter, softened
- 2 Tbsp ground peanuts

Directions

1. In a bowl, beat the cream until stiff peak and double in volume.
2. Melt the chocolate chips in a microwave for about 45 - 60 seconds; stir every 20 seconds.
3. Fold all ingredients in a whipped cream and beat for 2 - 3 minutes.
4. In a meanwhile, whip together peanut butter, coconut oil and butter.
5. Pour the mixture in molds or in cupcakes holders and freeze for 4 hours.
6. Keep refrigerated.

Nutritional Value:

Calories: 310 Carbohydrates: 7g Proteins: 5g Fat: 28g Fiber: 2g

495. Cinnamon - Nutmeg Fat Bombs

Serves: 8
Preparation: 10 minutes

Ingredients

- 1 cup almond butter (plain, unsalted)
- 1/2 cup almond milk (or coconut milk)
- 3/4 cup ground almonds or Macadamia nuts (unsalted)
- 1/2 tsp cinnamon
- 1 tsp vanilla extract
- 1/2 tsp ground nutmeg (optional)
- 2 Tbsp of natural sweetener (Stevia, Truvia, Erythritol...etc.)

Directions

1. Add all ingredients in your food processor, and process for 45 - 60 seconds.
2. Add more or less sweetener, to taste.
3. Grease your hands with oil and form dough into small balls.
4. Place on a baking pan covered with parchment paper and refrigerate for 2 - 3 hours.
5. Serve.

Nutritional Value:

Calories: 274 Carbohydrates: 6.5g Proteins: 11g Fat: 24g Fiber: 3.5g

496. Creamy Green Olives Fat Bombs

Serves: 8
Preparation: 20 minutes

Ingredients

- 1 lb cold cream cheese
- 1 cup whipped cream
- 1 1/2 cups green olives pitted
- 1/2 cup fresh parsley finely chopped
- 1 pinch of salt (optional)

Directions

1. Line a platter or baking pan with parchment paper; set aside.
2. Add cream cheese in a bowl and fast whisk with the spoon.
3. In a separate bowl, beat the cream to double in volume.
4. Combine the cream cheese and whipped cream; season with a pinch of salt.
5. Make balls from the cream cheese mixture, and insert one olive in a centre of each ball.
6. Roll each ball in chopped parsley and coat evenly from all sides.
7. Place the balls on prepared platter and refrigerate for 4 hours or overnight
8. Serve.

Nutritional Value:

Calories: 131 Carbohydrates: 2g Proteins: 2g Fat: 14g Fiber: 0.5g

497. Creamy Lime Fat Bombs

Serves: 10
Preparation: 10 minutes

Ingredients

- 3/4 cup coconut oil
- 1/2 cup fresh cream (yields 2 cups whipped)
- 1/2 cup cream cheese

- 1 tsp pure lime extract
- 10 drops natural sweetener (Stevia, Truvia, Erythritol...etc.)

Directions

1. In a bowl, beat the cream with a hand mixer.
2. Add all remaining ingredients and continue to beat for 45 - 60 seconds.
3. Pour the mixture into a silicone tray and freeze for several hours.
4. When hard enough, remove from the freezer, and from silicone tray and serve.

Nutritional Value:

Calories: 223 Carbohydrates: 1g Proteins: 1g Fat: 25g Fiber: 0g

498. Eggs with Gorgonzola Fat Bombs

Serves: 6

Preparation: 10 minutes

Ingredients

- 2 eggs, boiled
- 1/4 cup fresh butter, softened
- 1 cup cream cheese full-fat
- 3/4 cup Gorgonzola - blue cheese, grated

Directions

1. First, boil the eggs in a saucepan; remove from heat and set aside for 10 minutes.
2. In a meantime, line a baking pan with parchment paper.
3. Combine cream cheese, butter and grated Gorgonzola. Add the chopped eggs and stir well.
4. Make 6 - 8 balls and place them on a prepared pan.
5. Refrigerate for 2 - 3 hours and serve.

Nutritional Value:

Calories: 274 Carbohydrates: 2g Proteins: 8g Fat: 27g Fiber: 0g

499. Lemon Lilliputian Fat Bombs

Serves: 10

Preparation: 10 minutes

Ingredients

- 1/2 cup coconut oil, melted and cooled
- 1/4 cup heavy cream
- 1/4 cup cream cheese, full-fat
- 1 lemon, freshly squeezed
- 1 lemon zest (finely grated fresh)
- 1 tsp pure lemon extract
- 1/4 cup natural sweetener (Stevia, Erythritol...etc.)
- 1/2 cup coconut shredded, unsweetened

Directions

1. Melt the coconut oil in a microwave oven for 10 - 15 seconds. Set aside to cool for 2 to 3 minutes.
2. Whisk melted coconut oil with heavy cream, and with the cream cheese.
3. Pour the lemon juice and lemon zest and stir. Add stevia sweetener and stir well until sweetener dissolve completely..
4. At the end, add pure lemon extract and stir.
5. Pour the mixture in a candy molds or ice cube tray.
6. Freeze for two hours, and then remove your fat bombs on a platter.
7. Keep refrigerated.

Nutritional Value:

Calories: 165 Carbohydrates: .5g Proteins: 1g Fat: 17g Fiber: 1g

500. Maca and Vanilla Protein Fat Bombs

Serves: 10

Preparation: 15 minutes

Ingredients

- 1 cup coconut oil (melted)
- 1/2 cup coconut butter
- 1/2 cup coconut shreds
- 1/2 cup raw almonds, peeled and finely chopped
- 2 Tbsp of Maca root powder
- 1 scoop of vanilla protein powder
- 1 tsp vanilla extract
- 1/4 cup of natural sweetener (Stevia, Erythritol...etc.) or to taste

Directions

1. Melt the coconut butter in a microwave oven for 10 seconds; let it cool for 2 - 3 minutes.
2. Add melted coconut oil along with all other ingredients from the list above in a food processor.
3. Process until the mixture is well combined.
4. Make small balls and place on a platter lined with parchment paper.
5. Freeze for 2 hours, remove from freezer and serve.
6. Keep refrigerated in a container.

Nutritional Value:

Calories: 375 Carbohydrates: 7g Proteins: 4g Fat: 38g Fiber: 2g

501. Minty Chocolate Fat Bombs

Serves: 6
Preparation: 10 minutes

Ingredients

- 1/2 cup coconut oil melted
- 1/4 cup fresh butter, softened
- 2 Tbsp cocoa dry powder
- 1/4 cup natural sweetener (Stevia, Erythritol...etc.)
- 2 Tbsp fresh mint leaves, finely chopped)

Directions

1. Stir all ingredients in a deep bowl.
2. Pour the mixture into silicon cases or ice cube trays and freeze for 4 hours.
3. Store in a container and keep refrigerated.

Nutritional Value:

Calories: 228 Carbohydrates: 2g Proteins: 1g Fat: 26g Fiber: 1g

502. Monk Fruit Candy Fat Balls

Serves: 10
Preparation: 15 minutes

Ingredients

- 1 cup coconut oil, softened
- 1 cup almond butter
- 2 Tbsp avocado oil
- 1/2 cup cocoa powder, unsweetened
- 1/2 cup coconut shreds
- 2 Tbsp of monk fruit sweetener or to taste

Directions

1. In a small saucepan over medium-low heat, combine and stir the coconut oil, almond butter and avocado oil.
2. Add cocoa powder, coconut shreds and monk fruit sweetener; stir until all ingredients are combined well.
3. Pour the mixture in a freezer-safe container and freeze for 1 1/2 to 2 hours.
4. Remove the mixture from the freezer, and for into small balls.
5. Place balls on a plate and return in freezer for further 1 hour.
6. Serve immediately or keep balls refrigerated.

Nutritional Value:

Calories: 399 Carbohydrates: 3g Proteins: 2g Fat: 44g Fiber: 2g

503. Piquant Pepperoni Fat Bombs

Serves: 10
Preparation: 15 minutes

Ingredients

- 2 cups of cream cheese from the fridge
- 1 cup of whipped cream, cold from fridge
- 4 slices Pepperoni Sausages** finely chopped
- 3 slices bacon cut into pieces
- 1 chili pepper
- 1 tsp fresh thyme (chopped fine)
- 1/4 tsp hot paprika (or smoked paprika)
- 1 pinch salt and pepper or to taste
- 1/4 tsp garlic powder
- 1/4 tsp onion powder

Directions

1. Beat the cream cheese in a mixing bowl with the whisker.
2. Add whipped cream and continue to beat

for 30 - 45 seconds.
3. Add chopped Pepperoni sausages and bacon and stir well.
4. Add all remaining ingredients and give a good stir.
5. Form the mixture into 12 balls, and place them on a plate lined with parchment paper.
6. Refrigerate balls for 3 hours.
7. Serve immediately or keep refrigerated.

Nutritional Value:

Calories: 201 Carbohydrates: 2g Proteins: 5g Fat: 20g Fiber: 0.2g

504. Rumichino Almond Fat Bombs

Serves: 12
Preparation: 10 minutes

Ingredients

- 1/2 cup coconut oil (refined), melted
- 3/4 cup almond butter
- 3/4 cup fresh butter, softened
- 3 Tbsp of cocoa powder, unsweetened
- 1/2 cup natural sweetener such Stevia, Erythritol, Truvia,...etc.
- 2 Tbsp strong rum

Directions

1. Melt the coconut butter in a microwave oven for 15 - 20 seconds.
2. Pour the coconut oil in a bowl, and whisk along with almonds butter and fresh butter.
3. Add all remaining ingredients and whisk for 35 - 40 seconds to combine well.
4. Pour the mixture into molds and freeze for 2 hours or more.
5. Serve or store in container and keep refrigerated.

Nutritional Value:

Calories: 289 Carbohydrates: 4g Proteins: 4g Fat: 30g Fiber: 2g

505. Spicy Choco Fat Bombs

Serves: 12
Preparation: 10 minutes

Ingredients

- 3/4 cup fresh butter softened
- 3/4 cup coconut oil softened
- 3/4 cup almond butter
- 1/4 cup cocoa dry powder unsweetened (80% cacao solid)
- 1/4 cup natural sweetener Stevia or Erythritol (or to taste)
- 2 pinch of cayenne pepper or to taste

Directions

1. Softened coconut oil and fresh butter in a microwave safe bowl; heat in a microwave oven for several seconds.
2. Add all ingredients in a bowl, and stir with the spoon.
3. Pour the mixture into small cupcakes holders, muffin thin, etc).
4. Place in a freezer for 2 hours and serve.
5. Keep refrigerated in a container.

Nutritional Value:

Calories: 321 Carbohydrates: 4g Proteins: 4g Fat: 34g Fiber: 2.3g

506. Strawberry Fat Bombs coated with Ground Nuts

Serves: 8
Preparation: 10 minutes

Ingredients

- 1/3 cup butter softened
- 1/2 cup coconut oil
- 2 Tbsp strawberry extract
- 2 Tbsp cocoa dry powder, unsweetened
- 1/2 cup ground nut mixture (walnuts, hazelnuts, almonds...etc.)

Directions

1. In a saucepan, heat butter, coconut oil and cocoa powder over moderate heat; stir.
2. Remove from heat, and pour strawberry extract; stir. Set aside to completely cool.
3. Make small balls and roll in ground nut mixture.
4. Place balls on a plate covered with parchment paper and freeze for at least 2

hours.

Keep refrigerated.

Nutritional Value:

Calories: 245 Carbohydrates: 2g Proteins: 2g Fat: 26g Fiber: 1g

507. Vanilla Coconut - Nuts Fat Bombs

Serves: 8

Preparation: 10 minutes

Ingredients

- 1/2 cup coconut oil, melted and cooled
- 3 cups coconut shreds, unsweetened
- 1 cup natural sweetener (Stevia, Erythritol...etc.)
- 2 tsp vanilla
- 1 pinch of salt (optional)
- Toppings
- 2 Tbsp shredded coconut
- 2 Tbsp of chopped nuts such Macadamia, almonds, Brazilian...etc.

Directions

1. Add ingredients from the list above in your food processor.
2. Process until the mixture is compact and blended well.
3. Grease your hands with coconut oil and form balls.
4. Place fat balls on a platter lined with parchment paper and sprinkle with coconut shreds and chopped nuts.
5. Refrigerate for two hours and serve.

Nutritional Value:

Calories: 243 Carbohydrates: 4g Proteins: 2g Fat: 25g Fiber: 3g

508. Cheese Muffin Bombs

Serves: 12

Preparation: 10 minutes

Ingredients

- 1/4 cup coconut butter, softened on room temperature
- 2 cups cream cheese (full fat), softened
- 1 cup heavy whipping cream
- 3/4 cup natural sweetener (Stevia, Truvia, Erythritol...etc.)
- 1 1/2 tsp vanilla extract
- 1 pinch of sea salt

Directions

1. Prepare two muffin tins with 6 paper liners.
2. Add all ingredients in your blender; blend for 35 -50 seconds.
3. Pour the mixture in a prepared muffin tins evenly.
4. Freeze for 3 - 4 hours and serve.
5. Store in a container and keep refrigerated.

Nutritional Value:

Calories: 241 Carbohydrates: 2.5g Proteins: 3g Fat: 25g Fiber: 0g

509. Ground Turkey and Cheese Stuffed Tomatoes

Preparation Time: 25 minutes
Servings 4)

Nutritional Value:413 Calories; 28.2g Fat; 7.8g Carbs; 35.2g Protein; 4g Sugars

Ingredients

- 4 tomatoes
- 1 tablespoon olive oil
- 1/2 pound ground turkey
- 1/2 cup scallions, chopped
- 1 garlic clove, smashed
- 1 tablespoon fresh parsley, chopped
- 1 teaspoon fresh rosemary, chopped
- Seasoned salt and ground black pepper, to taste
- 1 cup Monterey Jack cheese, shredded
- 1 cup Romano cheese, freshly grated
- 1/2 cup chicken stock

Directions

1. Slice the top off of each tomato. Discard the hard cores and scoop out the pulp from the tomatoes with a small metal spoon.
2. Now, heat the oil in a cast-iron skillet that is preheated over a moderately high heat. Brown turkey meat for 3 to 4 minutes; reserve.
3. In the same skillet, sauté the scallions and garlic until they are just tender, about 4 minutes. Add reserved beef and tomato pulp; sprinkle with fresh parsley, rosemary, salt, and pepper.
4. Arrange tomatoes in a casserole dish. Divide the stuffing among tomatoes and top with cheese.
5. Pour chicken stock around tomatoes and bake in the middle of the preheated oven at 360 degrees F, approximately 18 minutes.Bon appétit!

510. Refreshing and Nutty Spring Salad

Preparation Time: 5 minutes
Servings 4)

Nutritional Value:184 Calories; 16.8g Fat; 5g Carbs; 2.1g Protein; 2.4g Sugars

Ingredients

- 1 medium-sized head lettuce, torn into bite-sized pieces
- 1/2 pound cucumber, thinly sliced
- 1 large-sized carrot, grated
- 1 cup radishes, thinly sliced
- 2 spring onions, sliced
- 1 ounce macadamia nuts, chopped
- 1/2 lime, freshly squeezed
- 3 tablespoons peanut oil
- 1 teaspoon chili sauce, sugar-free
- 1/2 teaspoon red pepper flakes, crushed
- Coarse salt, to taste

1. 1 tablespoon sesame seeds, lightly toasted

Directions

Add the vegetables along with macadamia nuts to a large salad bowl. Toss to combine.

In a small mixing dish, thoroughly whisk the lime juice, peanut oil, chili sauce, red pepper and salt. Dress the salad and serve sprinkled with toasted sesame seeds.

511. Spicy Cremini Mushroom Stew

Preparation Time: 30 minutes
Servings 4)

Nutritional Value:133 Calories; 3.7g Fat; 6.7g Carbs; 14g Protein; 2.4g Sugars

Ingredients

- 1 tablespoon olive oil
- 1 cup shallots, chopped
- 1 teaspoon chili pepper, finely minced
- 1 teaspoon garlic, minced

- 1 celery, chopped
- 2 carrots, chopped
- 1/2 pound Cremini mushrooms, chopped
- 2 ½ cups bone broth, low-sodium
- 1/4 cup dry white wine
- 1/2 cup water
- 2 ripe tomatoes, crushed
- Salt and ground black pepper, to taste
- 1/4 teaspoon ground ginger
- 1/2 teaspoon ground allspice
- 1/4 teaspoon ground cinnamon
- 2 bay leaves
- 1/2 cup fresh basil, chopped

Directions

2. Heat the oil in a large heavy pot that is preheated over a moderate flame. Now, sweat the shallots, peppers, garlic, celery, carrots, and mushrooms approximately 8 minutes.
3. Add the broth, tomatoes, and seasonings, except for basil; bring to a boil. Now, turn the heat to a medium and let it simmer for 18 minutes, stirring periodically.
4. Serve in individual bowls, garnished with fresh basil leaves. Bon appétit!

512. Absolutely Incredible Turkey Kebabs

Preparation Time: 30 minutes
Servings 6)

Nutritional Value:293 Calories; 13.8g Fat; 5.7g Carbs; 34.5g Protein; 2.9g Sugars

Ingredients

- 1 ½ pounds British turkey diced thigh
- 2 tablespoons butter, at room temperature
- 1 tablespoon dry ranch seasoning
- 2 orange bell peppers, sliced
- 1 red bell peppers, sliced
- 1 green bell peppers, sliced
- 1 zucchini, cut into thick slices
- 1 red onion, cut into wedges
- 1 cucumber, sliced
- 1 cup radishes, sliced
- 2 tablespoons red wine vinegar
- 1 tablespoon fresh parsley, roughly chopped

Directions

1. Rub the turkey with softened butter and toss with dry ranch seasoning. Thread the turkey pieces onto skewers.
2. Alternate with bell peppers, zucchini, and onion until all the ingredients are used up. Now, place your skewers in the refrigerator while you're lighting the grill.
3. Grill your kebabs, turning periodically, for 9 minutes or until they are cooked through.
4. In the meantime, toss the cucumbers and radishes with red wine vinegar and fresh parsley.
5. Serve kebabs immediately with the cucumber-radicchio salad on the side. Bon appétit!

513. Easy Grilled Chicken Salad

Preparation Time: 20 minutes
Servings 4)

Nutritional Value:408 Calories; 34.2g Fat; 4.8g Carbs; 22.7g Protein; 0.4g Sugars

- Ingredients
- 2 chicken breasts
- 1/2 teaspoon sea salt
- 1/3 teaspoon red pepper flakes, crushed
- 1/4 teaspoon dried thyme, or more to taste
- 1 large-sized avocado, pitted and sliced
- 2 egg yolks
- 1 tablespoon lime juice
- 1/2 teaspoon mustard powder
- 1/3 teaspoon sea salt
- 1/3 cup olive oil
- 1 tablespoon Worcestershire sauce

Directions

1. Preheat your grill on high. Season the

chicken breasts with salt, pepper and thyme. Now, grill the chicken for 3 to 5 minutes on each side.
2. Cut the grilled chicken into the strips.
3. Divide avocado slices among four serving plates.
4. Then, prepare the dressing. In a mixing dish or a measuring cup, thoroughly combine the remaining ingredients.
5. Place the chicken strips on the serving plates and drizzle with the prepared dressing. Enjoy!

514. Spicy Chicken Strips with Hemp Seeds

Preparation Time: 55 minutes
Servings 6)

Nutritional Value:420 Calories; 28.2g Fat; 5g Carbs; 35.3g Protein; 2.6g Sugars

Ingredients

- 3 chicken breasts, cut into strips
- 1/2 stick butter
- Salt and pepper, to taste
- 2 tablespoons soy sauce
- 3 teaspoons apple cider vinegar
- 1/2 teaspoon hot chili sauce, sugar-free
- 2 tablespoons tomato paste
- 2 cloves garlic, minced
- 2 eggs
- 1/4 cup hemp seeds

Directions

1. Preheat your oven to 410 degrees F. Lightly grease a baking dish with a nonstick cooking spray.
2. Now, rub chicken wings with the butter, salt, and pepper.
3. Drizzle with soy sauce, vinegar, chili sauce, tomato sauce and garlic. Let it marinate at least 30 minutes in your refrigerator.
4. In a mixing dish, whisk the eggs with hemp seeds. Dip each chicken strip in the hemp mixture. Transfer your chicken to the baking dish.
5. Bake for 20 to 25 minutes, turning once.

You can broil these chicken strips to make them crispy, if desired.

515. Serve garnished with fresh chives.

Chicken Fillets with Cream-Mustard Sauce
Preparation Time: 25 minutes
Servings 4)

Nutritional Value:311 Calories; 16.9g Fat; 2.1g Carbs; 33.6g Protein; 0.4g Sugars

Ingredients

- 1 pound chicken fillets
- Salt and pepper, to taste
- 1 tablespoon butter, melted
- 1/2 cup scallions, chopped
- 1 teaspoon garlic paste
- 1/4 cup dry white wine
- 1/4 cup low-sodium chicken broth
- 1/2 cup double cream
- 2 tablespoons whole grain mustard
- 1/2 cup fresh cilantro, roughly chopped

Directions

1. Rub the chicken fillets with salt and pepper to your liking.
2. Melt the butter in a saucepan that is preheated over a moderate flame. Now, cook the chicken fillets until they are just barely done. Transfer the chicken to a plate and set it aside.
3. Add the scallions and garlic paste to the saucepan; cook, stirring often, until it is aromatic or about 4 minutes.
4. Raise the heat to medium-high; pour in wine and scrape the bits that may be stuck to the bottom of your saucepan.
5. Next, pour in the broth; allow the liquid to reduce by about half. Stir in double cream and mustard.
6. Pour the sauce over the reserved chicken fillets and serve garnished with fresh cilantro. Enjoy!

516. Easy and Yummy Chicken Drumettes

Preparation Time: 30 minutes

Servings 4)

Nutritional Value:165 Calories; 9.8g Fat; 7.7g Carbs; 12.4g Protein; 3.9g Sugars

- **Ingredients**
- 2 tablespoons tallow
- 4 chicken drumettes
- Salt, to taste
- 1/2 cup leeks, chopped
- 1 carrot, sliced
- 2 cloves garlic, minced
- 1 teaspoon cayenne pepper
- 1 teaspoon dried marjoram
- 1/2 teaspoon mustard seeds
- 1 cup turkey stock
- 2 tomatoes, crushed
- 1 tablespoon Worcestershire sauce
- 1 teaspoon mixed peppercorns
- 1 thyme sprig
- 1 rosemary sprig

Directions

1. Melt the tallow in a saucepan over medium-high heat. Sprinkle the chicken drumettes with the salt.
2. Then, fry the chicken drumettes until they are no longer pink and lightly browned on all sides; reserve.
3. Now, cook the leeks, carrots and garlic in pan drippings over medium heat for 4 to 6 minutes.
4. Reduce the heat to simmer, and add the remaining ingredients along with the reserved chicken. Simmer, partially covered, for 15 to 20 minutes. Serve warm.

517. Chicken Sausage with Salsa

Preparation Time: 15 minutes
Servings 4)

Nutritional Value:156 Calories; 4.2g Fat; 5.1g Carbs; 16.2g Protein; 2.4g Sugars

Ingredients

- 2 teaspoons lard, room temperature
- 4 chicken sausage, sliced
- 1/4 cup Sauvignon Blanc
- 1 cup pureed tomatoes
- 1 teaspoon granulated garlic
- 2 bell peppers, deveined and chopped
- 1 minced jalapeno, chopped
- 1 cup onion, diced
- 2 tablespoons fresh cilantro,minced
- 3 teaspoons lime juice

Directions

1. Warm the lard in a heavy-bottomed skillet over moderately high heat.
2. Sauté the sausage until well browned; pour in the wine and cook an additional 3 minutes. Reserve.
3. Then, make the salsa by mixing pureed tomatoes, garlic, bell pepper, jalapeno pepper, onions, cilantro and lime juice.
4. Serve the sausage with the salsa on the side. Bon appétit!

518. Turkey Sausage with Bok Choy

Preparation Time: 50 minutes
Servings 4)

Nutritional Value:189 Calories; 12g Fat; 6.6g Carbs; 9.4g Protein; 2g Sugars

Ingredients

- 1 tablespoon butter
- 4 mild turkey sausages, breakfast links, sliced
- 2 shallots, chopped
- Coarse salt and ground black pepper, to taste
- 1 pound Bok choy, tough stem ends trimmed
- 1 cup chicken stock
- 1/2 cup full-fat milk
- 1/8 teaspoon freshly grated nutmeg
- 6 ounces Gruyère, coarsely grated

Directions

1. Start by preheating an oven to 360 degrees F. Melt the butter in a pan; now, brown the sausage for a couple of

minutes, stirring periodically; reserve.

2. Add the shallots, salt, pepper, and Bok choy. Add the chicken stock and cook until just tender, 2 to 3 minutes.
3. Spread the Bok choy mixture in a lightly greased baking dish. Top with reserved sausage.
4. In a mixing bowl, thoroughly combine chicken stock, milk, and nutmeg. Pour the mixture over the sausage.
5. Cover with a piece of foil and bake for 40 minutes. Remove the foil and scatter grated cheese over the top.
6. Bake in upper third of oven an additional 4 minutes or until bubbly.

519. Easy Herby Turkey Drumsticks

Preparation Time: 1 hour
Servings 2)

Nutritional Value:488 Calories; 24.5g Fat; 2.1g Carbs; 33.6g Protein; 0.5g Sugars

Ingredients

- 2 tablespoons apple cider vinegar
- 2 thyme sprigs, chopped
- 2 rosemary sprigs, chopped
- 1 teaspoon dried marjoram
- 1 teaspoon dried basil
- 1 teaspoon granulated garlic
- 2 tablespoons olive oil
- 2 turkey drumsticks
- Salt and black pepper, to taste
- 1/2 cup Taco bell sauce

Directions

1. To make the marinade, thoroughly combine apple cider vinegar, thyme, rosemary, marjoram, basil, granulated garlic, and olive oil in a mixing bowl.
2. Now, marinate the turkey at least 3 hours in the refrigerator.
3. Cook turkey drumsticks on a preheated grill for 45 minutes to 1 hour or until a meat thermometer has reached the temperature of 180 degrees F. Season with salt and pepper to taste.
4. Serve with Taco bell sauce on the side. Bon appétit!

520. Mediterranean Chicken Drumsticks with Aioli

Preparation Time: 35 minutes
Servings 4)

Nutritional Value:562 Calories; 43.8g Fat; 2.1g Carbs; 40.8g Protein; 1g Sugars

Ingredients

- 1 ½ tablespoons ghee
- 4 chicken drumsticks
- Sea salt and crushed mixed peppercorns, to taste
- 1 tablespoon fresh parsley, chopped
- 6 Kalamata olives, pitted and halved
- 1 cup Halloumi cheese, cubed
- 1 hard-boiled egg yolk
- 1 tablespoon garlic, finely minced
- 1 tablespoon lemon juice
- 1/2 cup extra-virgin olive oil
- 1/4 teaspoon sea salt

Directions

1. Preheat your oven to 395 degrees F.
2. Melt the ghee in a nonstick skillet.
3. Season chicken drumsticks with salt and crushed peppercorns; brown chicken drumsticks in hot skillet for 3 to 4 minutes.
4. Arrange the fried chicken on a baking sheet; scatter fresh parsley and olives over the top.
5. In the meantime, make Aioli by mixing the remaining ingredients, except for cheese, with an immersion blender. Mix until it comes together.
6. Now, spread Aioli over fried chicken. Bake in the preheated oven approximately 25 minutes. Add Halloumi on top and bake an additional 3 to 4 minutes. Serve warm.

521. Dinner Party Pork Gumbo

Preparation Time: 35 minutes
Servings 6)

Nutritional Value:427 Calories; 26.2g Fat; 7.6g Carbs; 35.2g Protein; 3.3g Sugars

Ingredients

- 2 tablespoons olive oil
- 1 pound pork shoulder, cubed
- 8 ounces pork sausage, sliced
- 2 shallots, toughly chopped
- 1 teaspoon beef bouillon granules
- Sea salt and freshly cracked black pepper
- 1 teaspoon gumbo file
- 1 teaspoon crushed red pepper
- 1 tablespoon Cajun spice
- 4 cups bone broth
- 1 cup water
- 2 bell peppers, deveined and thinly sliced
- 2 celery stalks, chopped
- 1/4 cup flaxseed meal
- 3/4 pound okra

Directions

1. Heat the oil in a heavy-bottomed pot that is preheated over a moderately high flame. Now, cook the pork until it is just browned; reserve.
2. Add the sausage and cook in pan drippings approximately 5 minutes; reserve.
3. Stir in the shallots and cook until they are softened. Add beef bouillon granules, salt, pepper, gumbo file, red pepper, Cajun spice and bone broth. Bring it to a boil.
4. Add the water, bell pepper and celery, and reduce the heat to medium-low. Cook an additional 15 to 23 minutes.
5. Afterwards, stir in the flax seed meal and okra; cook for a further 5 minutes or until heated through.

522. Pork Meatloaf with Homemade Tomato Sauce

Preparation Time: 45 minutes
Servings 6)

Nutritional Value:251 Calories; 7.9g Fat; 6.5g Carbs; 34.6g Protein; 3g Sugars

Ingredients

- Nonstick cooking spray
- 1 ½ pounds ground pork
- 1/4 cup pork rinds,crushed
- 1/3 cup flaxseed meal
- 2 shallots, chopped
- 3 cloves garlic, finely minced
- 1 large egg
- Sea salt and ground black pepper
- 1 teaspoon mustard powder
- For the Sauce:
- 2 ripe plum tomatoes, pureed
- 2 tablespoons ketchup
- 1 ½ tablespoons Swerve
- 1 tablespoon cider vinegar
- 1/2 teaspoon dried thyme
- 1 teaspoon fresh parsley

Directions

- Start by preheating your oven to 360 degrees F. Lightly spray a loaf pan with a nonstick cooking oil or line with foil.
- Add the pork mince, pork rinds, flaxseed meal, shallot, garlic, egg, salt, pepper, and mustard powder to a mixing dish. Thoroughly combine the ingredients until everything is well mixed.
- Press the meatloaf mixture into the pan.
- Next, cook the sauce ingredients over moderate heat. Pour the sauce evenly over the meatloaf. Bake for 40 minutes or until meat thermometer registers 165 degrees F.
- Allow it to cool down for a couple of minutes before slicing. Cut into 3/4-inch thick slices and serve immediately.

523. Pork Shoulder with Blue Cheese Sauce

Preparation Time: 30 minutes
Servings 6)

Nutritional Value:495 Calories; 36.9g Fat; 3.6g Carbs; 33.4g Protein; 1.1g Sugars

Ingredients

1. 1 ½ pounds pork shoulder, boneless and cut into 6 pieces
2. Salt and freshly cracked black peppercorns, to taste
3. 1 teaspoon dried thyme
4. 1 tablespoon butter
5. 1 onion, chopped
6. 2 garlic cloves, chopped
7. 1/3 cup dry sherry wine
8. 1/3 cup broth, preferably homemade
9. 1 teaspoon dried hot chile flakes
10. 1 tablespoon soy sauce
11. 6 ounces blue cheese
12. 1/3 cup double cream

Directions

1. Rub each piece of pork shoulder with salt, black peppercorns, and thyme.
2. Now, warn the butter in a sauté pan over a moderately high heat. Then, brown the pork on all sides about 18 minutes; reserve.
3. Next, sauté the onions and garlic until onions are caramelized. Add the wine and broth and stir, scraping up any brown bits from the bottom.
4. Turn the heat to medium and add the other ingredients; continue to simmer until the desired thickness is reached by evaporation.
5. Serve reserved pork with the sauce on the side.Bon appétit!

524. Carrot and Meat Loaf Muffins

Preparation Time: 35 minutes
Servings 6)

Nutritional Value:220 Calories; 6.3g Fat; 5.4g Carbs; 33.8g Protein; 2.9g Sugars

Ingredients

1. 1 pound pork, ground
2. 1/2 pound turkey, ground
3. 1 cup carrots, shredded
4. 2 ripe tomatoes, pureed
5. 1 ounce envelope onion soup mix
6. 1 tablespoon Worcestershire sauce
7. 1 tablespoon Dijon mustard
8. 1/2 teaspoon dry basil
9. 1 teaspoon dry oregano
10. Kosher salt and ground black pepper, to taste
11. 2 cloves of garlic, minced
12. 1 eggs, whisked
13. 1 cup mozzarella cheese, shredded

1. **Directions**
2. Start by preheating your oven to 350 degrees F.
3. Then, thoroughly combine all ingredients until everything is blended.
4. Spoon the mixture into a muffin tin that is previously coated with a nonstick cooking spray.
5. Bake for 30 minutes; allow them to cool slightly before removing from the tin. Bon appétit!

525. Hearty Pork Soup with Avocado

Preparation Time: 20 minutes
Servings 6)

Nutritional Value:423 Calories; 31.8g Fat; 6.5g Carbs; 25.9g Protein; 2.9g Sugars

Ingredients

- 2 tablespoons lard
- 1 medium-sized yellow onion, peeled and chopped
- 2 cloves garlic, peeled and minced
- 1 teaspoon Mezzeta pepper, seeded and minced
- 1 celery, chopped
- 1 ¼ pounds pork shoulder, cut into chunks
- 3 cups beef broth, less-sodium
- Sea salt and ground black pepper, to taste
- A pinch of dried basil
- 2 ripe tomatoes, undrained
- 1/4 cup fresh parsley, roughly chopped
- 1 medium-sized avocado, pitted and sliced

Directions

1. Melt the lard in a large-sized stock pot over a moderate flame. Next, sauté the

onion, garlic, Mezzeta pepper and celery for 2 to 3 minutes or until the onion is translucent.
2. Stir in the pork chunks and continue cooking for 4 minutes more, stirring continuously. Add the other ingredients.
3. Now, lower the heat and simmer for 10 minutes, partially covered; make sure to stir periodically.
4. Serve topped with fresh parsley leaves and sliced avocado.

526. Greek Souvlaki with Tzatziki Sauce

Preparation Time: 20 minutes + marinating time
Servings 6)

Nutritional Value:147 Calories; 4.8g Fat; 5.8g Carbs; 17.3g Protein; 4.2g Sugars

Ingredients

- 1/3 cup red wine vinegar
- 2 tablespoons cilantro, chopped
- 2 tablespoons fresh lemon juice
- 3 cloves garlic, smashed
- Sea salt and ground black pepper, to taste
- 1 teaspoon Greek oregano
- 2 pounds pork loin, trimmed of silver skin and excess fat, cut into 1-inch cubes
- Wooden skewers, soaked in cold water for 30 minutes before use
- For Tzatziki Sauce:
- 1 small-sized cucumber, shredded and drained
- 1 cup full-fat Greek yogurt
- 1 teaspoon garlic, smashed
- 3 teaspoons olive oil
- Sea salt, to taste
- 2 teaspoons fresh dill, finely minced

Directions

1. To make the marinade, thoroughly combine the vinegar, cilantro, lemon juice, garlic, salt, black pepper and Greek oregano.
2. Add the pork loin to the marinade. Let it marinate in your refrigerator for 3 hours. Now, thread the pork cubes onto the skewers.
3. Grill your souvlaki until they browned on all sides, about 8 to 12 minutes in total.
4. Mix all ingredients for Tzatziki sauce. Serve with souvlaki skewers. Bon appétit!

527. Kansas City-Style Meatloaf

Preparation Time: 1 hour 10 minutes
Servings 8)

Nutritional Value:318 Calories; 14.7g Fat; 6.2g Carbs; 39.3g Protein; 2.4g Sugars

Ingredients

- 2 pounds ground pork
- 2 eggs, beaten
- 1/2 cup shallots, chopped
- 1/2 cup chipotle salsa, bottled
- 8 ounces sharp Cheddar cheese, shredded
- 1 teaspoon garlic powder
- 1 teaspoon paprika
- Sea salt and freshly ground black pepper, to taste
- 1 teaspoon lime zest
- 1 tablespoon whole grain mustard
- 1/2 cup tomato paste
- 1 tablespoon Swerve

Directions

1. Start by preheating your oven to 360 degrees F.
2. In a mixing bowl, thoroughly combine the ground pork with eggs, shallots, chipotle salsa, cheddar cheese, garlic powder, paprika, salt, pepper, lime zest, and mustard.
3. Mix until everything is well incorporated. Press the mixture into a loaf pan that is previously greased with a nonstick cooking spray.
4. Then, whisk the tomato paste with Swerve; pour the mixture over the top of your meatloaf.
5. Bake about 65 minutes, rotating the pan once or twice. Place under the broiler during the last 5 minutes if desired.
6. Let your meatloaf stand 5 to 10 minutes

before slicing and serving.

528. Indian-Style Saucy Pork

Preparation Time: 1 hour 15 minutes
Servings 8)

Nutritional Value:369 Calories; 20.2g Fat; 2.9g Carbs; 41.3g Protein; 1.5g Sugars

Ingredients

- 1 tablespoon olive oil
- 2 pounds pork belly, cubed
- Salt and freshly ground pepper
- 1/2 teaspoon ground coriander
- A bunch of scallions, chopped
- 2 garlic cloves, minced
- 1/2 tablespoon curry powder
- 1/2 tablespoon ground cloves
- 2 tomatoes, pureed
- 1 bell pepper, deveined and chopped
- 1 Thai chile, deveined and minced
- 1/2 teaspoon fennel seeds
- 1/2 cup unsweetened coconut milk
- 2 cups bone broth

Directions

1. Heat the oil in a saucepan over a moderate heat. Sprinkle the pork belly with salt, pepper and ground coriander.
2. Cook the pork about 10 minutes, stirring frequently.
3. Next, cook the scallions, garlic, curry, and cloves in pan drippings. Scrape the mixture into the slow cooker. Add the remaining ingredients. Cook, covered, for 1 hour over low heat. Serve warm.

529. Pork Rib Chops with Spinach

Preparation Time: 25 minutes + marinating time
Servings 6)

Nutritional Value:234 Calories; 11g Fat; 2g Carbs; 29.8g Protein; 0.6g Sugars

Ingredients

- 1 ½ pounds pork rib chops
- Sea salt and ground black pepper, to taste
- 2 tablespoons oyster sauce
- 1 tablespoon cider vinegar
- 1 tablespoon fresh lime juice
- 1/4 cup Champagne wine
- 1 tablespoon garlic paste
- 2 teaspoons olive oil
- 1 red onion, sliced
- 1 celery stalk, sliced
- 1 bell pepper, chopped
- 2 cups spinach

Directions

1. Season pork rib chops with salt and pepper. In another small dish, make the marinade by whisking the oyster sauce, vinegar, lime juice, Champagne and garlic paste.
2. Add the pork to the marinade; let it stand for at least 2 hours.
3. Next, heat 1 teaspoon of olive oilin a large-sized pan that is preheated over a moderate flame; cook the onion, celery and bell pepper about 5 minutes, stirring frequently; reserve.
4. Heat another teaspoon of olive oil in the same pan. Add the pork, along with marinade, to the pan. Now, brown the pork for 3 to 5 minutes per side.
5. Add the reserved vegetables to the pan along with spinach. Cook until the spinach leaves are wilted, about 6 minutes. Serve warm. Bon appétit!

530. Breakfast Pork in a Mug

Preparation Time: 10 minutes
Servings 2)

Nutritional Value:327 Calories; 16.6g Fat; 5.8g Carbs; 40g Protein; 2.6g Sugars

Ingredients

- 1/2 pound ground pork
- 1/2 cup Asiago cheese, shredded
- 1/2 cup tomato sauce
- Salt and ground black pepper, to taste
- 1 teaspoon garlic paste
- 1/2 teaspoon onion powder
- 1/2 teaspoon cayenne pepper

Directions

1. Thoroughly combine all ingredients in a mixing bowl.
2. Divide the mixture among 2 microwave-safe mugs.
3. Microwave for 7 minutes and serve warm with pickles.Bon appétit!

531. Bacon-Wrapped Meatballs with Parsley Sauce

Preparation Time: 30 minutes
Servings 6)

Nutritional Value:399 Calories; 27g Fat; 1.8g Carbs; 37.7g Protein; 0.2g Sugars

Ingredients

- 1 pound ground beef
- 1 egg, beaten
- 1 ½ tablespoons olive oil
- 1/2 cup crushed pork rinds
- 1/4 cup fresh cilantro, chopped
- 2 cloves garlic, smashed
- Sea salt and ground black pepper, to your liking
- 1/2 teaspoon cayenne pepper
- 1/2 pound bacon slices
- Toothpicks
- For the Parsley Sauce:
- 1 cup fresh parsley
- 1 tablespoon almonds, toasted
- 1 tablespoon sunflower seeds, soaked
- 1/2 tablespoon olive oil
- Sea salt and black pepper, to taste

Directions

1. Preheat your oven to 390 degrees F.
2. Then, in a mixing bowl, thoroughly combine the ground beef, egg, olive oil, crushed pork rinds, cilantro, garlic, salt, black pepper, and cayenne pepper.
3. Shape the mixture into 1.5-inch meatballs. Wrap each ball with a slice of bacon; secure with a toothpick.
4. Arrange the meatballs on a baking sheet; bake in the preheated oven for 25 to 30 minutes.
5. In the meantime, make the parsley sauce. Pulse all ingredients in a food processor until uniform and smooth.
6. Serve warm meatballs with parsley sauce on the side and enjoy!

532. Sunday Flank Steak

Preparation Time: 20 minutes + marinating time
Servings 6)

Nutritional Value:350 Calories; 17.3g Fat; 2.1g Carbs; 42.7g Protein; 0.6g Sugars

Ingredients

- 2 tablespoons olive oil
- 2 tablespoons soy sauce
- 1 teaspoon garlic paste
- A bunch of scallions, chopped
- 1 tablespoon lime lemon juice
- 1/4 cup dry red wine
- 2 pounds flank steak
- Salt and cayenne pepper, to taste
- 1/2 teaspoon black peppercorns, crushed

Directions

1. In a mixing bowl, thoroughly combine the oil, soy sauce, garlic paste, scallions, lemon juice, and red wine.
2. Now, season the flank steak with salt, cayenne pepper and black peppercorns. Place the meat in a marinade; cover and refrigerate for 6 hours.
3. Preheat a nonstick skillet over a moderately high flame. Fry your steaks about 10 minutes, turning once. Bon appétit!

533. Father's Day Stuffed Avocado

Preparation Time: 20 minutes
Servings 6)

Nutritional Value:407 Calories; 28.8g Fat; 6.4g Carbs; 23.4g Protein; 2.4g Sugars

Ingredients

- 1 tablespoon avocado oil
- 3/4 pound beef,ground
- 1/3 cup beef broth

- 1/2 cup shallots, sliced
- Salt and black pepper, to taste
- 3 ripe avocados, pitted and halved
- 2 small-sized tomatoes, chopped
- 3/4 cup Colby cheese, shredded
- 3 tablespoons Kalamata olives, pitted and sliced
- 1/2 cup mayonnaise

Directions

1. Preheat an oven to 340 degrees F.
2. Het avocado oil in a pan over a moderate heat; now, brown the ground beef for 2 to 3 minutes, crumbling it with a wooden spatula.
3. Add the broth and shallots. Cook until the shallots turn translucent. Season with salt and pepper.
4. Then, scoop out some of the middle of each avocado. Mash the avocado flash that you scooped out along with chopped tomatoes.
5. Add the reserved beef mixture and stuff your avocado. Afterward, top with shredded cheese and sliced olives.
6. Place stuffed avocado on a roasting pan. Bake for 8 to 10 minutes in the preheated oven. Serve with mayonnaise and enjoy!

534. Beef Sausage and Vegetable Skillet

Preparation Time: 40 minutes
Servings 4)

Nutritional Value:250 Calories; 17.5g Fat; 5.4g Carbs; 6.8g Protein; 3.7g Sugars

Ingredients

- 2 tablespoons canola oil
- 4 beef sausages, sliced
- 2 shallots, chopped
- 2 spring garlic, minced
- 2 bell peppers, deveined and chopped
- 1 parsnip, chopped
- Salt and pepper, to taste
- 2 ripe tomatoes, pureed
- 2 tablespoons ketchup, sugar-free
- 1 ½ cups beef bone broth
- 1/4 cup dry red wine
- 2 thyme sprigs
- 2 rosemary sprigs

Directions

1. Heat the oil in a deep skillet over a moderate heat. Cook the sausage for 2 to 3 minutes, stirring periodically.
2. Stir in the shallots, garlic, bell peppers, and parsnip; season with salt and pepper. Cook approximately 7 minutes.
3. Add the remaining ingredients and bring it to a boil. Reduce the heat to medium-low. Let it simmer for 25 minutes. Serve warm.

535. Spicy Sausage and Vegetable Casserole

Preparation Time: 30 minutes
Servings 4)

Nutritional Value:424 Calories; 32.4g Fat; 6.8g Carbs; 23.7g Protein; 1.8g Sugars

Ingredients

- 1 tablespoon tallow, softened
- 4 beef sausages
- 1 banana shallot, sliced
- 1 cup broccoli, broken into small florets
- 1 carrot, sliced
- 1 celery stalk, chopped
- 1 bell pepper, sliced
- 1 dried Poblano pepper, crushed
- 2 garlic cloves, finely chopped
- Salt, to taste
- 1 teaspoon black peppercorns, freshly crushed
- 1/2 teaspoon smoked cayenne pepper
- 1 ¼ cups beef stock, preferably homemade

Directions

1. Melt the tallow in a nonstick skillet over a moderately high heat. Cook sausages until they are browned on all sides; reserve.

2. Now, cook the shallot, broccoli, carrots, celery, peppers, and garlic in the same skillet; cook for 6 to 9 minutes or until the vegetables are tender.
3. Season with salt, peppercorns and smoked cayenne pepper. Transfer the sautéed vegetables to a lightly greased casserole dish. Nestle the reserved sausages within the sautéed vegetables.
4. Pour in the stock and bake in the preheated oven at 350 degrees F for about 10 minutes. Serve warm garnished with fresh chives if desired.

536. Hamburger Soup with Cabbage

Preparation Time: 35 minutes
Servings 4)

Nutritional Value:307 Calories; 23.6g Fat; 6.4g Carbs; 14.8g Protein; 2.2g Sugars

Ingredients

- 2 tablespoons lard, melted
- 3/4 pound ground chuck
- 1/2 cup scallions, chopped
- 2 cloves garlic, minced
- 1 carrot, diced
- 1 cup cabbage,shredded
- 1 celery with leaves, diced
- 1 tomato, pureed
- 6 cups chicken broth
- 1 bay leaf
- Seasoned salt and ground black pepper, to taste
- 1 cup sour cream

Directions

1. Melt the lard in a stockpot. Cook the chuck until it is no longer pink; reserve.
2. Then, cook the scallions, garlic, carrot, cabbage, and celery in the pan drippings, stirring constantly.
3. Stir in the other ingredients along with reserved chuck, bringing to a rapid boil. Turn the heat to a simmer. Cook another 27 minutes, partially covered.
4. Taste and adjust the seasonings. Ladle into individual bowls; serve dolloped with full-fat sour cream.

537. Ultimate Thai Beef Salad

Preparation Time: 15 minutes
Servings 4)

Nutritional Value:404 Calories; 32.9g Fat; 8g Carbs; 12.8g Protein; 3.3g Sugars

Ingredients

- 1/2 pound beef rump steak, cut into strips
- 1/2 teaspoon sea salt
- 1/3 teaspoon freshly cracked black pepper
- 1 teaspoon soy sauce
- 2 tablespoons sesame oil
- 1 red onion, peeled and sliced
- 1 garlic clove, minced
- 1 bunch fresh mint
- 2 avocados, pitted, peeled and sliced
- 2 cucumbers, sliced
- 1 bunch fresh Thai basil, leaves picked
- 1 teaspoon minced Thai chili
- 2 tablespoons rice vinegar
- 1 tablespoon fresh lime juice
- 1/4 cup pumpkin seeds

Directions

1. Combine the beef with the salt, pepper and soy sauce.
2. Preheat the oil in a nonstick skillet over medium-low heat. Then, sauté the onion and garlic until tender and aromatic, about 4 minutes.
3. Cook the beef on a grill pan for 5 minutes or until cooked to your liking.
4. Arrange fresh mint, avocado slices, cucumber, Thai basil, and Thai chili in a nice salad bowl. Top with the beef slices. Add the onion-garlic mixture.
5. Drizzle with rice vinegar and lime juice. Sprinkle with pumpkin seeds and serve.

538. Hungarian Beef Stew

Preparation Time: 1 hour 25 minutes

Servings 4)

Nutritional Value:357 Calories; 15.8g Fat; 7g Carbs; 40.2g Protein; 4.2g Sugars

Ingredients

- 2 tablespoons olive oil
- 1 ¼ pounds chuck-eye roast, diced
- Celery salt and ground black pepper, to taste
- 1 tablespoon Hungarian paprika
- 1 tablespoon pear cider vinegar
- 1/2 cup Cabernet Sauvignon
- 4 cups water
- 2 tablespoons beef bouillon granules
- 1/4 teaspoon ground bay leaf
- 2 onions, peeled and chopped
- 1 celery with leaves, chopped
- 2 carrots, peeled and cut into 1/4-inch rounds
- 1 tablespoon flaxseed meal

Directions

1. Heat the oil in a heavy-bottomed pot. Then, cook the meat until no longer pink, for 3 to 4 minutes; work in batches and set aside. Season with celery salt, pepper, and Hungarian paprika.
2. Now, pour the vinegar and Cabernet Sauvignon to deglaze the bottom of the pot. Add the water, beef bouillon granules and reserved beef to the pot.
3. Stir in the ground bay leaf, onions, celery and carrots and cook an additional 1 hour 15 minutes over medium-low heat.
4. Add the flaxseed meal to thicken the liquid; stir constantly for 3 minutes. Serve in individual bowls and enjoy!

539. Za'atar Strip Steaks with Cabbage

Preparation Time: 20 minutes +marinating time
Servings 4)

Nutritional Value:321 Calories; 14g Fat; 7.3g Carbs; 36.7g Protein; 3.3g Sugars

Ingredients

- 1 pound New York strip steaks, cut into bite-sized pieces
- 1 tablespoon hoisin sauce
- 1 tablespoon fresh lemon juice
- Sea salt and ground black pepper, to taste
- 1 teaspoon Za'atar
- 2 tablespoons sesame oil
- 1 yellow onion, chopped
- 2 garlic cloves, chopped
- 1 cup cabbage, shredded
- 1 bell pepper, chopped

Directions

1. Toss strip steaks with hoisin sauce, fresh lemon juice, salt, black pepper and Za'atar seasoning. Marinate in the refrigerator for at least 3 hours.
2. Heat the oil in a skillet that is preheated over a moderately high heat. Now, brown strip steaks for 3 to 4 minutes, stirring occasionally.
3. Add the onions to the same skillet and cook until it is translucent. Add the garlic, cabbage and bell pepper and turn the heat to medium-low.
4. Simmer an additional 10 minutes and serve warm. Bon appétit!

540. Spicy Winter Sauerkraut with Ground Beef

Preparation Time: 20 minutes
Servings 4)

Nutritional Value:330 Calories; 12.2g Fat; 6.7g Carbs; 44.4g Protein; 3.6g Sugars

Ingredients

- 1 tablespoon tallow, melted
- 2 onions, chopped
- 2 garlic cloves, smashed
- 1 ¼ pounds ground beef
- 18 ounces sauerkraut, rinsed and well drained
- 1 teaspoon chili pepper flakes
- 1 teaspoon mustard powder
- 1 bay leaf
- Sea salt and ground black pepper, to taste

Directions

1. Heat a saucepan over a moderately high heat. Now, warm the tallow and cook the onions and garlic until aromatic.
2. Stir in ground beef and cook until it is slightly browned.
3. Add the remaining ingredients. Reduce the heat to medium. Cook about 6 minutes or until everything is thoroughly cooked.Bon appétit!
4.

541. Coconut Dip

Preparation time: 10 minutes
Cooking time: 0 minutes
Servings: 2

Ingredients:

- 1 cup coconut, grated
- ½ inch ginger, grated
- 1 green chili, chopped
- 20 curry leaves
- 2 teaspoons coconut oil, melted

Directions:

1. In your blender, combine the coconut with the ginger, chili, curry leaves and coconut oil, pulse really well, divide into 2 small bowls and serve as a dip.
2. Enjoy!

Nutritional Value:calories 129, fat 2, fiber 4, carbs 8, protein 4

542. Easy Coriander Dip

Preparation time: 10 minutes
Cooking time: 0 minutes
Servings: 2

Ingredients:

- 1 cup coriander leaves
- 1 green chili pepper, chopped
- 1 tablespoon ginger, grated
- 2 teaspoons lemon juice

Directions:

1. In your blender, combine the coriander with the chili, ginger and lemon juice, pulse well, divide into 2 small cups and serve as a dip.
2. Enjoy!

Nutritional Value:calories 90, fat 2, fiber 2, carbs 6, protein 7

543. Mint Dip

Preparation time: 10 minutes
Cooking time: 0 minutes
Servings: 4

Ingredients:

- 4 tablespoons cashew yogurt
- 1 cup coriander leaves
- 2 cups mint leaves
- 1 green chili, chopped
- 1 yellow onion, chopped
- 1 tablespoon ginger, grated
- 2 garlic cloves, minced
- 1 teaspoon cumin powder
- 1 teaspoon mango powder
- A pinch of salt and black pepper

Directions:

1. In your blender, combine the cashew yogurt with the coriander, mint, chili, onion, ginger, garlic, cumin, mango powder, salt and pepper, blend well, divide into cups and serve as a dip.
2. Enjoy!

Nutritional Value:calories 100, fat 2, fiber 3, carbs 7, protein 5

544. Easy Tomato Chutney

Preparation time: 10 minutes
Cooking time: 10 minutes
Servings: 2

Ingredients:

- 1 cup tomatoes, chopped
- 1 tablespoon ginger, grated
- 2 red chilies, dried and crushed
- A pinch of salt and black pepper
- 3 cloves
- 2 tablespoons water
- ½ tablespoon avocado oil
- 8 curry leaves, chopped
- ½ teaspoon mustard seeds
- 3 fenugreek seeds

Directions:

1. Heat up a pan with the oil over medium

heat, add tomatoes, ginger, chilies, salt, pepper, cloves and water, stir and cook for 7 minutes.
2. Add the curry leaves, mustard seeds and fenugreek ones, stir, cook for 3 minutes more, divide into bowls, leave aside to cool down and serve.
3. Enjoy!

Nutritional Value:calories 129, fat 1, fiber 3, carbs 9, protein 5

545. Fast Green Chutney

Preparation time: 10 minutes
Cooking time: 0 minutes
Servings: 1

Ingredients:

- 2 cups coriander leaves
- 2 green chilies, chopped
- 1 teaspoon ginger, grated
- ½ teaspoon lime juice
- ½ teaspoon cumin powder
- ½ teaspoon chaat masala
- 2 teaspoons water
- A pinch of salt

Directions:

1. In your blender, combine the coriander with the chilies, ginger, lime juice, cumin, chaat, water and salt, pulse well, transfer to a bowl and serve as a dip.
2. Enjoy!

Nutritional Value:calories 100, fat 1, fiber 2, carbs 5, protein 6

546. Papaya Spread

Preparation time: 10 minutes
Cooking time: 10 minutes
Servings: 4

Ingredients:

- 1 and ¼ cup papaya, peeled and grated
- ½ teaspoon mustard seeds
- ½ tablespoon olive oil
- 8 curry leaves, chopped
- ¼ teaspoon turmeric powder
- ¼ teaspoon stevia
- ¼ teaspoon lemon juice

Directions:

1. Heat up a pan with the oil over medium-high heat, add mustard seeds and curry powder, stir and cook for 3 minutes.
2. Add turmeric, stevia and lemon juice, stir and cook for 3 minutes more.
3. Add the papaya, stir and cook for 4 minutes, leave aside to cool down, divide into bowls and serve as a dip.
4. Enjoy!

Nutritional Value:calories 140, fat 2, fiber 2, carbs 8, protein 8

547. Chili Garlic Chutney

Preparation time: 20 minutes
Cooking time: 0 minutes
Servings: 1

Ingredients:

- 14 red chilies, dried
- 1 and ¼ cups water
- 10 garlic cloves, minced
- A pinch of salt

Directions:

1. In a bowl, mix the chilies with 1 cup water, leave aside for 20 minutes, drain well and chop.
2. In a blender, combine the chilies with the garlic, salt and ¼ cup water, pulse well, transfer to a bowl and serve as a hot dip.
3. Enjoy!

Nutritional Value:calories 100, fat 1, fiber 2, carbs 6, protein 7

578. Fast Onion Chutney

Preparation time: 10 minutes
Cooking time: 10 minutes
Servings: 2

Ingredients:

1. 1 yellow onion, chopped
2. 2 garlic cloves, minced
3. 2 red chilies, chopped
4. 2 teaspoons avocado oil

5. 1 teaspoon sweet paprika
6. A pinch of salt
7. ¼ cup water

Directions:

1. Heat up a pan with the oil over medium-high heat, add the chilies, garlic and onion, stir and cook for 5 minutes.
2. Add paprika, salt and water, stir, cook for 5 minutes more, divide into 2 bowls and serve.
3. Enjoy!

Nutritional Value:calories 121, fat 2, fiber 6, carbs 9, protein 5

549. Pomegranate Chutney

Preparation time: 10 minutes
Cooking time: 0 minutes
Servings: 4

Ingredients:

- 4 teaspoons pomegranate seeds
- ½ cup coriander leaves, chopped
- 1 yellow onion, chopped
- ¼ cup mint, chopped
- ½ teaspoon cumin, ground
- 1 teaspoon lemon juice
- 1 green chili, chopped
- ½ teaspoon stevia
- 3 tablespoons water

Directions:

1. In your blender, combine the pomegranate seeds with coriander, onion, mint, cumin, lemon juice, chili, stevia and water, pulse well, divide into bowls and serve as a dip.
2. Enjoy!

Nutritional Value:calories 90, fat 1, fiber 2, carbs 6, protein 6

550. Beets Spread

Preparation time: 10 minutes
Cooking time: 8 minutes
Servings: 4

Ingredients:

- 1 cup beet, peeled and grated
- 7 curry leaves, chopped
- 2 green chilies, chopped
- ½ tablespoon avocado oil
- 1/3 cup coconut, grated
- ½ cup water
- A pinch of salt

Directions:

- Heat up a pan with the oil over medium heat, add the beets, curry leaves, chilies, coconut, salt and water, stir, cook for 8 minutes, take off heat, whisk well, divide into bowls and serve as a party spread.
- Enjoy!

Nutritional Value:calories 111, fat 2, fiber 3, carbs 6, protein 4

551. Easy Tomato Salsa

Preparation time: 10 minutes
Cooking time: 12 minutes
Servings: 4

Ingredients:

- 3 tomatoes, halved
- 3 garlic cloves, peeled
- 1 red jalapeno pepper, chopped
- 1 yellow onion, roughly chopped
- 1 and ½ tablespoons lime juice
- A pinch of salt and black pepper
- 1/3 cup cilantro leaves

Directions:

1. Heat up a pan over medium heat, add tomatoes, garlic and jalapeno, cook for 6 minutes and transfer to your blender.
2. Heat up the same pan over medium heat, add onion, cook for 6 minutes and also transfer to your blender.
3. Add salt, pepper, cilantro and lime juice, pulse a bit, divide into bowls and serve.
4. Enjoy!

Nutritional Value:calories 166, fat 2, fiber 3, carbs 7, protein 6

Tomatillo Salsa
Preparation time: 4 hours

Cooking time: 0 minutes
Servings: 4

Ingredients:

- 2 cups tomatillos, chopped
- 1/3 cup green onions, chopped
- 1/3 cup cilantro, chopped
- 1 tablespoon lime juice
- 1 jalapeno, chopped
- 1 cup avocado, peeled, pitted and cubed
- A pinch of salt

Directions:

1. In a bowl, combine the tomatillos with the green onions, cilantro, lime juice, salt and jalapeno, toss, cover and keep in the fridge for 4 hours.
2. Add the avocado, toss and serve as a party snack.
3. Enjoy!

Nutritional Value:calories 151, fat 2, fiber 4, carbs 8, protein 5

552. Quick Apple Salsa

Preparation time: 10 minutes
Cooking time: 0 minutes
Servings: 12

Ingredients:

- 2 cups green apple, cored, peeled and cubed
- ½ cup red bell pepper, cubed
- ¼ cup red onion, chopped
- ¼ cup lime juice
- ¼ cup cilantro, chopped
- 1 tablespoon stevia
- A pinch of salt and black pepper
- 1 jalapeno pepper, chopped

Directions:

1. In a bowl, combine the apple with bell pepper, onion, cilantro, lime juice, stevia, jalapeno, salt and pepper, toss and serve as a snack.
2. Enjoy!

Nutritional Value:calories 87, fat 2, fiber 2, carbs 5, protein 8

553. Peach Salsa

Preparation time: 10 minutes
Cooking time: 0 minutes
Servings: 6

Ingredients:

- 2 cups watermelon, cubed
- 1 cup peaches, peeled and cubed
- ¼ cup basil, chopped
- ¼ cup chives, chopped
- 3 cups cherry tomatoes, halved
- A pinch of salt and black pepper

Directions:

1. In a bowl, combine the watermelon with the peaches, basil, chives, tomatoes, salt and pepper, toss, divide into small bowls and serve as an appetizer.
2. Enjoy!

Nutritional Value:calories 78, fat 1, fiber 2, carbs 5, protein 5

554. Party Cranberry Salsa

Preparation time: 30 minutes
Cooking time: 0 minutes
Servings: 4

Ingredients:

- 1 cup cranberries, dried
- 1 cup water
- ½ cup cucumber, cubed
- ½ cup purple onion, chopped
- ¼ cup cilantro, chopped
- 1 jalapeno, chopped
- 1 garlic clove, minced
- ¼ cup lime juice
- ½ teaspoon cumin, ground
- A pinch of salt and black pepper

Directions:

1. In a bowl, combine the cranberries with the water, leave aside for 30 minutes, drain and put them in a bowl.
2. Add the cucumber, onion, cilantro, jalapeno, garlic, lime juice, cumin, salt and pepper, toss, divide into smaller bowls and serve as a snack.

3. Enjoy!

Nutritional Value:calories 91, fat 1, fiber 2, carbs 7, protein 4

555. Fresh Party Salsa

Preparation time: 10 minutes
Cooking time: 0 minutes
Servings: 4

Ingredients:

- 2 cups cherry tomatoes, halved
- ¼ cup red onion, chopped
- 2 tablespoons cilantro, chopped
- 1 garlic clove, minced
- 2 tablespoons lime juice
- 1 jalapeno, chopped
- A pinch of salt and black pepper

Directions:

1. In a bowl, combine the cherry tomatoes with the onion, cilantro, garlic, lime juice, jalapeno, salt and pepper, toss, divide into bowls and serve as a snack.
2. Enjoy!

Nutritional Value:calories 87, fat 1, fiber 2, carbs 7, protein 5

556. Blueberry Appetizer Salad

Preparation time: 10 minutes
Cooking time: 0 minutes
Servings: 4

Ingredients:

- 1 cup blueberries, whole
- 2 cups blueberries, chopped
- 3 tablespoons cilantro, chopped
- ¼ cup lemon juice
- 2 jalapenos, chopped
- ¼ cup yellow onion, chopped
- ¼ cup red bell pepper, chopped
- A pinch of salt

Directions:

1. In a big bowl, combine the whole blueberries with the chopped ones, cilantro, lime juice, jalapenos, onion, bell pepper and salt, toss, divide into small bowls and serve as an appetizer.
2. Enjoy!

Nutritional Value:calories 90, fat 1, fiber 2, carbs 7, protein 8

557. Pineapple and Cucumber Appetizer Salad

Preparation time: 1 hour
Cooking time: 0 minutes
Servings: 4

Ingredients:

- 1 cucumber, peeled and cubed
- 2 cups pineapple, peeled and cubed
- 2 green onions, chopped
- 1 jalapeno pepper, chopped
- 1 tablespoon lime juice
- ¼ cup basil, chopped
- A pinch of salt

Directions:

1. In a bowl, combine the cucumber with the pineapple, onions, jalapeno, lime juice, basil and salt, toss and keep in the fridge for 1 hour before serving as an appetizer.
2. Enjoy!

Nutritional Value:calories 100, fat 2, fiber 3, carbs 9, protein 6

558. Cilantro Salsa

Preparation time: 10 minutes
Cooking time: 10 minutes
Servings: 2

Ingredients:

- ½ cup red onion, chopped
- 10 Serrano peppers, chopped
- 1 tablespoon olive oil
- 3 garlic cloves, minced
- ½ cup cilantro, chopped
- 1 teaspoon white vinegar
- ¼ teaspoon cumin, ground
- A pinch of salt and black pepper

Directions:

1. Heat up a pan with the oil over medium-

high heat, add the onion, the Serrano peppers and the garlic, stir and cook for 10 minutes.
2. Add cilantro, vinegar, cumin, salt and pepper, stir, divide into 2 bowls and serve.
3. Enjoy!

Nutritional Value:calories 121, fat 2, fiber 3, carbs 7, protein 6

559. Plum Appetizer Salad

Preparation time: 10 minutes
Cooking time: 0 minutes
Servings: 3

Ingredients:

- 1 cup plums, chopped
- 2 tablespoons basil, chopped
- 1 jalapeno, chopped
- 2 tablespoons red onion, chopped
- 2 teaspoons lime juice
- A pinch of salt and black pepper
- 2 tablespoons stevia
- ½ teaspoon cumin, ground
- 1 teaspoon olive oil

Directions:

1. In a salad bowl, combine the plums with the basil, jalapeno, onion, lime juice, salt, pepper, stevia, cumin and oil, toss, divide into small cups and serve as an appetizer.
2. Enjoy!

Nutritional Value:calories 137, fat 2, fiber 2, carbs 7, protein 5

560. Artichoke Appetizer

Preparation time: 10 minutes
Cooking time: 0 minutes
Servings: 10

Ingredients:

- 15 ounces marinated artichoke hearts, drained and ½ cup marinade reserved
- 2 tablespoons red vinegar
- 2 tablespoons olive oil
- 6 plum tomatoes, sliced
- 1 pound mozzarella, sliced
- 2 cups basil, chopped
- A pinch of black pepper

Directions:

1. Arrange artichoke heart, tomatoes, mozzarella slices and basil on a platter.
2. In a bowl, combine the vinegar with the oil, reserved marinade and black pepper, whisk well, pour over the artichokes mix and serve as an appetizer.
3. Enjoy!

Nutritional Value:calories 200, fat 7, fiber 1, carbs 6, protein 7

561. Shrimp Appetizer Salad

Preparation time: 10 minutes
Cooking time: 0 minutes
Servings: 8

Ingredients:

- 1 pound shrimp, cooked, peeled and deveined
- ¼ cup yellow onion, chopped
- 1 tomato, cubed
- 4 radishes, chopped
- 2 tablespoons lime juice
- ¼ cup cilantro, chopped
- 1 and ½ teaspoons jalapeno, minced
- A pinch of salt and black pepper

Directions:

1. In a large bowl, combine the shrimp with the onion, tomato, radishes, lime juice, cilantro, jalapeno, salt and pepper, toss and keep in the fridge until you serve it as an appetizer.
2. Enjoy!

Nutritional Value:calories 90, fat 1, fiber 1, carbs 2, protein 6

562. Fast Mango Guacamole

Preparation time: 10 minutes
Cooking time: 0 minutes
Servings: 12

Ingredients:

- 3 avocados, peeled, pitted and cubed
- 1 mango, peeled and cubed
- 1 tomato, cubed
- ¼ cup cilantro, chopped
- 1 red onion, chopped
- 3 tablespoons lime juice
- A pinch of salt and white pepper

Directions:

1. In a bowl, combine the avocados with the mango, tomato, cilantro, onion, lime juice, salt and pepper, toss, divide into small cups and serve as an appetizer.
2. Enjoy!

Nutritional Value:calories 87, fat 4, fiber 4, carbs 8, protein 2

563. Creamy Dill Dip

Preparation time: 10 minutes
Cooking time: 0 minutes
Servings: 10

Ingredients:

- 1 cup coconut cream
- ½ cup avocado mayonnaise
- 1 tablespoon yellow onion, chopped
- 2 teaspoons parsley flakes
- 2 teaspoons dill, chopped
- A pinch of salt

Directions:

1. In a bowl, combine the cream with the mayo, onion, parsley flakes, dill and salt, whisk well and serve with veggie sticks on the side.
2. Enjoy!

Nutritional Value:calories 102, fat 3, fiber 1, carbs 2, protein 2

564. Crab Dip

Preparation time: 10 minutes
Cooking time: 0 minutes
Servings: 12

Ingredients:

- 2 tablespoons natural grape juice
- 1/3 cup avocado mayonnaise
- 2 tablespoons yellow onion, chopped
- 2 tablespoons lemon juice
- 1 tablespoon garlic, minced
- 16 ounces cream cheese, cubed
- 1 pound crabmeat, chopped

Directions:

1. In a bowl, combine the grape juice with the mayo, onion, lemon juice, garlic, cream cheese and crabmeat and whisk well.
2. Divide into bowls and serve as a party dip.
3. Enjoy!

Nutritional Value:calories 100, fat 4, fiber 1, carbs 4, protein 4

565. Creamy Basil Dip

Preparation time: 10 minutes
Cooking time: 0 minutes
Servings: 10

Ingredients:

- 1 cup avocado mayonnaise
- 2 tablespoons basil pesto
- 1 tablespoon parmesan, grated
- 1 tablespoon basil, chopped
- 1 teaspoon lemon juice
- 1 garlic clove, minced

Directions:

1. In a bowl, combine the mayonnaise with the basil pesto, parmesan, basil, lemon juice and garlic and whisk really well.
2. Divide into bowls and serve as a dip.
3. Enjoy!

Nutritional Value:calories 100, fat 4, fiber 2, carbs 5, protein 3

566. Cheese and Bacon Spread

1. Preparation time: 10 minutes
2. Cooking time: 0 minutes
3. Servings: 12

Ingredients:

- 12 ounces bacon, cooked and crumbled
- ½ cup almonds, chopped

- 1 pounds cheddar cheese, soft and shredded
- 2 cups avocado mayonnaise
- 2 tablespoons sweet red pepper, chopped
- 1 yellow onion, chopped
- A pinch of salt and black pepper

Directions:

1. In a bowl, combine the bacon with the almonds, cheese, mayo, red pepper, onion, salt and pepper, whisk well, divide into small cups and serve as a party spread.
2. Enjoy!

Nutritional Value:calories 184, fat 12, fiber 1, carbs 4, protein 5

567. Smoked Salmon Spread

Preparation time: 10 minutes
Cooking time: 0 minutes
Servings: 10
Ingredients:

- 16 ounces cream cheese, soft
- 4 ounces smoked salmon, flaked
- 1 tablespoon lemon juice
- ¼ teaspoon Creole seasoning
- A pinch of salt and black pepper
- 1 tablespoon dill, chopped

Directions:

1. In a blender, combine the cream cheese with the salmon, lemon juice, Creole seasoning, salt, pepper and dill, pulse well, divide into bowls and serve as a party spread.
2. Enjoy!

Nutritional Value:calories 100, fat 8, fiber 2, carbs 2, protein 4

568. Easy Spinach Dip

Preparation time: 10 minutes
Cooking time: 0 minutes
Servings: 10

Ingredients:

- 2 cups coconut cream
- 1 ounce keto ranch dressing
- 10 ounces spinach, chopped
- ¼ cup yellow onion, chopped
- 1 teaspoon basil, dried
- ½ teaspoon oregano, dried

Directions:

1. In a bowl, combine the spinach with cream, ranch dressing, onion, basil and oregano, whisk well, divide into small cups and serve as a party snack.
2. Enjoy!

Nutritional Value:calories 161, fat 6, fiber 2, carbs 17, protein 5

569. Brussels Sprouts Appetizer

Preparation time: 10 minutes
Cooking time: 50 minutes
Servings: 20

Ingredients:

- 2 tablespoons ghee, melted
- 1 yellow onion, chopped
- 2 garlic cloves, minced
- 2 tablespoons stevia
- 2 tablespoons white vinegar
- 1 teaspoon chili powder
- 20 Brussels sprouts, halved
- 2 tablespoons olive oil
- 6 bacon slices
- A pinch of salt and black pepper
- 7 ounces favorite cheese, cut into squares

Directions:

1. Heat up a pan with the ghee over medium-high heat, add the onion, stir and sauté for 8 minutes.
2. Add the garlic, stevia, vinegar, salt, pepper and chili powder, stir, cook for 10-12 minutes more and take off heat.
3. Spread the sprouts on a lined baking sheet, season with a pinch of salt and black pepper, drizzle the olive oil over them, toss and bake in the oven and cook at 375 degrees F for 20 minutes.
4. Meanwhile, heat up another pan over medium-high heat, add the bacon, stir, cook for 8 minutes, drain excess grease

and cut it into squares.

5. Arrange a Brussels sprouts halve on a cutting board, top with a piece of bacon, then with a cheese piece, then add another Brussels halve and secure with a toothpick.
6. Repeat with the other Brussels sprouts and the rest of the ingredients and serve as an appetizer.
7. Enjoy!

Nutritional Value:calories 188, fat 2, fiber 3, carbs 9, protein 6

570. Cashew Hummus

Preparation time: 10 minutes
Cooking time: 0 minutes
Servings: 4

Ingredients:

- 5 tablespoons cashews, soaked for 12 hours
- 1 teaspoon apple cider vinegar
- 1 cup veggie stock
- 1 tablespoon water

Directions:

1. In a blender, combine the cashews with the vinegar, stock and water, pulse really well, divide into small cups and serve as an appetizer.
2. Enjoy!

Nutritional Value:calories 201, fat 6, fiber 5, carbs 9, protein 8

571. Chocolate Bundt Cake

Preparation Time: 30 MIN
Serves: 10

Ingredients:

- 1 cup almond flour
- ½ cup cocoa powder, unsweetened
- 3 tbsp. walnuts, unsweetened
- 4 large eggs
- 4 tbsp. coconut oil, melted
- ½ cup heavy cream
- 1 tsp baking powder
- 1 tsp powdered stevia

Directions:

1. Combine all dry ingredients in large mixing bowl. Mix well and then add eggs, coconut oil, and heavy cream. Using a hand mixer, beat until well combined.
2. Grease a 6-inches bundt pan with some cooking spray. Pour in the batter and set aside.
3. Plug in your instant pot and pour in 2 cups of water in the stainless steel insert. Position a trivet and place the bundt pan on top. Securely close the lid and adjust the steam release handle.
4. Press the "Manual" button and set the timer for 20 minutes. Cook on high pressure.
5. When you hear the cooker's end signal, press "Cancel" button and release the pressure naturally.
6. Open the pot and let it chill to a room temperature before serving.
7. Enjoy!

Nutritional Value:

Calories 137
Total Fats 12.9g
Net Carbs: 1.9g
Protein 4.6g
Fiber: 4.6g

572. bRaspberry Mug Cake

Preparation Time: 15 MIN
Serves: 3

Ingredients:

- 1 cup almond flour
- ½ cup fresh raspberries
- 1 tbsp. dark chocolate chips, unsweetened
- 3 large eggs
- 1 tbsp. swerve
- ¼ tsp vanilla extract, sugar-free
- ¼ tsp salt

Directions:

1. Mix together all ingredients in a large mixing bowl. Grease 3 mason jars with some cooking spray and evenly divide the mixture between them.
2. Plug in your instant pot and pour in 2 cups of water. Position a trivet in the stainless steel insert and place the jars on top. Cover each jar with aluminum foil and lock the lid.
3. Adjust the steam release handle and press the "Manual" button. Set the timer for 10 minutes and cook on high pressure.
4. When you hear the cooker's end signal, press "Cancel" button and turn off the pot. Perform a quick release of the pressure by turning the valve to a venting position.
5. Remove the jars from the pot and let it chill to a room temperature before serving.
6. Enjoy!

Nutritional Value:

Calories 151
Total Fats 10.2g
Net Carbs: 4.4g
Protein 8.7g
Fiber: 2.3g

573. Quick Chocolate Cake

Preparation Time: 17 MIN
Serves: 12

Ingredients:

- 1 cup applesauce, unsweetened
- 3 large eggs
- 1 cup dark chocolate chips, unsweetened
- 1 tsp vanilla extract, sugar-free
- ¼ cup raw cocoa powder, unsweetened
- ½ cup arrowroot powder
- 3 tsp coconut oil, melted
- ½ tsp salt

Directions:

1. Plug in your instant pot and pour 2 cups of water in the stainless steel insert. Position a trivet and place the ramekin filled with chocolate chips on top. Press "Sautee" button bring the water to a boil. Cook until melted and remove the ramekin from the pot.
2. In a large mixing bowl, combine eggs, vanilla extract, and applesauce. Mix until combined. Now, add cocoa powder, arrowroot powder, salt, and melted chocolate chips.
3. Brush 6-inches springform pan with melted coconut oil and pour in the previously prepared mixture. Place on top of a trivet and securely lock the lid.
4. Adjust the steam release handle and press the "Manual" button. Set the timer for 5 minutes. Cook on high pressure.
5. When done, perform a quick release of the pressure by turning the handle to a venting position. Open the pot and let it chill for 10 minutes.
6. Transfer the cake to a serving plate. Optionally, dust with some raw cocoa.
7. Enjoy!

Nutritional Value:

Calories 107
Total Fats 5.3g
Net Carbs: 13.3g
Protein 2.6g
Fiber: 0.7g

574. Orange Brownies

Preparation Time: 35 MIN
Serves: 10

Ingredients:

- 4 oz dark chocolate chips, unsweetened
- 2 large eggs
- ½ cup coconut flour
- 3 tbsp. raw cocoa, unsweetened
- ½ cup almonds, chopped
- ½ cup walnuts, chopped
- 1 cup swerve
- ½ cup coconut oil
- 2 tsp baking soda
- 1 tsp orange extract, sugar-free
- ¼ tsp salt

Directions:

1. Plug in your instant pot and pour in 2 cups of water. Position a trivet in the stainless steel insert. Add chocolate chips to a heatproof ramekin and place it in the pot. Press "Sautee" button and cook until melted. Remove from the pot and set aside.
2. Combine coconut flour, swerve, cocoa powder, baking soda, and salt in a large mixing bowl. Mix until combined and then add melted chocolate chips, eggs, coconut oil, and orange extract. With a paddle attachment on, beat until all well incorporated.
3. Line a 6-inches springform pan with some parchment paper. Pour in the butter and flatten the surface using a kitchen spatula.
4. Place the pan on top of a trivet and securely lock the lid. Adjust the steam release handle and press the "Manual" button. Set the timer for 15 minutes.
5. When done, perform a quick release by turning the handle to the venting position. Open the lid and let it cool for a while.
6. Carefully remove the pan from the pot using kitchen mitts. Cut the cake into small square brownies and enjoy.

Nutritional Value:

Calories 256
Total Fats 21g
Net Carbs: 8.6g
Protein 6.1g
Fiber: 6.3g

575. Almond Biscuits

Preparation Time: 18 MIN
Serves: 16

Ingredients:

- 3 cups almonds, minced
- 1 cup coconut flour
- 3 tbsp. chia seeds
- ½ cup almond oil
- 2 eggs
- ½ cup cocoa powder, unsweetened
- 2 tsp powdered stevia
- ½ tsp salt
- 1 tsp baking soda

Directions:

1. Combine all ingredients in a large mixing bowl. Mix until all well incorporated.
2. Knead the dough on a clean surface. Shape the biscuits into the desired size.
3. Line a springform pan with a parchment paper and transfer the cookies on top.
4. Plug in your instant pot and pour in 2 cups of water. Position a trivet in the stainless steel insert and place the springform pan. Close the lid.
5. Adjust the steam release handle and press the "Manual" button. Set the timer for 8 minutes and cook on high pressure.
6. When you hear the cooker's end signal, press "Cancel" button and turn off the pot. Perform a quick release of the pressure by turning the valve to the venting position. Open the pot and remove the springform pan.
7. Transfer the biscuits to a wire rack and let them chill to a room temperature.
8. Enjoy!

Nutritional Value:

Calories 223
Total Fats 18.5g
Net Carbs: 4.5g
Protein 6.5g
Fiber: 7.3g

576. Mug Blueberry Cheesecake

Preparation Time: 15 MIN
Serves: 3

Ingredients:

- ¼ cup heavy cream
- 1 cup cream cheese, softened
- 2 tsp lemon juice, freshly squeezed
- 2 large eggs
- 1 tsp blueberry extract, sugar-free
- 1 tsp stevia powder

Directions:

1. Combine all ingredients in a large mixing bowl. Mix until well incorporated and transfer to mason jars. Set aside.
2. Plug in your instant pot and pour in 2 cups of water. Position a trivet in the stainless steel insert and place the jars on top.
3. Securely lock the lid and adjust the steam release handle. Press the "Manual" button and set the timer for 10 minutes. Cook on high pressure.
4. When you hear the cooker's end signal, press "Cancel" button and turn off the pot. Perform a quick release of the pressure by turning the valve to the venting position.
5. Open the pot and let it cool to a room temperature.
6. Enjoy!

Nutritional Value:

Calories 357
Total Fats 34g
Net Carbs: 2.9g
Protein 10.3g
Fiber: 0g

577. Creamy Raspberry Cake

Preparation Time: 20 MIN
Serves: 8

Ingredients:

- ½ cup coconut flour
- ¼ cup heavy cream
- ½ cup fresh raspberries
- 5 egg yolks
- ¼ cup butter
- 3 tsp powdered stevia
- 1 tsp baking powder
- 1 tsp vanilla extract, sugar-free
- ¼ cup coconut oil

Directions:

1. Combine all dry ingredients except raspberries in a large mixing bowl and mix until combined. Add all wet ingredients and beat until fully combined.
2. Line a 6-inches springform pan with some parchment paper and pour in the batter. Spread the raspberries on top by tucking them into the batter.
3. Plug in your instant pot and pour in 2 cups of water. Position a trivet in the stainless steel insert and place the pan on top.
4. Securely close the lid and adjust the steam release handle. Press the "Manual" button and set the timer for 10 minutes. Cook on high pressure.
5. When done, press "Cancel" button and perform a quick release of the pressure by turning the valve to the venting position.
6. Open the pot and let it chill for a while before serving.

Nutritional Value:

Calories 222
Total Fats 18.3g
Net Carbs: 5.3g
Protein 3.9g
Fiber: 6.5g

578. Strawberry Chocolate Fudge

Preparation Time: 25 MIN
Serves: 8

Ingredients:

- 2 cups almond flour
- ½ cup dark chocolate, unsweetened
- ½ cup raw cocoa powder
- 2 tsp powdered stevia
- ½ cup almond milk, unsweetened
- 1 tsp baking powder
- 1 tsp baking soda
- 5 eggs
- 1 tsp strawberry extract, sugar-free
- ½ tsp salt

Directions:

1. In a large mixing bowl, combine all dry ingredients and mix until combined. Now, add all the remaining ingredients. With a paddle attachment on, beat until all well incorporated.
2. Plug in your instant pot and pour in 2 cups of water. Position a trivet in the stainless steel insert. Pour in the previously prepared mixture into a greased springform pan. Place the pan on top of a trivet and close the lid.
3. Adjust the steam release handle and set the timer for 15 minutes. Cook on high pressure.
4. Once done, press "Cancel" button and turn off the pot. Open the lid and let it chill for a while before serving.

Nutritional Value:

Calories 242
Total Fats 18.6g
Net Carbs: 6.2g
Protein 8.5g
Fiber: 4.9g

579. Apple Lemon Pie

Preparation Time: 35 MIN
Serves: 10

Ingredients:

- 2 small Granny Smith's apples, peeled and thinly sliced
- 1 cup coconut flour
- ½ cup almond flour
- 1 tsp baking powder
- ½ tsp salt

- 1 tbsp. lemon juice, freshly squeezed
- 1 tsp lemon extract, sugar-free
- 1 tbsp. instant gelatin
- 3 tbsp. coconut oil, melted

Directions:

1. Combine apples, lemon extract, and lemon juice in a large bowl. Mix until apple slices are well coated. Transfer all to a springform pan lined with some parchment paper. Set aside.
2. Now, combine all dry ingredients in a large bowl and mix until combined. Add all wet ingredients and mix with a kitchen spatula until dough is formed. Using your hands, flatten the dough into a circle crust. Place the dough on the top of the apple mixture. Set aside.
3. Plug in your instant pot and pour in 2 cups of water. Position a trivet in the stainless steel insert. Place the pan on top and securely lock the lid. Adjust the steam release handle and set the timer for 20 minutes. Cook on high pressure.
4. When done, press "Cancel" button and turn off the pot. Release the pressure naturally.
5. Open the pot and let it chill for a while. Once cooled, turn the pan upside down and remove the parchment paper. Cut into slices and serve immediately.

Nutritional Value:

Calories 132
Total Fats 6.9g
Net Carbs: 7g
Protein 3.2g
Fiber: 7.3g

580. Rum Custard

Preparation Time: 30 MIN
Serves: 4

Ingredients:

4 oz cream cheese
½ cup heavy whipping cream
4 large eggs
¼ cup almond milk
1 tsp powdered stevia
1 tsp rum extract
For the topping:
2 tbsp. butter
1 tbsp. swerve
1 tbsp. cocoa powder, unsweetened

Directions:

1. In a large mixing bowl, combine cream cheese, heavy whipping cream, eggs, almond milk, stevia, and rum extract. With a whisking attachment on, beat until smooth and creamy. Pour the mixture into 4 ramekins and cover the top with some aluminum foil. Set aside.
2. Plug in your instant pot and pour in 2 cups of water. Position a trivet in the stainless steel insert. Place the ramekins on top and close the lid. Adjust the steam release handle and set the timer for 10 minutes.
3. When you hear the cooker's end signal, press "Cancel" button and turn off the pot. Perform a quick release of the pressure by turning the valve to the venting position.
4. Carefully remove the ramekins from the pot and let it chill for a while.
5. Meanwhile, combine all topping ingredients in another ramekin and place in the pot. Close the lid and adjust the steam release handle. Press the "Manual" button and set the timer for 3 minutes.
6. Once done, perform a quick release of the pressure and open the pot. Pour the melted sauce over the cheese custards. Refrigerate for 20 minutes before serving.

Nutritional Value:

Calories 315
Total Fats 29.9g
Net Carbs: 2.9g
Protein 9.4g
Fiber: 0.7g

581. Almond Strawberry Squares

Preparation Time: 18 MIN
Serves: 8

Ingredients:

- 1 ½ cup almond flour
- ¼ cup almonds, ground
- 1 tbsp. cocoa powder, unsweetened
- 1 tsp baking powder
- ½ cup heavy cream
- ½ cup almond milk
- 1 large egg
- 1 tsp vanilla extract
- For the strawberry layer:
- ½ cup fresh strawberries, chopped
- 1 cup whipped cream
- 2 tbsp. Greek yogurt

Directions:

1. In a large mixing bowl, combine almond flour, ground almonds, and cocoa powder. Mix until well combined
2. In a separate bowl, whisk eggs, heavy cream, and vanilla extract. Now, combine dry and wet ingredients and mix together until well incorporated.
3. Plug in your instant pot and pour in 2 cups of water. Position a trivet in the stainless steel insert. Line a 6-inches springform pan with some parchment paper. Spread the previously prepared mixture evenly and place the pan on top of a trivet. Securely lock the lid and adjust the steam release handle. Press the "Manual" button and set the timer for 8 minutes. Cook on high pressure.
4. When done, perform a quick release and open the pot. Carefully transfer the pan to a wire rack and let it cool completely.
5. Meanwhile, combine all strawberry layer ingredients in a food processor. Pulse until creamy. Spoon this mixture onto chilled crust. Using a kitchen spatula, spread the mixture evenly.
6. Refrigerate for 45 minutes, or freeze for 20 minutes. Cut into squares before serving.

Nutritional Value:

Calories 171
Total Fats 15.8g
Net Carbs: 3.2g
Protein 3.9g
Fiber: 1.7g

582. Chia-Almond Bars

Preparation Time: 20 MIN
Serves: 10

Ingredients:

- 1 cup raw almonds, minced
- ¼ cup raw hazelnuts, mince
- ¼ cup cocoa powder, unsweetened
- ½ cup almond flour
- ½ tsp cinnamon
- 1 cup almond butter
- 3 tbsp. chia seeds
- 3 tbsp. swerve
- ¼ tsp salt

Directions:

1. Combine almonds, hazelnuts, cocoa powder, almond flour, salt, cinnamon, swerve, and almond butter in a food processor. Process until smooth.
2. Transfer the mixture to a large bowl and add chia seeds. Mix well and transfer to a baking dish lined with some parchment paper. Loosely cover with aluminum foil and set aside.
3. Plug in your instant pot and pour in 1 cup of water. Set the trivet at the bottom of the stainless steel insert and put the baking dish on top.
4. Seal the lid and set the steam release handle to the 'Sealing' position. Press the 'Manual' button and set the timer for 15 minutes.
5. When done, release the pressure naturally and open the lid.
6. Remove the pan and cool to a room temperature. Slice in 10 bars before serving.

Nutritional Value:

Calories 144
Total Fats 11.5g
Net Carbs: 7.3g
Protein 5.2g
Fiber: 4.8g

583. Quick Blackberry Brownies

Preparation Time: 25 MIN
Serves: 6

Ingredients:

- 4 tbsp. coconut flour
- ¼ cup almond yogurt, sugar-free
- 3 tbsp. swerve
- 4 tbsp. coconut oil
- ½ cup blackberries, fresh
- ¼ tsp cinnamon, ground
- ¼ cup almond butter
- For the chocolate topping:
- ½ cup unsweetened dark chocolate chunks
- ¼ cup unsweetened almond milk

Directions:

1. Brush a small baking dish with some oil and line with parchment paper. Set aside.
2. Plug in your instant pot and pour in 1 cup of water. Set the trivet in the stainless steel insert.
3. In a large mixing bowl, combine all ingredients. With a dough hook attachment, beat well for 3 minutes.
4. Transfer the mixture to the prepared baking dish and press with your hands to flatten the surface.
5. Place the pan in the instant pot and seal the lid. Set the steam release handle and press the 'Manual' button. Set the timer for 3 minutes on high pressure.
6. When done, perform a natural release for 15 minutes. Open the lid and remove the pan. Chill for a while.
7. Press the 'Sautee' button and add chocolate. Gently melt and pour in the milk. Simmer for 2-3 minutes. Drizzle over chilled brownies and refrigerate for 1 hour before slicing them.

Nutritional Value:

Calories 249
Total Fats 20.8g
Net Carbs: 6.6g
Protein 3.8g
Fiber: 5.5g

584. Creamy Strawberry Cupcakes

Preparation Time: 20 MIN
Serves: 6

Ingredients:

- 1 cup strawberries, chopped
- 1 cup cream cheese
- 1 cup whipped cream
- 2 tbsp. plain Greek yogurt
- 3 eggs
- 2 egg whites
- ½ tsp salt
- 3 tbsp. almond flour
- 3 tbsp. swerve

Directions:

1. In a large mixing bowl, combine eggs, egg whites, and swerve. With a whisking attachment on, beat well for 1 minute. Now add cream cheese, whipped cream, Greek yogurt, and salt. Optionally, add one teaspoon of vanilla extract. Continue to mix until light and fluffy mixture. Finally, add almond flour and strawberries. Mix until fully combined.
2. Divide the mixture between 6 silicon muffin cups. Place them in a round baking dish and loosely cover with aluminum foil.
3. Plug in your instant pot and pour in 1 cup of water. Set the trivet and place the baking pan with cupcakes. Seal the lid and set the steam release handle.
4. Press the 'Manual' button and set the timer for 10 minutes.
5. When done, perform a quick release and open the lid.
6. Carefully remove the pan and aluminum foil. Chill cupcakes to a room temperature.
7. Optionally, sprinkle with some shredded coconut before serving.

Nutritional Value:

Calories 254
Total Fats 22.8
Net Carbs: 4.3g

Protein 8.4g
Fiber: 0.7g

585. Chocolate Orange Bars

Preparation Time: 20 MIN
Serves: 4

Ingredients:

- 2 cups almond flour
- 2 tsp orange extract
- ½ cup unsweetened almond milk
- ½ cup almond butter
- 1 tbsp. cocoa powder, unsweetened
- ½ unsweetened dark chocolate, cut into chunks
- 1 large egg
- 1 tsp stevia powder

Directions:

1. Plug in your instant pot and pour in 2 cups of water. Position a trivet in the stainless steel insert. Line a small baking dish with some parchment paper and set aside.
2. Combine the ingredients in a food processor and process until smooth. Transfer the mixture to the prepared baking dish and press with your hands to flatten the surface.
3. Wrap tightly with aluminum foil and place in the instant pot. Seal the lid and set the steam release handle. Press the 'Manual' button and set the timer for 12 minutes.
4. When you hear the cooker's end signal, perform a quick release and open the lid.
5. Using oven mitts, carefully remove the pan from the instant pot and cool to a room temperature.
6. Slice into bars and refrigerate for 1 hour before serving.

Nutritional Value:

Calories 141
Total Fats 10.6g
Net Carbs: 2.7g
Protein 5.6g
Fiber: 2.5g

586. Strawberry Scones

Preparation Time: 20 MIN
Serves: 6

Ingredients:

- 1 cup strawberries, chopped
- 1 cup almond flour
- 2 large eggs
- ½ cup almond butter, melted
- 1 tsp powdered stevia
- ½ tsp salt
- 2 tsp baking powder
- 1 tsp cherry extract, sugar-free

Directions:

1. In a large mixing bowl, combine all dry ingredients. Stir well until combined. Now, add eggs, almond butter, and cherry extract. With a paddle attachment on, beat until well incorporated. Using a kitchen spatula, stir in the strawberries.
2. Form 6 triangular-shaped scones and place them on a round baking pan lined with parchment paper.
3. Plug in your instant pot and pour in 2 cups of water. Position a trivet in the stainless steel insert and place the pan on top. Adjust the steam release handle and press "Manual" button. Set the timer for 10 minutes.
4. When done, perform a quick release of the pressure by turning the valve to the venting position. Open the lid and carefully transfer scones to a wire rack. Chill to a room temperature before serving.
5. Enjoy!

Nutritional Value:

Calories 69
Total Fats 4.7g
Net Carbs: 2.8g
Protein 3.5g
Fiber: 1.2g

587. Lemon Egg Bars

Serves: 8
Preparation Time: 1 hour

Ingredients

- 1¾ cups almond flour
- ½ cup butter, melted
- 1 cup Erythritol, powdered
- 3 large eggs
- 3 medium lemons, juiced

Directions

1. Preheat the oven to 350 degrees F and grease an 8-inch baking pan.
2. Whisk together butter, almond flour, Erythritol, and salt in a bowl.
3. Transfer this mixture to a pan and press firmly.
4. Place in the oven and bake for about 20 minutes.
5. Dish out and allow it to cool for 10 minutes at room temperature.
6. Mix the rest of the ingredients in a separate bowl and spread evenly over the baked crust.
7. Bake again for 25 minutes in the oven and slice the bars after removing from oven.
8. Serve and enjoy.

Nutritional Value:

Calories: 282
Carbs: 9.4g
Fats: 25.1g
Proteins: 8g
Sodium: 117mg
Sugar: 0.7g

588. Blackberry Lemon Tart

Serves: 8
Preparation Time: 30 mins

Ingredients

- 2 (9" tart molds with loose bottoms)
- 1 tablespoon sliced almonds
- 1 cup blackberries
- 1 cup lemon curd
- Almond Flour Pie Crust
- ½ cup coconut flour
- 4 tablespoons cold butter, unsalted
- 1½ cups almond flour
- 4 tablespoons Erythritol, powdered
- 2 eggs

Directions

1. Preheat the oven to 350 degrees F and grease two tart molds.
2. Mix together all the ingredients for almond flour pie crust to form a dough.
3. Divide the dough into two equal sized balls and place in the tart molds.
4. Make a few holes into each dough layer with a fork and transfer in the oven.
5. Bake for about 15 minutes and remove from the oven to cool.
6. Fill both the crusts equally with lemon curd and top with berries, Erythritol, and almond slices.
7. Serve and enjoy.

Nutritional Value:

Calories: 321
Carbs: 8.1g
Fats: 12.9g
Proteins: 5.4g
Sodium: 28mg
Sugar: 1.8g

589. Caramel Bars

Serves: 8
Preparation Time: 55 mins

Ingredients

- For the Cracker Base:
- 1 cup almond flour
- ¼ teaspoon salt
- ¼ teaspoon baking powder
- 1 egg
- 2 tablespoons grass-fed salted butter, melted
- Caramel Sauce:
- ½ cup butter
- ½ cup Swerve
- ½ cup heavy cream
- 1 teaspoon caramel extract
- ¼ teaspoon salt
- ½ teaspoon vanilla essence
- Toppings:

- 1 cup pecans, chopped
- 2 cups chocolate chips
- 1 cup coconut, shredded

Directions

1. Crackers: Preheat the oven to 300 degrees F and grease a baking pan.
2. Combine baking powder, salt, and almond flour in a bowl.
3. Whisk eggs and butter in a bowl and combine with the flour mixture.
4. Place the dough on the working surface layered with parchment paper.
5. Cut the dough into a rectangle then cover it with a parchment paper.
6. Spread it using a rolling pin into 1/8 inch thick dough sheet.
7. Transfer it to the baking pan and bake for about 35 minutes.
8. Increase the temperature of the oven to 375 degrees F.
9. Caramel sauce: Put butter, Swerve, vanilla, cream, and caramel extracts in a saucepan.
10. Combine well and spread the sauce over the baked crackers base.
11. Drizzle chocolate chips, coconut, and pecans over it and transfer in the oven.
12. Bake for another 5 minutes and remove from the pan.
13. Allow it to cool and slice to serve.

Nutritional Value:

Calories: 358
Carbs: 7.4g
Fats: 35.2g
Proteins: 5.5g
Sodium: 178mg
Sugar: 1.1g

590. Strawberry Vanilla Tart

Serves: 3
Preparation Time: 25 mins

Ingredients

- Coconut crust:
- ¾ cup coconut flour
- ½ cup coconut oil
- 2 eggs
- 1 teaspoon powdered sweetener
- 1 teaspoon vanilla essence
- Cream Filling:
- 2 eggs, separated
- 1 cup strawberries
- 1 cup mascarpone
- 1 teaspoon vanilla essence
- 2 tablespoons Stevia, powdered

Directions

1. Crust:
2. Preheat the oven to 350 degrees F and grease a baking pan.
3. Whisk together eggs in a bowl and add rest of the ingredients.
4. Spread this dough in between two sheets of parchment paper.
5. Place this dough sheet in a greased pan and pierce holes in it with a fork.
6. Transfer in the oven and bake for about 10 minutes.
7. Cream Filling:
8. Whisk the egg whites in an electric mixer until frothy.
9. Stir in mascarpone cream, egg yolks, sweetener, and vanilla and beat for about 3 minutes.
10. Spread this filling evenly in the baked crust and top with Stevia and strawberries.
11. Place the pie in the refrigerator for about 30 minutes and serve hot.

Nutritional Value:

Calories: 236
Carbs: 7.6g
Fats: 21.5g
Proteins: 4.3g
Sodium: 21mg
Sugar: 1.4g

591. Peanut Butter Bars

Serves: 8
Preparation Time: 15 mins

Ingredients

- Bars
- 2 oz. butter
- ¾ cup almond flour
- ¼ cup Swerve
- ½ teaspoon vanilla extract
- ½ cup peanut butter
- Topping
- ½ cup sugar-free chocolate chips

Directions

1. Preheat the oven to 300 degrees F and grease a baking pan.
2. Put all the ingredients for the bars in a bowl and mix well.
3. Spread this mixture in the pan and top with chocolate chips.
4. Transfer in the oven and bake for about 15 minutes.
5. Remove from the oven and transfer the pan in the refrigerator for about 1 hour.
6. Remove the base from pan and slice to serve.

Nutritional Value:

Calories: 214
Carbs: 6.5g
Fats: 19g
Proteins: 6.5g
Sodium: 123mg
Sugar: 1.9g

592. Cheesecake Jam Tarts

Serves: 6
Preparation Time: 45 mins

Ingredients

- Crust
- ½ cup almond flour
- 1½ tablespoons butter, melted
- Filling
- 1 small egg
- ½ teaspoon vanilla essence
- 1/8 teaspoon salt
- 6 oz. cream cheese
- 1/8 cup Erythritol
- ½ tablespoon fresh lemon juice
- Toppings
- 1/8 cup strawberry jam, sugar-free
- 1/8 cup blueberries

Directions

1. Preheat the oven to 340 degrees F and grease muffin tins.
2. Mix butter and almond flour in a bowl and pour this mixture into the muffin tin.
3. Transfer in the oven and bake for about 8 minutes.
4. Meanwhile, beat cream cheese in an electric mixture along with an egg.
5. Stir in Erythritol, vanilla essence, salt, and lemon juice and combine well.
6. Divide this filling into the muffin crust and transfer in the oven.
7. Bake the tarts for 20 minutes and allow it to cool after removing from oven.
8. Top with jam and blueberries and refrigerate overnight to serve.

Nutritional Value:

Calories: 175
Carbs: 2.8g
Fats: 16g
Proteins: 9g
Sodium: 8mg
Sugar: 1.8g

593. Chocolate Dipped Granola Bars

Serves: 4
Preparation Time: 35 mins

Ingredients

- 3 tablespoons coconut oil
- 1 oz. sesame seeds
- 1½ oz. walnuts
- 1 oz. pumpkin seeds
- 1 teaspoon cinnamon, ground
- 1½ oz. sugar-free dark chocolate
- 1 egg
- 1½ oz. almonds
- ¼ teaspoon flaxseed
- 1 oz. coconut, shredded, unsweetened
- 1 oz. sugar-free dark chocolate

- 2 tablespoons tahini
- ½ pinch sea salt
- ½ teaspoon vanilla essence

Directions

1. Preheat the oven to 340 degrees F and grease a baking pan.
2. Put all the ingredients in a food processor, except chocolate, and coarsely grind.
3. Spread the ground mixture in the baking pan and transfer in the oven.
4. Bake for about 20 minutes and remove from oven.
5. Allow it to cool at room temperature and slice it into small squares.
6. Melt the chocolate in a microwave and pour over the bars.
7. Arrange the bars over a baking sheet and refrigerate them for about 30 minutes to serve.

Nutritional Value:

Calories: 313
Carbs: 9.2g
Fats: 28.4g
Proteins: 8.1g
Sodium: 39mg
Sugar: 3.1g

594. Pumpkin Almond Pie

Serves: 8
Preparation Time: 1 hour 15 mins

Ingredients

- Almond Flour Pie Crust
- 4 tablespoons butter, melted
- 2 cups almond flour
- 1 teaspoon vanilla
- ½ teaspoon cinnamon
- 1 egg yolk
- Pumpkin Spice Filling
- 1 cup heavy cream
- 2 teaspoons pumpkin pie spice
- ⅔ cups Swerve
- 8 ounces cream cheese
- 4 eggs
- 1 teaspoon vanilla
- ¼ teaspoon salt

Directions

1. Preheat the oven to 400 degrees F and grease a pie pan.
2. Mix together all the ingredients for the crust in a bowl and transfer into the pie pan.
3. Press this mixture and transfer into the oven.
4. Bake this crust for about 12 minutes and keep aside.
5. Filling: Whisk together eggs and cream cheese until it turns frothy.
6. Add rest of the ingredients and stir well to combine.
7. Spread this filling evenly into the baked crust and return the stuffed pie to the oven.
8. Bake for another 45 minutes and allow to cool for 10 minutes.
9. Slice and enjoy.

Nutritional Value:

Calories: 285
Carbs: 3.5g
Fats: 27.3g
Proteins: 7.2g
Sodium: 165mg
Sugar: 0.4g

595. Key Lime Pie

Serves: 8
Preparation Time: 40 mins

Ingredients

For Crust:

- ½ cup coconut flour, sifted
- ¼ cup butter, melted
- ¼ teaspoon salt
- ½ cup almond flour
- ¼ cup Erythritol
- 2 organic eggs

For Filling:

- ½ cup Erythritol
- 2 teaspoons xanthan gum

- 3 organic egg yolks
- 2 tablespoons unsweetened dried coconut
- ¾ cup unsweetened coconut milk
- ¼ cup heavy cream
- 1 teaspoon guar gum
- ¼ teaspoon powdered Stevia
- ½ cup key lime juice

For Topping:

½ lime, cut into slices

1 cup whipped cream

Directions

1. Preheat the oven to 390 degrees F and grease a 9-inch pie dish.
2. For crust: Mix together all ingredients in a bowl to form a dough.
3. Arrange the dough between 2 sheets of wax paper and roll into 1/8-inch thick circle.
4. Place the dough in the pie dish and press firmly.
5. Pierce the bottom and sides of crust with a fork at many places.
6. Transfer in the oven and bake for about 10 minutes.
7. Remove from the oven and allow it to cool.
8. Reset the oven to 350 degrees F.
9. For filling: Put coconut milk, heavy cream, egg yolks, lime juice, erythritol, guar gum, xanthan gum and Stevia in a food processor.
10. Pulse until well combined and spread the filling mixture evenly over crust.
11. Transfer in the oven and bake for about 10 minutes.
12. Remove from oven and allow to cool for about 10 minutes.
13. Freeze for about 4 hours and top with whipped cream and lime slices to serve.

Nutritional Value:

Calories: 255

Carbs: 13.1g

Fats: 24.8g

Proteins: 5.2g

Sodium: 147mg

Sugar: 8.9g

596. Meringue Pie

Serves: 10

Preparation Time: 1 hour

Ingredients

- 2 tablespoons coconut flour
- 1 tablespoon granulated Swerve
- ¼ teaspoon salt
- 4 tablespoons ice water
- 1¼ cups almond flour
- 2 tablespoons arrowroot starch
- 1 teaspoon xanthan gum
- 5 tablespoons chilled butter, cut into small pieces

: *For Filling*

- 1½ cups plus 2 tablespoons water, divided
- ¼ teaspoon salt
- 3 tablespoons butter
- 1 tablespoon grass-fed gelatin
- 4 large organic egg yolks
- 1 cup granulated Swerve
- 2 teaspoons fresh lemon zest, grated
- 1/3 cup fresh lemon juice
- ½ teaspoon xanthan gum

For Meringue Topping:

1. ¼ teaspoon cream of tartar
2. ¼ cup powdered Swerve
3. ½ teaspoon organic vanilla extract
4. 4 large organic egg whites
5. Pinch of salt
6. ¼ cup granulated Swerve

Directions

1. Preheat the oven to 335 degrees F and grease a pie pan.
2. For crust: Put the flours, butter, arrowroot starch, Swerve, xanthan gum, and salt in a food processor until combined.
3. Add ice water slowly to form a dough and transfer into a pie pan.
4. Press gently and pierce holes in the crust with a fork.

5. Transfer in the oven and bake for about 12 minutes.
6. Remove from the oven and keep aside to cool completely.
7. Reheat the oven to 300 degrees F.
8. For filling: Whisk together egg yolks in a bowl and slowly add ½ cup of water, beating until well combined.
9. Boil Swerve, salt and lemon zest in 1 cup of the water in a pan.
10. Whisk in the egg yolks mixture slowly into the pan, beating continuously.
11. Lower the heat and cook for about 1 minute, stirring continuously.
12. Remove from the heat and stir in the butter and lemon juice until smooth.
13. Top with xanthan gum and beat vigorously with a wire whisk until well combined.
14. Meanwhile, dissolve the gelatin into remaining 2 tablespoons of water in a small bowl.
15. Keep aside for about 2 minutes and add the gelatin mixture into hot lemon mixture.
16. Beat until well combined and cover the pan to keep aside.
17. For topping:
18. Whisk together the egg whites, cream of tartar, and salt in a large bowl and beat until frothy.
19. Add the powdered Swerve, granulated Swerve, and vanilla extract slowly until stiff peaks form.
20. Pour the warm filling evenly over the crust and top with meringue.
21. Transfer in the oven and bake for about 20 minutes.
22. Remove from the oven and keep aside to cool.
23. Refrigerate for at least 3 hours and serve chilled.

Nutritional Value:

Calories: 215
Carbs: 7.2g
Fats: 18.5g
Proteins: 6.7g
Sodium: 159mg
Sugar: 1.1g

597. Keto Meat Pie

Serves: 8
Preparation Time: 25 mins

Ingredients

- The Filling
- 1 garlic clove, finely chopped
- 20 oz. ground beef
- 1 tablespoon dried oregano
- ½ cup water
- ½ yellow onion, finely chopped
- 2 tablespoons butter
- Salt and black pepper, to taste
- 4 tablespoons tomato paste
- Pie Crust
- 4 tablespoons sesame seeds
- 1 tablespoon ground psyllium husk powder
- 1 pinch salt
- 4 tablespoons water
- ¾ cup almond flour
- 4 tablespoons coconut flour
- 1 teaspoon baking powder
- 3 tablespoons olive oil
- 1 egg
- Topping
- 7 oz. cheddar cheese, shredded
- 8 oz. cottage cheese

Directions

1. Preheat the oven to 350 degrees F and grease a springform pan.
2. Heat olive oil in a pan and add onion and garlic.
3. Sauté for about 3 minutes and add ground beef, dried oregano, salt and black pepper.
4. Cook for about 4 minutes and add tomato paste, psyllium husk powder and water.
5. Lower the heat and allow to simmer for at least 20 minutes.

6. Meanwhile, make the dough for the crust by mixing all the dough ingredients in a food processor.
7. Spread the dough in the pan and transfer in the oven.
8. Bake for about 15 minutes and remove from the oven.
9. Fill the meat in the crust and top with cheese.
10. Transfer in the oven and bake for about 40 minutes.
11. Serve hot.

Nutritional Value:

Calories: 467
Carbs: 12.7g
Fats: 30.5g
Proteins: 36.9g
Sodium: 368mg
Sugar: 2.4g

598. Keto Silk Pie

Serves: 4
Preparation Time: 15 mins

Ingredients

- For the crust:
- ½ teaspoon baking powder
- 1/3 cup granulated Stevia
- 1½ teaspoons vanilla extract
- 1½ cups almond flour
- 1/8 teaspoon salt
- 3 tablespoons butter
- 1 medium egg
- 1 teaspoon butter, for greasing the pan
- For the filling:
- 4 tablespoons sour cream
- ½ cup + 2 teaspoons granulated Stevia
- 16 oz. cream cheese, room temperature
- 4 tablespoons butter
- 1 tablespoon +1 teaspoon vanilla extract
- ½ cup cocoa powder
- 1 cup whipping cream

Directions

1. Preheat the oven to 375 degrees F and grease a 9-inch pie pan with some butter.
2. Combine baking powder, almond flour, salt, and 1/3 cup Stevia in a bowl and add butter.
3. Stir in egg and vanilla extract and knead until the dough forms into a ball.
4. Transfer the dough into the pie pan and spread it covering the bottom and sides of the pan.
5. Pierce the holes in the crust and transfer in the oven.
6. Bake for about 15 minutes and remove crust from the oven to cool.
7. For the filling: Place sour cream, cream cheese, butter, vanilla extract, cocoa powder, and ½ cup stevia in a blender.
8. Blend until fluffy and place the whipping cream in a separate bowl.
9. Add 2 teaspoons granulated stevia and 1 teaspoon vanilla extract to the cream and beat to form stiff peaks.
10. Mix the whipped cream mixture into the sour cream mixture.
11. Scoop this mixture into the crust and cover to refrigerate for at least 3 hours before serving.

Nutritional Value:

Calories: 449
Carbs: 9.3g
Fats: 43.6g
Proteins: 9.5g
Sodium: 267mg
Sugar: 2.3g

599. Pie Banana Cream

Serves: 10
Preparation Time: 45 mins

Ingredients

Crust
1 batch Low Carb Walnut Pie Crust
Banana Cream Filling
1/3 cup almond milk
1/8 teaspoon xanthan gum
2 large eggs
1 teaspoon banana extract
½ teaspoon Stevia

1 cup heavy cream
1/3 cup Erythritol
2 tablespoons cornstarch
3 large egg yolks
1 teaspoon vanilla
1 pinch salt
2 tablespoons butter
For Filling and Topping
Stevia, to taste
1½ cups heavy cream

Directions

1. Preheat the oven to 325 degrees F and grease a 9-inch pie pan.
2. Banana Cream Filling: Mix together all the ingredients in a saucepan on medium-low heat.
3. Allow to simmer and remove from heat.
4. Refrigerate overnight and fill in the readymade low carb crust.
5. Transfer it in the oven and bake for about 20 minutes.
6. Dish out and keep aside.
7. Mix Stevia in heavy cream and pour over the pie.
8. Refrigerate at least 4 hours before serving.

Nutritional Value:
Calories: 478
Carbs: 9g
Fats: 47g
Proteins: 9g
Sodium: 145mg
Sugar: 3.8g

600. Chayote Squash Mock Apple Pie

Serves: 16
Preparation Time: 1 hour

Ingredients

1. Crust
2. 1½ cups almond flour
3. ½ teaspoon salt
4. ½ cup butter, melted
5. ¾ cup coconut flour
6. 4 eggs
7. 1 tablespoon whole psyllium husks
8. Filling
9. ¾ cup stevia
10. ¼ teaspoon ginger
11. 1 tablespoon lemon juice
12. 1/3 cup butter cut in small pieces
13. 5 medium chayote squash, peeled and sliced
14. 1½ teaspoons cinnamon
15. 1/8 teaspoon nutmeg
16. 1 tablespoon xanthan gum
17. 2 teaspoons apple extract
18. Topping
19. 1 tablespoon Stevia
20. 1 egg

Directions

1. Preheat the oven to 375 degrees F and grease a 9-inch pie pan.
2. Mix together crust ingredients to form a dough ball.
3. Transfer the dough ball into the pie dish and press firmly.
4. Filling: Boil sliced chayote and drain completely.
5. Add Stevia, apple extract, lemon juice, and xanthan gum to cooked chayote squash.
6. Pour chayote mixture into pie pan and top with butter.
7. Topping: Brush egg on pie top and sprinkle with Stevia.
8. Bake for about 35 minutes and dish out to serve.

Nutritional Value:

Calories: 187
Carbs: 6.6g
Fats: 16.7g
Proteins: 2g
Sodium: 204mg
Sugar: 0.5g

601. Low-Carb Banoffee Pie

Serves: 12
Preparation Time: 40 mins

Ingredients

- 1 cup organic almond flour

- 1 cup Stevia
- 6 tablespoons organic butter
- 2 cups + 2 tablespoons organic heavy cream
- 1 tablespoon banana flavor

Directions

1. Preheat the oven to 300 degrees F and grease a 9-inch pie pan.
2. Melt the butter over low heat and add almond flour and 1/3 cup stevia.
3. Press the dough firmly into a pan and transfer in the oven.
4. Bake the crust for about 20 minutes and keep aside.
5. Put ¾ cup + 2 tablespoons of the heavy cream and 2/3 cup Stevia in a saucepan and stir well.
6. Boil this mixture on a medium heat stirring constantly until the mixture thickens.
7. Remove the pan from heat and add banana flavor.
8. Allow to cool in the fridge and spread the toffee on the crust.
9. Top with the remaining whipped cream and serve chilled.

Nutritional Value:

Calories: 323
Carbs: 11.5g
Fats: 27.8g
Proteins: 3.3g
Sodium: 70mg
Sugar: 0g

602. Brownie Truffle Pie

Serves: 10
Preparation Time: 55 mins

Ingredients

- Crust:
- 3 tablespoons coconut flour
- 5 tablespoons butter, cut into small pieces
- 1¼ cups almond flour
- 1 tablespoon granulated Swerve
- ¼ teaspoon salt
- 4 tablespoons ice water
- Filling:
- 6 tablespoons cocoa powder
- 1 teaspoon baking powder
- ¼ cup melted butter
- ½ cup almond flour
- 6 tablespoons Swerve Sweetener
- 2 large eggs
- 5 tablespoons water
- 1 tablespoon Sukrin Fiber Syrup
- 3 tablespoons sugar-free chocolate chips
- ½ teaspoon vanilla extract
- Topping:
- 2 tablespoons Swerve Sweetener
- ½ ounce sugar-free dark chocolate
- 1 cup whipping cream
- ¼ teaspoon vanilla extract

Directions

Crust: Preheat the oven to 325 degrees F and grease a pie pan.

1. Mix together almond flour, coconut flour, water, Swerve, butter, and salt in a bowl to form a dough.
2. Press evenly into the pie pan and transfer in the oven.
3. Bake for about 12 minutes and remove from the oven.
4. Filling: Whisk together the cocoa powder, almond flour, Swerve, and baking powder in a bowl.
5. Add water, eggs, butter, chocolate chips, and vanilla extract until well combined.
6. Pour this batter into the pie crust and transfer in the oven.
7. Bake for about 30 minutes and allow to cool.
8. Topping: Mix together cream, vanilla extract, and Swerve in a large bowl.
9. Beat until stiff peaks form and layer over cooled filling.
10. Top with dark chocolate and chill until completely set.

Nutritional Value:

Calories: 374

Carbs: 5.7g
Fats: 33.9g
Proteins: 8.5g
Sodium: 280mg
Sugar: 0.8g

603. Low Carb Grasshopper Pie

Serves: 8
Preparation Time: 25 mins

Ingredients

- ½ cup cocoa powder
- ½ teaspoon baking powder
- ¼ cup coconut oil
- 2 tablespoons chocolate syrup
- 2 cups ground flax seeds
- 3 teaspoons Stevia powder
- Pinch of salt
- ½ cup smooth almond butter
- 2 eggs
- Mint ice cream, sugar-free

Directions

1. Preheat the oven to 350 degrees F and grease a large pie dish.
2. Mix together all dry ingredients in a bowl and keep aside.
3. Mix almond butter, eggs, chocolate syrup and coconut oil in another bowl.
4. Combine the two mixtures to form a crumbly dough and press in the pie dish.
5. Transfer in the oven and bake for about 12 minutes.
6. Allow to cool and fill with sugar-free mint ice cream to serve.

Nutritional Value:

Calories: 358
Carbs: 15.2g
Fats: 26.5g
Proteins: 11g
Sodium: 51mg
Sugar: 4.3g

30-DAY MEAL PLAN

DAY	BREAKFAST	LUNCH/DINNER	DESSERT
1	Nutty Cocoa Cereal	Mini Egg Muffins	Chocolate Bundt Cake
2	Cheesy Boiled Eggs	Spanish Salsa Aioli	Chia-Almond Bars
3	Batter Coated Cheddar Cheese	Chili Chicken Breasts Wrapped in Bacon	Almond Strawberry Squares
4	Keto Oatmeal	Goat Cheese Muffins with Ajillo Mushrooms	Rum Custard
5	Breakfast Protein Bread	Berry Pancakes with Coconut Topping	Strawberry Chocolate Fudge
6	Sweet & Creamy Eggs	Vanilla-Coconut Cream Tart	Apple Lemon Pie
7	Frozen Ketoccino	Carrot & Cheese Mousse	Creamy Raspberry Cake
8	Autumn Keto Pumpkin Bread	Zucchini with Blue Cheese and Walnuts	Mug Blueberry Cheesecake
9	Anchovy, Spinach and Asparagus Omelet	Prosciutto & Cheese Egg Cups	Almond Biscuits
10	Cheesy Bacon and Chive Omelet	Garlick & Cheese Turkey Slices	Orange Brownies
11	Pizza Waffles	Cajun Crabmeat Frittata	Quick Chocolate Cake
12	Breakfast Tacos	Bacon Balls with Brie Cheese	Raspberry Mug Cake
13	Anaheim pepper Gruyere Waffles	Jamon & Queso Balls	Chocolate Orange Bars
14	Smoked Turkey Bacon and Avocado Muffins	Cilantro & Chili Omelet	Creamy Strawberry Cupcakes
15	Mahón Kale Sausage Omelet Pie	Juicy Beef Cheeseburgers	Quick Blackberry Brownies
16	Breakfast Chia Pudding	Baked Chicken Legs with Cheesy Spread	Strawberry Scones
17	Bok Choy and Eggs Mix	Cheesy Bites with Turnip Chips	Keto Silk Pie
18	Sausage Casserole	Herbed Keto Bread	Meringue Pie
19	Green Onions Omelet	Creamy Cucumber Avocado Soup	Keto Meat Pie
20	Bell Pepper and Ham Omelet	Creamy Vegetable Stew	Key Lime Pie
21	Baked Ham and Kale Scrambled Eggs	Vegetable Greek Mousaka	Pumpkin Almond Pie
22	Adorable Pumpkin Flaxseed Muffins	Zucchini Lasagna with Ricotta and Spinach	Chocolate Dipped Granola Bars
23	Vesuvius Scrambled Eggs with Provolone	Cauliflower Gouda Casserole	Cheesecake Jam Tarts
24	Apple Bowls	Pureed Broccoli with Roquefort Cheese	Peanut Butter Bars
25	Monterey Bacon-Scallions Omelet	Crabmeat & Cheese Stuffed Avocado	Strawberry Vanilla Tart
26	Hot n' Spicy Scramble	Ginger & Walnut Porridge	Caramel Bars
27	Breakfast Bread Pudding	One-Pot Cheesy Cauliflower & Bacon	Blackberry Lemon Tart
28	Chorizo Breakfast Peppers	Chorizo Egg Balls	Lemon Egg Bars
29	Creamy Chocó & Avocado Mousse	Italian Cakes with Gorgonzola and Salami	Banana Cream Pie
30	Sour Cream Cheese Pancakes	Cheese Ciabatta with Pepperoni	Chayote Squash Mock Apple Pie

CONCLUSION

You now hold the golden ticket to living the Ketogenic Diet life of your dreams and are well on your way to losing weight, keeping it off, and living a healthier lifestyle. From breakfast to soups, appetizers to poultry and fish dishes, and even desserts, you have one of the most comprehensive guides to going Keto available on the market today! So, say farewell to that old dread you once carried around in swimsuit season, because those feelings are a thing of the past, my friend! With the Ketogenic Diet, you can start seeing real results and finally start living life as the happiest and healthiest version of yourself.

Manufactured by Amazon.ca
Bolton, ON